Russian Eurasianism

Russian Eurasianism

An Ideology of Empire

Marlène Laruelle

Translated by Mischa Gabowitsch

Woodrow Wilson Center Press
Washington, D.C.

The Johns Hopkins University Press
Baltimore

EDITORIAL OFFICES

Woodrow Wilson Center Press
Woodrow Wilson International Center for Scholars
One Woodrow Wilson Plaza
1300 Pennsylvania Avenue, N.W.
Washington, D.C. 20004-3027
Telephone: 202-691-4029
www.wilsoncenter.org

ORDER FROM

The Johns Hopkins University Press
Hampden Station
P.O. Box 50370
Baltimore, Maryland 21211
Telephone: 1-800-537-5487
www.press.jhu.edu/books/

2 4 6 8 9 7 5 3 1

*The Library of Congress has cataloged the hardcover
edition of this book as follows:*

Laruelle, Marlène
  Russian Eurasianism: an ideology of empire / Marlène Laruelle ; translated by Mischa
Gabowitsch.
  p. cm.
  Includes bibliographical references and index.
  ISBN 978-0-8018-9073-4 (cloth : alk. paper)
  1. Eurasian school. 2. Russia (Federation)—Politics and government—1991—Philosophy.
3. Post-communism—Russia (Federation). 4. Geopolitics. I. Title.
  DK510.763 L37613   2008
  320.54′9095—dc22

2008008569

ISBN 978-1-4214-0576-6 (pbk. : alk. paper)

Contents

Acknowledgments   xi

**Introduction: Eurasianism—Marginal or Mainstream
in Contemporary Russia?**   **1**
  The Historical Roots of the Eurasianist Idea   2
  Neo-Eurasianism and Its Place in Post-Soviet Russia   4
  Neo-Eurasianist Doctrine and Russian Foreign Policy   7
  Marginal or Mainstream?   9
  Premises of This Study   12
  Plan of the Book   14

1 Early Eurasianism, 1920–1930   **16**
  The Life and Death of a Current of Thought   17
  A Philosophy of Politics   25
  A Geographic Ideology   31
  An Ambiguous Orientalism   40
  Conclusions   46

2 Lev Gumilëv: A Theory of Ethnicity?   **50**
  From Dissidence to Public Endorsement:
    An Atypical Biography   51
  "The Last Eurasianist"?   55
  Gumilëv's *Episteme:* Subjecting the Humanities to the
    Natural Sciences   60

Theories of the *Ethnos* or Naturalistic Determinism   65
The Complex History of the Eurasian Totality   70
Xenophobia, Mixophobia, and Anti-Semitism   74
Gumilëv, Russian Nationalism, and Soviet Ethnology   77
Conclusions   81

3 **Aleksandr Panarin: Philosophy of History and the
   Revival of Culturalism**   **83**
Is There a Unified Neo-Eurasianist Theory?   84
From Liberalism to Conservatism: Panarin's
   Intellectual Biography   86
"Civilizationism" and "Postmodernism"   89
Rehabilitating Empire: "Civilizational" Pluralism and
   Ecumenical Theocracy   95
Highlighting Russia's "Internal East"   101
Conclusions   105

4 **Aleksandr Dugin: A Russian Version of the European
   Radical Right?**   **107**
Dugin's Social Trajectory and Its Significance   108
A Russian Version of Antiglobalism: Dugin's
   Geopolitical Theories   115
Traditionalism as the Foundation of Dugin's Thought   120
The Russian Proponent of the New Right?   126
Fascism, Conservative Revolution, and National
   Bolshevism   131
A Veiled Anti-Semitism   135
Ethno-Differentialism and the Idea of Russian Distinctiveness   138
Conclusions   141

5 **The View from "Within": Non-Russian Neo-Eurasianism
   and Islam**   **145**
The Emergence of Muslim Eurasianist Political Parties   146
The Eurasianist Games of the Russian Muftiates   155

Tatarstan: The Pragmatic Eurasianism of Russia's
    "Ethnic" Regions   162
Conclusions   169

6 Neo-Eurasianism in Kazakhstan and Turkey   171

Kazakhstan: Eurasianism in Power   171
The Turkish Case: On the Confusion between Turkism,
    Pan-Turkism, and Eurasianism   188

Conclusion: The Evolution of the Eurasian(ist) Idea   202

The Unity of Eurasianism   204
Organicism at the Service of Authoritarianism:
    "Revolution" or "Conservatism"?   209
Nationalism: Veiled or Openly Espoused:
    The Cultural Racism of Eurasianism   211
Science, Political Movement, or Think Tank?   214
Is Eurasianism Relevant to Explanations of Contemporary
    Geopolitical Change?   217
Psychological Compensation or Part of a Global Phenomenon? 219

Notes   223
Bibliography   255
Index   269

Acknowledgments

I am deeply grateful to the Woodrow Wilson International Center for Scholars and to the Kennan Institute at the Center for the very generous conditions they provided me as a fellow in 2005–6, during which time I wrote this book. I am very appreciative of my colleagues at both institutions for making them such intellectually exciting and welcoming places. My sincere thanks go to Blair Ruble and Joe Brinley for their wonderful enthusiasm and encouragement. I also would like to thank the two reviewers of the manuscript, who provided advice and critical remarks on an earlier draft of the book. I am much indebted to Mischa Gabowitsch, who, in addition to being a brilliant translator, is a remarkable specialist on Russian nationalism and provided me with numerous invaluable comments. Finally, I would like to thank Sebastien for the countless hours he spent helping me with the project. This work is dedicated to him.

Russian Eurasianism

Introduction: Eurasianism—Marginal or Mainstream in Contemporary Russia?

The terms "Eurasianism" and "Eurasia" have once again come to the fore on the post-Soviet political and intellectual scene since 1991. This Eurasianist terminology suggests that Russia and its "margins" occupy a dual or median position between Europe and Asia, that their specific traits have to do with their culture being a "mix" born of the fusion of Slavic and Turko-Muslim peoples, and that Russia should specifically highlight its Asian features. Eurasianism thus conflates the center and the middle. It rejects the view that Russia is on the periphery of Europe, and on the contrary it interprets the country's geographic location as grounds for choosing a messianic "third way."

What has come to be known as *Neo*-Eurasianism is the most elaborate of the various conservative ideologies that emerged in Russia in the 1990s. It maintains that Europe is not in an advanced state of development but represents a specific mode of development that cannot be reproduced: Russia must "unlearn the West" and reject the imperialism of European identity. The Eurasianist doctrine has been attractive to many intellectuals and politicians because it helps them formulate an explanation for the collapse of the Soviet Union and to restore a sense of Russia's continuity from its troubled history by recasting it in spatial rather than temporal terms.

Since the beginning of the 2000s, however, the term "Eurasia" has undergone a profound transformation. It has grown beyond the purely intellectual circles to which it had been confined for about a decade, entering a larger public space. The idea of "Eurasia" has become the victim of its own success, because it is now being used as a catchall vision of Russia. Though Eurasianist theories as such remain little known, the idea of a Eurasian entity encompassing the center of the Old Continent, in which Russia would

1

be "at home," is becoming ever more widespread. As a result, Neo-Eurasianism is undergoing significant ideological twists and losing its homogeneity. Some of its themes are being profoundly transformed and appropriated by new social milieus with diverse objectives.

Not only are the doctrines and concepts of Eurasianism little known; the term itself refers to historical and contemporary currents of thought that are often difficult to identify. It is beset with numerous ambiguities, paradoxes, and contradictions. "Eurasianism" may stand for a number of things: the Romantic philosophy of empire developed by the original Eurasianists of the 1920s and 1930s; the theories of ethnogenesis elaborated by the Orientalist Lev N. Gumilëv (1912–92); the fascistic geopolitics of the fashionable theorist Aleksandr Dugin (1962–); the philosopher Aleksandr Panarin's (1940–2003) defense of a multipolar world; the literary assertion of Kazakh national feeling in the writings of the poet Olzhas Suleimenov (1936–); calls for a better recognition of national minorities, as advanced by the Spiritual Boards of the Muslims of Russia; or plans for the constitution of a Russo-Turkish axis that would rival the European Union as a magnet for Europe's Eastern margins. Given this diversity of meanings, is Eurasianism a strictly Russian phenomenon, is it a more generally post-Soviet one, or is it part of the general surge of cultural fundamentalism that has been sweeping across all continents since the end of the East/West divide?

This book is the final volume of a three-part study of Russian imperial ideologies. The first book examined the doctrine of Eurasianism as it emerged among interwar Russian émigrés,[1] and the second studied nineteenth-century Aryanist theories, which can be considered a form of proto-Eurasianism because they presented Russian expansion in Asia as natural.[2] This volume focuses on the present. But first, it is helpful to look at the roots of Eurasianism.

The Historical Roots of the Eurasianist Idea

The roots of the Eurasianist idea go back to the nineteenth century. Starting with the Slavophiles, many Russian intellectuals saw Europeanness as the main problem of Russia's nationhood. The fact that Russia's identity was developed under, through, and for Western eyes provoked profound resentment and prompted many to turn toward regions where Russia would be recognized as the dominant power. Pëtr Chaadaev remarked as early as 1829: "We do not belong to any of the great families of the human race; we are neither of the West nor of the East, and we have not the traditions of either."³ Much of what underlies all debates about the Russian nation is expressed in Chaadaev's maxim and in Fyodor Dostoyevsky's retort from 1881: "In Europe we were Tatars, but in Asia we too are Europeans."⁴ Does this mean that these intellectuals favored the idea of cultural rapprochement with Asia? Whereas the conquest of the Caucasus had provoked no real interest outside the realm of literature,⁵ the advance into Asia and the Far East at the end of the nineteenth century gave rise to more elaborate attempts at intellectual legitimation and prompted reflections about the nature of Russia: Was it a European state with Asian colonies, or was it a special Eurasian state? Much was at stake in this search for a definition; it reflected changes in Russia's position in the international arena, a new attitude toward the administration of the country's national minorities, and a different view of Russia's past and its conflict-laden relationship with Turkic and Mongol nomads.

Immediately after the Crimean defeat in 1855, Tsar Alexander II's foreign affairs minister, Prince Aleksandr Gorchakov (1798–1883), called upon the tsar to turn his back on Europe and promote Russian expansion in Asia. After the Berlin Treaty of 1878, perceived as a humiliation in Russia, several intellectuals disappointed with Pan-Slavism decided to turn their gaze eastward. Their aims were ambiguous; they were looking for new allies but also engaging in a purely imperialist quest.⁶ These so-called Orientalizers (*vostochniki*) were the first to take the country's imperial character into account in a definition of its identity. They thereby anticipated the theory of the "median world" (*srednii mir*) elaborated by the Pan-Slavist linguist Vladimir I. Lamansky (1833–1914), who was the first to grant the empire's geographic location and ethnic diversity a major role in a definition of Russian identity.⁷ His contemporary Konstantin Leont'ev (1831–91) went even further in opening up Russia toward the Asian world and anticipated, in a still-equivocal fashion, the Eurasianists' future eastward turn. He considered that Russia would only be able to find the resources necessary for a rejection of Europe if it learned to think of itself as "Turanian" rather than Slavic.⁸

From the *vostochniki* to Lamansky and Leont'ev, these nationalist-minded intellectuals thus opted for a more Asian view of Russian identity: They no longer defined the nation through its linguistic affiliation with the Slavic world, as the Slavophiles had, but on the basis of its imperial policies in Asia. But they remained ambiguous on many points, and they still considered the Christian and "Aryan" character of the Russians more important than the empire's national and territorial reality. Although this reality began to be considered relevant to thinking about Russian identity, there remained a deep-seated feeling that an Asian destiny was being imposed upon Russia by a disdainful Europe. For the *vostochniki* as well as for Lamansky, opening up Russia toward Asia was a mere geostrategic palliative for Russia's failure in Europe, rather than an acknowledgment of the natural links between Russia and Asia. For these Russians, the attraction to Asia was only a mirror, a way of challenging the West's centrality. They incessantly warned against the risk of intellectual colonization by the "Romano-Germanic" world.

The purported Asianism of the late nineteenth century must therefore be taken with a pinch of salt; before Eurasianism in the 1920s, no Russian intellectual movement displayed a real openness to the Turko-Mongol world. Asia was only ever highlighted under the aspect of Aryanism; it was a mere detour to reinforced claims of Europeanness. Most of those theorists who sought to comment on Russia's alleged distinctiveness, from the Slavophile Aleksandr Khomiakov in 1840 to the Symbolist poet Aleksandr Blok in 1918, painted Russia's identity in identical terms, embodied by Scythia; for them, the Russians were descended directly from the Asian cradle of the European peoples. Even the best-known Pan-Slavists, such as Nikolai Danilevsky (1822–85), claimed to prefer Asia over the "Romano-Germanic" world, Islam or Buddhism over Catholicism, and the Turks over the Latins. The idea was that it was Europe's errors and lack of understanding, the European allegation that the Slavs were "Turanian,"[9] that forced the Russians to take this "slanted-eyed" view of Russia, in Aleksandr Blok's poetic phrase.[10] Thus it took the shock of the Revolution of 1917 and exile to really prepare the ground for Eurasianism's claims of Asianness.

Neo-Eurasianism and Its Place in Post-Soviet Russia

Eurasianist ideas resurfaced in the USSR in the 1980s within Pamiat', an organization that at the time encompassed most of the Russian nationalist movement. Outside a narrow circle of specialists, the term "Eurasianism" was rediscovered during the final years of perestroika and seeped into public debates through the weekly *Den'*, then the dominant newspaper in the nationalist scene. By 1992, the term "Eurasia" had become sufficiently commonplace for several political movements to mention it and for the newspaper *Moskovskie novosti* to use it as rubric for its news about the republics of the newly formed Commonwealth of Independent States. However, relations between the so-called national-patriotic forces and the Neo-Eurasianist movement remained complex, crystallizing around the figure of Dugin, who supported Eurasianism as a member of *Den''*'s editorial board. Sergei Kurginian (1949–), the director of the Experimental Creative Center, one of the think tanks created toward the end of perestroika to avert the disintegration of the Soviet Union, vehemently rejected Eurasianism as early as 1993, stating that it fostered Turko-Muslim separatism and endangered the Russian people. The famous journal *Molodaia gvardiia,* a mouthpiece of Russian nationalism since the 1960s, accused the Eurasianists of Zionist-Masonic plots and lambasted Dugin's admiration of the Western New Right and the Third Reich, recalling that antifascism and anti-Germanism are considered crucial parts of the Russian patriotic heritage.

Nationalist movements have been ambiguous in their interpretation of Eurasianist rhetoric ever since its rediscovery, not least due to Vadim Kozhinov (1930–2001), a well-known nationalist literary scholar. To him, the Eurasianist idea was not engendered by the October Revolution but was a response to Russia's destiny of being a synthesis between East and West. Thus it is fully compatible with all versions of Russian nationalism, whether they hanker for the Tsarist Russian Empire or Stalinism, and there is no need for debate on whether the founding fathers of Eurasianism were "White" or "Red." However, Kozhinov had a very Russocentric Eurasianism in mind when making those comments; he condemned the so-called Turkic tradition of the 1920s movement and supporters of what he called Euro-Asianism (*evropoaziatstvo*).[11] In his interpretation, the Russians constitute the only matrix for Eurasia; their destiny lies not in the Orientalization advocated by the original interwar movement but in a renewed awareness of the country's imperial calling. Eurasianism's place within the Russian nationalist spectrum has remained paradoxical due to the fact that it can be interpreted in either a "Russocentric" or a "Turkocentric" way. However, the paradox is not simply in the eye of the outside beholder; it has also divided the Neo-Eurasianists, who have accused each other of advocating the supremacy of one people over another. The diverging interpretations of Russia's specific place inside Eurasia constitute the movement's founding ambiguity: Although on the surface they praise the national and religious diversity of what they call Eurasian space, all theorists of Eurasianism in fact espouse a fervent Russian nationalism.

From 1993 onward, Neo-Eurasianism began to spread more widely, being partly disseminated by the two main nationalist parties of the time, Vladimir Zhirinovsky's Liberal-Democratic Party (LDPR) and Gennady

Ziuganov's Communist Party of the Russian Federation (CPRF). Both leaders stressed the geopolitical aspects of Neo-Eurasianism, bracketing out the other levels of the doctrine. Zhirinovsky, known for his political escapades and provocative statements, advocates an Orthodox Pan-Slavism, expressed most openly during the Yugoslav wars of the 1990s, coupled with southeastward expansionism. In his book *The Last Thrust to the South,* published in 1993, he announced that Russian soldiers would "dip their boots into the Indian Ocean" and the Mediterranean, for Russia's future lay partly on Islamic territory.[12] He also took up Dugin's idea that the expansion of the great powers is now no longer "horizontal" but "vertical," that is, follows a north-south axis; in that view, Russia is destined to control Iran, Turkey, Afghanistan, and India.

As for the CPRF, it includes an ideologically diverse array of movements, among them Stalinists, internationalists, Tsarists, Orthodox Christians, and Neo-Eurasianists.[13] Ziuganov has therefore sought to assert the continuity of the Russian state in spite of the breaks between the Tsarist, Soviet, and post-Soviet periods, and he has seized Dugin's idea that Russia has always been, irrespective of its political regime, the pivotal state of Eurasia. He also borrows from Dugin the idea that Russian nationalism is not at odds with the self-expression of national minorities, and he presents the CPRF as a great champion of, say, Tatar nationalism or Kalmyk Buddhism. His book *The Geography of Victory: The Foundations of Russian Geopolitics* (1999) was directly inspired by Dugin's ideas on the specific features of Russian geopolitical science and the revival of Russia as the guarantor of stability in the world at large and in Eurasia in particular.[14]

Despite these more or less recurrent Neo-Eurasianist allusions, these two parties cannot be considered political mouthpieces of Eurasianism and will not be treated in this book; both the LDPR and the CPRF draw on a number of other doctrines beside Eurasianism, and their electoral activities are unrelated to their endorsement of Eurasianist ideas is the strict sense of the term. My aim is not to look for traces of Neo-Eurasianism in all the statements made by different Russian politicians since the collapse of the Soviet Union. Before 2001, no political party openly and fully espoused Neo-Eurasianism, and the two parties that tried to do so after that date failed in the legislative elections of December 2003. However, the impact of Neo-Eurasianism has little to do with political parties, their electoral representation, or their sociological profile, and much more with ideological "entryism" into state bodies and intellectual life. Neo-Eurasianism must therefore be studied through its think tanks and the intellectual fashions it has engendered, because many aspects of its doctrine have largely succeeded in penetrating into Russian public life and influencing what the New Right would call the "field of metapolitics."

Neo-Eurasianist Doctrine and Russian Foreign Policy

Since the beginning of the 2000s, the term "Eurasianism" has begun to be used more and more often to comment on the development of Russian foreign policy. Yevgeny Primakov's important role as minister of foreign affairs (1996–98) and prime minister (September 1998–May 1999) is often mentioned by Neo-Eurasianists; he was one of the very few politicians of the Boris Yeltsin era to promote closer relations with the Asian powers. Since Vladimir Putin came to power in 2000, several of his presidential addresses reopening the question of Russia's place between Europe and Asia have fueled Neo-Eurasianists' hopes for greater prominence. Thus Dugin has referred to Putin's speeches on several occasions, as have the Kazakh leadership and the whole set of institutions responsible for promoting economic rapprochement between the post-Soviet republics.

The Neo-Eurasianists regularly cite Putin's official visits, for example, his participation in the Asian Summit in Brunei in November 2001. Just before his departure, the president declared: "Russia has always felt herself to be a Eurasian country. Never have we forgotten that the greatest part of Russian territory is in Asia. But it must be said in all honesty that we have not always made use of this advantage. I think the time has come to mate words with deeds together with the countries of the Asia-Pacific region and build up economic, political, and other links. Russia today has all that is required to do so."[15] In October 2003, Putin took part in a meeting of the Organization of the Islamic Conference in Malaysia, to the joy of the Neo-Eurasianists, who insist that Russia is an Islamic power. They were also very pleased when Russia signed a Treaty of Friendship and Cooperation with the Association of Southeast Asian Nations in November 2004, and they applauded the president's stated intention of making Russia adhere to the interregional forum known as Asia-Europe Meeting. They regretted that Moscow was marginalized at the first East Asia Summit in Malaysia in December 2005, where Putin only had observer status.

However, it is doubtful whether this aspect of Russian foreign policy really has much to do with Eurasianism. First of all, it should be noted that Putin and other foreign policy decisionmakers call Russia a "Euro-Asian country" (*evro-aziatskaia strana*), almost never using the term "Eurasian" or "Eurasianist" (which are identical in Russian). Calling the Federation "Euro-Asian" amounts to a mere acknowledgment of an undeniable geographic reality, whereas mentioning "Eurasian" features would be a first step toward an ideological interpretation of that reality. Neither Yeltsin nor Putin has ever made *Eurasianist* statements in the sense of using a culturalist terminology to argue that Russia has an Asian *essence*. Wanting to be respected in Asia is not tantamount to thinking of oneself as an Asian culture. Stressing that Siberia and the Far East are geographically Asian, and pursuing an active diplomacy in favor of regional integration in the most dynamic part of the world is no more than political common sense. Moreover, several Anglophone countries with a European culture and a Christian religious tradition, such as Australia, New Zealand, and the United States with Hawaii, are also adjacent to Asia. By virtue of that location, they are members of regional bodies in the Asia-Pacific region, which Russia could also join. But that has nothing to do with the belief in a country's specifically *Eurasian* or *Asian* national essence. For this reason, I shall not, in this book, use the expression "pragmatic Eurasianism" to describe Russia's desire to accentuate its political and economic presence in Asia.[16]

The idea of Russia as a "great power" (*derzhava*), which is clearly becoming dominant in Russia today, is not strictly synonymous with Eurasianism either. In foreign policy, stating that Russian interests do not automatically coincide with those of the West—wanting to play a major role in international crises, for example, in the Middle East, at eye level with the United States, or supporting Serbia or Iran on certain issues—are not really expressions of Eurasianism. In domestic policy, the authoritarian tendencies of the Putin regime as well as official talk about the special features of "Orthodox civilization" and the insurmountable distinctiveness of the "Russian national character" express the revival of a certain kind of nationalism and the elevation of a new patriotic ideology to the rank of official doctrine. But this is not a direct result of Neo-Eurasianism; nor does it confirm the success of authors such as Dugin. These ideologies are not specific expressions of Eurasianism but are common to all nationalist movements, whose views of contemporary Russia are heavily influenced by nostalgia for the great power that was the Soviet Union.

The idea that Russia will only become a great power once again if it regains its imperial pride is one of the most classic clichés of Russian nationalism in general. Its most radical supporters want the Russian Federation to recover its political preeminence in the former Soviet Union (by reconstructing a suprastate unity), while more moderate proponents want it to wield greater geopolitical clout (by having its sphere of influence in "Eurasia" internationally recognized) or exercise economic influence (by bringing the weak economies of the new post-Soviet states under its control and shaping their economic choices). Anatoly Chubais's statements on "liberal empire" (*liberal'naia imperiia*) indicate to what extent the belief in Russia's natural imperial destiny, far from being a defining feature of Eurasianism, is also espoused by "Westernizers."[17]

In an opinion poll carried out by VTsIOM in November 2001, 71 percent of respondents said they believe Russia to be a one-of-a-kind civilization, "Euro-Asian or Orthodox," while only 13 percent stated that it belongs to Western civilization.[18] Can this really be interpreted as the result of direct Eurasianist influence? A feeling of "distinctiveness" does not necessarily signify adhesion to Eurasianism as a doctrine, and many Russian citizens probably had in mind the tautological idea that what is special about Russia is that it is *Russian* (and Orthodox, because the question did not allow respondents to state whether the distinctiveness resides in "Euro-Asianism" or in "Orthodoxy") rather than close to Asian cultures. Thus, though Neo-Eurasianism has found a place for itself in the general revival of patriotic discourse, it has only done so as one element among many rather than as the driving force behind the whole movement.

Marginal or Mainstream?

Eurasianism as studied here, therefore, is neither an element of Russian foreign policy nor the theoretical base of the big nationalist parties, the LDPR and the CPRF. Nor is it identical with the new patriotism promoted by the political regime. Because any interpretive model is necessarily reductionist, for the purposes of this study, "Eurasianism" is defined as a doctrine, that is, a systematic set of theoretical conceptions upheld as true and promoted primarily by intellectuals. Many of them hold important academic positions; those who do not belong to a university or academy of sciences, such as Dugin, are trying to obtain a comparable status to gain academic legitimacy. Indeed, Eurasianism often claims to be a *science* whose message about Russia does not depend on personal considerations but is a methodical and *objective* analysis of Russian interests. This is why it seems fair to say that, whereas Eurasianism does not account directly for Russian foreign policy or the new patriotism, it is not a marginal phenomenon in any sense.

Far from it. It is contributing to the diffusion of a strictly ethnic and cultur-alist justification for the feeling of failure prevalent in Russian society as a response to the upheaval of the 1990s; it offers a simplistic reading of the conflicts of the post-bipolar world and of Russia's place on the international scene; and it elaborates a pseudo-scientific jargon that allows it to circum-vent the political and social breaks of twentieth-century Soviet history and to justify authoritarianism through culture.

The great theorists of Eurasianism wield considerable influence in Rus-sia and the neighboring republics. Lev Gumilëv, for example, is one of the scholars best known among the general public. Since his death in 1992, he has become a cult figure, and his words are perceived as dogmas that are above criticism. His books are best-sellers; the publishing houses that ac-quired the rights produce them in hundreds of thousands of copies, and they are on all school and university reading lists in the humanities and social sciences. His peculiar vocabulary dominates virtually all history, ethnology, and "culturology"[19] textbooks, without its scientific relevance ever being questioned. Thus the terms *ethnos, superethnos, ethnosphere, ethnogenesis,* and *passionarity* have become so common that many scholars or teachers no longer even perceive them as conscious references to Gumilëv's theo-ries. The special "ethnic" or even "racial" features of a particular group, the "mentality" of an *ethnos,* the "invariants of biosocial organization," and so on are considered legitimate research topics in Russia and other post-Soviet countries, largely though not exclusively due to Gumilëv.[20]

Beyond academic circles, the acknowledgment of Gumilëv's theories extends to the political authorities. Thus the new Kazakh State University founded in 1996 was named after him, and the Kazakh president Nursultan Nazarbaev is proud to display his familiarity with Gumilëv's works. During a visit to Astana on October 10, 2000, Putin publicly applauded this institu-tional recognition and recalled that "many call him the great Eurasianist of our times."[21] He described Gumilëv as a great historian and ethnologist with a celebrated intellectual legacy: "His scholarly works are a brilliant contribution not only to thinking about history but also to the assertion of the centuries-old community and interrelation between the peoples who in-habit the vast expanses of Eurasia, from the Baltics and the Carpathians to the Pacific Ocean. The instructive potential of Eurasianism is especially significant today, as we are building genuinely equal relations between the countries of the Commonwealth of Independent States."[22] The Kyrgyz president Askar Akaev (ousted in March 2005 by the "Tulip Revolution") relies on Gumilëv's theories in his book on the history of the Kyrgyz and has repeatedly acknowledged that Gumilëv was a source of inspiration for him in analyzing the peoples of the steppe.[23] In August 2005, the thousandth anniversary of the city of Kazan provided Tatarstan with an occasion to express its respect for Gumilëv officially by unveiling a bust of the great man and lauding his role as a defender of the Turkic peoples and especially the Tatars. Once more, Putin lent his support to these statements during a visit to Kazan.

Dugin, the most publicized Neo-Eurasianist, occupies a more complex place in Russian public space. He seems to exert real influence on certain military and political circles and part of the presidential administration. He was an adviser to Gennady Seleznev, the speaker of the State Duma from 1996 to 2003. Later, Dugin became the chairman of the Geopolitical Expertise Section of the Duma's consultative National Security Council. His Center for Geopolitical Expertise and his lectures at the Military Academy of the General Staff have earned him financial support from military circles. He has access to the Duma and supporters in all the parties represented in parliament, and his book on geopolitics is used as a textbook in many institutions of higher education. Aleksei Podberëzkin and his Spiritual Heritage (*Dukhovnoe nasledie*) organization, which long functioned as the Communist Party's main think tank, regularly quotes Dugin and acknowledges that he inspired several of Gennady Ziuganov's books.

However, it would be wrong to present Dugin as the ideological "guru" of the Putin regime, as some scholars and journalists have done. His influence actually remains largely limited to certain academic and student circles, mainly in the fields of philosophy, "culturology," political science, and international relations, where he is often presented as a great theorist. His geopolitical writings are extremely fashionable, and the claim that Russia has no choice *in principle* but to oppose the United States has become one of the most "commonplace" ideas, as even Dmitry Trenin of the Carnegie Moscow Center recognizes.[24]

Aleksandr Panarin seems less known among the general public, but he was a respected figure in Russian political science whose influence should not be underestimated. In 2002 he received the prestigious Solzhenitsyn Prize for his last book, *Orthodox Civilization in a Globalized World,* which got rave reviews from nationalist-minded authors and was presented as one of the most fundamental works to have appeared in post-Soviet Russia. Many of his colleagues consider his extreme culturalist claims, his definition of Russia as the only possible model for a multipolar world, and his view of religion as the basis of all cultures to be indisputable scientific truth rather than debatable presuppositions. As for "non-Russian" Eurasianism, it is extremely influential among academics in Turkic-speaking republics, and the idea of "Eurasia" is constantly referred to by the political authorities of these republics, whether they are part of the Russian Federation (Tatarstan, Bashkortostan, Altai, Buryatia, Yakutia-Sakha, Kalmykia, etc.) or have been independent since 1991 (Kazakhstan, Kyrgyzstan), as well as by those in institutions representing post-Soviet Islam.

Paradoxically, the real effect of Eurasianism has less to do with the dissemination of intricate doctrines on the nature of the relation between Russia and Asia; that remains a minor topic in claims about Russia's distinctiveness. Its impact is more subtle and has more to do with the theoretical presuppositions of its doctrine: Today's conflicts result not from economic and social struggles but from a clash between the cultural essences of peoples; religion is the foundation of civilizations and provides them with an unchangeable nature; and civilizations, rather than individuals or social groups, are the true driving force of history. Eurasianism also draws much of its social appeal from its commitment to the creation of new academic disciplines: geopolitics, culturology, conflictology, conspirology, ethnoconflictology, ethnopolitology, ethnopsychology, and so on. This essentialist interpretation of the world serves an undisguised political objective: to show that the Western model is not applicable to the post-Soviet countries because civilizations cannot adopt anything from the outside. Thus, Eurasianism has acquired a nonnegligible influence over the political and social climate in post-Soviet countries in general, and Russia in particular, by disseminating the idea that culture constrains the liberty of the individual: Individuals must respect the essence of their national group (often expressed in an ethnicist terminology), not try to oppose it. The Neo-Eurasianist "sciences" thus serve to justify a kind of cultural fundamentalism.

Premises of This Study

The phenomenon of nationalism has been interpreted in many different ways, which can be schematically divided into two large categories: primordialist and constructivist. This study adopts the latter perspective, questioning the unity of national identity from the outset and highlighting its constructed nature: Identity is not unchangeable, it is not a given but a human-made construct. It is constantly remodeled and makes use of diverse symbols and constructions that change over time; a "nation" exists because there are people who say and think so. Research on the construction of collective identities must therefore take into account the mode of elaboration, and the conditions of production, of discourse on Russia's purported uniqueness. The aim is not to look for a "truth" outside the texts, to link Neo-Eurasianism as an ideology of nationhood to the "Eurasian" reality of Russia, but to spell out the doctrine's internal logic, its aims, and the ways in which it tries to prove its basic hypothesis.

Thus, as Patrick Sériot has rightly noted, "It is less important to ask whether the Russians are a *world unto themselves* than to try to explain why they believe that they are."[25] Indeed, it is hard not to be puzzled by the feeling, widespread among Russian academics, that they are engaged in a "different science." From my perspective, the content of Eurasianist declarations is less important than how knowledge claiming to be scientific is produced. This task is all the more important because in Russia, epistemological and scientific refutations have always gone hand in hand with a *cultural* rejection of Western innovations, perceived as foreign. In this book, I therefore dissect a corpus of sources and dive into a particular set of arguments and sources. As a disclaimer, it may be worthwhile quoting Maurice Olender: "To portray an author who expresses the political mindset of his times, to attempt a description of the windings of his thought, implies neither agreement nor adherence."[26]

Today, Neo-Eurasianism is too often equated with foreign policy discourse or the new Russian patriotic ideology. On the contrary, it must be grasped in its historical and philosophical context to take its rightful place in Russian intellectual history, whatever our judgment on it. Only a precise analysis of its doctrines will allow us to measure the spread of these radical culturalist theories and the political changes linked to them. Therefore, this book analyzes Neo-Eurasianism without judging it, for two reasons. First, I do not think one may, either methodologically or ethically, judge and analyze at the same time. Knowledge is a prerequisite of argument, but the former must precede the latter. Second, as Pierre-André Taguieff has remarked, "There is no need to put words into an author's mouth or demonize him in order to critically examine theses that one believes must be opposed."[27]

Eurasianism uses a highly flexible terminology that hides a variety of currents, which are distinct both ideologically and sociologically. That is why this book analyzes the movement in its diversity by examining its main theorists and currents separately.[28] Though Lev Gumilëv, Aleksandr Panarin, and Aleksandr Dugin share many Neo-Eurasianist references, they actually espouse highly different doctrines. Moreover, Western research has focused mostly on the works of Dugin, the most publicized of the Neo-Eurasianists, leaving aside other figures who are just as relevant, if not more so. Debate has mainly centered on Dugin's influence on the presidential administration. This ignores the fact that Gumilëv and Panarin are highly regarded in their respective academic fields and have probably had a much greater impact because their theories, presented as the scientific norm, are being taught to tens of thousands of students. Thus Gumilëv is probably more relevant than Dugin to an understanding of contemporary Russia. Finally, non-Russian versions of Neo-Eurasianism also remain little known, although they play a major role in political and ideological discourse in the regions, countries, and institutions concerned. They must therefore be considered part and parcel of the phenomenon of Neo-Eurasianism as a whole, thus highlighting one of the movement's crucial aspects: its inability to distinguish between what is Russian in the ethnic sense (*russkii*), Russian in the sense of pertaining to Russia (*rossiiskii*), and Eurasian (*evraziiskii*), and to state precisely what place it reserves for the "small peoples" and Islam in its conception of Russia.

Plan of the Book

Chapter 1 of this book is devoted to an analysis of original interwar Eurasianism and its significant contribution to theories of "Russian distinctiveness." Its theorists elaborated complex doctrines that marshaled political, geographic, cultural, and historical arguments in the hope of demonstrating the existence of an entity called "Eurasia" and proving that Russia's presence in Asia is natural. Chapter 2 focuses on the life and work of Lev Gumilëv, who may chronologically be considered the link between the original Eurasianism and post-Soviet Neo-Eurasianism. In his case, however, claims about the existence of "Eurasia" can only be understood in the context of his focus on ethnic issues and his search for a biological, and therefore total, account of human history. Chapter 3 deals particularly with the philosopher Aleksandr Panarin. Though he is the least known of the Neo-Eurasianist thinkers, he remains closest to the theories of original interwar Eurasianism in his philosophy of history, his culturalism, and his commitment to a multipolar world.

In chapter 4, which is devoted to the inevitable Aleksandr Dugin, I try to assess the importance of his references to doctrines other than Neo-Eurasianism. The man, his intellectual biography, and his current political activities cannot be understood without an appreciation of his debts to Guénonian Traditionalism, German occultism, and the theories of the Western New Right. Dugin is also the only Neo-Eurasianist who has managed to penetrate into politics and is trying to act as a rallying figure for the other Neo-Eurasianist movements. His active overtures to Islam make it important to study the emergence of a "non-Russian" Eurasianism. Thus, chapter 5 deals with the development of a Muslim Eurasianism, as manifested in the emergence of political parties claiming to draw on both Islam and Eurasianism, in the ideological battles between Russia's different Muslim Spiritual Boards, and in the emergence of Euro-Islamic views in Tatarstan. In these three cases, Eurasianism is seen as an expression of "friendship among peoples" and allows non-Russian intellectuals and politicians to claim a fundamental role for their people in the future of the Russian Federation. Chapter 6 deals with the importing of Neo-Eurasianism into Kazakhstan and Turkey. In both countries, references to the idea of Eurasia may both compete with classical nationalist ideas about Kazakh or Turkish identity and merge with them in different ways, depending on the idea's exponents. A conclusion sums up the analysis.

This wide-ranging survey thus intends to depict the true breadth of Eurasianism, its political presuppositions, and its intellectual impact, and to analyze what this "cultural fundamentalism" is trying to say about Russia.

Chapter 1

Early Eurasianism, 1920–1930

The ideology of Eurasianism is often associated with Russian currents of thoughts such as Slavophilism, nineteenth-century Pan-Slavism, and early-twentieth-century Asianism—and rightly so. No less fundamentally, however, Eurasianism must be compared with Western intellectual trends of the interwar period. First, this comparison moves us beyond the idea that Eurasianism is nothing but the inevitable upshot of Russian thinking about the supposed differences between Russia and Europe. Second, it is important to place Eurasianism back into its international historical context: Russian narratives on identity do not make any claims unheard of in any other country. Russian intellectuals' thinking about politics never departs from an ideological framework that is of Western origin. Even the Eurasianists, the most brilliant defenders of insurmountable national distinctiveness, are, unwittingly, part and parcel of European intellectual history. Exposing Eurasianism's subtle intellectual genealogies is thus not an end in itself; rather, it should enable us better to assess the current popularity of the term "Eurasia" across the entire post-Soviet region and to challenge essentialist interpretations of Russian identity.

Analyzing Eurasianism through its Western influences can help us understand how the ideas of the Russian émigrés were, crucially, a *philosophy in exile,* developed in different places across the planet but coming together in debates that crisscrossed the entire Euro-Asian continent, from the West through Central Europe to the Far East. Eurasianism was also a philosophy *of* exile, because its ideas, and especially the Asianism espoused by some in the movement, could only emerge among intellectuals who found it difficult to accept being torn from their homeland and were going through a process of *self-estrangement.* This led them to develop exceptionally radical and iconoclastic views on Russia's identity. Approaching the discourse of national distinctiveness "via the West" thus reveals the extent to which its mechanisms are unwittingly modeled on Western examples. It is part of a mode of thought that was widespread at the time and was fueled by disappointment with the contemporary West. Eurasianism must therefore be understood within a Western context. Indeed, there is no better proof of the Europeanness of Russian intellectual history.

This detour via the intellectual sources of Eurasianism allows us to grasp the richness of the movement as well as its paradoxes. Eurasianism is complex: It is heir to a long tradition of thinking about Russia's "otherness" and its relation to Europe; it takes the millenarian and eschatological aspects of early-twentieth-century literary Asianism to their conclusion; it articulates the Russian intelligentsia's attraction to utopia and totalitarian ideologies; and it expresses a mystical understanding of the Revolution of 1917. It thus reveals the complexes and difficulties of an exile community in search of a place in the West and a mission in Russia, a community whose nationalism is a gesture toward the Soviet Union. The short but tumultuous history of Eurasianism illustrates its internal difficulties: scientific eclecticism unified around the theme of "Eurasia," a diversity of interpretations of the Soviet experience that finally lead to breakup, hesitation between a spiritual and a political definition of the movement, and so on. These paradoxes manifested themselves in the day-to-day activities of the movement, accelerating its collapse. Nevertheless, they are above all intellectual; the general philosophy of Eurasianism blends multiple traditions and does not balk at contradictions, although it cloaks them in a language that is simultaneously metaphysical and scientific.

The Life and Death of a Current of Thought

The Russian exile community was highly politicized and deeply divided. It was brimming with factions. With the exception of communism, the entire political spectrum was represented: ultraconservatives, supporters of constitutional monarchy, Cadets, liberals, socialists, anarchists. There were some acts of violence (suicides and terrorism), but on the whole the émigrés' activities were mainly verbal. They had a diversified press and a rich and eventful political life. The initial ideological struggles between monarchist and constitutionalist exiles were aggravated, rather than resolved, by new parties that appeared in the early 1920s. These new ideologies called for reconciliation with Soviet Russia; they were impressed with the global reach of the new Russian state and attached to an idea of national greatness whose mythical appeal was increased by the fact that it was irrevocably lost. Realizing that they would not return to Russia and that the Bolshevik regime was set to remain in power, these Russians, despite their White background, sought a rapprochement with the Soviet Union.

The one event that forced the émigrés to make clear political choices was the advent of Nazism in Germany; the alternatives were an alliance with Hitler, in the hope that he would overthrow the communist regime, or a reconciliation with the Soviet Union, which was at that time playing the card of traditional Russian nationalism. The failure of the German and Hungarian revolutions made the Soviet Union abandon the idea of world revolution, opt for "socialism in one country," and, in its turn, elaborate a discourse on Russian distinctiveness that appealed to part of the exile community. Different Russian versions of the principle of a "third way" thus emerged: a rejection of both communism and Western parliamentary regimes; a combination of fascistic talk with an acceptance of the Soviet revolutionary adventure; and ideological hesitations between fascism, monarchism, and socialism.

The Eurasianist movement was also born of a psychological need to compensate for an impasse considered intolerable by a young, cultivated, and impatient elite that refused to accept that their fatherland was declining, deplored the humiliating terms of the Soviet-German peace treaty, and blamed the West for the difficulties of Russia's historical development.[1] Eurasianism was complex; it continued the Russian intelligentsia's long tradition of thinking about Russian otherness and its relation to Europe that stemmed from the Slavophiles; it expanded upon the ideas of the Russian "geographic ideology" school of thought about Russia as a "third continent" (V. I. Lamansky, 1833–1914; V. V. Dokuchaev, 1846–1903; et al.)[2] and the millenarian and iconoclastic aspects of early-twentieth-century literary Asianism, pan-Mongolism, and Scythism.[3] But above all, the movement was impressed by the emotional and intellectual violence represented by October 1917 and the mystical catharsis of early Soviet discourse that announced an end of history of sorts—a modernized, social millenarianism.[4] The diversity of the Eurasianists' biographies illustrates the diversity of the movement. Its strength as well as its weakness lay precisely in the multiplicity of its supporters' interests and ways of thinking. The Eurasianist movement was able to bring together high-level intellectuals with a wide range of interests and specializations: geography, economics, ethnography, linguistics, philosophy, history, religion, and Oriental studies. This encounter between different disciplines and worldviews was to give birth to an ideology with a total, global ambition, and with an internal logic of its own that brought these disciplines together around the concept of "Eurasia."

The movement included numerous important figures of the Russian exile community: the geographer and economist Pëtr N. Savitsky (1895–1968), the ethnographer Nikolai S. Trubetzkoy (1890–1938), the aesthetic critic Pëtr P. Suvchinsky (1882–1985), the linguist Roman Jakobson (1896–1982), the philosopher Lev P. Karsavin (1882–1952), the historian George V. Vernadsky (1887–1973), the religious thinker Georges V. Florovsky (1893–1979), and the legal philosopher N. N. Alekseev (1879–1964). Among its lesser-known adherents were the historian M. V. Shakhmatov, the literary critic Dmitry P. Sviatopolk-Mirsky, the orientalist V. P. Nikitin, the (self-described) Jew Ia. A. Bromberg, and the (self-described) Mongol E. Khara-Davan.[5] This diversity, which accounts for the strength and resilience of Eurasianism in Russian intellectual history, was also the source of its difficulties: Can Eurasianism be considered a unified system of thought, or is it a diversified and thus contradictory current?

All these intellectuals contributed, to differing degrees, to the development of Eurasianism, but most of them were specialists whose professional reputation stemmed from other works. Savitsky was the only one to dedicate his entire life and work to Eurasianism. The others—Jakobson, Trubetzkoy, Karsavin, and Vernadsky—can by no means be entirely identified with the Eurasianist movement; the former two were the founders of phonology and created the Prague Linguistic Circle; Karsavin remains well-known as a medievalist and philosopher; and Vernadsky is heavily referenced in American research on Russia. Yet, in spite of their diversity, during their Eurasianist period these thinkers saw all their intellectual activities as part of one and the same logical whole.

We cannot understand Eurasianism unless we bear in mind the disappointments and disillusionment suffered by the Russian intelligentsia during the events of 1905 and February 1917: Russia seemed incapable of replicating the Western political system. Exile was therefore not only a physical expatriation; it also revealed that the identity of both the émigrés and the new Russia was at an impasse. Eurasianism was thus born in the context of a crisis, in an atmosphere of eschatological expectations: Its proponents had the feeling of standing at a turning point in human history. Their attempts to theorize these expectations made them look toward the future.[6] The first Eurasianist collection of articles (published in Sofia in 1921), an avant-gardist and consciously provocative volume, was titled *Iskhod k Vos-toku,* meaning "Exodus to the East"—to the Orient. The authors played on the double meaning of the Russian word *iskhod,* which means both "exo-dus" or "exit" and "outcome" or "solution."[7] The title also stressed their op-position to the Russian intelligentsia's exodus—in both a literal and a figu-rative sense—to the West. This collection of articles was intended as a manifesto announcing a new era in thinking about Russian identity and the future of Soviet Russia. Though the futurism of the first issue tapered off rather quickly, Eurasianism continued to see itself as eminently modern: "Any inclination toward Eurasianism is an inclination toward modernity, and, conversely, any decline in modernity is a decline in Eurasianism."[8]

For almost a decade, Eurasianism was at the political and cultural fore-front of the émigré scene, in particular due to the quality and diversity of the young intellectuals who embodied it. At the height of its activity in the mid-1920s, the Eurasianist movement had approximately one hundred members engaged in an array of intense activities: congresses; meetings; lecture series; weekly seminars in Paris, Prague, Brussels, and Belgrade; and the publication of the *Chronicle,* a weekly newspaper, and *Versty,* a prestigious literary journal. The Eurasianists' dynamism was a continuation of Russia's bustling intellectual life in the early twentieth century. Eurasian-ism proved attractive, especially to Russian youth in Czechoslovakia and the Balkans. The Eurasianist periodicals carried numerous book reviews and conference reports, illustrating the extent to which the movement was in touch with the intellectual trends of its era. The Eurasianists also con-tributed to the first issue of *Put'* (The Path), which presented itself as "the organ of Russian religious thought," in the words of its editor, Nikolai Berdiaev; Trubetzkoy, Karsavin, Kartashëv, Il'in, Savitsky, Suvchinsky, and Florovsky wrote for it, entering a debate with Berdiaev in response to his famously harsh article about Eurasianism. In 1925, the prestigious In-stitut Saint-Serge invited Florovsky, Karsavin, and Il'in to Paris. The Eurasianists were then at the peak of their activities and influence. They were also close to *Versty,* whose three issues were published in Paris in 1926–28 by Prince Sviatopolk-Mirskii, Suvchinsky, and Sergei Efron, fea-turing the most prestigious names of the Russian literary world, such as Lev Shestov, Marina Tsvetaeva, and Aleksei Remizov. This encounter between Russian émigré literature and Eurasianism was made possible by Sviatopolk-Mirskii, who was at the time professor of Russian literature in London. The central idea of the journal was seductive for the Eurasianists: *Versty* wanted to demonstrate the unity of the finest accomplishments of Russian, Soviet, and émigré literature.

The Eurasianist publications can be divided into three categories. The first series of collected articles, called *Evraziiskii vremennik* (Eurasianist Annals), ran to ten volumes of three to four hundred pages each, published roughly every two years. The second, *Evraziiskaia khronika* (Eurasianist Chronicle) saw thirteen issues of about one hundred pages each, distributed over more than a decade (1925–37). The third category of publications encompasses single-author books, mainly by the leaders of the Eurasianist movement (Savitsky, Trubetzkoy, and Vernadsky). The *Vremennik* carried articles on issues of fundamental importance, whereas the *Khronika* was more journalistic and geared toward current affairs, although it kept a certain balance between politics, history, religion, and Oriental studies. The movement also produced a range of occasional publications: the very anti-Catholic collection *Rossiia i latinstvo* (Russia and the Latin Creed), numerous propaganda booklets,[9] responses to attacks, leaflets for the general public, and the like.

Even in the 1920s, Eurasianism did not really have a common ideological platform; it was an atmosphere, an outlook on the world. The need to take a stand on the Soviet experience produced discord within the movement. Certain Eurasianists, such as Savitsky and Trubetzkoy, never really sided with the Soviet Union, but the movement as a whole remained ambiguous on this topic. The acceptance of the Soviet regime accelerated the division of the movement into two factions. The first faction, based in Prague (Savitsky, Alekseev, Trubetzkoy), kept its distance from the USSR; while the second faction (Karsavin, Suvchinsky, Sviatopolk-Mirskii), based in Paris, was close to the new regime. The latter published the Marxist weekly *Evraziia* (Eurasia) in 1928–29, and a Belgian version, *Evraziets* (The Eurasian)—which often limited itself to republishing articles from *Pravda*—from 1929 until 1934. From 1924 the Eurasianist movement was infiltrated by the State Political Directorate (Aleksandr Langovoi, among others).[10] A tragic destiny awaited those Eurasianists who chose to return to the Soviet Union, such as A. Durnyi and Sviatopolk-Mirskii: They were welcomed upon arrival and given leading posts in the literary hierarchy, but at the end of the 1930s, after the death of Maksim Gorky deprived them of their protector, they ended up in camps or in front of firing squads.

This schism within the Eurasianist movement between allies and opponents of the Soviet Union was not strictly political. It was representative of two more general tendencies of Eurasianism: the first was mainly interested in philosophical and religious questions, while the second paid more attention to contemporary political problems. The "idealists" called for a literary, essayistic, and purely intellectual Eurasianism, whereas the "realists" wanted a more organized and ideological approach. This cleavage concerning the very nature of the movement paralleled the political divisions; the moderate Eurasianists found refuge in academic and scholarly careers, whereas the radical ones offered their services to the USSR. Underlying the different attitudes toward the Soviet experience were different conceptions of Eurasianism: Was it to be an intellectual current or a political party?

Since its first issue, on November 24, 1928, the weekly *Evraziia,* published in the Parisian suburb of Clamart, defined its aim very clearly: to link Eurasianism's historical conception of Russia with an awakening Marxist political conscience. The first issue featured all the big names of Eurasianism, including Savitsky and Trubetzkoy. Later the paper mainly published young and little-known pro-Soviet Eurasianists. The editorial board included both people who had been more or less close to early Eurasianism (L. Karsavin, V. Nikitin, S. Sviatopolk-Mirskii, P. Suvchinsky, P. Arapov, P. Malevskii-Malevich, S. Efron) and newcomers. Suvchinsky, who was close to Gorky and the National Bolshevist Nikolai Ustrialov, was the leader of this Marxist Eurasianism at the time, opposing Savitsky ideologically. *Evraziia* quickly began to borrow from Soviet rhetoric, denouncing opponents of the Soviet Union as "bourgeois" and "materialistic egoists." A third of the newspaper was reserved exclusively for—then already self-glorifying—official Soviet news, mainly on economic (five-year plan success rates, etc.) and organizational issues (reports on the different Soviets, etc.). The articles on political philosophy remained very dogmatic and attempted to make all the principles of Eurasianism compatible with communism.[11] The poet Sergei Efron, although he was not yet working for the Soviet secret service, accepted dubious sponsorship (probably from the Lubianka) for *Evraziia.*

Such loyalty to the Soviet Union quickly drew censures from Eurasianism's founding fathers, who were disconcerted by the number of individuals moving "to the left." In a small booklet,[12] Savitsky, Alekseev, and Il'in denounced the weekly as a non-Eurasianist publication and refused to enter a debate with it. Savitsky decided no longer to write in the newspaper. *Evraziia* contemptuously called this reaction an "infantile disorder of the Eurasianist ideas"[13] and compared it to the critical texts Florovsky wrote when he left the movement in 1923. Prince Trubetzkoy chose to resign from all Eurasianist organizations. He explained his choice in a public letter written on December 31, 1928; according to him, *Evraziia* had corrupted the Eurasianist teachings by introducing alien and incompatible elements, such as Marxism or the ideas of Nikolai Fëdorov (1828–1903).[14] He declared himself no longer responsible for any Eurasianist publications with the exception of his own writings, which he listed in the letter.[15]

The editors of *Evraziia* tried not to dramatize this rupture, hoping that Trubetzkoy's departure would be temporary. They reaffirmed their view that Eurasianism had indeed changed, but in response to new challenges. The paper would be innovative but remain faithful to the logic of Eurasianism. However, they went on to condemn the founding fathers, who, they wrote, were rooted in a nationalistic, right-wing way of thinking that not only endangered the movement but was also sterile and limited to an idealization of Muscovy and Orthodoxy. According to *Evraziia,* Eurasianism must, on the contrary, react to the Russian Revolution, whose universal aim was to reorganize society against anarchy to recreate natural order. Eurasianism was thus of necessity ontologically revolutionary: "Eurasianism recognizes the discrepancy between a material culture that is becoming more and more universal and the individual forms of culture. It understands the Russian revolutionary process as a heroic attempt to transcend these forms and to find newer, more adequate ones."[16] Eurasianism was based on a philosophy of Russian history, but it now had to develop a theory of revolution. Its interest in forms of social organization "naturally" drew it closer to other theoretical systems, such as Marxism or Fëdorov's ideas.

Crucially, the Clamart current also had a very different conception of the organization of Eurasianism, calling for the constitution of a Eurasianist political party or at least a tightly knit structure modeled on Bolshevism. Its members talked about an "organized" and institutionalized Eurasianism; to be a "Eurasian" would be a title assigned by a higher organ, and no longer an individual feeling shared by people with sometimes incompatible interests. The Clamart current thus illustrates Eurasianism's internal tensions. The movement as a whole never managed to decide what it wanted to be; wavering between setting up a political party and remaining an intellectual current, as well as between the status of a dogmatic or more informal community, it necessarily produced schisms and dissensions.

Whereas Eurasianism was dominated by cultural and historical topics during the 1920s, in the 1930s a new, more political atmosphere emerged in the movement. Trubetzkoy abandoned Eurasianist cultural theory for strict political philosophy and more or less explicit condemnations of Nazi racial thought.[17] *Evraziiskie tetradi* (The Eurasianist Notebooks), which were published between 1934 and 1936, differed from the traditional Eurasianist publications; after the departure of Il'in and Sezeman, the small editorial board no longer included many big names (only Savitsky and Alekseev remained), the movement produced little, and the journal only published the very Bolshevik-sounding resolutions of the Eurasianist Organization and exclusively political articles about the USSR. The movement was forced to publish smaller journals, covering topics that were more diverse and less specifically Eurasianist. In the 1930s, Eurasianism was both intellectually and organizationally on the retreat. In 1926, the members of the Committee of the Eurasianist Organization had met in Prague to elect a Politburo. However, no further steps were taken to create a Eurasianist "party" that would at least terminologically correspond to the Bolshevik model. Disagreement set in; Karsavin refused to join the committee of the Eurasianist organization and condemned the institutionalization of the movement, although he was recognized as its main philosopher after the departure of P. M. Bitsilli and, later, Florovsky. In 1932, there was a short-lived burst of activity, when the movement organized a Eurasianist Congress that reaffirmed the primary importance of Orthodoxy as the basis of the new Russia's social organization. The desire to create a rigid organization resembling a political party created more problems than it solved; the Eurasianists were mired in debates about whom to exclude, whom to deny the title of Eurasianist or grant it with qualifications,[18] and so on.

The networks of social contacts that had ensured the success of Eurasianism in the 1920s also disappeared almost entirely:[19] Eurasianist groups continued to exist only in Paris and Prague; the pro-Soviet Brussels group became completely autonomous; and the "Clamart schismatics," who only published *Evraziia* for a year and a half, no longer even considered themselves Eurasianists. Eurasianism got bogged down in political debates and cut off from intellectual circles in the strict sense of the word, its original cradle. This change of environment proved fatal to the movement; Eurasianism had been "meaningful" as an intellectual current whose informal nature made it all the more productive. It was out of place amid party political struggles, where its complexity, its nuances, and its profound contradictions put it at a disadvantage, particularly at a time when the Russian exile community had to choose between fascism and communism. Savitsky and, to a lesser extent, Trubetzkoy and Suvchinsky, remained the only real day-to-day promoters of Eurasianism. By 1935, the movement had nearly disappeared, and it survived only in Prague, revolving around the indefatigable

Savitsky. World War II signaled the end of Eurasianism, marked by Trubetzkoy's death in 1938, the return of the Marxist Eurasianists to the USSR, and Jakobson's and Florovsky's departure to the United States. Savitsky remained isolated in Central Europe. Only Vernadsky continued to develop a "Eurasian" vision of the Russian history after 1945.

Although fertile and active, the movement thus collapsed at the turn of the 1930s, not only because of its internal divisions but also because of the change in political atmosphere; the rise of Nazism in Europe and the end of the New Economic Policy in the Soviet Union called for a politicization and a radicalization that had negative consequences for the complexity of Eurasianist thought. Eurasianism had developed thanks to the unique conjunction between an intellectually fertile Russian émigré community and exceptionally receptive Western surroundings. It proved unable to outlive these circumstances. Eurasianism was the only truly original ideology to emerge among the émigrés; nevertheless, it remained a product of exile—unable to act, the émigrés vented their hopes in an extremely complex discourse of Russian messianic identity. For the Russian exiles as a whole and for Eurasianism in particular, writing served as a substitute for action; words replaced deeds.

It seems evident that the Eurasianists' focus on the topic of national identity and their willingness to stress their distinctiveness from the host culture were inversely proportional to their opportunities for real action. The Eurasianist doctrine must be grasped in its fundamentally provocative character. It was born of the malaise of young nationalists who were reluctant to integrate into the host culture and who refused to resign themselves to the thought that links with the homeland were definitely broken. Their rejection of Europe can only be understood if we remember that it was elaborated in the West by those Russians who, culturally speaking, were the most Europeanized.

A Philosophy of Politics

Eurasianism was a conservative utopia born of a desire to take into account the fact of the Revolution, yet it called for a "revolutionary reaction"[20] that would differ from the political conservatism shared by the Russian right in exile. The Eurasianist ideology was the Russian version of Western currents known as the "third way."[21] Like them, Eurasianism was attracted to the Italian Fascist model and intrigued by the Bolshevik adventure, and it condemned Mussolini's narrow nationalism, as well as communism, which it associated with the West. However, the Eurasianists stressed their differences with these Western currents by upholding Russian cultural distinctiveness. If Russia must choose a third way between capitalism and socialism and between liberalism and dictatorship, they argued, this is not a strictly political choice, because Russia is, in its very "essence," a third continent. Eurasianism was an original variety of the idea of conservative revolution in that it considered itself a non-European current of thought, aloof from all classical Western debates. In the Eurasianists' interpretation, the "third way" was no longer the solution for a Europe stuck between the expansion of communism and the purported failure of the liberal Western model, but rather a statement of Russia's cultural irreducibility to the West. In spite of this culturalist facade, Eurasianism merely adapted Western precepts to the Russian case; rooted in German, French, and Italian schools of thought of the time, it had no specific political originality.

The editorial board of *Evraziia* was overtly inspired by the Bolshevik experience, but the other Eurasianists' attitude toward the Soviet Union was more ambiguous. The chasm between Eurasianism and Marxism was insurmountable—above all on the religious level: Bolshevism was considered to be a destructive and iconoclastic movement, whereas Eurasianism saw itself as constructive and fundamentally religious. The new political authorities were deeply disturbing for the Eurasianists because of the materialistic doctrine that was at the basis of Marxism's philosophy of history. For them, Marxism was a religion of atheism, and the Soviet antireligious policies were unacceptable. Marxist materialism denied the autonomy of ideas, a fundamental tenet of Eurasianism. However, very few Eurasianists openly joined the White movements; even those most opposed to the USSR, such as Trubetzkoy and Savitsky, eventually qualified their initial anticommunist stance. Eurasianism defined itself as White only in its early texts, when some émigrés in the Balkans (more than in Prague or Paris), such as Savitsky, were still close to Denikin and Wrangel. But the Eurasianists never wholeheartedly supported the idea of a political volte-face and constantly criticized the monarchist movements; to be useful, the reaction needed to transcend the revolution positively, rather than simply negating it:[22] "The emotional counterrevolution has so far not managed to become a deliberate, willful reaction."[23]

Eurasianism's alliance with communism was therefore complex. At first it was based on negation; the Eurasianists were united against the West, sympathized with non-European cultures *by definition,* and condemned the

European experience *out of principle.* Bolshevism wanted to make a clean sweep of the past, and Eurasianism also banned the period of the Romanovs' imperial rule from the annals of Russian history.[24] The two movements had the same ideological enemies—the political and social realities of the West: "Eurasianism agrees with Bolshevism in rejecting not just certain political forms, but the entire culture that existed in Russia immediately before the revolution and continues to exist in the countries of the Romano-Germanic West, as well as in demanding a radical reconstruction of that entire culture. Eurasianism agrees with Bolshevism in its call for the liberation of the peoples of Asia and Africa who are enslaved by the colonial powers."[25] Yet this "third-worldism" *avant la lettre* and the dismissal of the West that were common to both movements were founded on different ideological presuppositions. The Eurasianists approved of the anti-European discourse of Russian communism, but they rejected, for example, the distinction it made between bourgeois and proletarians; for them, these two concepts remained Western and excessively social. The real issue, for the Eurasianists, was necessarily a national one. Though they took a positive view of the new Soviet culture, they dismissed its internationalism as illusory, for culture could only be the expression of a nation and its faith.

Nevertheless, Eurasianism always strove to be very pragmatic toward the Soviet Union, and it did not hesitate to acknowledge the features it shared with its regime. For example, it applauded the idea that justice should be dependent on the state; supported the creation of a Russian proletariat; approved of the various plans for an accelerated industrialization of the country and of the principle of economic planning, which it considered a necessary remedy for the natural chaos of human activity; and called for national economic autarky. In the early 1920s, the end of War Communism and the more liberal period of the New Economic Policy greatly influenced this positive attitude. Eurasianism also genuinely interiorized the Soviet leitmotif of social justice, juxtaposing religious truth and social truth as embodiments of Russia's double mission: Following a Russian tradition started by the Slavophiles, the Eurasianists stressed the similarities between the construction of a new society and a renewal of religious sentiment.[26]

Eurasianism acknowledged that it was postrevolutionary, and it wished to be an innovative, not a reactionary, movement within the Russian exile community. The events of 1917 were not only an accomplished and accepted fact but also a reality that provided the framework for all thinking on Russia. "To interpret the Russian revolution is to interpret Russian history, and vice versa: By clarifying the meaning of the revolution we are clarifying the meaning of history."[27] It was therefore necessary to make one's peace with the Revolution, which presupposed presenting it as a natural and redeeming event; Eurasianism saw 1917 as a healthy cataclysm that put an end to Russia's duality. The Revolution embodied the historical contradiction in which Russia had lived for two centuries; it constituted the peak of its Europeanization and, at the same time, its departure from a Western framework of thought, the self-dissolution of imperial, European Russia. This view engendered an attitude that had both positive and negative aspects: The Revolution was seen as a European phenomenon, because Marxism was a Western-centered ideology born of the industrial revolution; and it was an Asian event, a symbol of Russia's reunion with the Orient and with itself.

Although the Eurasianists rejected Marxism, Bolshevism was seen as eminently national. Thus the need for a positive reading of painful events spawned a philosophy of downfall, a euphoria about ruins, an appeal to elementary forces. Eurasianism took on a Faustian tinge. Evil will breed good; "in perishing, Russia came alive in spirit."[28] Eurasianism adopted Marxism's dialectic approach, turning the idea of humanity evolving in stages against communism; Russia would thus go "from capitalism as a thesis and communism as an antithesis to Eurasianism as their synthesis."[29] Because Eurasia was supposed to be a median world, Eurasianism sought to become a third way between capitalism and communism on the economic level, although it acknowledged that it was closer to the latter, judged "oriental," while capitalism was equated with Western culture. This proximity with communism was seen as residing in practice, in organization. For the Eurasianists, communism is not a genuine ideology, because its materialist presuppositions keep it from reaching down to the essence of things and the true nature of historical events.[30] According to the Eurasianists, "in Soviet reality, communism plays the role not of an ideal, but of a method."[31] Thus the status of ideology is reserved for Eurasianism, while communism is nothing but a method of management devoid of meaning and waiting to be vested with Eurasianism. In the future, practice would be communist and totalitarian, while the ideal would be Eurasian. The two principles would no longer be competing but complementary.

Eurasianism was thus an eminently modern movement. It clearly rejected monarchy,[32] and it was in favor of a kind of republic, but one that would be "demotic" rather than democratic. Besides, the issue of the form of government was of no interest to the Eurasianists, who considered it a facade of Western legalism. National sovereignty was seen as organic, and the state as above all a spiritual entity that corresponds to the national character. The Western model was thus to be rejected: Universal suffrage does not reveal the national essence; it is a mechanical game played by political parties using amorphous masses, an arithmetic conception of power through elections, the dangerous illusion that "public opinion" exists.[33] What was needed, on the contrary, was an organic order representing needs, knowledge, and ideas; even in the West, beyond changes of government, there is a constancy of the nation, and it is this essence that must be formulated and elevated as the principle of power: "We must look for the future forms of Russian statehood in the principle of people's autocracy, which optimally combines popular sovereignty with the principle of people's will. Only the combination of these two principles can create a strong and organic regime."[34]

The Eurasianists therefore advocated an extreme form of statism: "But in the sphere that is distinctly its own, government is absolute; otherwise, it would not be government."[35] This absolutization of the state naturally went hand in hand with a monist conception of law. In the Eurasianist state, law, morals, and faith would fuse into one; there would be no distinction between the different powers, justice would have no autonomy, and there would be no private law that could be used against the state. Politics is seen as organic: It is spontaneously self-regulating, moved by an internal dynamic; it is free and not artificial; and it is singular, self-expressing, and self-totalizing. As with certain German Romanticists who inspired the Eurasianists, the state is considered an ideal sphere, the theoretical location of totality, an all-embracing whole that does not put society at odds with itself. It is humanity's nontranscendable natural environment.[36] For the Eurasianists, "demotism" is the political system that best represents the nation. Eurasian citizens must not be mere subjects of power; they are called upon to invest themselves in the res publica. The movement thus called for the formation of an estate-based society of a new type, not modeled on feudalism, democracy, or theocracy, but corresponding to Russia's distinctive features.[37] Class differences would be transcended through professional corporations, councils of "elders," and functional groups based on ethnicity, territory, religion, and the like. These estates would be able to voice their opinions, their partial vision of the national organism, but they would not be entitled to make political decisions; that right would be reserved for the Eurasian ruling class.

This ruling class would constitute the government of the future Eurasian state. It would be united by a belief in the power of the "idea"—an idea that would obviously be national and reveal the essence of the people. The political discourse of Eurasianism thus took its earlier philosophical postulates to their logical conclusion: The state is an organic expression of the nation and encompasses society in a totalitarian fashion; individuals derive their meaning from something that is superior to them and organizes them hierarchically; and power belongs solely to those who master the philosophy of Eurasian history. Eurasianism fully subscribed to the commonplace interwar idea of the collapse of the West and classical culture. For Eurasianism, Europe had reached an impasse, as proven by the West's internal divisions during World War I and by the October Revolution born of this war. Eurasianism harshly criticized Western democracies: Their parliamentarianism was not representative; they were rife with corruption, political games, and indecision; their public opinion was illusory; and so on.

Thus the Eurasianists rejected Europe without fully adhering to communism. This prompted them to consider the other dissident Western political movements of the 1920s. Italian Fascism intrigued them. They criticized it for its "practical" mistakes (deification of the Italian people and nationalism) but not in its principle: Fascism, for them, was a rough implementation of ideocracy that needed to be improved. It constituted "the most serious attempt to overcome Europe's cultural and political crisis without leaving the framework of multinational capitalism."[38] Many of their texts reveal an awareness of the proximity between fascism and Eurasianism, especially regarding the nature of the questions asked and the solutions proposed: statism, a mass movement, a single party, a ruling class, a new corporatist social organization, and organicism. The Eurasianists' discourse illustrates the extent to which, in the 1920s, the young Italian Fascism was perceived primarily as revolutionary and social rather than "right wing." "In spite of deep differences, one can observe that fascism shares numerous essential correspondences with Russian Bolshevism."[39] Unlike fascism, Nazism received little attention in the publications of the Eurasianist movement, which was already in its death throes when Hitler took power. Nevertheless, the last Eurasianist texts, which were openly supportive of the Soviet Union, mentioned Nazism several times; their authors were interested in the questions it asked and even in its—simultaneously social and national—solutions, but they clearly condemned its pan-Germanism and Aryanism, which were opposed to Russia.[40]

Eurasianism was sometimes accused by its opponents of thinking *racially.* It would be more accurate to call their conceptions *organicist:* They endowed peoples, cultures, and territories with an almost human reality and saw them as living or even thinking entities, as active subjects of the historical process. This organicism is reminiscent of fascism, especially in the context of a political discourse about expressing the national will. However, the Eurasianists never thought in racial terms and did not conceive of cultures as hierarchically arranged into "superior" and "inferior" ones; they did not believe in relevant genetic differences between peoples or nations. According to Eurasianism, peoples are not biological entities but rather cultural, religious, and territorial ones; miscegenation guarantees universalism; and history is the realization of ideas, not a sinister fight for survival between peoples. The geographical or biological determinism of fascist ideologies is thus different from, and less subtle than, Eurasianist determinism, which was centered on the idea of common "tendencies," a teleology shared by different peoples living in the same space.

On a philosophical level, Eurasianism borrowed from German Romanticism, although politically it was closer to the modernity of Italian Fascism and Soviet totalitarianism. It was literally imbued with German thought (despite officially rejecting it as "Romano-Germanic"), both of the nineteenth and of the early twentieth centuries. Although it considered itself genuinely innovative and purely national, rooted solely in the Russian experience, Eurasianism was actually part and parcel of the European history of ideas, from *Naturphilosophie* to conservative revolution, and it embodied a fusion between the Russian imperial past terminated by the Revolution and the Western crisis of the interwar period.

A Geographic Ideology

Eurasianism claimed to provide a global explanation of the world, a Weltanschauung. Its basic tenet was a condemnation of the "epistemological imperialism" of the West; by applying its own concepts to the rest of the world, the Eurasianists argued, Europe obfuscates the diversity of civilizations and establishes a benchmark for measuring political and economic backwardness. However, Europe does not represent a *state* of development that all nations must reach but a specific *mode* of development that cannot be reproduced. Seen through the historicist Western prism, Russia is a backward country; but the Eurasianists suggested that Russia should unlearn the West and perceive itself *geographically:* History, they argued, is the mode in which Europe expresses its identity; geography is Russia's.

The Eurasianist movement aimed to put an end to the "cultural hege-

mony of the West"[41] by asserting the superiority of the East. The Eurasianists subscribed to a third-worldism *avant la lettre;* they were persuaded not
only of non-Western cultures' right to differ, but also, and above all, of their
ultimate superiority and Europe's decline. The development of a nation
can—and must—only be organic; cross-cultural assimilation is impossible.
Thus every nation has its own mode of development and its own organic
epistemology; sciences are inevitably "national," "applied," and at the service of the state, and they converge in a system of thought that encompasses
them and provides a nation with its ideology.

Eurasianism asserted the existence of a third continent within the Old
World. Eurasia "is neither a European nor one of the Asian cultures, nor a
sum or mechanical combination of elements of the former and the latter";[42]
it has a distinctive geographic individuality of its own. Territory must lend
meaning to the nation and to history; it has a "transparent"[43] structure that
reveals Russia's nature and destiny and the "trends" that are common to the
soil and peoples living on it. The structural unity of Eurasia and its inerad-
icable distinctiveness from the rest of the world were thus established
through a language that was at once geographical, economic, and geopolitical, and also through the creation of a specific terminology for the Eurasian
sciences. For the Eurasianists, there was an organic link between a geographic territory, the specific development of a culture, and the peoples living on this territory; between environment and culture there is interaction,
mutual influence, and tension. Eurasianism saw itself as deeply rooted in
the soil. It endeavored to theorize its ideology geographically to an extent
that made this "territorialized" aspect one of the main targets of its critics.
Shirinskii-Shikhmatov, for instance, accused the Eurasianists of naturalism
and criticized the fact that, to them, "it seems that . . . Russia's path is determined not by a spiritual, but by a material factor (geography)."[44]

Savitsky's concept of topogenesis—or "place-development" (*mestorazvi-
tie*)—aimed to prove scientifically the mystical link the Eurasianists saw between territory and culture, and it illustrated their teleological conception
of the relationship between humanity and nature. From this encounter between history and territory, a geographical being was born, which is presented as a living organism. Topogenesis thus expressed Eurasianism's subtle determinism. Although reminiscent of the vocabulary of naturalism,
topogenesis posits not the subjection of humanity and history to territory
but a reciprocal and equal interaction between the natural and the sociohistorical environments. For the Eurasianists, the discipline of geosophy—a
Russian word coined on the model of historiosophy (philosophy of his-

tory)—confirmed the idea of a distinct historical destiny that was specific to the Eurasian space. The soil exposes the hidden meaning of events and destinies; it reveals Russia to itself. Territory thus possesses an eschatological and philosophical value. Geosophy analyzes territory not as a simple object of the natural sciences but as an element of the humanities that is intrinsically linked to history and its philosophical interpretation, as well as national identity.

According to the Eurasianists, the unity of Eurasian territory is visible in its geometric and systemic nature (*zakonomernost'*, from the German *Gesetzmäßigkeit*), in the degree to which it lends itself to rationalization and explanation, and in its subjection to demonstrable scientific principles. Eurasia, they argued, is the only country whose climate, soil, flora, and fauna are so perfectly harmonious, so much in conformity with a scientific "law" that Eurasianism offers to discover and formulate. As Savitsky put it, "Moving from the south to the north, nowhere on our planet can we observe a more regular alternation of different types of plants and soils than in crossing the plains of Russia-Eurasia."[45] Thus all the scientific data adduced only became meaningful through their spatial coincidence; the unity of Eurasia was proved by its natural "regularity."

Savitsky was, accordingly, one of the pioneers of structural geography, complementing the nascent structural linguistics of Jakobson and Trubetzkoy. According to him, a comparative analysis of several criteria (temperature, flora, fauna, soil, linguistic features, etc.) proves, by revealing their coextensiveness, the structural existence of a Eurasian whole and the spuriousness of the purported border between Europe and Asia in the Ural Mountains. For the Eurasianists, Eurasia is divided into four botanical and pedological (i.e., soil) strips, which are horizontal, stretching from west to east: tundra, taiga, steppe, and desert. These strips are transversely intersected by three plains: the plain connecting the White Sea to the Caucasus, the Siberian plain, and the plain of Turkistan. Savitsky tried to demonstrate the mutual closeness of the three plains and disprove any continuity between the European and Russian plains.[46]

Eurasianism did not grant all these strips the same role in the construction of Eurasia. The steppic strip is Russia's geopolitical "flesh," its chief element, its explanatory principle. The steppe is the linchpin of Eurasia; it is the only strip that spreads across the whole Eurasian space from east to west and links the different civilizations of the Old Continent.[47] The steppe alone gives "meaning" to Russia and reveals its essence: The Russian equivalent to the West's oceanic adventure is the advance into the steppe, a radical assertion of continentalism; Russian agricultural practice is marked by extensiveness, a peculiarly steppic mode; Russia's eastward geographic depth encourages economic autarky and political isolationism; control over the steppes secures Russia's geopolitical position as the world's heartland, because "he who controls the steppe easily becomes the political unifier of the whole of Eurasia."[48]

Thus Eurasia is defined in geographic terms, and the Eurasianists must now explain that Russia's main feature is to be a "horizontal" power. Whereas the European countries are said to have found a "vertical" embodiment of their political identity (in the development of democratic systems), Russia, the Eurasianists claim, finds its fulfillment in its "horizontality," whose political expression is the country's imperial structure; being *geographic*, Russia's territorial expansion is thus the *natural* expression of its identity. Eurasia therefore has to be a structural whole that can be explained out of itself, rather than from interaction with the outside world: "In many respects, Russia-Eurasia is a closed circle, a perfect continent and a world unto itself."[49] If Eurasia is a "natural" space, then it cannot accept the severance of any of its parts; this would be a violation of nature: "The nature of the Eurasian world offers as little scope as possible for different kinds of 'separatisms,' be they political, cultural, or economic."[50] An interest in geopolitics is therefore inherent in Eurasianism; geography is a *scientific* means of restoring *political* power.

The second aspect elaborated upon by the Eurasianists to justify the existence and unity of Eurasia was the cultural closeness of the Eurasian peoples: "How many people are there in Russia who have no Khazar or Polovtsian, Tatar or Bashkir, Mordvin or Chuvash blood in their veins?"[51] The idea of a third geographic and political continent was intrinsically linked to the idea of its cultural unity; to exist as a continent distinct from Europe and Asia, Russia must be an empire based on common features shared by all its peoples. Consequently, both linguistics and ethnology were called upon to confirm the unity of Eurasia. This fully reveals the epistemological premises of the movement; the linguistic and ethnographic discourse of Eurasianism was, fundamentally, *both* a means to demonstrate the unity of Eurasia *and* a Eurasianist science-to-be that was an end in itself.

Whereas Pan-Slavism had endeavored to demonstrate the unity of the Slavic world and the crucial role of the Russian people, the Eurasianists stressed their difference from the Slavophile tradition by clearly stating their rejection of a Russian identity subordinated to Slavdom, which for them belonged to Europe. However, Prince Trubetzkoy remained more balanced than his friends concerning the cultural affiliation of the Slavs. He considered them to be an independent component of the Western world, which is not limited to the "Romano-Germanic" peoples. Being Slavs, the Russians, despite their difference from the other, exclusively European Slavic peoples, belong as much to Slavdom as to the world of the steppes. They are linked to the former by language and religion but remain part and parcel of the Turanian world by virtue of blood ties, character, and culture. "The Russians, along with the Ugro-Finnic and the Volga Turkic peoples, constitute a special cultural zone that is closely linked with both Slavdom and the 'Turanian' East, and it is difficult to say which of these links is stronger and more stable."[52] This wish to put the Slavic and Turanian elements of Russia-Eurasia on an equal footing completes the conception of this space as a third continent, a middle ground between Europe and Asia.

· However, the Eurasianists' writings on the subject are contradictory. Several texts, even some of Trubetzkoy's, object to equating "Slavic" with "Orthodox": The western Slavs are of Romano-Germanic culture; in Russia, Slavic culture has developed and taken root as an expression of Orthodoxy, not of Slavdom. As Trubetzkoy explained, "Slavdom is not an ethnopsychological, ethnographic or cultural-historical concept, but a linguistic one. Language, and language only, links the Slavs to each other. Language is the only link that links Russia to Slavdom."[53] The idea of topogenesis is used to underpin this denial of the Slavic features of the Russian space. The Eurasianists considered genetic and racial kinship or proximity irrelevant to identity. What really mattered was *where* a culture or a language developed; linguistic groups are shaped by geocultural affiliation, rather than origin. Russia belongs exclusively to the Eurasian topogenesis.[54]

· Thus the unity of the Russians and the peoples of the steppe not only results from their sharing the same territory; it is also expressed linguistically and ethnographically. Jakobson endeavored to demonstrate the unity of the Eurasian languages.[55] The three criteria he considered important were tone, correlation of palatalization, and territorial continuity. This phonological analysis led him to both geographic and cultural conclusions: Eurasia is an area characterized by lack of tone and the correlation of palatalization, surrounded by more or less concentric geographical zones lacking such characteristics. This linguistic argument thus corroborated Eurasianist physical geography. The languages of Eurasia may have heterogeneous origins, but they are nonetheless all evolving in the same direction. What is important, therefore, is not their linguistic kinship but only their geographic relations. As Jakobson expressed it: "The principle of place-development prevails over the principle of genetic closeness";[56] the affinity between languages is not a state but a dynamic process due to spatial contact (the principle of topogenesis).

    · Jakobson's theory was meant to be teleological; it is more important to know where the languages "are headed" than where they "come from": "The unity of phonological 'purpose,' the movement in one common direction is what welds the languages of Eurasia together."[57] For the Eurasianists, the evolution of languages is neither incoherent nor random. To the contrary, they evolve in a definite direction that can be subjected to analysis and argument; there is a philosophy of the history of language, because language evolves just like a living organism. According to Savitsky, "All Slavic, Romance, Hindu, Finno-Ugric, Turkic, Mongolian and North Caucasian languages that are found inside Eurasia and have developed a system that distinguishes between soft and hard consonants, are languages with common tendencies, despite their different origins. . . . It [this tendency] has a philosophical aspect. The peoples of Eurasia are peoples with a 'common tendency,' not just in the sphere of linguistics."[58]

    This linguistic approach to the unity between Russia and the steppe facilitates an imperceptible transition to ethnographic discourse; the Eurasianists drew up long lists of cultural "facts" of all kinds that were supposed to support their linguistic claims. The cult of nomadism was at the heart of Eurasianism's iconoclastic call to reject European values; the nomads symbolize movement, permanent regeneration, nonhistory, and a unique human psychology. For the Eurasianists, the person of the steppe possesses qualities and a psyche different from those of sedentary people.[59] The Eurasianists disparaged the sedentary, and more particularly urban, way of life; they refused to view it is an ideal, because it breeds insalubrious sanitary conditions. Western culture is petrified and leads humanity to an impasse, even on the level of hygiene. Nomadism, on the contrary, is described as a school of bodily culture; the Eurasianists even went as far as to give physical descriptions of the nomads and their morphological features, extolling their sense of direction, their healthy food, the fresh air they breathe, their perfect adjustment to their environment, their symbiotic relation with nature,[60] and so on.

    Of all the Eurasianists, Trubetzkoy was the one who took the interpretive parallels between linguistics, psychology, and sociopolitical behavior the farthest. He argued that the distinctiveness of the Turanian languages resides in their regularity;[61] they have a structure organized around a few rudimentary basic principles, and thought is submitted to this syntactical and phonetic regularity: "the comparative poverty and rudimentarity of the material and their total submission to simple and schematic laws, which welds this material into a single whole and gives this whole a certain schematic clarity and transparency."[62] Trubetzkoy went on to draw psychological conclusions from his linguistic analysis. First of all, the Turkic linguistic system sheds light on Turkic society itself and explains both the nomads' common law and their clan system. It also reveals the identity, the essence of "the Turk," in the broad sense of a person belonging to the Turkic peoples.

Despite this rudimentary and regular nature, the Turanian psychological type, Trubetzkoy writes, has not developed abstract thought, whether philosophical or creative. According to him, the Turks have borrowed from Arab-Persian Islam, and the Mongols from Buddhism and Chinese culture, but neither people has added anything new to the ideas of these cultures; they only reproduced them in a schematic way. The Turks have no value outside the Eurasian world, outside their interaction with Russia. What Trubetzkoy called the Turanians' "subconscious philosophical system"[63] precludes any dichotomy between life and thought, habits and ideology: "The Turanian psyche imparts a cultural stability and force to the nation, upholds cultural and historical continuity, and creates the conditions for an economy of the nation's strength."[64] Thus the qualities ascribed to the Turanians served to legitimize an ideocratic and autocratic regime and the concept of a cultural, political, and religious equilibrium, a favorite idea with the Eurasianists, who considered that Russia, having borrowed it from the Mongols, forgot this concept in the course of its Europeanization in the eighteenth and nineteenth centuries. Russia must emulate the nomadic world, which symbolizes the Eurasianists' cultural relativism and belief in the indelibility of identities.

This illustrates one of the central ambiguities of Eurasianist thought: its hesitation between exalting and dismissing steppic and Turanian culture. The two attitudes alternate in the texts of the Eurasianists. They sometimes put the Turanian world on an equal footing with the familiar European or Asian civilizations and demand to do justice to its culture. But the "absence" of a distinctive Turanian culture may also serve as a positive argument in favor of the Eurasianists' authoritarian conception of power and, above all, to defy Eurocentric clichés by extolling the savage, the barbarian, the nomad unspoiled by culture.

The Eurasianists' iconoclastic theories have very often drawn accusations either of "betrayal" of the fatherland or of Turkocentrism. However, the opponents of Eurasianism have rarely noticed the numerous ambigui-

ties of this discourse; though the Eurasianist view of national identity differed profoundly from the more traditional nationalism shared by most
White Russians, it was nevertheless a modernized but still messianic expression of Great Russian nationalism. The discourse on the linguistic and
cultural unity between Russia and the steppes was thus two-sided, and this
ambiguity must be highlighted: Eurasianism posited the existence of a
Eurasian nation rooted in the fusion and the equality of all the peoples of
the empire, but it also equated Eurasia with the Russian world.

Eurasianism's praise of Russia's proximity with the East stemmed from
its iconoclasm; the Eurasianists took pride in shocking readers by claiming
that "in every Russian there is a drop of yellow blood."[65] However, defining the *cultural* unity of Eurasia was the greatest challenge for the movement; this unity cannot be ethnic, nor is it a unity of citizens, as in a French-
type nation-state. It takes the form of a common destiny: "[The whole is]
neither a class, nor the people, nor humanity. But between the all-too-
concrete people and all-too-abstract humanity there is the concept of a
'world apart.' All of the peoples who inhabit the economically self-contained [autarkic] place-development and are connected to each other not by
race but by a community of historical destiny, the joint creation of a common culture or a common state—they are that whole."[66] Eurasian unity is
symbolized by concentric circles, allowing affiliations with multiple communities, with mutually compatible "individuations" inside Eurasia; one
can be all at once Buryat, Russian (*rossiisky*), and Eurasian. Russia-Eurasia is therefore a cultural whole not so much because of its actual, demonstrable unity and uniqueness but because its different elements are intertwined and possess no reality outside the whole.

As Trubetzkoy stated, "It is not an obliteration of the individual features
of each part that creates the unity of the whole, but the continuity of the rainbow network itself."[67] The unity of Eurasia thus results from the relation of
each component to the whole (vertical relationship), not from a systematic
correlation between the components (horizontal relationship); it is even
possible for the parts to have in common only their belonging to the whole,
rather than any specific cultural characteristics. This approach presupposes,
however, that there is an identifiable discontinuity between Eurasia and the
other topogeneses. Whereas the borders of Eurasia with Europe are hermetic,
the borders with the East are penetrable. The Russian world and the world
of the steppes are connected by strips of "rainbow" defined only by their relation to the Eurasian whole and without any clear limits between them:
"This culture's eastern and south-eastern boundaries with the (Turkic-

Mongolian) 'steppic' culture and, through it, with the cultures of Asia, are so gradual as to be imperceptible."[68] This purportedly seamless connection remained ambiguous. One the one hand, it served to justify a boundless Orientalization, or even Asianization, of Russian identity, and to put Russia on a par with the other peoples with regard to their relation to the Eurasian totality. On the other hand, it allowed the Eurasians to deny the existence of a natural eastern border for the Russian empire. As a consequence of Eurasia's oriental connections, Russia has a certain claim to Asia.

  According to this theory, Eurasia's history is distinct from Russia's, both geographically and temporally, because Eurasia transcends Russia, precedes it historically, and exceeds it geographically. Russian history is therefore part of Eurasia's, and Eurasian history contains a non-Russian element. We may notice, however, a constant confusion between a state, Russia, with its history, people, and religion, and a territory, Eurasia, praised for its diversity. The word "Eurasian" is thus supposed to designate not only the Russians but also all the Turanian peoples. Yet "the history of the expansion of the Russian state is to a large degree the history of the Russian people's adjustment to its place-development, Eurasia, and of the adjustment of the entire space of Eurasia to the economic and historical needs of the Russian people."[69]

  In general, the Eurasianists used the words "Russia" and "Eurasia" interchangeably, as synonyms; but they did distinguish between them when it served their purpose. The Russian people are in fact unlike any other people in Eurasia because they serve as the connecting element of Eurasian national diversity; without them, there would be no movement from one Eurasian element to another, there would be no whole giving meaning to its components. It is therefore solely under the aegis of the Russian people that the Eurasian nation is constituted. "The role of the Russian people in the construction of Russia-Eurasia is not limited to national self-determination. It is Russian culture, supplemented with elements of the cultures of other Eurasian peoples, that must become the basis of the supranational (Eurasian) culture which would serve the needs of all the peoples of Russia-Eurasia without constraining their national specificities."[70]

  Eurasia is not a symbiosis of civilizations because it unifies different peoples and cultures, some of them European and others Asian, but only because the Russian people blend all the identities of the Old Continent; Russia is Eurasian in its very principle, with or without Eurasia. The Eurasian supranationality actually constitutes a new expression of Russianness, which already includes national diversity. What becomes, then, of the other peoples of the Empire, especially the Turanians? If they are not acculturated to Russia, are they also called "Eurasians" or simply "Asians"? Do they have a recognized existence outside the discourse on Russia's Orientalness, given that the Russians are declared "first among equals"[71]?

An Ambiguous Orientalism

The Eurasianists were aware and particularly proud of being the first to highlight so openly the existence of Asian elements in Russian culture. This aspect of their ideas was indeed innovative. Throughout the nineteenth century, Russian intellectuals with nationalist leanings were sensitive to the idea of an Asian influence on Russia. But they remained ambiguous about the topic, and stressing the Christian and "Aryan" characteristics of the Russians was still considered more important than any analysis of the national and territorial reality of the empire. It seems that the shock of the revolutions, the civil war, and exile was what cleared the ground for the Eurasianists to make their Asianist claims, portraying Asia as a nomadic and Turkic-Mongolian community that goes against the grain of European values.

Paradoxically, Eurasianism was born out of the personal experience of its authors, who first rejected Europe and then tried to theorize that rejection. The first book that could be called Eurasianist, even before the famous collection *Exodus to the East* in 1921 and the formation of the movement as such, is Prince Trubetzkoy's *Europe and Mankind* (*Evropa i chelovechestvo*), published in 1920; though at this point the author did not yet advocate the idea of Eurasian unity, he did endeavor to deny the West any universal value. As the first thinker to apply the colonialist framework to the Russian situation, Trubetzkoy argued further for the need for decolonization and the right to national self-determination for Russia.[72] This book shows how the early reasoning of the Eurasianists was negative and would only later be transformed into a constructive discourse. The movement thus denounced Europe before promoting Eurasia. As he expressed it, "My book does not have the ambition to put forward concrete positive and directive principles. It must only help to overthrow certain idols and, after confronting the reader with empty pedestals, force him to rack his brains for a solution."[73]

Eurasianism allows us to understand that discourse on cultural otherness does not boil down to a mere acknowledgment of difference. The "civilizational" perspective it offers is intended as a means of self-revelation. At first sight, the Eurasianist theoreticians make positive claims about Russia's

Easternness; Russia, for them, is closer to Asia than to Europe, and Orthodoxy is closer to the oriental religions than to the two major Western Christian confessions. Yet, these general remarks remain ambiguous; upon closer
inspection, the Eurasianist texts on the East are in fact limited to exalting
the steppe. They take no interest in Asia itself, for their aim is not an "exodus to the East" but Russia's realization of its own Easternness, which is
simply a way of rejecting the West. It can therefore only be a Russian East,
an "internal" exoticism; the world of the steppe is a mirror of Russia, and it
is to be distinguished from Asia proper, which represents a real otherness
with which Eurasianists do not know how to deal.

In their writings on historiography, the Eurasianists attack the classic
Kiev–Moscow–Saint Petersburg triad in Russian history, which they consider Eurocentric. Rehabilitating the East entails formulating a new theoretical grid: Eurasian history is divided into five dialectical stages (from opposition to domination and then to symbiosis) by "rhythms" resulting from the
meeting of two principles: forest and steppe. Eurasian history is, on this account, composed of two elements, the Russian and the Turanian: "Slavdom's
cohabitation with Turandom is the central fact of Russian history."[74] Ancient
Russian history is, on this reading, a depiction of the dominance of the nomads and their acculturation of the early Slavs. Kievan Rus' and the Saint
Petersburg period are denounced as expressions of a European rather than a
Eurasian Russianness. Eurasianist historiography thus focuses on the Mongol period and on fourteenth- through sixteenth-century Muscovy.[75]

The Mongol Empire represents a key element in Eurasianist theory, for
it is situated at the very junction of the Eurasianists' history/historiosophy
and their geographic ideology of the steppe. As a many-faced symbol, it is
present in every Eurasianist argument and may be used to advocate both the
relativism of Russian culture against Europe and its universality for the rest
of the non-Western world. Consequently, the function of the Mongol Empire is to have revealed Russia's identity. For the Eurasianists, the Mongol
Empire was incarnated in the figure of Genghis Khan, who, they claim,
brought out Russia's hidden identity: power, control over both territory and
circumstances, a universal perspective in thought and action, and so on. The
Mongol Empire crystallized an experience of self-realization, formulated
Eurasian identity geographically, and thus became the true driving force of
Russia's entry into history, having given an ideological expression to Rus-
sia's intrinsic telluric force.

The Mongol Empire gave Russia an identity that manifests itself in a
variety of fields.[76] It endowed the country with a temporality all of its own,

expressed in its cyclical and repetitive history, but also with a unique spatiality, which is the basis of its geographic identity.[77] The Mongol world is also an inverted symbol of the geographic and temporal smallness of Europe; for the Eurasianists, Genghis Khan surpasses Napoleon and Alexander the Great, his achievement being impossible to assess on the scale of Western civilization, which is narrowed down by the dominance of European thought.[78]

. The Mongol Empire is also what gives Russia its universality. The Eurasianists argue that only those countries that exhibit a dual nature, both Eastern and Western, can be centers of the world. Their duality is a guarantee of universal reach. The Mongol Empire was the arbiter and mediator between the Indo-Chinese and Mediterranean worlds, and it formulated the unity of the Old Continent in its own way: "Genghis Khan's ideal was to create a United Empire of Mankind"[79]—and he thus carried on the tradition of universality of the first and second Roman Empires, turning it to his advantage. The nomadic world has replaced the sedentary cultures as the center of the Old World, and the steppe has taken over from the Mediterranean.[80] This prestigious lineage can thus be continued by Russia itself, because it is heir to the Mongols. The Eurasianists take up and modify the notion of Moscow as Third Rome; along with the religious connection between Constantinople and Moscow, a geographic legacy of centrality is passed on from Byzantium via the Mongols to Moscow, validating Russia's messianic claims.

' Finally, the Mongol Empire is a religious model for Russia. Although the Eurasianists praise its tolerance of other religions, the empire exemplifies the absence of separation between the spiritual and temporal spheres. It is considered to have prefigured Russia's political principles: Through its centralism, it expressed the "natural" authoritarianism of Eurasia; through its postal system it demonstrated its complete control over territory, and particularly over the steppe; and through its hierarchical organization of society, a synthesis of social and military hierarchies, it subjected the individual to the community and to political authority. Consequently, everyone knows his or her exact place in a totality that transcends the individual, and people are simply cogs in the machine of the state. The Mongol Empire confirms the Eurasianists in their view that the rule of an "idea" will give meaning and order to the world, to Russia, and to each individual; this reign is the only possible answer to the individualist chaos born out of anarchy, to superficial legalism, and, above all, to European secularism.

: Whether on a national, political, or religious level, the Mongol Empire alone gave Muscovite Russia its distinctiveness and an awareness of its territorial and ideological essence. Hence the Mongol period was not, according to the Eurasianists, a difficult period or a blank page in the nation's history but, on the contrary, the founding moment of an autonomous Russian culture, the expression of an almost divine will that announced the uniqueness of Russia's fate: "Without the Tatar period Russia would not exist,"[81] because Muscovy was born of the Mongol Empire as from a "mother's bosom."[82]

This long-term mutual acculturation of the Tatar-Mongol and Russian worlds is by no means seen as limited to the construction of a common state; it goes much further than that, shaping ways of life and thinking, and fusing the two peoples into one ethnic whole. "Concurrently with the Russification of the Turanians there was also a certain Turanification of the Russians, and the organic fusion of these two elements created a peculiar new whole, the Russian national type, which is essentially Slavic-Turanian rather than simply Slavic."[83] If Muscovy's new identity was fashioned through acculturation to the Tatar world, then it must also embody continuity with the empire of the steppe in the sphere of international politics: "The political collapse of the Turko-Mongol world soon after Tamerlane's death . . . caused the political initiative in Eurasia to pass into the hands of the Russian people."[84] The Eurasianists thus view the Russian advance to the East as Muscovy's realization of its role as heir to the empire. After the collapse of the khanates, Moscow was no longer one of the numerous states succeeding the Golden Horde but the unifying link between the different Genghizid *uluses,* including the Timurid one; the integration of the Caucasus, Central Asia, and the Far East into the Russian state is thus described as a voluntary, natural, and nonviolent act.

Tatar rule also made Russia aware of its own Easternness and of its mission as a state. It is at the origin of a national trait that, for the Eurasianists, constitutes the very essence of Russian identity: religion, or, more exactly, religiosity. As Savitsky puts it, "This religiosity as such, and the way it has nourished and continues to nourish Russian spiritual life, was created during the Tatar period."[85] According to the Eurasianists, the Mongols played the role of a "divine punishment"[86] by purifying and sanctifying Russia as well as by unveiling its identity; since Mongol times, the Russian state has drawn its legitimacy from religion, and absorbed Mongol statehood by combining it with its own Byzantine religious traditions.

The Eurasianists believe that the Orthodox Church did not suffer from Mongol rule; the conquerors were tolerant, the Church had a metropolitan at Saray (the capital of the Golden Horde), and many Tatars converted to Christianity. Although the Mongols are praised for the religious neutrality of their shamanism and even their openness to Nestorian Christianity, it is Tatar Islam that is deemed the main component in the religious fusion between Russia and the steppes: "This integration [of the Tatar khanates] created an even stronger bond between the two peoples, since the Tatars, thanks to a popular psyche that resembles our own, turned the kind of Islam that was assimilated by their ethnographic type into a religion of everyday life."[87] This cult of religion as an element of everyday life is at the very core of the Eurasianist doctrine. It fits in with the discourse on the "Turanian psyche" and Mongol ideology: Ways of life, faith, culture, and state ethics make up but one whole, one ideology, preserving the indelible originality and the messianism of the Russian nation.

This understanding of religious beliefs, unlike any "Western" thinking on faith, is considered by the Eurasianists as the only true expression of Christianity. Being Russian would be a global and homogeneous way of living, of trying to perfect the interior self, of sacralizing everyday life. It is ritualism, as the Old Believers would understand it: "Life in Russia was an everyday confession of one's faith; everyday life was the form of Russian religiousness, 'the true contemplation of God,' and this was what the church leaned on."[88] Russia borrowed its dogmas from Byzantium, but it anchored them in the steppe and in Eurasia as a whole, obliterating the theological differences between the religions. The space to which Russian religious experience brings its newly territorialized faith is the space of a mythical Turanian East, where religious gesture takes precedence over any intellectual approach to faith, and religion is merged with the ideals of the state. For the Eurasianists, this experience is the very symbol of the transfer of power from the Golden Horde to Muscovy: Russia has a Genghizid legitimacy.

The example of Muscovy's state morals shows the extent to which the Eurasianists consider ideology synonymous with faith: It must be the founding principle of daily life, lifestyle, the structure of society, politics, and the state, and finally of religion. According to them, in Russia power is strength combined with faith; ideocracy is thus supposed to implement the collective principle, the *sobornost'*, of the Russian church on a political level. Ideology must be as total as possible to become an intellectual embodiment of the material and geographic reality of the Eurasian whole. A Eurasia that is aware of itself cannot tolerate a secular, lay space inside itself.

This paradox is particularly ostensible in matters of religion. Thus, the Eurasianists never abandon a strong Christian feeling; their talk of the proximity between the Orthodox and Eastern religions is mere facade. They do not display any particular sympathy toward Confucianism, whose polytheism troubles them: "The religion of China, based on the veneration of deceased ancestors, on a cult of demons and forces of nature, is too alien to our religious psychology."[89] As for Islam, it is blamed for having disfigured the principles of the Mongol Empire: "But when we read the Koran looking for confirmation of our religious aspirations, we feel disappointed. The dogmas of Islam turn out to be poor, stale, and banal; its morals, crude and basic; and none of us may in good faith become an orthodox Muslim."[90]

Buddhism is among the religious doctrines that are most violently disparaged by Eurasianist thinkers—it is likened to a kind of polytheism, because several people can claim the status of Buddha. Trubetzkoy considers the concept of "nirvana" to be spiritual suicide rather than a search for the divine. As a religion lacking a transcendent God, "Buddhism is strikingly artful in making its repulsive, gloomy teachings look attractive."[91] The Eurasianists also made considerable efforts to describe their attitude toward Hinduism. Without the concept of a unique God, Hinduism is only a magic and superstitious rite, because "from a Christian point of view the entire history of India's religious development is marked by the uninterrupted sway of Satan."[92] From the point of view of a doctrine as Christian in spirit as Eurasianism, this accusation of Satanism is devastating.

Any synthesis between Russian Christianity and Eastern religions is thus impossible. The "exodus to the East" promoted by the Eurasianists cannot by any means be a religious exodus; the non-Christian East is for Russia the very embodiment of otherness, of strangeness. To shock the West and distinguish themselves from it, the Eurasianists cultivated paradoxes and iconoclasm, calling those peoples who are both non-European and non-Eurasian "uncultured," "primitive," and "Satanist"; but in fact they simply rejected them in favor of Russia and Orthodoxy. Thus the Eurasianists' stance on Asia could not be more ambiguous, on the level of politics and identity as well as religion: "Eurasianism holds in high esteem the cultures of the Asian peoples but it has never felt tempted to consider itself an integral part of these cultures."[93] The Eurasianists' openness to Eastern religions seems thus to be pure theory; Eurasia is depicted as a multinational and polyconfessional space, but the Orthodox Church alone is considered worthy of representing the ideology of the future Eurasian state. Thus the Eurasianists highlight only those "oriental" aspects deemed compatible with the image they want to give of Russia, a Russia that would be as far removed from the West as possible.

Conclusions

Eurasianism claimed to be the logical conclusion of Russian thinking about identity, which until then had been limited either to an acceptance of the West or to its all-out rejection in the name of Slavicness. Eurasianism was the only movement that ventured to take a positive view of Russia's otherness, braving criticism and schism. It asked questions that are fundamental to the nation's identity: Whence can a country that aspires to be both a European state and a distinctly Eastern empire derive its legitimacy? How can one go beyond the traditional theories on Russia, which can never dispense with terms such as "lagging behind the West" or the "Slavic soul"? How can the empire be preserved or restored without giving in to Tsarist nostalgia?

Although Eurasianism claimed to be a geographically ideological way of thinking (partly to earn the status of a natural science), it actually viewed the diversity of the Old Continent from a cultural standpoint: geography (Europe-Asia) and culture (West-East) are not coextensive. Is Eurasia the third continent or a Euro-Asian fusion? It is not linked to Europe by "rainbow arcs" and cannot therefore represent a real fusion of European and Asian elements. To the vagueness of this terminology corresponds the ambiguity of Eurasianist ethnography; *the East* or *Orient,* equated with the steppe, is depicted as a world of movement, regeneration, and brutal change, whereas *Asia* is praised as a world of hierarchy, historical immobility, and a cosmic unity that prevents "chaos." Eurasianism never ceased to waver between these two symbols. In fact, the absence of narrative borders between the Orient and Asia leaves the door open to any new enlargement of the Empire to the East. "We are at home in Asia, and that is not just a phrase."[94]

The crucial goal of Eurasianist thought is to demonstrate that the territory Russia covers is naturally its own and that the need for an imperial structure is evident. Russia's history is the history of its expansion to the East, to the North and to the South; the history of Eurasia is the history of its incessant striving for unification. Geography consequently takes a clear precedence over Orthodoxy, for it is what gives Eurasia its legitimacy, in spite of anything the Eurasianists have to say about religion. Control over territory is synonymous with self-awareness—the Eurasianists' calls for self-awareness are nothing but calls to recognize empire as the only viable structure for Russia. Eurasianism does not stop short of demanding an imperial system. Trubetzkoy asserted that Turkic thought is driven by "a striving for expansion,"[95] which is a subtle way of legitimating the expansion of Russian territory and its organic "horizontality" by drawing parallels between ethnography and politics. Hence Eurasianism's reification of space is an essential condition for its legitimation of empire: Empire is merely the political expression of Eurasian space; the strips of the "rainbow" may be Eurasian, but the whole remains thoroughly Russian.

Fëdor Stepun portrayed the Eurasianist thinkers as futuristic Slavophiles.[96] Eurasianism is indeed the most forward-looking, the most modern, the most postrevolutionary of all Russian émigré intellectual movements, offering Russia a retroactive utopia. It is a paradoxical system of thought, both pragmatic and utopian. The movement wanted to be realistic, programmatic, waiting to take power in the Soviet Union, while being at the same time a philosophy of history and religion and a reflection on identity. These constant hesitations between metaphysical discourse, culturalism, and politics generated internal tensions. This is why the Eurasianists could never decide whether they were an intellectual movement, a religious order, or a political party.

The internal logic of Eurasianism does not presuppose a reality check based on external truth; its arguments only strive for *internal* truthfulness. This utopian quality is expressed not only on a methodological level but also in its thinking on identity and culture; Eurasianism conceives of Russia as a self-legitimating whole whose parts acquire their meaning in relation to the overall structure and owe their existence to seclusion from other areas. A closed utopia as totalitarian as Eurasianism requires a total space. The spatial closure of Eurasia is the geographic expression of its cyclical history, its utopian thought, and its eschatology.

Eurasianism cultivates paradox; it is a self-legitimating rhetoric. It attempts to theorize what is above all an experience and a feeling: the experience of young men in exile who feel humiliated by the defeat of the Whites and try to understand the reality of the motherland and stay in touch with it. Its steadfast scientism, so strongly asserted in its conceptions of geography and linguistics as well as of ethnology and history, is paradoxically opposed to its rejection of empiricism and Western rational argument and to its belief in telluric forces that give meaning to things. To the Eurasianists, "Western" secular and objective knowledge cannot account for a reality that belongs to the field of religion and identity. Eurasianists are not interested in details, rigorous analysis, or facts. They are heirs to *Naturphilosophie* with its belief in the superiority of synthesis; the power and validity of science, they hold, depend only on its capacity to create systems, ideologies.

Eurasianism thus relies on a twofold presentation of its thought. On the one hand, new sciences are needed to express the nature of Eurasia; on the other hand, the study of the Orient serves a certain philosophy of history. Each political or ideological argument is given a "civilizationist" illustration, an Orientalizing legitimacy on the levels of ethnography, history, and geography. The epistemological premises of Eurasianism and their closely knit relationship with Orientalism thus represent the real originality of Eurasianist theory. In Russia, totalitarianism often goes hand in hand with a discourse on Asia.

Even though the great tendencies in Russian thought have their distinctive features, they are inseparable from the history of Western European ideas. Eurasianism is no exception; on the contrary, it illustrates that rule all the more relevantly by its rejection of Europe, its values and its sciences, however brilliantly formulated and theorized. All its intellectual roots come from the Western cultural heritage. Its philosophy of history is Hegelian in its dialectics, its finalism, and its stress on "ideas"; its antidemocratic political conceptions and its cultural pessimism are typical of their times; its legitimation of empire, its dreams of exoticism, and its clichés on Asia are all part of nineteenth-century European Orientalism; and its paradoxical attraction to the model of the natural sciences *as well as* a return to the irrational and metaphysics is shared by many contemporary Western intellectuals. Eurasianism's attempt to think of the parts only in their relation to the whole, to perceive humanity and history in symbiosis with nature and the divine, links it to Romanticism and to a form of Hegelianism mixed with Neoplatonism.

Eurasianism aims to find a homegrown definition of Russia in its relationship with Europe. Despite their thinking about Asia, Europe is in fact the only real challenge for Russian intellectuals and is at the root of this Orientalist discourse. Eurasianism thus provides a different perspective on the intimate relationship between Russia and its "colonies," perhaps precisely because they are not colonies and because Russia holds them to be the realization of its "geohistoric being." The notion of identity becomes more important than the would-be civilizing mission that underpinned Western imperialism.

Because of its messianism, Eurasianism's philosophy of history conforms with the standard of Russian intellectual history. The movement is conceived as iconoclastic and radically novel because it calls attention to the role of the East in Russia's history, geography, and identity. The Eurasianists' Orientalism is embedded in a national philosophy that is common in Russia. The yearning for Western technologies and knowledge is coupled with a derogation of its values and a rejection of its models. Russian thought thus borrows many of its schemes and questions from Western European thought while stressing the uniqueness and national distinctiveness of its doctrine. The radical novelty that Eurasianism claims to represent must therefore be put in perspective. Its philosophical and political ideas on the nature of the state, culture, and humankind turn Eurasianism into a total, perhaps even a totalitarian, theory. This fundamentalism is one of the possible answers to modernity (embodied in Russia by the shock of the Revolution), which Eurasianism does not want to reject. As a result, it becomes an integral part of European developments, even if it attempts to exclude Russia from them. Its willingness to theorize empire makes Eurasianism one of the main Russian exponents of the "European crisis of consciousness."

Chapter 2

Lev Gumilëv: A Theory of Ethnicity?

Visitors to contemporary Russia are often struck by the massive popularity of the works of Lev Gumilëv (1912–92). His disciples consider his theories definitive; scholars of no mean standing use references to him as evidence of scientific quality; and whole institutions base their activities on his work. Articles on Gumilëv are often hagiographic; as both a scholar and poet, he is said to have provided an unrivalled explanation of ethnic relations, to have definitively elucidated the relationship between the humanities and exact science as well as the inherent opposition between Russia and Europe, and to have perfected the originally vague ideas of Eurasianism. "Gumilëv ascertained the natural and historical conditions of the birth of the Eurasian *super-ethnos;* he demonstrated the organic character of its unity in diversity; he described the stages of its growth; and he discovered the natural side of its being. . . . Thus Gumilëv's teachings take social philosophy and Eurasianism to their logical conclusion."[1]

Chronologically, Gumilëv is the link between the original Eurasianism of the 1920s and 1930s and the Neo-Eurasianist currents that made their appearance in the 1990s. Intellectually, he is the prism through which many of the academics and politicians who profess Eurasianism or an interest in it perceive that doctrine; for a long time, his books were read as substitutes for the works of the first Eurasianists, which remained inaccessible until the 1980s. Even now that those texts are being republished in massive editions, the Neo-Eurasianists often appear to be more familiar with his terminology than with that of the interwar Russian émigrés. Yet Gumilëv was not a Eurasianist in the strict sense of the term; he went beyond trying to prove the existence and unity of an entity called "Eurasia," elaborating an idiosyncratic worldview and philosophy of history. Though his Eurasianist ideas are disputed by some Russian nationalists, his ethnic theories are immensely popular; many post-Soviet scholars consider them to be scientifically proven. Gumilëv's numerous disciples, especially in Saint Petersburg, use the prestigious aura of the Russian émigrés and domestic dissidence to proclaim their master's theories unassailable. However, having been a victim of the Soviet regime is no guarantee of infallibility. A person who spent fourteen years in camps deserves respect but is not safeguarded against error. Gumilëv was a poetically talented eccentric, which makes him even more difficult to assess, because in his writings emotions are inextricably intertwined with a wide range of scientific claims. Finally, his high self-esteem ("I am a genius, but no more than that"[2]) does not facilitate a calm appraisal of his theories, covering analytic tracks to this day. The fact that it has become nearly impossible to criticize his theories in Russia is precisely an indication of their unscientific quality. They are embedded in an ideological belief in the existence of nontransient truths that may not be reconsidered or reformulated, especially by "Western" critics. Thus his work needs to be understood not only against the background of the Eurasianist theories that flourished in exile but also in the light of the Soviet ethnology of the 1960s through 1980s. It is as an advocate of a primordialist and even biological view of the nation that Gumilëv is most successful; the boundary between his view of Russia as a Eurasian state and his radical theories of ethnicity is blurred.

From Dissidence to Public Endorsement:
An Atypical Biography

Lev N. Gumilëv was both an official Soviet intellectual and a dissident. The son of two famous poets of the Silver Age, Nikolai Gumilëv (1886–1921) and Anna Akhmatova (1889–1966), Gumilëv bore the mark of his prestigious parentage throughout his career; as a stigma during Soviet times, and as an element of his myth ever since. His father was killed by the Bolshevik authorities in 1921 and was only rehabilitated as late as 1990. Young Lev was separated from his mother during childhood and adolescence, and he only joined her in Leningrad in 1929. He hoped to embark on higher education the same year, but the university refused to admit him because of his ideologically unwelcome family origins. He volunteered for research expeditions in Siberia and Crimea, and in the early 1930s he worked for the epidemiological services responsible for fighting the spread of malaria in Tajikistan.

He was arrested for the first time in 1933 but was soon released and succeeded in obtaining admission to Leningrad University's History Faculty. However, he was arrested again, together with his stepfather Nikolai N. Punin, for antirevolutionary activities and for reading an anti-Stalin poem by Osip Mandelstam. Anna Akhmatova and Boris Pasternak wrote to Stalin personally, obtaining the release of the two men and Gumilëv's readmission to the university. After his third arrest in 1938, he was sentenced to serve five years in a labor camp and sent to the White Sea–Baltic Canal construction project and thence to Norilsk. In 1943, he volunteered for the front and later took part in the Battle of Berlin, a fact that always filled him with great pride. The end of the war offered him a brief respite; having matriculated at university in 1934, he was at last allowed to pass his examinations between 1945 and 1947, and in 1949 he defended his first doctoral thesis (*kandidatskaia dissertatsiia*) at the Institute of Oriental Studies. Unexpectedly, he was arrested again that same year, in part because Akhmatova had fallen out of favor, having been criticized by Zhdanov and Stalin himself. Gumilëv was sent to Karaganda and then to Omsk, to be liberated only during the de-Stalinization that followed the Twentieth Party Congress in 1956.[3]

In the second half of the 1950s and throughout the 1960s, his living conditions remained highly unstable. He was forty-three years old when released from the labor camp, and he found work at the Hermitage Museum's library and became acquainted with its director, Mikhail Artamonov, a specialist on the Khazars. Artamonov took Gumilëv on several expeditions on the Volga between 1959 and 1961, giving him an opportunity to work out his own theses on the Khazars. In 1960, Gumilëv published his first book, *The Huns,* and the following year defended his second thesis (*doktorskaia dissertatsiia*) on the Old Turkic peoples, written in the camp at the same time as *The Huns.* Having obtained a doctoral degree in history, Gumilëv was at last given a teaching position at Leningrad University's Institute of Geography and Economics in 1963. His first publications, partly written during his confinement, were about the history of the steppe in ancient times: *The Huns* is devoted to the first great nomadic empire, founded in the third century BCE; *The Old Turks* (1967) is a study of the sixth-century-CE Turkic khaganate; and *The Huns in China* (1974), a sequel to his first book, concentrates on the difficult relations between the peoples of the steppe and the Central Kingdom.

Apart from this first trilogy about the pre-Mongol Turkic world, Gumilëv also published two books that focused on the Western part of the Eurasian steppes: *The Discovery of Khazaria* (1966), about the Khazar khaganate, and *One Thousand Years around the Caspian,* which attempts to chart the supposed interaction between climate fluctuations and the history of the nomadic peoples of the Caspian Sea Rim. The book came out very late, in 1990, but Gumilëv managed to publish several articles on this subject in the 1970s. *In Search of the Imaginary Kingdom,* published in 1970, was his only book specifically devoted to the Mongol period. According to him, the Crusaders justified their refusal to help Genghis Khan's Central Asian Nestorian Christians, who had come to fight the Infidels, by belittling the Eastern (Nestorian and Orthodox) Christian confessions and depicting the Mongols as worse enemies than the Muslims.

Although Gumilëv remained interested in the history of the Turko-Mongol peoples, most of his publications from the 1970s onward were about the theory of ethnicity. His first article on this subject appeared in 1965, but his theory of ethnogenesis was not fully developed until the second half of the 1970s. At the time, Soviet ethnology was vividly debating the status of the *ethnos* within the discipline, and Gumilëv tried to take part in these debates by offering his views on ethnogenesis and the ethnosphere. However, his theories attracted few comments; leading figures at the Institute of Ethnology of the Academy of Sciences were irritated. In 1970–71, one of the central debates on Gumilëv's theories took place in the journal *Priroda;* Leningrad-based authors close to Gumilëv argued with the director of the Institute, Iulian Bromlei (1921–90), and his close associate, Viktor I. Kozlov (1924–). Both of them criticized Gumilëv for diverging from the ideological standards of Marxism-Leninism. In 1974, Kozlov published another anti-Gumilëv article in the prominent journal *Voprosy istorii,* in which he denounced Gumilëv's theories as biological.[4] Gumilëv's reply, although accepted by the journal's editorial board, was not published due to pressure from Bromlei.[5] Kozlov's criticism was so harsh that no other academic journal risked publishing Gumilëv's articles, and he was no longer invited to any official conferences. In the early 1980s, he nevertheless managed to reopen debate on his theories with articles in the magazines *Ogonëk* and *Dekorativnoe iskusstvo SSSR,* published respectively in September and December 1980. In November 1981, the nationalist essayist Vadim Kozhinov (1930–2001) approvingly reviewed Gumilëv's ideas in an article in the well-known journal *Nash sovremennik.*

Despite these publications, Gumilëv could not resign himself to his institutional situation, and he suffered from the fact that he was shunned by the Soviet intellectual establishment. In 1974, he attempted to bypass the rigid academic system by defending another doctoral thesis, this time in geography, titled *Ethnogenesis and the Biosphere of the Earth.* However, the defense report was negative, and publication of the manuscript was prohibited. After several fruitless publication attempts, he decided, in 1979, to deposit it at the Institute for Scientific and Technical Information, enabling those who wished to read it to request an individual reprint. It appears that over 2,000 copies of the book were printed in this way,[6] and thus thousands of colleagues read it before it was first officially published in 1989. Gumilëv remained in an ambiguous position between official recognition and dissidence throughout his career. Thus between the second half of the 1960s and the early 1980s, he managed to publish five books with very low print runs and about thirty articles. But with the exception of an article in *Druzhba narodov* in 1977, he was limited to semipublic periodicals, for example, Leningrad-based journals where he had supporters.[7] In biographical interviews, he recalled having succeeded in publishing sixteen articles between 1975 and 1985, while about eighty were rejected.[8]

Gumilëv's "revenge" came during perestroika, when he quickly became a leading figure in Soviet public life and academia. On April 13, 1988, at the height of glasnost, the newspaper *Izvestiia* published an interview with him, signaling his recognition as "politically correct." All his main works were republished between 1987 and 1989, with print runs of dozens of thousands of copies. His central work, *Ethnogenesis and the Biosphere of the Earth,* was published for the first time in 1989 with the support of the head of Leningrad University, the physicist V. N. Krasil'nikov, and Gumilëv's patron A. I. Luk'ianov, by then a close associate of Mikhail Gorbachev. During this period of public recognition, Gumilëv wrote several general works on the issue of relations between Russia and the peoples of the steppe. *Old Rus' and the Great Steppe,* published in 1989 with a preface by the celebrated academician Dmitry Likhachev (1906–99), paints a positive picture of relations between the Russian principalities and the peoples of the steppe. *The Black Legend,* a collection of articles published in the same year, denounces Western historiography's mistaken view of the supposed "Mongol yoke." A few months before his death, Gumilëv finished his last popularizing book, *From Rus' to Russia,* which sketches over a thousand years of Russian history and presents the Tsarist Empire and the Soviet Union as natural heirs to the empires of the steppes.

Upon his death in 1992, even his long-standing opponent Viktor Kozlov felt obliged to publish a positive obituary. The Mir–L. N. Gumilëv Foundation, created in 1992 and based in Saint Petersburg, oversees publications, a radio station, and television broadcasts on Eurasianism and news from the Commonwealth of Independent States.[9] Since 1993, a yearly conference series, the *Gumilëvskie chteniia* (Gumilëv readings), has been held by his disciples in the room where he taught. Many of them, for example, K. P. Butusov and V. A. Michurin, study cosmic influences and try to combine Gumilëv's theories with Vladimir Vernadsky's writings on the noosphere. The year 1993 also saw the publication of *Rhythms of Eurasia: Eras and Civilizations,* a collection of Gumilëv's articles. In 1996, the journal *Istoriia,* very popular among teachers, devoted a special issue to him, opening with a hagiographic description of his life and work. In the same year, his last book, *From Rus' to Russia,* was republished with a circulation of 25,000 copies, as a textbook for teachers and students at universities and even high schools.[10]

The early 2000s witnessed the publication of more hagiographic texts (Sergei Lavrov's monograph being the best-known) and several memoirs by his friends, students, and fellow inmates. On the Internet, his disciples rallied around the Web site *Gumilevica*[11] and the online magazine *Evraziiskii vestnik,* created in 2001 by I. S. Shishkin, who defines his mission as the dissemination of "the teachings of L. N. Gumilëv [which] turned Eurasianism into a complete scientific theory that may and must be taken as the basis for a national and state ideology which would take full account of the interests of the Russians and the other native peoples of Russia."[12] To this day, Gumilëv occupies a colossal place in school and university textbooks; his works are included in virtually all reading lists for students of history, ethnology, culturology, and psychology, and have gone through print runs of several hundreds of thousands of copies. The same goes for the autonomous regions of the Russian Federation, such as the Turkic republics of Tatarstan and Bashkortostan, where he is presented as a national hero, as well as the new post-Soviet states, especially Kazakhstan, and Kyrgyzstan.

"The Last Eurasianist"?

Several scholars who admire one of the layers of Gumilëv's theories insist on the two-part structure of his work, distinguishing between his works on the history of the steppe and theoretical texts on ethnogenesis. However, this formal distinction is difficult to pin down to specific texts, and it has little relevance on the level of methodology; the strength and the paradox of

Eurasianism reside precisely in the inextricable interconnectedness between these two sets of arguments. It will not do to suggest, as many post-Soviet authors have done in their replies to critics, that Gumilëv's scientific arguments were always correct though his conclusions were sometimes wrong. This duality is organic to Gumilëv's thought; it anticipated how his biological understanding of peoples would later be integrated into a more traditional Eurasianism, such that today, many people fail to see the differences between the two currents.[13]

The view that Gumilëv is simply "the last Eurasianist," as claimed in the title of a famous article from 1991 based on an interview with him, is staunchly upheld by his disciples. This supposed lineage contributes to the myth of Eurasianism's resilience throughout the twentieth century and to the legend of a supposed Eurasianist anti-Soviet counterculture. It also allows its proponents to lend historical credibility and scientific sanction to Gumilëv's writings. In fact, on several occasions he did call himself a Eurasianist, but that acknowledgement was largely passive: "Some people call me a Eurasianist, and I don't deny it."[14] His disciples have very artificially turned this lineage to their own advantage; it allows them to legitimize his theories by "proving" that the founding fathers of Eurasianism themselves recognized him as one of their own.

This intellectual usurpation took off in the 1990s, after Gumilëv's death, so he cannot be made responsible for it; in fact, he even contradicted the legend of his meeting with Pëtr Savitsky. This story has it that the two men met in the Gulag in the 1950s; the supposed intellectual lineage is thus further ennobled with the aura of dissidence. However, Gumilëv did confirm an entirely different account: He got in touch with Savitsky after his release from the camps in 1956 with the help of Matvei Gukovsky, a colleague at the Hermitage who had been a fellow inmate of Savitsky's in Mordovia. Savitsky had been arrested in Prague in 1945 by the Soviet secret services for his "White" activities during the civil war[15] and sentenced to ten years in labor camps. The correspondence between Gumilëv and Savitsky only began in 1956, when the latter, discreetly rehabilitated and living in Moscow, asked for and soon obtained permission to move back to Czechoslovakia. This correspondence, which consists of over a hundred letters, lasted twelve years, until Savitsky's death in 1968.[16] Their first meeting took place in 1966, when Gumilëv was invited to an archeological congress in Prague. Apart from this exchange of letters with Savitsky, Gumilëv also had a relatively extensive correspondence with the historian George Vernadsky, the founder of the Yale school of Russian studies, but he had no contact with the other central figures of the Eurasianist movement, who had all died by that time.

The story of the meeting between Gumilëv and Savitsky in a camp is a myth; but so is the idea that they knew each others' works and theories. Gumilëv discovered the Eurasianist theories in the 1930s, as a first-year history student, during a discussion with A. Bernshtam (1910–56), a specialist on the Kyrghyz.[17] When he started corresponding with Savitsky, he knew little about the works of the Eurasianists, because he had no access to the works of Trubetzkoy, Savitsky, and Alekseev, or to interwar Eurasianist periodicals such as *Evraziiskii vremennik* and *Evraziiskaia khronika*. He later acknowledged that he only managed to get hold of three Eurasianist books on the steppes.[18] These works were crucial for his research because they mirrored his own historiographic interests, that is, his belief in the historic role of the nomads. However, they did not enable him to grasp the breadth and variety of Eurasianism, which was not merely a historiography of the steppe. He had no knowledge of the Eurasianists' ideological texts, their philosophical and religious postulates, their literary output, or the atmosphere of Russian thought in exile.

This lack of knowledge was mutual. During his exchange of letters with Savitsky, Gumilëv only succeeded in publishing a few articles, as well as *The Huns,* his most empirical and least theoretical book. His theory at the time was limited to the claim that landscape influenced the ancient nomadic peoples; he had not yet developed any of the key concepts of his thinking, such as ethnogenesis, passionarity, or biochemical energy. Thus Savitsky could not have commented on Gumilëv's system such as it appears today: so the founding fathers never sanctioned a theory that came into being well after the demise of the original Eurasianism. The belief that the Eurasianists and Gumilëv were working at the same time is one of the central elements of the intellectual usurpation undertaken by his disciples. Yet in 1956, when the two scholars began their correspondence, Eurasianism had been defunct for two decades. Thus the only person with a rightful claim to the title of "last Eurasian" was Savitsky, who had participated in the movement since its inception in 1921 and remained its last surviving representative.

Moreover, in his letters to Gumilëv, Savitsky makes few references to the interwar Eurasianist movement, which he considers a thing of the past; he mainly tries to direct Gumilëv's scholarly attention to the Turko-Mongol peoples. This encouragement seems to have given a boost to the morale of his colleague, who was still enduring intellectual marginality and hardship at the hands of the Soviet regime. As the often intimate tone of the correspondence confirms, the parallels between their situations helped create a sense of closeness between the two scholars. Savitsky openly expressed his admiration for Gumilëv's work; he did see him as his intellectual successor, but only in his quality as a specialist on the nomads, not as a Eurasianist in the strict sense. Savitsky invested him with the mission of finding scientific proof of the Eurasianists' intuitions, which they had been unable to substantiate because as émigrés they had had no access to sources: "Knowing that a congenial, attentive mind is doing what I . . . should have done as early as the Thirties . . . will make my life easier. Be a Yermak to this world!"[19]

Gumilëv was writing in the second half of the twentieth century. Both the post-Stalinist Soviet Union and Europe as a whole had changed considerably since the interwar period: The intellectual context was profoundly different. The original Eurasianism can only be understood against the background of the first years of the Bolshevik Revolution, the catharsis of civil war and exile, and the high hopes pinned on the New Economic Policy. The central features of its political philosophy were borrowed from Western theories of conservative revolution or even fascism, neither of which was directly relevant to Gumilëv's work. Gumilëv's fundamental texts, written in the 1970s, embodied the ethnic determinism then dominant in Soviet ethnology. Thus Gumilëv was not Savitsky's Soviet counterpart or disciple but an original author whose theories came into being long after the end of Eurasianism. Moreover, Gumilëv himself presented them as profoundly novel.

In fact, Gumilëv made very few references to the Eurasianists; he only took a stand on them in one article, "Notes of the Last Eurasianist," and in his introduction to a new edition of Prince N. S. Trubetzkoy's works. Gumilëv remained critical or even aloof in his attitude toward the founding fathers; they had never developed what he considered to have been his main scholarly contribution, an understanding of history and ethnography as natural sciences as well as the use of a biological terminology to explain the history of nations. As he expressed it, "I agree with the main historical and methodological conclusions of the Eurasianists. But they had no knowledge of the key element in the theory of ethnogenesis: the concept of passionarity. They lacked a background in natural science."[20] Thus Gumilëv defined the natural-scientific aspect of his thought as its greatest novelty. This insistence on the natural sciences made him relativize his links with the original Eurasianists, and his self-esteem was too high to allow him to acknowledge precursors. Moreover, he said that he owed more to Vladimir

Vernadsky, a physicist, geochemist, and theorist of the biosphere, than to his son George, the historian of Eurasia.

Furthermore, in those cases where Gumilëv did attempt to appropriate the ideas of the Eurasianists, he introduced terminological changes that distort them. Thus he confuses Trubetzkoy's "person" (*lichnost'*) with his *ethnos*, Eurasia's "multinational personality" with the *super-ethnos*, "mutual sympathy" between peoples with his idea of biological complementarity, and so on.[21] When the Eurasianists spoke of a symbiosis between the Russians and the peoples of the steppe, they defined it as a predisposition to common tendencies, whereas Gumilëv was a staunch advocate of endogamy, even inside each people of the Soviet Union. When they identified "catholicity" or "conciliarity" (*sobornost'*) as the basis for the unity of Eurasia as a state and a nation, they were referring to a key concept of Orthodoxy and Slavophilism rather than a biological entity of any kind. Though the theorists of Eurasianism had tried to prove that Russia's presence in the East was organic, their naturalism, inspired by German Romanticism, was not of the biological or genetic variety found in Gumilëv's texts. It should also be noted that Gumilëv's science is based on the principle of ethnic essences, whereas the original Eurasianism was mainly a "geographic ideology."[22] The founding fathers had remained close to *Naturphilosophie;* they had a teleological conception of the harmony between humanity and nature, and they believed in a parallel between the specific historical and cultural features of peoples and the geographic reality of their territory. So whereas in the original Eurasianism, territory gives meaning to national identity, Gumilëv employs a much more resolutely biological determinism; for him, spatial proximity is insufficient for symbiosis, because the *ethnoi* are closed entities. Thus his determinism is opposed to the fundamental idea of Eurasianism, namely, that territory, which unites groups that may have the most diverse origins, is much more important than the original relations of kinship.[23]

The Eurasianists and Gumilëv share an interest in the nomadic world, but their approach to it is also very different. Thus, in their correspondence, Savitsky repeatedly distanced himself from what Gumilëv wrote about the nomadic world being inferior to the great civilizations.[24] Moreover, unlike the Eurasianists, as a historian Gumilëv specialized in the Old Turks rather than the Mongols. He vehemently condemned Islam, which the founding fathers strongly appreciated despite a number of ambiguities. He saw Tamerlane as a representative of the Islamic world rather than that of the steppe (according to his own terminology), whereas for Savitsky, Tamerlane was a scion of Genghis Khan's tradition.[25] Gumilëv also criticized the Eurasian-ists for never having insisted on the Mongols' Nestorianism and conse-quently misunderstanding the fusion between Mongol statehood and Or-thodoxy,[26] which doomed their exotic Orientalism.[27]

That Gumilëv should be an intellectual descendant of the original Eurasianists is thus far from obvious, contrary to what is widely believed in Russia today. Savitsky, who died in 1968, and Vernadsky, who died in 1973, could give neither full appreciation nor intellectual sanction to Gumilëv's theories of ethnogenesis, which emerged mainly in the second half of the 1970s and are now being cultivated by his disciples. Though many post-Soviet intellectuals claim Gumilëv as their own, that claim should be taken at face value rather than as a reference to the "last Eurasianist."[28] Moreover, Gumilëv's disciples are above all developing his theories of ethnicity rather than his Eurasianist ideas. Thus, at the annual "Gumilëv readings" in Saint Petersburg, discussions mainly revolve around the idea of ethnic comple-mentarity and the influence of cosmic energy on peoples, rather than fo-cusing on any specific event in the history of the steppe. Finally, Gumilëv's disciples see no common ground with the Neo-Eurasianism of Aleksandr Panarin or Aleksandr Dugin, and they refuse to be amalgamated with them into a single ideological movement.

Conversely, the theorists of Neo-Eurasianism also have a complex atti-tude toward Gumilëv. Panarin repeatedly rejected Gumilëv's ethnicism and claimed that he had not been entirely Eurasianist. As for Dugin, who holds extremely ethnicistic or even racialist views, he is mainly inspired by Western theories rather than Gumilëv or Soviet ethnology. The other Neo-Eurasianists, however, do seek to use Gumilëv, posthumously, to sanction their own rather meager theories. Thus both Eduard Bagramov's journal *Evraziia: Narody, kul'tury, religii* and the publications of the Kazakhstani Eurasianists are full of references to Gumilëv and his theories of ethnogen-esis. However, this does not at all imply that they agree with him on those questions. In any case, Gumilëv died too early to have been able to take a stand on Neo-Eurasianism, be it positive or negative.

Gumilëv's *Episteme:*
Subjecting the Humanities to the Natural Sciences

The original Eurasianism, born in the 1920s of the shock of Revolution and exile, had developed a militant philosophy of history that considered hu-

manity capable of turning the world upside down. This almost eschatological sense of witnessing the dawn of a new era is diametrically opposed to
Gumilëv's philosophy. Gumilëv draws a dark picture of the world that
barely leaves room for humankind; in his view, humanity is but an unconscious cog in nature's gigantic machine, which leaves no space for human
action. In this vision of humankind, history is relegated to the rank of an
auxiliary to the all-powerful natural sciences; its sole function is to collect
facts, not to analyze them critically. This negation of the humanities is not
a late addition to Gumilëv's thought; in the camps, as early as 1942, he met
the future astronomer Nikolai Kozyrev (1908–83), who convinced him of
the superiority of the hard sciences over the humanities and stirred up his
interest in the cosmos.

  Inspired by nineteenth-century scientism, Gumilëv believed that humanity is subject to the same laws of development as the rest of nature.
Among his basic presuppositions is the idea that any human phenomenon
obeys certain laws and patterns (*zakonomernost'*): "History has been driven
by that very 'force of things' that exists in history independently of our will
and shapes the patterns of the historical process."[29] The scholar's task is to
discover these laws in order to gain access to the hidden meaning of things.
For Gumilëv, humanity does not shape events, even involuntarily; even
where a person can intervene, his or her actions can only be negative, because he or she can only see appearances. Gumilëv unflinchingly condemns
human actions that run counter to the definite sense of history, and he ad-
vises against breaking the natural order of things: "Without the utmost necessity it is better not to attempt to change history, for any such change will
always come at a great cost, and its results cannot be foreseen."[30] Thus Gumilëv's history offers no room for human will. The "facts" are the only real,
living, and conscious subjects of the historical process; they are the ontological reality of the world.

  Humanity is not the master of events; Gumilëv's conceptual framework
includes *time* (the time of nature or the *ethnos*) but no human *history*. Because history is governed by laws, everything that happens in history *had*
to happen. Chance is but a disturbance of the higher logic of nature, and any
contradiction must be overcome through a dialectic principle of the synthesis of opposites. However, Gumilëv cannot be entirely deterministic, for
that would make it impossible to justify historical exceptions to his rules.
He is thus compelled to recognize what he calls "the X factor," something
that cannot be defined in advance that changes the course of history, thereby
allowing Gumilëv to escape the internal contradictions in his theories. Nev-

ertheless, once the "law" of history has been discovered by the scientist and theorized like a mathematical formula, the future may be partly predicted. "The pattern discovered by the historian not only explained the past, but also enabled him to make predictions."[31] Thus history is a prognostic discipline, and Gumilëv does not hesitate to compare it to statistics or meteorology with their supposed objectivity. "We have a meteorological service that predicts the weather and in many ways helps us avoid its pernicious consequences. My theory of ethnogenesis may likewise be used as an applied science."[32] Thus Gumilëv makes no secret of the extent to which his interest in history is due to current events and to his desire to prevent ethnic conflict. He more or less explicitly calls upon the political authorities to put his theories at the service of the state: "To deny the objective laws of ethnogenesis, which are independent of the laws of social development and the desires of individual officials, is to deliberately preclude a true understanding of the principles and mechanisms of ethnic conflicts."[33]

History barely belongs to humankind; but neither does historiography as an academic discipline belong to the historian. Gumilëv adopts an extremely restricted definition of history, calling it a mere "science of events,"[34] a neutral and objective chronology. The historian's role is minimal, because he does not interpret events but "discovers" them. His subjectivity makes him a disruptive factor: Events have a logic of their own, an objective sense that does not depend on the way one looks at them. "Facts only appear clearly in their relations with each other when reduced to a logical sequence of cause and effect and brought down to a single scale. This eliminates the bias and insufficiency of the document."[35] Thus a critical approach to historical sources is needed not because they bear the mark of their author's subjective approach but because they distort the "facts," which are considered real. This is a far cry from current thinking about history, which sees it as the study of a person in his or her time, as the historian's meeting with people of other times, informed by an awareness of his or her own historical subjectivity and the inevitably personal nature of interpretations of the "facts."

Thus, in all his books, Gumilëv constantly criticizes classical historiography for its inability to answer what he believes to be the fundamental question: "What is a people?" He is pessimistic about the future of the discipline; historians are too specialized, they have lost a sense of the convergence of the sciences and want to participate in the process of history creation through their subjectivity. By contrast, he calls for an essentialist reading of history and for the elaboration of a synthetic science, a discipline that would endow all other disciplines with the meaning they are lacking. However, his thinking on this is paradoxical; though he believes that reality consists of raw facts that are independent of human perception and can be discovered by the historian, he also thinks they must be interpreted. For all the talk of facts, Gumilëv deems his theory to be, at heart, philosophical; because history has laws, humankind develops in a certain direction, which must be revealed. Western historiography is thus doubly deficient: Not only does it overemphasize the personality of the historian and presents the "facts" as being constructed by the beholder; it also seeks to show *how* things happen, rather than *why* they happen—whereas to Gumilëv, answering the latter question is the only way of gaining access to the meaning of history.[36] Nevertheless, the philosophy of history he calls for is not a worldview; humanity is not the author of that philosophy, which transcends it and is inherent in the phenomena themselves. It is the law of nature or God. Thus Gumilëv continues one of the fundamental traditions of organicist thought: the wish to reach a synthesis, to consider a science "successful" only if it yields an all-embracing understanding of human destiny and answers questions formulated in the language of essentialism.[37]

In fact, Gumilëv's writings are not historiographical; readers are not presented with the sources of his theses on history, and the footnotes only mention secondary works. In a letter to Savitsky, he even acknowledges that certain parts of *The Huns* were written with very little use of primary sources, in a free style justified by the hypothetical thrust of his thought.[38] Despite his call for a synthetic science that would reveal the "laws" of history, Gumilëv does not hesitate to write a history of the steppe that is analytical rather than synthetic, and monographic rather than interpretive; his history of the steppic states is utterly classical in its approach, and battles, political conflicts, and dynastic change are the core subject matter analyzed. The appendixes to his books often feature dozens of pages of year-by-year chronology, as well as synchronic or diachronic tables. For him, these tables are not merely auxiliary material for the historian; they have an intrinsic value: Every one of them is presented as a "cardiogram" of an ethnic group, expressing the distinctive features of its way of life.[39] The historian has nothing to add to these chronologies, which carry their own meaning and do not stand in need of further analysis.

The human aspect of research must be limited to a strict minimum; the "facts" must be reconstructed without bringing in the people who orchestrated or suffered them, without the people who documented them in writing or left traces pertaining to them, and without the people who reflect upon

them as historians who are children of their own times. Unwittingly, Gumilëv informs the reader about his way of treating the sources and his contempt for the humanities: "Only the establishment of a certain number of
indisputable facts, which can be extracted from the source and inserted into
a chronological table, . . . will be positive. The geographer, the zoologist,
the soil scientist never have more data at their disposal, and yet their sciences are developing. . . . In other words, the natural sciences have overcome the silence of the sources and have even used it to the benefit of
science. . . . So why shouldn't historians? If we use nature as a source, we
must also use the appropriate method of study; and this opens up magnificent perspectives."[40] He repeatedly states that he approaches the subject
matter of the humanities as a natural scientist rather than as an historian.
The distinctive features of Gumilëv's thought may indeed be expressed in
the formula "naturalism against humanism."

Having thus criticized historiography, Gumilëv cannot consistently define himself as an historian. His epistemological approach expresses a view
of the natural sciences as a model for all other areas of knowledge. This is
where his self-definition as an ethnologist comes in. His disciples often
present him as "the founder of a new science, ethnology,"[41] even though he
hardly ever had an opportunity to carry out fieldwork. His ethnology is a
discipline without a past; it is neither a continuation of the great schools of
Russian ethnography nor a Soviet version of a discipline that also exists in
other European countries. The methods of Gumilëv's new ethnology are not
those of the Western discipline of the same name but those of the natural
sciences, and more specifically biology: It is "a science that processes the
subject matter of the humanities using the methods of the natural sciences,"[42] "the science of the behavioral impulses of ethnic groups, just like
ethology is the science of animal behavior."[43]

For Gumilëv, reality may be divided into three principles: geographical
(landscape), ethnic (peoples), and political and social (the state). The first
two principles are essential and are studied by the natural sciences. The
third, which is superficial and entirely derived from the other two, is the subject matter of the humanities. Historiography, in Gumilëv's view, is an auxiliary discipline of geography and ethnology. He thus rejects the usual division into natural sciences on the one hand and humanities on the other
hand: Humanity and human activities fully belong to the realm of natural
science, just like nature and (in)organic matter.[44] He glorifies the "pure"
natural sciences, and he appends to them those disciplines that study the
"mixed" character of humanity as both a natural and a cultural being, such

as geography. But he is happy to leave the study of intellectual activity and politics to the humanities, for, while "ethnology is a natural science, history belongs to the humanities."[45]

Gumilëv also reaffirms that the goal of any science is to consider its object as a totality. History cannot attain that goal, because it takes humanity as its end. Biology and ethnology can, because they grasp humanity in its dependence on nature: "Our goal is to understand world history as the formation of one of the Earth's outer layers: the ethnosphere."[46] Thus Gumilëv regularly refers to the great thinkers of ancient times and of the Renaissance —times when knowledge was unified, and scholars were both philosophers and astronomers. One has to be a natural scientist, he believes, to go beyond the superficial aspects of humanity and grasp it in its totality. Ethnology reinterprets the material that history has not been able to understand, and it seeks to answer the question "Why?" It therefore fulfils all Gumilëv's conditions of scientific rigor. His epistemology is paradoxical in the extreme; referring to ethnology, it presents itself as a confirmation of the superiority of the natural sciences and their methodology over the humanities, which are not scientific at all. However, he holds on to a teleological and essentialist view of history and is keen to find a philosophical interpretation of the natural or divine "laws" that govern humanity. His rejection of history as a profession parallels his dismissal of the role of human will in history. This desire to explain history through laws that give a meaning to the apparent chaos of humankind leads him to elaborate a pseudo-scientific ideology that turns the nation into an object of biology, physics, and chemistry.

Theories of the *Ethnos* or Naturalistic Determinism

Gumilëv's thinking about human nature is fundamentally pessimistic; not only can humans not develop their personalities in the circumstances of their choice, because they choose neither the time nor the place of their birth; they are also driven above all by their instincts. Nevertheless, people are provided with something Gumilëv calls a "zone of freedom," a highly restricted space within which they can make choices. Yet even that space is illusory: "The only distinctive thing about freedom is that Man can make the right choice or make a mistake, and in the latter case he is doomed."[47] According to Gumilëv, humankind has two handicaps: the weight of responsibility (its choice can bring about its disappearance), and a total lack of real liberty (if people want to live, they have only one possible choice).

Thus human history knows no variants; both possibilism and perfectibility are ruled out. Ethnic diversity signifies the disappearance of those whose choices are contrary to nature's plans. Gumilëv's determinism is absolute.

The original Eurasianists had been more subtle determinists; rather than seeing humanity as unilaterally dependent on nature, they believed that the two interact. Gumilëv deviates from this tradition, for despite his talk of the *ethnos'* intrinsic dependence on its landscape, he carried out little geographical analysis. His only elaborate theory on this question concerns the interaction between the movements of nomads on the one hand and variations of humidity and climate in the steppe on the other hand, as described in *One Thousand Years around the Caspian.*[48] For Gumilëv, territory is but the first element of a more complex determinism, and one of the least important ones at that; the characteristic features of the *ethnos* are grounded not in soil but in physics, chemistry, biology, and genetics. In several of his books, he criticizes the geographical determinism of classic authors such as Montesquieu, Bodin, and Herder, who thought that national psychology depends on the natural milieu. For him, territory is not a sufficient condition for the emergence of an *ethnos;* humanity depends on the entire cosmic and terrestrial environment, of which territory is but a minor part.[49] Unlike the founding fathers of Eurasianism, Gumilëv does not seek to establish the Eurasian totality with the help of geographic arguments. He does not draw up maps showing the superposition of different data; nor does he talk of the internal and external symmetry of the space of Eurasia or theorize the existence of a geographical "third continent": Russia, for him, strides the two continents of the Old World, Europe, and Asia.[50]

Thus, in Gumilëv's theories, Eurasia is not a totality that draws its meaning from geography but a framework for that in which he is really interested: ethnogeneses. Gumilëv's determinism is physical rather than geographical: Humanity must be studied not as part of his immediate spatial environment but in a planetary and cosmic perspective. For him, *ethnoi* originate from natural phenomena; they are born of a burst of energy coming from the creatures that inhabit the surface of the Earth, as well as of geological and mineral activity, of the circulation of energy between plants and animals, and of solar activity. Gumilëv's writings are interspersed with physical and chemical metaphors intended to explain the nature of people and nations.[51] He believes he has founded a new discipline, which he calls "socionatural history," a branch of his ethnology that studies humanity's relationship with natural and planetary activity. Though the humanities can only graze the surface of human nature, socionatural history goes to its very core, because the *ethnos* "is not only biological, but also physical and chemical, that is, part and parcel of planetary patterns."[52]

This theory of cosmic energy is borrowed from one of Gumilëv's inspirations, Vladimir I. Vernadsky (1863–1945). A geochemist by training, Vernadsky was, in his time, a scientist with a European-wide reputation. He was particularly interested in interaction between humanity and the biosphere, and he used the concept of a "noosphere." The term "biosphere" as popularized by Gumilëv is defined as the interaction between animate and inanimate matter. According to him, the biosphere is currently entering a new geological era, that of the noosphere, which will be based on the power of the human intellect: "The process of ethnogenesis as such is finite; it is linked to a certain form of energy discovered by our great compatriot, V. I. Vernadsky."[53] Gumilëv offers no detailed discussion of the idea that humankind's original force is of cosmic origin, but one may wonder whether this idea may have been a cautious way of asserting the existence of God or a vague belief in the presence of extraterrestrial forces, a conviction later shared by many of his disciples.

Gumilëv's supporters explain this interest in things cosmic by stressing his profound ecological awareness. Indeed, some of his ideas seem to be inspired by an ecological sentiment, for example, when he wrote: "We are not alone in the world! The Cosmos participates in the protection of nature, and it is our duty not to destroy it. It is not only our home; it is us."[54] His dissertation in geography, *Ethnogenesis and the Biosphere of the Earth,* is also full of cosmist implications. Cosmism was one of the main currents in early-twentieth-century Russian religious philosophy. It attempted to recover a conception of faith that would be universal and resonate with an archetype of human thought: that the visible heaven is also where God resides. The thinking of Nikolai Fëdorov (1828–1903), Vladimir Vernadsky, Konstantin Tsiolkovsky (1857–1935), and A. L. Chizhevsky (1897–1964) was dominated by the idea that the development of space travel may help regenerate humanity through the cosmos.[55] Chizhevsky even sought to prove that cosmic phenomena, and in particular solar eruptions, have demonstrable sociohistorical effects. This new discipline, called "historiometry," claims to have ascertained the existence of solar cycles of about eleven years that divide human history into political periods ranging from stability to war or revolution.

The extreme expression of Gumilëv's naturalization of humanity is "passionarity," one of his key theoretical concepts. According to him, the theory of passionarity has "for the first time linked the existence of *ethnoi* as col-

lectives of people with the ability of men as organisms to 'absorb' the biochemical energy of the biosphere's living substance."[56] Beyond humanity's
primordial needs (eating and dwelling), all other human activities—the pur-
suit of glory or happiness, victory, the accumulation of wealth or values, the
development of culture or religion, and so on—result from passionarity,
which is the opposite of the survival instinct, because it can lead a person
to die for his or her ideas. It is a purely physical phenomenon, a surplus of
chemical or cosmic energy that drives certain people. According to Gumilëv, every individual may be classified on a scale of passionarity; some
were great passionaries (the great men, among whom he mentions Alexander the Great, Jan Hus, Joan of Arc, Avvakum, and Napoleon), and others
were subpassionaries. Every people possesses a set ratio of passionaries and
subpassionaries, which may be predicted on the basis of Gumilëv's assessment of its biological age: "The start [of an ethnogenesis] is marked by a
burst of passionarity, a dissipation of the energy of the living substance of
the biosphere."[57] However, Gumilëv cannot accept the idea that individuals may be the agents of their history; passionaries are merely unconscious
bearers of a collective energy that transcends them.[58]

   Thus passionarity is presented as a genetic attribute, passed on heredi-
tarily within an *ethnos,* that accounts for phenomena that are not based on
rational deliberation. Thus the traits usually taken to distinguish humans
from animals boil down to an expression of biological phenomena. The cultural aspects of humanity simply express natural features, because biochemical processes influence the human subconscious and emotions: "The
ethnic phenomenon is material; it exists outside and independently of our
mind, although it is localized in the activity of our soma and higher nervous activity."[59] Thus the feeling of belonging to a national collectivity is in-
born rather than acquired, and every human being genetically belongs to the
collectivity of his parents: "The process of ethnogenesis is linked to a specific genetic attribute."[60] Gumilëv relegates the classic definitions of community used in political science (peoples, nations) or ethnography (tribes,
clans, kinship) to the rank of errors committed by the humanities because
of their inability to reach the absolute certainty of the natural sciences. The
social aspect of humanity is redundant; it is far removed from underlying
human reality as a product of nature. The *ethnos* is a unique form of collectivity of *homo sapiens,* an invariant of human nature: "*Ethnoi* have existed continuously, ever since the emergence of *homo sapiens.*"[61]

   Thus, for Gumilëv, the *ethnos* is an objective reality, not a speculative
category. Its emergence is not arbitrary; it is situated within places and cy-

cles governed by "laws" that he claims to have discovered.[62] He believes
he has developed universal concepts valid for all civilizations, and he de-
votes long passages of his works to the non-Eurasian world to prove his hypotheses. However, his theory is ambiguous on this point; his global cata-
logue contains only thirteen instances of ethnogenesis, and all of them are
limited to Europe and Asia: "The phenomena of ethnogenesis are arranged
on a single strip stretching in a straight line from Mecca to Xi'an."[63] The
other continents are implicitly relegated to a form of nonhistory. This historical phenomenon is also limited in time, because no ethnogenesis is said
to have taken place since the thirteenth century, allowing him to avoid pro-
nouncing on the history of the European nation-states and the global expansion of the West.[64]

 Ethnogenesis is what Gumilëv calls the history of *ethnoi*. Born of a burst
of chemical energy that transmits passionarity to men, ethnogenesis is a
process that takes place over approximately sixty generations, giving each
ethnos a lifespan of 1,200 to 1,500 years. "Once it emerges, an *ethnos* goes
through a series of predetermined stages that may be likened to the ages of
a human being."[65] Ethnogenesis is divided into several stages: a stage of
ascent that takes about 300 years; a stage of acme, which lasts another 300
years; a pivotal phase of about 150 years, during which human pressures
are destructive; a stage of inertia of approximately 600 years, during which
the *ethnos* accumulates technological means and ideological values yet dies
internally; a stage of eclipse, during which the *ethnos* no longer has any cultural or natural concerns; and finally a stage of homeostasis, during which
the dying *ethnos* expires piteously in isolation, in a quasi-return to savagery.
In the end, the *ethnos* either disappears or becomes what Gumilëv calls a
"relic," such as the Bushmen, the Australian aborigines, and the Paleo-
Siberian peoples. This evolution is intrinsic to the species; features ensuring survival are reinforced, whereas negative traits disappear over time. Humanity is bound by absolute Darwinistic laws; for Gumilëv, the history of
humankind is a struggle for the survival of the fittest.

 Like the older Eurasianists, Gumilëv believes that the national collectivity is by nature superior to the individual. These theorists think that in
Western thought, society is mechanistically seen as the sum of atomized
citizens; Eurasianism, by contrast, highlights the collective as a structure, a
totality. For Gumilëv, "the *ethnos* is not a sum of people but a complex
systemic totality."[66] This organicism is rooted in *Naturphilosophie* and in
the Romantic conception of an ontological unity between humanity and
nature. Gumilëv is also inspired by the classic theories of conservative Pan-

Slavists such as Nikolai Danilevsky,[67] for whom civilizations are closed "historico-cultural types." The structure of a civilization may evolve over time while remaining the same by "nature," but it is permanently shut off from the other systems. As Gumilëv states, "However mosaic the *ethnos* may be, and however varied its structure, at the level considered here it is a totality."[68] Gumilëv's theory is systemic. He elaborates a strict hierarchy of ethnic entities: *sub-ethnoi,*[69] *ethnoi, super-ethnoi,*[70] and *meta-ethnoi.*[71] Obviously, he gives no precise definition that would permit classifying peoples systematically in this hierarchy. Nor does he advance arguments that would clarify the relationship between polarity and totality: How can the *ethnos* be divided into *sub-ethnoi* without losing its systemic unity? How can *ethnoi,* which are supposed to be irreducible to each other, unite into a *super-ethnos*?

Gumilëv defines the ethnos as a "biosocial" organism, a definition that enraged Soviet ethnologists. In line with Marxist historiography, they officially rejected any biological account of the *ethnos,* considering it a phenomenon of social history. In practice, however, many other Soviet scholars pushed their primordialism all the way to biologization. Gumilëv tried to respond to Bromlei's and Kozlov's accusations of biologism by claiming that the *ethnos* is determined by its "behavior" (*povedenie*), which cannot be explained by that of neighboring *ethnoi.* But however social that term may sound, the *ethnos* is still a product of nature rather than culture; behavior is itself a biological phenomenon, because "the stereotypes of behavior are the highest form of Man's active adaptation to the landscape."[72] Gumilëv's disciples, especially Viacheslav Ermolaev, later took this thinking further by developing a "behaviorist" science (*bikhevioristika*), which, despite being prima facie an analysis of behavior, is in many ways close to American sociobiology.

The Complex History of the Eurasian Totality

Gumilëv's system-building ambition is reflected in his political writings on Eurasia. He directly continues the Eurasianist tradition, which favors the metaphysical totality over a folkloric cult of diversity. Although he defines Eurasia as "the Great Steppe which stretches from the Yellow River almost to the banks of the Arctic Ocean,"[73] in most of his texts he equates it with the territory of the Soviet Union, sometimes adding Tibet and Mongolia. This parallel between Eurasia and the Soviet Union does, not, however, presuppose the existence of a single *super-ethnos*. He enumerates seven of them: Russian, Steppic, Circumpolar, Muslim, European, Buddhist, Byzantine (or Caucasian Christian), and Jewish. Thus the position of the "Soviet people" in his theories of ethnogenesis is not made explicit: Does the alliance between several *super-ethnoi* lead to the emergence of a superior entity, close to the *meta-ethnos* he sometimes mentions?

Gumilëv believes that only two *super-ethnoi*, the Russian and the Steppic, dominate the territory of the Soviet Union, for they are the only ones for whom Eurasia is the only habitat, whereas the others stride civilizational zones. Thus the history of the Russian Empire is the history of these two *super-ethnoi*'s slow convergence in the steppe, whose geographic centrality is unique in the world and revelatory of the identity of Eurasia: "The Great Steppe is a geographic totality, inhabited by diverse peoples with different economic structures, religions, social institutions, and mores. Nevertheless, all its neighbors have always perceived it as a kind of unified entity, although neither ethnographers, nor historians, nor sociologists have been able to determine the content of the dominant principle."[74] Just like the original Eurasianists and the Neo-Eurasianists, Gumilëv remains highly ambiguous on the distinction between *russkii, rossiiskii,* and *evraziiskii* (ethnically Russian, pertaining to the Russian state, and Eurasian), and in his writings he never signals transitions from one to the other.

His historiography of Russia as well as his opinions on the centrality of Eurasia clearly place Gumilëv in the Eurasianist tradition. For him, Russian history is not linear but dual; after a first ethnogenesis in the first century CE (the future Kievan Rus'), there was a second one in the twelfth century (giving birth to Muscovy). This national continuity can only be explained by the continuity of religion, which was transmitted from the first *ethnos* to the second: "It was the new system of behavior, created on the basis of the old religion, Orthodoxy, which helped Russia assert herself in the history of Eurasia."[75] Thus the Mongols played a crucial role in Russian history by ensuring continuity between the two *ethnoi.* As in traditional Eurasianism, Kievan Rus' is judged to have been a stranger to Eurasia because of its excessive European orientation; its downfall is attributed to internal factors rather than to the Mongol invasion. However, because of its long-standing history of contacts with the steppe, it nonetheless presaged Russia's Eurasian identity; unwittingly, it anticipated Russia's coming fusion with the Tatar-Mongol world.[76]

The different stages of the second—Muscovite—ethnogenesis follow the traditional Eurasianist chronology. The stage of the *ethnos*' ascent cor-

responds to the period of Mongol domination, which Gumilëv views positively because he believes that the origins of the Russian Empire lay in
Genghis Khan's principles of statehood. The fifteenth and sixteenth centuries witnessed an upsurge of passionarity, which led to the birth of sub-
systems (the Judaizers and the followers of Nilus of Sora) and *sub-ethnoi*
(the Sibiriaks, Russian settlers in Siberia; and the Cossacks). The seventeenth through nineteenth centuries were a period of decadence, during
which Russia was more European than Eurasian and experienced a Ger-
manization of mores, a profound religious schism,[77] the emergence of
subpassionaries in search of material welfare (e.g., the Strel'tsy), a pro-
European and therefore unconstructive foreign policy, and so on. Nevertheless, this point of view does not keep Gumilëv from being just as ambiguous as the original Eurasianists about the Romanov period; though he
criticizes it for its Europeanness, he nevertheless appreciates it for further
expanding into Asia.

In keeping with Eurasianist presuppositions, Gumilëv affirms that the
Mongol threat was merely a myth created by the West to conceal from the
Russians that their real enemies were in the Romano-Germanic world,
particularly the Balts, Poles, and Swedes. To justify his theories, Gumilëv
worked extensively on the *Lay of Igor's Host,* presenting it as historical
proof of Russia's fundamentally Eurasian character,[78] a tradition that was
later continued by Olzhas Suleimenov. However, contrary to the original
Eurasianist tradition, Gumilëv was particularly critical of Islam. For him,
the conversion of the Golden Horde to Islam in 1312 severed the symbiosis between Russia and the Mongol world. By adopting Islam as the khanate's
state religion, Mamai attached the Tatars to the Muslim *super-ethnos,* although by ethnic origin they belonged to the Eurasian Steppic *super-ethnos.*
Thus, after the Golden Horde adopted Islam, Muscovy remained the only
legitimate heir to the empire of the steppes.

This historiography, considered by many post-Soviet scholars to be one
of Gumilëv's irrefutable scholarly contributions, is in profound contradiction with his theories. Why is Russian history longer than the maximum life
span accorded to every *ethnos?* How can it be the result of two ethnogeneses if Gumilëv's "laws" rule out two thrusts of passionarity on the same territory? How can there be continuity between the products of these two
ethnogeneses if types of "behavior" are said to die with their *ethnos?* Although it is presented as biological, Russia's passionarity remains intrinsically linked to religion: "Conservative Orthodoxy channeled the growing

passionarity of the Russian people into the single undertaking of building Holy Russia."[79] Despite his search for new types of scientific legitimacy for Eurasia, Gumilëv subscribes to Russian nationalism's classic clichés about the key role of Orthodoxy in Russian history.

The original Eurasianism advocated closure because of the impossibility of horizontal communication between civilizations. Gumilëv adds the new idea of a vertical difference in time. Thus any comparison between the Russian and the European *ethnoi* is pointless, because the former is five hundred years younger than the latter. Russia is not lagging behind or backward; it is young and dynamic, and heading toward a glorious future, whereas Europe is old and decaying. As for the Mongols, their violence should be "excused" not because their civilization was intrinsically different from that of the Europeans but because they were three hundred years younger than the West.[80] Thus Gumilëv seems to espouse a linear understanding of time, even though this runs counter to the postulates of Eurasianism. Furthermore, as its name indicates, "Eur-Asia" is meant to be a place of meeting, of equilibrium, between Europe and Asia; yet like all Eurasianists, Gumilëv asserts Eurasia's centrality without ever accepting any element of European culture: "The Turks and the Mongols can be genuine friends, but the English, the French and the Germans, I am convinced, can only be cunning exploiters. . . . Let me tell you a secret: If Russia will be saved, then only as a Eurasian power, and only through Eurasianism,"[81] because "harm has always come to us from the West."[82]

On the one hand, Eurasia only appears central, because Gumilëv entirely rejects Europe. But on the other hand, the only reason why Russia is turned toward the East is that it is synonymous with it. Even though Gumilëv was a specialist of the nomadic world, he did not fully accept the alterity of the steppe, whose only meaning, to him, is to be an organic part of the Russian Empire. The nomads are not Russia's Other; they are part of its identity. "Whatever may distinguish them from the Russians, the Tatars are a people that is not outside us, but inside us."[83] Gumilëv constantly upholds the unity, irreducible distinctiveness, and universality of the Eurasian world, and he claims that its permanence guarantees it a glorious future. Adequate analysis of contemporary problems, he asserts, requires an awareness of this permanence. The entire Eurasianist historiography serves to demonstrate that Russia's eastward expansion is not a conquest but a natural phenomenon: "Any territorial question can only be resolved on the basis of Eurasian unity."[84] Any kind of secessionism is condemned in advance as violating nature.

Xenophobia, Mixophobia, and Anti-Semitism

Gumilëv perceived the *ethnoi* as closed entities, but he was often obliged to pronounce on processes of meeting and symbiosis between collectivities. His judgment was peremptory: He virulently criticized assimilation and miscegenation. *Ethnoi,* he believed, cannot mix without being destroyed. This opinion led him to support endogamy, which would stabilize every people's "gene pool" (*genofond*) and guarantee the respect of its traditions. Thus, according to him, children born of exogamous marriages have two stereotypes of behavior at their disposal, and because they cannot fully embrace either of them, they bring about the destruction of the ethnic collectivity: "Endogamy is necessary for the preservation of ethnic traditions, because the endogamous family hands down a perfected stereotype of behavior to the child, whereas the exogamous family gives him two mutually destructive stereotypes."[85]

Yet Gumilëv cannot rule out the very possibility of contact between *ethnoi*. This forces him to recognize the existence of what he calls "positive complementarity." This (always reciprocal) feeling of closeness between two *ethnoi*—he implies the Russian and steppic *super-ethnoi*—is rooted in a form of biological correspondence and can therefore not be the product of a culture or a historical event. However, this complementarity should not be seen as grounds for miscegenation; the two *ethnoi* must remain impenetrable to each other.[86] Gumilëv gives a strange definition of symbiosis: "The optimal kind of ethnic contact is symbiosis, when *ethnoi* live side by side, preserving peaceful relations, but not interfering with each other's affairs."[87] Gumilëv's symbiosis, in which the two entities coexist without ever meeting, looks like the opposite of what is usually meant by that term. Totalities may be contiguous or even superposed, but they always remain closed; there is no room for otherness.

On the basis of this understanding of totality, Gumilëv approaches the realm of religion by outlining two irrevocably opposed worldviews: systemism and antisystems. In the first, people recognize that they are part of nature, and they accept the ethnic and political consequences of that understanding; in the second, people reject the material world, considering it as the source of all evil, and uphold the "lie"[88] that humanity is free from the influence of nature. According to him, the first conception is at the heart of the great monotheistic religions; the second informed heretic movements: Manichaeism, Mazdaism, Ismailism, Bogomilism, Catharism, and the like. These religious movements are condemned not only for their supposedly false conceptions of nature but also for their implicit challenge to the temporal authorities. Gumilëv praises total and all-encompassing religions. Faith is the expression of the *ethnos* and its current stage of ethnogenesis; it is a national, not an individual, affair. Religious excommunication is therefore tantamount to political condemnation and exclusion from the ethnic group.

   This fear of contact and exogamy informs Gumilëv's unequivocal stance on "cosmopolitanism," which he sees as destructive of ethnic totalities and symbolized, very classically, by the Jews.[89] At the turn of the 1960s, Gumilëv took part in several archeological field trips to the Lower Volga in search of remnants of the Khazar kingdom. Under the influence of his colleague and friend Mikhail Artamonov—whose anti-Semitic *History of the Khazars* (Istoriia Khazar, 1962) he edited—he centered his anti-Semitism on the Khazar myth, dedicating his *Discovery of Khazaria* to Artamonov.[90] Contrary to the original Eurasianists, he does not directly include Khazaria in Eurasia; for him, it is a mere "colony of Levantine culture on Eurasian territory."[91] However, the Khazars played a key role in the formation of one of Russia's main *sub-ethnoi,* the Cossacks, whom Gumilëv considers to be their more or less direct descendants.[92]

   For Gumilëv, Khazaria is the most revealing historical example of what he calls a "chimera" (*khimera*); any symbiosis between *ethnoi* may only be illusory and lead to disintegration, because the ethnic minority will always end up by dominating the majority.[93] Like Artamonov, Gumilëv rejects the widely accepted theory that the mainly Turkophone native elites converted to Judaism in the eighth century. He believes that Khazaria was originally populated by Scythians, Caucasians, and Turks of different creeds, including Nestorian Christians. Then Jews, coming from the Middle East, settled there in large numbers, refusing to assimilate to the local population. Those hailing from Byzantium, whom he presents as urban traders particularly influenced by Rabbinic thought, constituted a mixed population layer that did not belong either to the Turkic community or to the original Jewish *super-ethnos.* They intermarried with members of the local princely families, leading the Khazar elites to adopt Judaism and persecute both Islam and Christianity. This Jewish *super-ethnos,* Gumilëv goes on to write, consisted of *ethnoi* with widely differing modes of behavior and stereotypes, which explains why their system collapsed at the first blow dealt by Prince Sviatoslav in 965 and became what he calls a relic *ethnos.*

   Gumilëv's view of the Khazar Khaganate of the eighth and ninth centuries clearly reveals his anti-Semitism. Lacking a natural native landscape, the Jewish *super-ethnos,* he says, is fundamentally cosmopolitan, creating "zigzags unprovided for either by nature or by science"[94] and upsetting his preformed scientific patterns. With their predatory approach to indigenous nature and peoples, whom they gradually annihilated, the Jews created a *deviation* in the region's natural history. Incapable of adapting to their environment, they lived as parasites, consuming and destroying their host organism. Moreover, their high level of passionarity is due to distinctive biological features, which, according to Gumilëv's theory, explains their unusual capacity for survival within other ethnic groups: "When individuals of a certain population simplify their morphological structure, they sharply raise their level of bio-geochemical energy, that is, the bio-energetic migration of their atoms, improving their chances in the struggle for survival."[95] Thus, Gumilëv recasts the traditional opposition between Christianity and Judaism as an biological conflict, implying that the Jews' inferiority (the supposed simplification of their morphological structure) enables them to destroy other peoples' "ethnic force."

This virulent anti-Semitism distinguishes Gumilëv from the original Eurasianists, for whom Khazaria was, on the contrary, the symbol of the Jews' Easternness and of their legitimate place in Eurasia. The Khazar euphemism as a historical cover for anti-Semitism was not invented by Gumilëv,[96] and it even predated Soviet anti-Zionism, of which it was part. Gumilëv's "chimera" is simply a subtle equivalent of the "Jewish-Masonic plot" or "world Zionism," and so it was not an accident that he defended his second dissertation, "Ethnogenesis and the Biosphere of the Earth," in the early 1970s, during an upsurge of official anti-Zionism. This anti-Semitism corroborates the fundamentally biological character of the *ethnoi* as he defined them. He takes up the physiological metaphors of late-nineteenth-century Western anti-Semitism, combining them with a condemnation of capitalism in line with official Soviet ideology. Thus, having defined the Jews as merchants hailing from zones of miscegenation at the margins of Europe, he compares them to "bacteria that devour the entrails of the *ethnos,*"[97] and he states that capitalism was born precisely of undesirable ethnic and racial blending. The myth of a "Khazar yoke" imposed by the Jews upon the Russian people was later taken up by Vadim Kozhinov, and it is supported by Igor' Shafarevich (1923–), who mentions it in his famous pamphlet *Russophobia.*[98] A victim of Soviet authoritarianism, Gumilëv seems to have been unable to avoid the equation of Bolshevism with Judaism that was popular with part of the Russian nationalist spectrum at the time. With his historical research on Khazaria, he wittingly informed the conspiracy theories that are so fashionable in Russia today.

Gumilëv, Russian Nationalism, and Soviet Ethnology

Several types of criticisms have been leveled against Gumilëv's theories. They may be divided into three generations and categories. Chronologically speaking, the first series of criticisms, starting in the second half of the 1960s, came from the Institute of Ethnology and was centered on the anti-Marxist character of Gumilëv's writings on ethnic issues. The second wave, in the second half of the 1970s and the early 1980s, came from Russian nationalists who condemned Gumilëv's Turkophilia and interpreted his view of Russia as Russophobic. Third-generation critics are contemporary scholars inspired by the Western constructivist model, such as Viktor Shnirelman, Sergei Panarin, and Vladimir Koreniako.[99] The first two categories of criticisms concern superficial elements of Gumilëv's theories, and in fact they share many of his presuppositions. Only the third category, which is very recent and wields little influence in contemporary Russia, targets Gumilëv's theories in their entirety by attacking their very philosophical foundations. Gumilëv's disciples believe that only Marxists and ethnocentric nationalists dare challenge their master's thought. This alleged political bias dispenses them from responding. They ignore the third-generation criticisms, which they consider to be imports of Western theories and therefore irrelevant to a distinctively national realm of knowledge that does not need to justify itself according to any universal theoretical standards.

In the second half of the 1970s, when Russian nationalism was firmly entrenched within powerful institutions such as the Union of Writers, the Communist Party apparatus, and organizations close to the Komsomol,[100] Gumilëv became a bone of contention between different currents of nationalism. Put simply, Tsarist, Neo-Slavophile, and ethnocentric nationalists all virulently criticized Gumilëv, whereas Stalinists and advocates of an outspoken Russian imperialism appreciated his talk of Russia's natural great power. His theories of ethnogenesis were generally accepted, at least passively; the debate essentially raged over his positive assessment of relations between the Russians and the peoples of the steppe. Thus he was much criticized by the medievalist Boris Rybakov (1908–2001) for casting the legend of Prester John as a negative Western myth. The writer Vladimir

Chivilikhin (1928–1984), in his famous novel *Memory* (*Pamiat'*), accused him of geographical determinism and biologism. Finally, Apollon Kuz'min (1928–2004), one of the leading Neo-Slavophile nationalist historians, attacked his Turkophile analysis of the *Lay of Igor's Host.*

In the 1990s, after the disappearance of the Soviet Union, Gumilëv's heritage commanded a broader consensus, and many of his former critics went over to his side, although certain nationalist authors, such as Ksenia Mialo, continue to denounce him. But his anti-Semitic historiography, his vehement rejection of any Western influence in Russia, his belief in a gene pool specific to each people, and his idea that certain *ethnoi* are more dangerous than others have all become major elements of contemporary nationalist discourse—all having been endowed by him with scientific legitimacy.

Gumilëv's disciples consistently refuse to view him as a theorist of Russian nationalism, and they try to present his writings as independent of any commitment to a national cause. Indeed, developing theories of ethnic history is not the same as being a convinced nationalist. However, a close reading of Gumilëv's works clearly reveals not only his anti-Semitism but also his desire to present Eurasia as a distinctive entity destined for a glorious future. His last books especially are inspired by the most classic Russian and Soviet messianism. His apparently scientific discourse in fact serves to cast the Soviet Union as a developing *super-ethnos.* His theories have a precise ideological objective: to validate the Soviet mode of ethnic coexistence, and to stress the special complementarity of the Russian and Turkic *super-ethnoi,* contrasting them with the intrinsic and eternally irreconcilable opposition between Russia and the West. As one of his main disciples, Viacheslav Ermolaev, states in his introduction to *The Black Legend:* "This book clearly shows a key truth: West Europeans' deep-seated antipathy toward the inhabitants of Eurasia is an inalienable element of the West European attitude toward the world. Like any other stable emotional disposition, this antipathy is unconscious; it is generated by the natural differences between the two *super-ethnoi.*"[101]

Despite the numerous accusations of Russophobia and Sovietophobia leveled by his opponents, Gumilëv was undoubtedly a patriot.[102] Although he condemned Marxism for having violated the fundamental principles of the biosphere, he perceived the violence of the Soviet period as necessary for the survival of the Russian *ethnos,* and he saw perestroika as an attempt at national salvation that was crucial for the preservation of Eurasia. "Salvation has come in the form of perestroika, . . . the result of long and terrible preparations. . . . It leads to a recombination of elements that saturate the ethnic field, preparing it for transition to a more durable phase of stable movement, of favorable culture."[103] His final book, *From Rus' to Russia,* published posthumously and written during the country's collapse in 1991, expressed his profound attachment to the Soviet Union, and the final chapter defends the country's political experience against the "steamroller" of the West. Moreover, many witnesses relate that Gumilëv suffered a psychological breakdown because he was unable to accept the disintegration of the USSR.[104] While he was neither a communist in politics nor a Marxist in science, he was very clearly pro-Soviet, a stance shared by many in contemporary Russia, who consider that the ideological disappearance of the regime should not have led to the demise of the country.

That nationalists of Neo-Slavophile hue, in the 1980s, attacked Gumilëv as a traitor prepared to sacrifice the Russian people in the name of its unity with the Turkic Muslims, does not mean that he did not himself profess another variety of Russian nationalism—an imperial and Eurasian one. To this day, many scholars take "Russian nationalism" to include only ethnocentric currents that hanker after Tsarism and are obsessed with the idea that the Russians paid their empire dearly and were robbed by the other Soviet peoples. However, there is another nationalist tradition, which is proud of Russia's imperial past, nostalgic about the Soviet Union, and convinced that Russia as a great power can only exist if it becomes aware of the naturalness of its Eurasian expansion. Gumilëv very clearly belongs to this strand of thought.

But what about the first category of criticisms? Being associated with the great figures of official Soviet ethnology, they allow Gumilëv's disciples to present him as a victim of the regime or even a dissident, and to claim that his theories of ethnicity had nothing to do with Soviet science. Although Gumilëv was much criticized in official ethnology well into the 1980s, he cannot strictly speaking be considered a "dissident," because from the 1960s onward he was allowed to pursue his profession. He was not forced to perform manual labor, was not confined to a psychiatric hospital, and was not stripped of his civil rights. Moreover, even his long camp confinement in the 1930s through 1950s was due to his being the son of "cursed poets" rather than to his academic work. Though this does not exculpate the Soviet regime or efface Gumilëv's suffering, it does mean that his works should not be adorned with the halo of the Gulag. Finally, Soviet realities, especially in academia, were not as black and white as this simplistic picture suggests.

The fact that Gumilëv found it very difficult to publish his research, did not obtain the academic status that he thought was his due, and suffered hardship throughout his life does not mean that he was simply a victim of the regime's ideological vagaries. From the late 1960s onward, Gumilëv had a circle of disciples at Leningrad University and at the Russian Geographic Society, where he regularly gave lectures. In the 1970s, he managed to publish some articles, albeit with difficulty, and he became a prestigious if scandalous figure in Leningrad academic circles. According to all available accounts, his lectures were well attended; he was appreciated by students for his free thinking, and he sparked many a passionate debate. His reputation as a marginalized intellectual thus helped him to find a real audience of students who now occupy academic positions. This prestige is not obliterated by the fact that he was never a member of the official academic establishment.

The search for a definition of Gumilëv's place in Soviet science is a corollary of the debates on whether he was a direct intellectual heir to the original Eurasianists. From the point of view of his disciples, his status as the "last Eurasianist" confirms his role as a dissident within the Soviet ethnology of the time. But although his theories were not fully in tune with the Marxist-Leninist view of *ethnoi* as being founded on productive forces and social relations, he was in agreement with the official idea that *ethnoi* are "natural." The conceptual divergences between Sergei Shirokogorov (1887–1939), Bromlei, and Gumilëv in their analysis of the adaptation of ethnic behavior to the natural milieu should not obscure the fact that they all had a strictly deterministic view of the *ethnos*. Even if the *ethnos* is seen as a historical rather than a biological phenomenon, all these writers thought that once ethnic identity exists, it becomes absolute: It is transmitted from one generation to the next; it cannot be shed by individuals; it cannot be combined with other ethnic identities; and it does not change over time: "No matter how hard he tries, Man cannot change his ethnic affiliation; everyone belongs to an *ethnos,* and to one only."[105]

Thus, although Gumilëv was justified in accusing his colleagues of having overtly boycotted him and for all their disagreement on certain theoretical issues,[106] they did share a common approach. This included, in particular, their conception of ethnology as the science of the *ethnos* and ethnic processes; their belief in the naturalness of the *ethnos,* seen as a given rather than a construct; their admiration of the exact sciences, which they believed must inspire research in the social sciences; their disparaging view of miscegenation; their rejection of multiple identities; and their hope that ethnology might be able to make predictions and ethnologists might provide expertise to the political authorities. Thus Gumilëv shared some of the

Soviet regime's ideological presuppositions, because he buttressed the thesis of the unity of the Soviet peoples and subscribed to scientific postulates that were in tune with the social Darwinism of Marxist-Leninist doctrine. He internalized the idea of having to look for "laws" of human development, and he engaged in the theorization and classification of human phenomena following the model of the exact sciences. Thus the debate on how to define the *ethnos* was internal to Soviet scholarship; all the positions were based on a set of entirely shared essentialist postulates. Gumilëv, no less than Bromlei, was an advocate of ethnicistic and naturalistic conceptions fully in line with the tradition of late Soviet ethnology.

Conclusions

Gumilëv was not the "last Eurasianist." He was the founder of a variety of Neo-Eurasianism, and he developed a theory of his own, which is now immensely successful in Russian academic circles. He did, of course, share a certain conception of Russian identity and Russia's imperial destiny with the original Eurasianists and the contemporary Neo-Eurasianists: they all believe that the peoples living on the territory of the Eurasian entity share a "community of destiny" that persists over time, through all political vagaries; that their unity is based on a Turko-Slavic alliance, historically embodied in the "Tatar-Mongol yoke," and on the rejection of the West; and that a glorious future is in stock for Eurasia, which will show the rest of humankind how to sail around the riffs of Europe. However, Gumilëv differs from the founding fathers in his extreme determinism. He introduces new ethnicistic hypotheses into the Eurasianist tradition, and he caricatures their complex views on mutual influences between people and territory. His rejection of possibilism and human perfectibility as well as his obsession with the exact sciences run counter to the underlying humanism of the original Eurasianists, who considered people to be masters of their own destiny. His contempt for the humanities is opposed to the philosophical and literary feel of 1920s Eurasianism, and his moral conservatism contrasts with the futurism of the first Eurasianist publications.

Like all the other Eurasianist theorists, Gumilëv does not believe in the universality of humanity. For him, this idea is a product of Western ideology, "since from an ethnic point of view historical mankind does not represent any kind of phenomenological community. This is why talk of 'the priority of values common to all mankind' is naive, though not harmless."[107]

He thinks that once Russia becomes aware of its Eurasianist, that is, imperial destiny, its mission will be to rebut that universalism. Russia must become the champion of relativism on a philosophical level, and of multipolarity on the level of politics. Both the first Eurasianists and the Neo-Eurasianists believe that individual elements draw their meaning from their relationship to a totality. Gumilëv's theory of the biological nature of humanity says the same thing. Thus he takes up the original Eurasianists' organicism and radicalizes it, using numerous biological or even genetic metaphors with far-reaching political implications. He does not, strictly speaking, develop a political theory; and unlike the other currents of Eurasianism and Neo-Eurasianism, he cannot be considered a partisan of conservative revolution. Nonetheless, he is part of a fundamentally conservative strand of thought holding that social evolution is degeneration. His theories of ethnogenesis imply a thirst for "normality"; he believes that upholding the norms of sexuality (endogamy), family life (respect for the elderly), society (respect for the nation), culture (respect for religious institutions), and politics (the rejection of any challenge to the powers that be) is necessary for the survival of the *ethnos*. His deterministic science thus serves a reactionary vision of contemporary developments.

Gumilëv was not a brilliant Oriental scholar but an ideologist: He developed a philosophy of history rather than a methodology or discipline, and he was full of contempt for the historical and archeological sources at his disposal. Like the original Eurasianists and the various currents of Neo-Eurasianism, he used a supposedly innovative science to justify his philosophical postulates. He never went beyond realism: He rejected the idea that objects of study may be social constructs; on the contrary, he sought to sacralize his object.[108] The fundamentally dogmatic character of his writings and the extreme scientism of his models make him the least intellectually relevant and the least original (Neo-)Eurasianist. To the difference of both his interwar predecessors and his successors, Aleksandr Panarin and Aleksandr Dugin, what is striking about Gumilëv's works is his ignorance of Western theories and his lack of general education. His theories read as if they had been elaborated in a vacuum, in a world entirely cut off from the outside, rather than in the actual Soviet Union of the 1970s. Decades of political marginality made him turn his back on a society that refused to recognize the relevance of his theories; and his thought, the product of this intellectual solitude, was fundamentally autistic.

Chapter 3

Aleksandr Panarin: Philosophy of History and the Revival of Culturalism

After the Soviet Union's unexpected demise in 1991, some intellectuals and politicians set out to seek a new substitute ideology that would allow them to come to terms with the rapid changes. Over the course of the 1990s, the difficult transition to a market economy and disillusionment with Russia's new democracy gradually prompted others to join the ranks of the original nostalgists for Soviet grandeur. The Neo-Eurasianists agreed with this group that the collapse of a specific regime, that of "real socialism," did not entail the collapse of the country; for them, the change of ideology did not justify the territorial contraction of the Soviet Union, which they more or less consciously equated with Russia. Thus the disappearance of the USSR was attributed to treason by its elites and by the West and was perceived as a negation of Russia's imperial nature. In striving for imperial reconstruction—on a narrative level, because it was unattainable as a political goal—the Neo-Eurasianists reinterpreted the intellectual framework established by the émigré founding fathers of Eurasianism and by Lev Gumilëv in the Soviet Union. Thus Neo-Eurasianism is a fundamentally *restorationist* movement.

Ever since the early 1990s, Neo-Eurasianism has never been anything like a unified force or ideology; rather, it is a motley and fragmented constellation of people with competing ambitions. Not all of Eurasianism's currents are institutionalized, and indeed it profits from the diffuseness of its culturalist terminology. It draws its strength from its capacity to present itself as a new ideology for the post-bipolar world, based on a civilizational worldview and the idea of an emergence of new, "postmodern" values. The inclusion of Neo-Eurasianist rhetoric into alter-globalization[1] theories is largely due to the intellectual endeavors of one of the main Neo-Eurasianist thinkers, Aleksandr S. Panarin (1940–2003), as well as those of lesser-known academic figures such as F. Girenko or V. Ia. Pashchenko.[2] Like the founding fathers in the 1920s and 1930s, Panarin sought to portray Russia as a "substance" and explain political reality using arguments about the original "essence" of civilizations. He wished to rehabilitate the notion of empire by presenting it not only as the historically natural type of regime for Russia but also as the main driving force behind any alternative to United States–led globalization: According to him, Russia's return to greatness will allow humanity to leave behind the Western model of development. Thus Neo-Eurasianism is part and parcel of the Russian messianic tradition, with its religious and political manifestations, and modernizes it by linking it to theories of a multipolar world.

Is There a Unified Neo-Eurasianist Theory?

Although they have certain well-defined ideological postulates in common, the Neo-Eurasianists are split into so many currents that it may well be more accurate to speak of Eurasianisms, all the more so because the various movements are not really intent on establishing links with each other. Nevertheless, certain disciples of Neo-Eurasianism have attempted, retrospectively, to trace an intellectual continuity across the entire twentieth century. They have done so by presenting their ideology as one of the major countercultures of that period—even though they take a positive overall view of the Soviet experience—and by adorning themselves with the prestige of the great currents of turn-of-century literature and also with that of émigré culture and of the Gulag. They draw on the early-twentieth-century Asianism of symbolists such as Aleksandr Blok, on the Russian exiles of the 1920s, and on the (mistaken) belief that Gumilëv met Savitsky in one of Stalin's labor camps. They have stressed Gumilëv's dissident credentials, his (genuine) meeting with the father of the poet Olzhas Suleimenov in a camp, and the like. Its historical inaccuracies aside, this mythical genealogy serves little to explain why the different currents of Neo-Eurasianism were so fiercely opposed to each other throughout the 1990s, or why they are still unable to unite at least to the extent of agreeing on the basics of a common ideological platform.[3]

This chapter concentrates on Panarin, but other important figures, such as Eduard Bagramov and Timur Pulatov, also need to be mentioned, however briefly. Bagramov (born 1930), who was a consultant of the Central Committee of the Communist Party of the Soviet Union, embodies the fraction of the Soviet elites that has converted to Eurasianism.[4] Working at the Institute of Political and Social Research of the Russian Academy of Sciences, in 1993 he founded the (irregularly published) journal *Evraziia: Narody, kul'tury, religii.*[5] It publicizes a folkloric view of Soviet ethnic diversity and argues that loyalty to Russia is the best way of protecting the national identity of the different Eurasian peoples. Its authors extol the diversity and coexistence of Slavic and Turkic peoples as well as of Orthodoxy and Islam, and they take up the Soviet rhetoric of "friendship between peoples," claiming that the inhabitants of Eurasia have a "common historical destiny."[6]

Timur Pulatov edits the journal *Literaturnaia Evraziia,* published since 1998 by the Union of Writers of the USSR, later renamed the International Community of Writers' Unions. Pulatov, a Tajik writer from Bukhara who was forced to leave Uzbekistan in the 1990s for political reasons, manages his journal with an iron hand.[7] It is the only Eurasianist periodical published in Russia that is edited by a non-Russian, and it is also the only one centered not on the Turkic world but rather on Tajikistan, celebrating it for its Zoroastrian and Aryan past. The journal presents itself as a place where the literary and spiritual space destroyed by the collapse of the Soviet Union is reassembled, and it promotes a cult of respect for national specificities. Every issue features sections such as "The Dialogue of Cultures" or "World Religions in Eurasia," presenting translations of foreign poetry, especially Chinese, Indian, and Iranian. The choice of authors, who have included Ayatollah Khomeini and Mao Zedong, is obviously ideological.

Literaturnaia Evraziia has a penchant for official figures, and it is proud to count presidents of the region's countries among its contributing authors, including Askar Akaev (Kyrgyzstan, ousted in March 2005), Nursultan Nazarbaev (Kazakhstan), Emomali Rakhmonov (Tajikistan), Aleksandr Lukashenka (Belarus), and Geidar Aliev (Azerbaijan, died 2003). The journal makes no secret of its nostalgia for the Soviet Union, has published strongly worded articles to protest "NATO aggression" against Serbia, and has called on the Eurasian world to become aware of its cultural and spiritual unity in order to resist Western dominance. Although much of the journal is devoted to Tajikistan, its definition of Eurasia is not free of ambiguity. Though the term is mostly used as a synonym for the post-Soviet region, it may sometimes embrace all of Asia, including India, Iran, and China. In fact, in both Bagramov's and Pulatov's journals, the relationship between Russia and Eurasia is difficult to pin down. Both journals defend imperial Great Russia, which, they argue, protected the small cultures of Eurasia without assimilating them. Nevertheless, despite this rhetorical cult of national diversity, Russians are granted pride of place in the post-Soviet world. In the words of *Literaturnaia Evraziia,* "We consider Russian literature to be the link between the literatures of all the peoples of Russia and the [Commonwealth of Independent States]."[8]

All these currents consider themselves to be in competition with each other, refusing to be seen as part of a single ideology and often denying the others any Eurasianist legitimacy. In the 1990s, the only explicit link between any two currents of Neo-Eurasianism was that between Bagramov's journal and Kazakhstan's official Eurasianism. President Nazarbaev, always in search of a mouthpiece in Russia, decided to finance the journal.[9] *Evraziia* was the only Neo-Eurasianist group to openly call for cooperation between the different post-Soviet integrationist ideologies and to highlight the Turkic peoples' contribution to Russian history. However, in the early 2000s, Aleksandr Dugin managed to reduce the diversity of the Neo-Eurasianist camp by creating a Eurasianist political party, relegating the other currents to a strictly intellectual niche and confronting them with the politicization of Neo-Eurasianism as a fait accompli. Faced with what he saw as a choice between joining Dugin or disappearing, Bagramov accepted to take part in the founding congress of the Evraziia Party in 2002, and he seems thereby to have publicly acknowledged Dugin's uncontested leadership of Neo-Eurasianism in Russia. Throughout the 1990s, however, Dugin's strand had to face competition from Panarin, whose writings many Russian scholars consider to have been clearly superior in intellectual quality to Dugin's.

From Liberalism to Conservatism: Panarin's Intellectual Biography

As the occupant of the political science chair at Moscow State University's philosophy department, Aleksandr S. Panarin was a prolific essayist known for his erudition and subtle analysis, and he was respected among political scientists with nationalist leanings, especially at his university. He wrote several standard university textbooks, including *The Philosophy of Politics* (1996) and *A Handbook of Political Science* (2002).[10] In 1998, he published a highly successful book called *The Revenge of History,* which, as its name indicates, was intended as a response to Francis Fukuyama's famous "end of history" thesis.[11] In 2002, only a few months before his death, he was awarded the prestigious Solzhenitsyn Prize for his book *Orthodox Civilization in a Globalized World,* where he announced the revenge of an economically backward but spiritually advanced Russia against a West that is losing itself in a technological frenzy. His biography is highly revelatory of the evolution of large parts of Russian academia: After the hopes raised by perestroika, the disillusionment caused by Boris Yeltsin's political and economic reforms prompted many intellectuals to support the communist and nationalist circles they had previously opposed.

In Soviet times, Panarin occupied a semidissident position. In his student days, he was expelled from the Komsomol and university for belonging to a social democratic circle. During perestroika, he supported the liberalizing movement initiated by Mikhail Gorbachev and called for a political, economic, social, and cultural reform of the Soviet Union. A convinced Occidentalist (rather than a Westernizer, a distinction that will be clarified below), he advocated the gradual introduction of a democracy that would offer the advantages of market economy, for example, by legalizing private property and entrepreneurship, while preserving Soviet achievements in matters of social policy, for example, the sense of equality prevalent in the Soviet Union. Nevertheless, he quickly grew disappointed with the Yeltsinist elites' choice of "shock therapy," and he was offended by the social brutality of the first post-Soviet governments' reforms. By the end of 1992, he was denouncing the elitist character of the reforms; he felt that the Westernizers were engaged in an assault on Russian society, degrading national culture by their boundless admiration for the West, and creating a blend of capitalism, corruption, savage privatization, and theft of the country's resources.

Between 1992 and 1995, Panarin tried to theorize a special path for Russia, defined as "people's capitalism." This mode of development would have taken into account Russia's specific national features, would not have thrown the advantages of the previous regime overboard, and, most importantly, would have been a genuine *reform,* as opposed to the *revolution* advocated by the Yeltsin regime.[12] These ideas made Panarin move closer to centrist groups who condemned the emergence of an oligarchic class and the dismemberment of the Russian state through privatization: The "people's capitalism" he imagined could only be realized by a strong state that would not sacrifice its own control over the country's resources to a cult of the market. He thus became interested in conservative political circles, which refused to accept the weakening of the Russian state on either the domestic or the international front. For instance, he agreed on many issues with the foreign minister and later prime minister Yevgeny Primakov, whom he especially appreciated for having initiated a foreign policy turned toward the great Asian powers and no longer obsessed with Russia's relationship with the West.[13]

Panarin became an even more radical advocate of conservative capitalism in the late 1990s: the NATO bombings of Yugoslavia, the dismissal of Primakov, and Western criticism of the Second Chechen War drew him closer to his former enemies, the communists and nationalists. Thus, at the beginning of the 2000s, faced with what he perceived as the failure of Russian parliamentary democracy, he affirmed that Russia's salvation now lay in a strong presidential regime with authoritarian features, and in a return to the nation's autocratic (*samoderzhavnye*) traditions. A former Occidentalist, Panarin thus ended up by accusing the West of being responsible for Russia's ills and leading humankind to destruction. In his eyes, the September 11, 2001, terrorist attacks were further proof that the American superpower was clinging to delusions. In the books he wrote in the early 2000s, Panarin upheld the modernity of Slavophilism, arguing that it remained relevant to an understanding of Russian identity. His political radicalization made him grow distant from the regime of Vladimir Putin, with whom he may otherwise have sympathized, and pushed him to advocate the restoration of both Orthodox spirituality and Stalinist statehood.

Thus, Panarin occupied a highly peculiar position inside the Neo-Eurasianist movement. As early as 1993, he wrote several articles about Eurasianism for *Znamia, Vostok,* and *Voprosy filosofii,* and in 1995 he published a book, *Russia in the Civilizational Process.* Between 1993 and 1996, he coedited—with his friend Boris S. Erasov (died 2001), a member of the Russian Academy of Natural Sciences—four collections of articles specifically devoted to Russia's relationship with the East.[14] In the first half of the 1990s, Panarin promoted what he then called a "civilized Eurasianism," presenting it as the exact opposite of Dugin's variety. However, Panarin hardly ever referred to the founding fathers of the movement in the 1920s and 1930s, and he was later openly critical of what he considered their "geographical determinism."[15] He also constantly criticized Gumilëv and his naturalist views of the peoples of the Russian Empire.[16] Despite this criticism, he shared the original Eurasianists' intellectual roots: He was in search of a philosophy of history rather than a conception of geopolitics, and, unlike Dugin, he never left the sphere of intellectual endeavors for politics. He was trying to continue and modernize a Russian Pan-Slavic tradition inspired by thinkers such as Nikolai Danilevsky and Konstantin Leont'ev (1831–91).[17]

Despite having been fiercely opposed to Dugin in the 1990s, Panarin eventually decided to move closer to him; his political evolution toward conservatism led him to take a more positive view of Dugin's ideas. Thus, for example, Panarin began to publish articles in Dugin's journals, such as *Evraziiskoe obozrenie*,[18] and he adopted Dugin's geopolitical vocabulary of an opposition between tellurocracies and thalassocracies and of the "restoration of the Continent's prerogatives as a program for the future."[19] Panarin also appeared to endorse Dugin's best-selling book, *The Foundations of Geopolitics* (1997). He even agreed to take part in the founding congress of the Evraziia movement and became a member of the party's Central Council in 2002.[20] Dugin later claimed that Panarin had agreed to write a foreword to one of his latest books, *Philosophy of War* (2004), but the professor's illness and death put an end to this unlikely cooperation.[21]

 However, Panarin's works cannot be reduced to Eurasianism, in the strict sense of the term. Though he constantly claimed that Russia was to become a Eurasian empire once again, he largely stopped expressing Eurasianist views after the 1990s, shifting to more "classical" themes of Russian nationalism, such as Orthodoxy's contribution to the distinctiveness of Russian civilization. His main books, such as *The Temptation of Globalism* (2000) and *Strategic Instability in the 21st Century* (2002), are works of political philosophy concerned with analyzing contemporary globalization. However, it was his successful inclusion of Eurasianist themes into a larger set of arguments that ensured his popularity. In his version, Eurasianist ideas are integrated into more general views on "Orthodox civilization" or on Russia's mission in the resistance to American globalization. For him, the idea that both Russia's expansion in Asia and its imperial character are "natural" is merely one ideological element among others in the discourse of "traditional" Russian nationalism; it is no longer perceived as a distinctive ideology that may be accepted or rejected.

"Civilizationism" and "Postmodernism"

 As in the original Eurasianism, the intellectual matrix of Neo-Eurasianism is based on a rejection of the West. Europe is invariably seen as synonymous with capitalism; its mindset is hedonistic and consumption-oriented; and while the Neo-Eurasianists are envious of Europe's technological advancement, they also criticize it for valuing "abstract techno-rationality"[22] over ethical and religious values. According to Panarin, the European political model is similar to the historical experience of Athens, because its success is based on enslaving the rest of the world: Europe stands for "a democratic racism"[23] because it considers democracy from the point of view of white Catholics or Protestants. He also rejects Europe on a level that could be called methodological; universality can only be the result of the hegemony of one particular culture, that of the West, which colonizes the other civilizations from within by offering them a Eurocentric and therefore inevitably distorting yardstick. Thus, according to Panarin, Eurocentrism presupposes unilateral development and a cultural hierarchy that distinguishes between donor and recipient countries; it is "dangerous for the moral health of peoples, because it instills a complex of nonachievement, debasing their own values."[24]

Nevertheless, in his attitude toward the West, Panarin remains the most subtle of the Neo-Eurasianists. As a former Occidentalist, he seeks to nuance his rejection of Europe by differentiating between two terms, "Occidentalism" (*zapadnichestvo*) and "Westernization" (*vesternizatsiia*). The former refers to the rule of law, a democratic regime, law-governed international politics, and the philosophical traditions of European liberalism. The latter is equated with savage capitalism, moral and social decline, and pure and simple imitation of Western culture. Though Westernization is seen as an ongoing process initiated by the United States, Occidentalism is associated with the European philosophical heritage. However, some European countries feature both of these phenomena. Thus, Panarin insists on an opposition between two Europes—one Atlantic and universalistic (the "Roman idea"), and the other continental and national ("the German idea"). In doing so, he takes up the traditional worldview of geopolitics, with its opposition between a continental and an Atlantic space and a third sphere, the "Rimland," divided between the two and embodied by Europe—which, in different historical contexts and in different countries, has wavered between the two models.

For Panarin, cultures develop cyclically, in thrusts. The West, however, is peculiar in that it has a linear conception of time, expressing its belief in historical progress. From a Western point of view, Panarin argues, only temporality (with "lags" and "advances") can account for the differences between civilizations, which are classified on a scale reaching from archaic to modern. In contrast, he proposes restoring the category of space to analytic favor and using it in support of non-European nations' right to differ; for him, cultural specificity is not temporal or vertical but spatial and horizontal. This places him squarely in the tradition of the original Eurasianists, although he does not refer to the geographic theories of Pëtr Savitsky.[25] Panarin holds that civilizations are irreducible to each other, because they constitute closed structures that cannot communicate with each other. Thus, civilizations that are different cannot "catch up" with others, because the difference constitutes an "essence" rather than a "lag." Though civilizations are the basic agents of history, they nevertheless remain ahistorical: Their internal structure is impervious to evolution; they represent unchangeable forms of social construction.[26]

, Thus the Neo-Eurasianists remain rooted in a fundamentally Herderian type of thinking: Every civilization has a transcendent idea of its own and is the bearer of a portion of divine truth; should such a unique character disappear, all humankind would be left impoverished. As Panarin's friend and associate Erasov states: "Every civilization exists separately and has its own distinctive character. Civilizational diversity manifests itself in different contents of spiritual life as well as structures and historical destinies."[27] Panarin's conception is an extreme form of cultural relativism, because he maintains that no nation can judge another nation; it has neither the right to do so nor has it the conceptual means required, for its thought is inevitably governed by the logic of its own civilization. Thus the concept of civilization acts as the theoretical matrix of his writings. He upholds "the postulate of the primacy of culture over all so-called objective determinants of the social world" and even speaks of "culturological transcendentalism."[28] Apart from its references to nineteenth-century German *Naturphilosophie* and Schellingian thought, Neo-Eurasianism also partakes of the fashion for "culturology."

The scientific credentials of Neo-Eurasianism partly hinge on the concept of civilization. Neo-Eurasianism claims a glorious and, paradoxically, Western intellectual ancestry. Panarin rarely refers to conservative Pan-Slavists such as Danilevsky or Leont'ev, but he constantly quotes Karl Marx, Max Weber, Arnold Toynbee, Oswald Spengler, Lucien Febvre, Fernand Braudel, and other exponents of the *Annales* School.[29] He is in search of unchanging features to counter the traumas of twentieth-century Russian history. He thinks that only a perspective based on the *longue durée* ("the long term," an idea he borrows from Braudel) produces an awareness of the essence of historical phenomena; it is Panarin's belief that civilizational factors, perceived as more important than individual human lives, are in fact what shapes the destiny of peoples. Erasov agrees that "these types of interaction [between civilizations] seem more significant than political or social struggles, which are subject to the influence of constantly changing local circumstances."[30] Thus these thinkers consider intercultural differences to be epistemological: The dynamic political history of the West contrasts with the permanence of the non-Western civilizations; beneath the brutal

change in end-of-century Russia, Panarin discerns the stable, almost im-
mobile essence of Eurasian space, massive and continental.

Along with these great Western classics, Panarin also draws on area studies and stresses the importance of Oriental, African, and Islamic studies.
Though Panarin claims that these disciplines were originally founded to
serve colonial objectives, they have become an independent sphere of
scholarship, an approach toward non-European cultures that does not apply
European standards.[31] Thus, his project of having the study of civilizations
recognized as a full-fledged science requires a reference to Europe (even
though the "science" is far from being universally recognized as such in the
"West" itself): He believes that his use of European branches of learning
proves his neutrality and bolsters Eurasianism's claim to the status of an
academic discipline. However, his appropriation of the Western scholarly
heritage is not a neutral endeavor; it serves an ideological project.

Panarin acknowledges that culturological studies developed after the
collapse of the philosophical systems of the twentieth century; they seek to
replace those systems and to derive the meaning of facts of life from a transcendent whole. The decline of the West is a recurrent theme in his culturalism. For him, any alternative to globalization requires an awareness that
the conflicts of the contemporary world are no longer ideological but civilizational, and that the history of humankind has gone from social inequality to historical inequality.[32] Francis Fukuyama's claim that the formation
of civilization models has come to an end is wrong, Panarin argues, because
the European paradigm of liberalism and parliamentary democracy has
failed. A renewal of civilizational awareness—that is, awareness of the
world's inherent diversity—will provide an alternative to the Western model.
He also argues that unless we are prepared to accept that the failure of
European civilization is tantamount to the failure of humanity, the right to
differ must be elevated to the rank of a philosophical principle. Thus the
Eurasianist "science" of civilizations is not a branch of scientific knowledge
but a philosophy of history and the nation.

This confusion between scientific analysis and political punditry can be
found in another discipline Panarin seeks to theorize, which he calls "global
political prognostication." Its subject is both the study of globalization in
its historical dynamics and also the conditions for "prognosticating a qual-
itatively different future."[33] According to Panarin, globalization creates a
democracy limited to a small group of privileged, extraterritorial people, the
rest of humankind being relegated to low-intensity conflicts and a permanent "ecocide."[34] Whereas geopolitics is the study of the spatial factor,

prognostication takes time as its object and belongs to the realm of "chronopolitics." Panarin's conception of civilization is thus based on one of the major presuppositions of Neo-Eurasianist thought, what he calls the "plurality [*mnogovariantnost'*] of history."[35] Panarin describes his new discipline as concentrating on the study of historical junctions and different possible scenarios, and reflecting upon the openness of the future. Thus he seems to be seeking to theorize possible alternatives to American globalization, which, he claims, "privatizes" the future of the world,[36] and to reject any kind of historical determinism that would rule out the possibility of other modes of development. For him, analyzing globalization and denouncing it are both parts of one and the same intellectual endeavor.

Panarin constantly refers to *The Clash of Civilizations.*[37] Though he agrees with its author, Samuel Huntington, that the concept of civilization can be used to explain the post-bipolar world, Panarin accuses the Europeans and North Americans of positing a false dilemma under the heading of the so-called death of ideologies: a choice between the unification of the world within a single framework inspired by American liberalism, and wars and political strife due to "ethno-confessional" differences. For Panarin, of course, this view stems from blinkered thinking: Both Western individualism and its opposite, ethnocentrism, need to be rejected, because they are in fact merely two sides of the same coin, two expressions of resistance to any centralized supraethnic body (i.e., empire). Arguing against European cosmopolitanism and its attendant humanism, which postulates that all human beings resemble one another, Panarin maintains that the fatherland is the only entity that provides access to the universal. Instead of the local, ethnic homeland or the Western-type nation-state, he emphasizes the "big" fatherland that makes every human being part of a civilizational area, which for him is synonymous with empire.

Panarin thus postulates that there must be a happy medium, a third way, between the West's egalitarian universalism and the ethnic particularism of the non-European world: "There is a clash between the idea of a common space based on the civilizational principle of supraethnic communities directly linking the individual with the 'world at large,' and the idea of a multitude of small, particular 'sovereignties' on a regional and ethnic scale, based on the assumption of a common collective destiny that enslaves the individual."[38] Thus the division of the world into cultural areas—exemplified by, but not limited to, the European Union—must be encouraged. Nevertheless, Panarin affirms that his definition of Orthodox civilization is not based on "cultural types" as outlined by Danilevsky or Huntington, because transcendence takes precedence over cultural reality; that is, Orthodoxy is primarily a faith rather than an element of Russian culture.[39] He draws inspiration from the great thinkers of early-twentieth-century Russian religious philosophy, frequently citing Vladimir Solov'ëv, Vasilii Rozanov, Sergei Bulgakov, and, among contemporary authors, the philosopher Sergei Khoruzhii and the philologist Sergei Averintsev.

In his willingness to appropriate strands of thinking traditionally classified as "left-wing," Panarin resembles certain authors of the New Right. It is no accident that he refers to Alain de Benoist in several of his books.[40] Panarin ridicules, pell-mell, the Romantic image of the barbarian, the West's gratuitous Orientalism, the myth of the noble savage, the new "Oriental" religions, and, more generally, the New Left's idealization of the developing world following its disappointment with Soviet Marxism. However, he rejects any myth of original cultural unity as vain and backward-looking, and he condemns any reactionary approach to civilization, proposing instead to consider a modernized understanding of the concept of barbarity.[41] Barbarity, for him, is not a heritage of the preindustrial societies but the solution adopted by resolutely postmodern ones: The future belongs to those who are still lagging behind, to the "young" peoples—a Hegelian and Herderian notion—who will be able to avoid the mistakes of industrial society by overtaking it.

Panarin's conservatism is neither backward-looking nor reactionary, and is thus fully in line with the original Eurasianist tradition, whose authors had never hoped for any kind of restoration of Tsarism and saw themselves as resolutely facing modernity, particularly in its totalitarian variety. According to Panarin, only contemporary Russia—precisely because it is doubly modern, being simultaneously postindustrial and post-totalitarian—may criticize modernity without being traditionalistic. The original Eurasianism had long played with the iconoclastic image of the nomad who is untainted by culture and thus solely capable of reviving decadent societies; Neo-Eurasianism resumes this cult of barbarity by turning the habitual criteria upside down: "Total barbarity is not the product of an archaic heritage but the result of 'postcivilizational' experiences of overcoming the contradictions and tensions"[42] of the modern world.

Thus, for Panarin, Western society is fundamentally "Faustian"; it has failed on a spiritual level but also in its striving to control technology; it has destroyed human relations as well as nature. Communism, with its cult of technology, also testifies to the failure of the West, rather than Russia.

Panarin's pessimistic vision of the future of the human race is rooted in an eschatological feeling that is common to all currents of Neo-Eurasianism. For example, he makes regular use of ecological arguments: Industrial society is the sick man of this century, and what humankind needs to get out of this impasse is moral, rather than physical or technological, strength. The "postmodernism" Panarin calls for would be characterized by a downgrading of economic criteria in favor of cultural and religious values—what he calls "the revenge of the natural against the artificial."[43]

Neo-Eurasianism's messianism derives from the metaphysical principle of a double reality: Russia's apparent lag is actually a sign of a significant lead. "Postindustrial civilization—and therein lies its central paradox—is the most soil-based, the most culture-centric—in accordance with the spiritual imperatives of postmodernism—and simultaneously the most ecumenical and universal civilization, based on a dialogue between world cultures."[44] Though Eurasia is backward by Europe's industrial criteria, it is advanced in terms of the criteria of postmodernism, using its position between West and East to bring opposites together; it is thanks to its "archaic nature" that Russia will be the first to face the onset of postmodernity.

Rehabilitating Empire: "Civilizational" Pluralism and Ecumenical Theocracy

In Panarin's view, Russia acts as a global safeguard of polycentrism. By its very existence, it demonstrates that the West is not the sole driving force of development: "In many ways, the future of the postindustrial era depends on Russia's future. If Russia becomes the Third Rome once again, postindustrial society will have better chances of becoming an alternative to the industrial ghetto."[45] Adopting the Western model would amount to geopolitical and cultural death; the only way Russia can avoid that fate is by rejecting the false dilemma of global North versus South and globalization versus ethnicity and by reestablishing what Eurasianism sees as the primordial dichotomy: that between West and East. As one of Panarin's disciples stipulates, "The nature and essence of any culture and civilization can only be understood by determining their place in this global dual system of West and East."[46] By presenting itself as the East (which Panarin, like Dugin, equates with the "second world," a term that used to refer to the socialist countries), Russia could refuse to become part of the South in economic terms, while rejecting the North in terms of politics and culture. Thus Neo-Eurasianism subtly exploits the presuppositions inherent in such geographical metaphors.

Wherever they may "locate" Russia, Panarin and Erasov vehemently condemn ethnic nationalism, which they present as a pagan and telluric sentiment that jeopardizes Eurasian unity, for "the logic of ethnic sovereignty takes us back to premedieval times."[47] National sentiment is also seen as an expression of alien political values: The nation-state is a creation of revolutionary France; it is the symbol of industrial society and the republican system. Because the two authors make no distinction between the ethnic and the national, they provide no grounds for their condemnation of the French-style nation-state, simply associating it with the pejorative idea of ethnicity. Their criticism of ethnic feeling goes hand in hand with a rejection of Gumilëv's ethnicism and Dugin's geopolitics. For Panarin, those varieties of geopolitics run counter to the Eurasianist philosophy of history because they postulate that humanity is dependent on nature and genes; they are blindly deterministic and assert the existence of physical constants. According to him, the reality of Eurasia is based, not on any kind of ethnic complementarity, but on the shared past of its peoples, on their common statehood, and even more on a strictly political imperial will. In Erasov's words, "the Empire was more universal than its official religion or its culture. It is precisely the Russian Empire's degree of universalism that set it apart from the other empires of its time and made it heir to the first and second Rome."[48]

Thus Panarin's and Erasov's definition of the relationship between Russia, its state, and its territory does not involve any ethnic criteria. On the contrary, "a large state means, above all, self-restriction and the repudiation of ethnocentrism and xenophobia, of cultivating small-scale ethnic traditions on the state level."[49] The state is considered the sole bearer of the nation's essence: Eurasian unity is not rooted in the cultural unity of its peoples; it is based on the reality of the state that dominates the Eurasian space. Being a Russian nationalist therefore means resolutely supporting the state: "In historical reality, statehood as a civilizational matrix has been linked to despotism. That is our tragedy,"[50] for the fall of Soviet totalitarianism should not have entailed the collapse of Russian statehood. In order to dissociate the Soviet regime from the territory that was once the USSR, and thus to propose restoring the boundaries of the latter without recreating the former, Panarin seeks to eliminate the traditional connection between an imperial system and repression of ethnic diversity. He also maintains that the Romanov Empire should no longer be considered a relevant model for contemporary Russia.

Panarin attempts to define a distinctively Eurasian pluralism, one that is "civilizational" rather than political. He argues that Europe gives primacy to individual rights to the detriment of collective rights, whether regional, ethnic, or religious. Europe upholds pluralism for individuals, but has a unitarian and hegemonic approach to relations between nations. Eurasia is the exact opposite of the European model; the absence of Western-type political democracy is tantamount to the recognition of a right to autonomy for the empire's regions and nations, a cult of the diversity of ways of life: "The principle of cultural pluralism, as well as attention toward and tolerance for different ethnocultural experiences are combined with a monist political authority that tolerates no opposition."[51] According to Panarin, these two possible definitions of the concept of pluralism are embodied in two different political experiences: the republican, which provides individuals with a framework for sociopolitical democracy; and the imperial, which offers "civilizational" democracy. The former approach, he argues, is formalistic, narrow, and mechanical, whereas the latter is based on the prestigious model of the Roman Empire and offers a more authentic reading of the democratic principle.[52]

Thus Panarin has several reasons to consider an "empire" as legitimate. First, an empire is the only political system able to respond to the challenges of "postmodern" society, because it promotes awareness of civilizations in a world divided along regional and ethnic lines and provides an ideology of order as a bulwark against the chaos of the modern world. Second, an empire would be the political embodiment of the horizontal nature and spatial extension of Eurasia, thereby legitimizing it as a "natural" entity. Panarin believes that the predominance of territory over time makes Russia evolve cyclically; he calls this the "idiom of space."[53] Finally, an empire is a response to Eurasia's national and religious diversity, "as a political form of organization of the coexistence of a heterogeneous ethnic and confessional conglomerate, of peoples who do not have any other basis for a set of universal norms and a legal order."[54]

Thus Eurasian civilization dissolves all national and social differences in a great whole inspired by a fundamental imperial idea. This idea necessarily has a religious basis, for Panarin believes that only faith can transcend national differences and propose a structured and generally acceptable vision of the world: "Religion institutionalizes supraethnic cultural and moral universals and creates a type of spiritual community that, in certain respects, transcends the localism inherent in any specific political regime, ethnocentric tradition, or natural landscape."[55] In other words, the claim to the status of a civilization is grounded in religion, understood broadly as a set of moral values that legitimize the state, for "ideology sacralizes political acts."[56] Thus Panarin draws a subtle distinction that serves his political convictions, between what he considers an (irreligious and even pagan) totalitarian regime and an authoritarian regime whose ideology is openly based on (some) religion. He believes that post-Soviet Eurasia should move from the first model to the second. Because religion constitutes the essence of a civilization, Russia enters the new century with a unique asset: Its high spirituality ensures that Eurasia will be one of the great civilizations of "postmodernity," whose main feature will be a renewal of asceticism and repentance in the industrial world.

Russia's contemporary difficulties should therefore be seen as a victory rather than a failure, and *The Revenge of History* thus centers on the idea that asceticism will be the new value of the postindustrial world: Humanity will grasp the necessity of curbing its own consumerism for the sake of higher moral goals. Thus Panarin calls for a vindication of the Indo-Buddhist tradition of nonviolence and respect for animal life. He does not conceal his profound attachment to the institution of religion, which he considers to be one of the major elements in the rediscovery of historical identities in the post-Soviet space. Like the original Eurasianists, however, he treats religion as pertaining to nations rather than individuals; what matters is neither theological dogma nor the transcendental aspect of faith but a ritualized and "nationalized" religion, a secularized version of the sacred texts of the Eurasian religions.

Although Panarin calls for a clear distinction between the temporal and the spiritual spheres, his apparently secular state would not amount to a secularization of society; the practical management of the state would remain neutral, but its ideological foundations must be rooted in a secularized version of religion. As he states, "In Russia, state power depends to an extraordinary degree on spiritual power—power over minds. . . . In this sense, state power in Russia is never really secular."[57] Thus Panarin affirms that political power must be ideocratic, that is, based on an ideology that would be intrinsically linked to the "esotericism of supreme historical knowledge."[58] He proposes to turn the sacred texts into an ethic of civilization, which he calls the Great Tradition (*Velikaia Traditsiia*) and which must be put at the service of the state. This Great Tradition is presented as a form of Orthodox theocracy. However, he also has great esteem for Islam as a guarantor of social stability, capable of transcending national differences by virtue of its concept of *umma*. According to Panarin, Islamic dogma allows a harmony of lifestyle, religion, culture, and political views—a harmony that Russians would be well advised to borrow from their Muslim neighbors. Thus the Great Tradition of the future Eurasian state cannot be limited to Eastern Christianity; it must blend Orthodoxy and Islam and extract the essence of the two religions. A fusion between the Bible and the Koran will make the Eurasian idea one and indivisible. He proclaims: "We need a new, powerful world-saving idea that would ensure a consensus between Orthodox and Muslim culture for the benefit of a common higher goal."[59]

This desire to combine the religions of Eurasia recalls the postulates of the founding fathers of Eurasianism: The religious unity of the Eurasian space is a key element in the assertion of the continent's dual nature. Ever since the original Eurasianist movement in the 1920s, the idea of the existence of a third continent has, implicitly yet inextricably, implied the idea of an economic and social third way—neither East nor West, but also neither capitalism nor communism, neither parliamentary democracy nor totalitarianism. Neo-Eurasianism also toys with the idea of conservative revolution; despite his criticisms of the entire European political spectrum, Panarin recognizes his proximity to the neoconservatives, who are more prone to civilizational thinking than the liberal and Atlanticist right: "The Eurasianist project is postmodern, and in this it recalls the neoconservative wave in the West. It expresses itself in a kind of 'revenge of the provinces,' a rehabilitation of the values of rootedness. It does not distinguish between regional cultures in a hierarchic fashion (separating them into 'modern' and 'non-modern' ones) but perceives them from the point of view of an inalienable diversity that is valuable for its own sake."[60]

Panarin calls for a hybrid political regime that he claims would preserve the advantages of different types of regimes while getting rid of their disadvantages. This regime would have a market economy that would safeguard the social achievements of communism, a powerful state with a strong presidential political administration, a modernizing economic nationalism coupled with conservative values, an official ideology imbued with national salvation and mystical theism, "a sectoral economic bureaucracy, and nationally minded intellectuals"[61]—and it would enter a strategic union with China and India. Without being reactionary, Panarin's Eurasian state would have to be authoritarian and imperious, for it would embody a forceful civilizational idea: "In the sphere of domestic and foreign policy, it [the

Eurasianist scenario] means a significant reinforcement of authoritarian tendencies as well as a renewed distance from the West. However, authoritarianism necessarily looks artificial and backward unless it is based on 'strong ideas.' "[62] In his last articles, the philosopher also mentions his admiration for Stalin, whom he considers to have been one of the "fathers" of the Russian nation and its power (*derzhavnik-otets*), and he does not hide his rejection of Khrushchev's de-Stalinization, which he denounces as an unacknowledged Oedipal complex.[63]

As a corollary of his rapprochement with nationalists and communists, Panarin's view of the Jews became more radical at the turn of the 2000s. He claimed that the Jews were prone to destroying their host cultures, and that the current globalization was but a form of the "Judaization of the world."[64] Nevertheless, Panarin, like Dugin, remained receptive to the Jewish messianic tradition. In *Orthodox Civilization* (2002), he devoted many pages to a comparison between Russians and Jews, describing the former as nomads in time and the latter as nomads in space.[65] He believed that the two peoples are different from the rest of humanity, but also in competition with each other, for both are bearers of a messianic idea and claim to be a chosen people. According to Panarin, however, the messianism of the Jews became "normalized" when they accepted the West's lifestyle and way of thinking and established their own country.[66] Thus the Russian people are now the only bearer of hope for a different humanity: Russia cannot become a normal and pragmatic state guided by national egoism, because the Russians are inherently messianic.[67]

Panarin's religious conceptions also evolved at the end of the 1990s, when he started granting preeminence to Orthodoxy. The idea of a Great Tradition, shared by Orthodoxy and Islam, receded into the background as Eastern Christianity became the central topic of *Orthodox Civilization*. His objective in that book is to demonstrate that Russia's nature resides in what he defines as Orthodox civilization. This definition includes a more assertive view of the role of religion in Russian identity, but also the belief in a natural link between Orthodox Slavs: The traumatic experience of the NATO bombardment of Slobodan Milošević's Serbia played a part in Panarin's turn to Pan-Slavism, which in his case is actually an expression of pan-Orthodox feelings. According to him, what distinguished Orthodoxy from the two Western branches of Christianity was its relation to the cosmos and its constant search for the sacred and the universal. In support of this view, he cites the hesychastic tradition and the teachings of Gregory Palamas, who insisted on the mystical and initiatory character of the divine revelation as against the logical understanding of faith developed in the West since the Middle Ages.

Whereas Catholicism and Protestantism are sociocentric and technocentric, Orthodoxy, Panarin argues, is both cosmocentric and anthropocentric because it gives pride of place to the transcendental relationship between humanity and the divine.[68] However, Panarin does not seem to be satisfied with contemporary institutionalized Orthodoxy, and he calls for a sweeping reform of the Orthodox Church that should enable it to take up the two great challenges it faces. The domestic challenge consists in overcoming the internal schism that has existed since Peter the Great's reforms between Westernized elites and "Oriental" masses. The international challenge is to bring Christianity's idea of resurrection back to the fore, because, Panarin thinks, this is the key notion that will allow Russia to save humankind.[69] In Panarin's writings, however, this Russian messianism is always largely based on the idea that there is a Eurasian empire that links the Slavs with the "Oriental" world, and that Russia's fundamental nature is to be "median."

Highlighting Russia's "Internal East"

All the Eurasianists extol Russia's internal diversity and wish to see it cultivated as an incarnation of the divine totality. This diversity is not only due to Russia's intermediate geographic and cultural position but also to the fact that it has an "internal East inside the space of its state as well as that of its spirit."[70] Often, however, this Eurasianist cult of diversity is mere rhetoric, superseded by the feeling that only totality and structure really matter. Thus Russian culture is seen as the only one in Eurasia that has an imperial potential, because it is the only one that links the different national elements to the whole. Panarin's Eurasianism sees no contradiction in upholding a cult of diversity while also defining Eurasia as the space in which Russia expresses itself: "The Russian idea [*russkaia ideia*] is largely the same as the Rossian idea [*rossiiskaia ideia*], and its existential content is multiethnicity and the organic coexistence of different peoples, cultures, traditions, confessions, etc."[71] Neo-Eurasianism does nothing to clarify the confusion between ethnic Russianness, Russian statehood, and Eurasian identity, rendering its conception of the East even more ambiguous.

For Panarin, the Russian people remains the only historical driving force behind Eurasia. He thus takes up the founding fathers' hypothesis that the myth of Moscow as the Third Rome developed concurrently with Russia's eastward advance. However, Neo-Eurasianism offers a less developed historiography than the original Eurasianism. Although Panarin is more receptive to historical reasoning than Dugin, his views on history are less theoretically sophisticated than those of the interwar Eurasianists. For example, Panarin does not take up Vernadsky's and Savitsky's central idea that the "rhythms" of Russian history reveal a dialectic between forest and steppe and constitute the formal expression of the concordance between territory and national consciousness that are characteristic of each period. Neo-Eurasianism is also more traditional in holding on to a positive interpretation of the Romanov Empire.[72] However, Panarin stresses several components of Eurasia that had been given scant attention by the original Eurasianists: Buddhism, which he puts on a par with Islam as a Eurasian religion; Central Asia, a symbol of the voluntary accession of the Timurid space to Russia; the Cossacks, as the embodiment of a steppic Slavic identity; and Siberia, which enables the authorities to present their imperial conquests as "natural."

Panarin's variety of Eurasianist historiography rejects Kievan Rus'—which he considers to have been more European than Eurasian and therefore doomed to disappear—and concentrates on the Mongol period. He depicts the Tatar "yoke" as a boon that enabled Russia to become an empire and master the steppes; the true Russia, he argues, was born in the Muscovite period from a combination of Orthodoxy and Mongol statehood, a fusion of Russians and Tatars. As in all Eurasianist theories, the Turkic world is presented as Russia's main Oriental element. Russia, he writes, was the only Christian country to integrate large numbers of Muslims—and he approvingly points out the four centuries of coexistence of the two religions. He even claims that the Muslims made a fundamental contribution to the country's constitution and the revelation of its "civilizational idea," for it was precisely at the end of the sixteenth century, after the fall of the khanates of Kazan and Astrakhan, that Russia acquired an imperial structure.

Nevertheless, Panarin's view of the Turkic peoples remains ambiguous. He sees them as both internal and external to Russia, and he calls upon them to become aware of their identity and cultivate it, but only in the framework of an alliance with Russia. Indeed, he thinks that there are two possible Eurasianist projects: a northern one, driven by Moscow; and a southern one, directed from Ankara, which would entail partitioning the Russian Federation along the Urals: "The Eurasian continent breathes like a single organism, and preserves in its deep cultural memory the archetype of original unity. It is for this precise reason that the southern, pan-Turkic project more and more actively conflicts with the northern Eurasianist project, which is weakened by Russia's civilizational self-denial."[73] He is thus opposed to any kind of pan-Turkism; a non-Russian Eurasia would herald the death of Russia itself. Russia must therefore "win the contest of civilizational projects in Eurasia" against a potentially hostile Turkic/Turkish world.[74] This statement is indicative of the main ambiguity of Eurasianism: It takes a positive view of the Turko-Muslim world, but only as an element of Russian identity, not for its own sake. The same goes for Islam, which is presented both as a real ally and as a virtual competitor. Panarin warns Russia's Muslim elites that any inclination toward independence would signify their disappearance in an entity dominated by Turkey and the Arab countries: "Without the Muslims, Russia cannot resist the West; without Russia, our Muslim brothers cannot resist the East and the South."[75]

If Neo-Eurasianism's "internal East" corresponds to the Turko-Muslim world, its definition of the "external East" is more ambiguous. Panarin is the only Neo-Eurasianist who regularly refers to Buddhism, Confucianism, and Taoism. The East he dreams about is no longer the exotic East of classical Orientalism; it is a modern, postindustrial East. According to him, Russia must choose "not the exotic East of theocracies and Islamic fundamentalism, but the new, Pacific East, which has proven its ability to assimilate Enlightenment without lapsing into decadence."[76] The Asian experience remains important for all the Neo-Eurasianists; despite the economic crisis of 1997–98, the East Asian Tigers attract them with their combination of unbridled and thriving capitalism with an authoritarian political regime. This successful blend between technological modernity and what Panarin interprets as a rejection of cultural Westernization is the reason why he thinks Asia is currently the experimental scene of a new world.

Panarin attempts to show that Russia is particularly open to this Asian world. To make this point, he uses the metaphor of the trade routes crossing the Old Continent; Russia, he writes, controlled not only the Silk Road to the Muslim world and the "Route from the Varangians to the Greeks" toward the Mediterranean and Europe but also the Siberian roads taken by the Cossacks and, later, the Trans-Siberian Railroad and the Baikal-Amur Highway to the Asia-Pacific region. He thus adds the so-called Confucian-Buddhist axis to the original Eurasianists' Russian-Turkic one. Eurasia, he argues, should now emphasize the fusion between the Russian and Far Eastern worlds, rather than that between the Slavic and Turkic ones, and Orthodoxy's link with Buddhism or Confucianism, rather than Islam. The Muslim world had already aroused the suspicion of the first Eurasianists and

Gumilëv, and it is a cumbersome ally for the Neo-Eurasianists, or even an enemy on a par with Europe. Panarin explains that Russia must reorganize its alliances: "To the West's hegemonic ambitions and to Islamic expansionism in the South, Russia can respond by uniting with China and the Far Eastern tigers."[77]

Nevertheless, though the interwar Eurasianists were unequivocal in their rejection of Europe and its values, Panarin takes a more nuanced view, seeking partly to appropriate European universalism. He thus insists on Russia's role as an interface between Europe and Asia: Russia is not only an East for the West, but also a West for the East.[78] "On Russia's dual sociocultural strategy: a 'Eurasian face' for the West, and an 'Atlantic' one for its 'internal East,' . . . Russia can realize its strategic aims only with the help of a geopolitical paradox. . . . In its relations with the West, it must adhere to a European policy that constantly stresses its civilizational distinctiveness. . . . Russia is in an entirely different situation in its relations with the near abroad. Here Russia is the country that most often plays the part of a donor culture. Consequently, it profits from an 'Atlantic' policy that favors an open sociocultural space and 'de-ideologization.' "[79] Russia, therefore, has a civilizing mission in the East that legitimizes its own universalistic and imperial ambitions, while denying the West any right to such ambitions.

In *Global Political Prognostication* (2002), Panarin also mentions the importance of the Indo-European heritage for Russia, a country that to him represents Eastern Christianity against the Latin heresy, defends the South against the North, and modernizes the "non-West" (*ne-Zapad*), partly because the "Indo-European idea enables Russia to reconstruct its Europeanism, its Petrine heritage, so as to recover the original sense that the great founder endowed it with: to promote the construction of a great Russia as an avant-garde of Eurasia."[80] This rare reference to the Indo-European idea stems not from Dugin's German-inspired Aryanism but from the ideas of nineteenth-century Slavophilism about the Aryan myth as a means of reconciling Slavophiles and Westernizers, an attempt to embrace European universalism without dissolving in it.[81]

Thus Panarin is more subtle than many of his fellow Neo-Eurasianists: "I personally do not doubt that universalism, the logic of the creation of a world civilization, is the pivotal idea of world history. But this logic appears, not in a linear and progressive time, but in cyclical time."[82] and will result from the revival of a "civilizational" consciousness. This cult of diversity, whose political expression is a multipolar world opposed to American dominance, amounts to a "new sacralization of the world."[83] Russia would take the lead in this process because its experience of totalitarianism in conjunction with its messianic traditions allows it to go from "from progressive utopianism to eschatological realism."[84] Thus, far from taking a negative view of Russia's alleged incompleteness compared with the West, Panarin sees it as a guarantee of its glorious future: "Russia's territory is precisely the space where the global fortunes of the modern era are decided."[85]

Conclusions

Despite their ideological differences and personal rivalries, the Neo-Eurasianists share a certain set of philosophical presuppositions, which Panarin expressed in a particularly sophisticated way: an extreme expression of the fashion for cultural relativism; a belief in the existence of cultural constants capable of explaining the deep meaning of contemporary political events; the search for a Western-type scientific legitimacy; a rhetorical cult of national diversity, which, however, they prove unable to consider in any but Russocentric terms, refusing to grant real autonomy to minorities; the conviction that empire is natural and its disappearance is a short-term historical "error"; a dual view of Russia's relationship with the rest of the world (its border with the West being hermetic, and its border with Asia, porous); and an implicit but invariable view of the cultural differences between East and West as paralleling their political bipolarity.

In this respect, Panarin's focus on political philosophy marks him as an heir to the original 1920s Eurasianists. He draws on Johann Gottfried von Herder and the traditional metaphysical idea of a double reality, and he fully subscribes to Romantic *Naturphilosophie*, with its view of the totality as an organic political whole. Despite these Western sources, Panarin thus continues the tradition of Pan-Slavic conservatives such as Danilevsky, and he proposes a modernized version of Slavophilism. He is closer than Gumilëv's biological theories or Dugin's extreme-right geopolitics to the ideas of early Eurasianists such as Pëtr Savitsky and Prince Trubetzkoy, despite a rapprochement with Dugin toward the end of his life. Like the early Eurasianists, Panarin proves unable to square his desire to define Russia as an "Orthodox civilization" with his offer to incorporate the non-Russians, and particularly the Muslims of Russia, into this identity. But if Eurasia turns out to be strictly synonymous with Orthodox civilization, then Eurasianism is merely a means of expressing classical Russian nationalism, and the empire is no more than the manifestation of Russia's unwillingness to abandon its Eastern margins.

Panarin's theories also prompt questions about the "scientific" status of these essayistic writings in search of legitimacy. Is it possible to use the concept of "Eurasia" as an epistemological framework without thereby acknowledging that Eurasianism is a science rather than a political ideology? May different branches of knowledge be broken up geographically into civilizational areas, and, if so, how would one then justify the boundaries between the disciplines or measure the risks involved in studying every culture as a priori constituting a self-contained whole? Panarin's analysis of globalization seems inherently linked with the search for an alternative, thus obliterating the boundary between scholarly research and political views. The way in which Neo-Eurasianism is rooted in a Russian variety of alter-globalization theories illustrates the need felt by some Russian intellectuals to find a new global explanatory theory, but it also reveals their desire to provide scientific legitimacy for Russia's claim to distinctiveness. An analysis of these theories allows us to understand better the intellectual tradition, reaching back to the nineteenth century, which holds that Russia is a world unto itself in identity, science, and politics.

Chapter 4

Aleksandr Dugin: A Russian Version of the European Radical Right?

In studying contemporary Russian Eurasianism—both as a doctrine and as a political movement—one constantly comes across Aleksandr Dugin. One of the main reasons why he is relevant to any such study is the quasi-monopoly he exercises over a certain part of the current Russian ideological spectrum. He is simultaneously on the fringe and at the center of the Russian nationalist phenomenon. He provides theoretical inspiration to many currents and disseminates precepts that can be recycled at different levels. Above all, he is striving to cover every niche in the current ideological "marketplace." He proceeds from the assumption that Russian society and Russia's political establishment are in search of a new ideology and that he therefore owes it to himself to exercise his influence over all the ideological options and their possible formulations.

Beyond the doctrinal qualities that make him stand out among the spectrum of Russian nationalism, Dugin is noteworthy for his frenzied and prolific output of publications that began in the early 1990s. He has published over a dozen books, either original texts or thematically rearranged articles initially printed in various journals or newspapers. He has also edited several journals: *Elementy* (nine issues between 1992 and 1998), *Milyi Angel* (four issues between 1991 and 1999), *Evraziiskoe vtorzhenie* (published as an irregular supplement to the weekly *Zavtra*, with six special issues in 2000), and *Evraziiskoe obozrenie* (eleven issues from 2001 to 2004.[1] In 1997, he wrote and presented a weekly one-hour radio broadcast, *Finis Mundi*, which was prohibited after he commented favorably on the early-twentieth-century terrorist Boris Savinkov.[2] In 1998, he took part in the creation of the "New University," a small institution that provides Traditionalist and occultist teach-

107

ings to a select few, where he lectures alongside noted literary figures such as Yevgeny Golovin and Yuri Mamleev. Since 2005, he has been appearing on the new Orthodox television channel Spas created by Ivan Demidov, where he anchors a weekly broadcast on geopolitics called *Landmarks* (*Vekhi*).[3] He also regularly takes part in roundtable discussions on Russian television and occupies a major place in the Russian nationalist Web.[4] Several intellectual tendencies manifest themselves in his thought: a political theory inspired by Traditionalism,[5] Orthodox religious philosophy,[6] Aryanist and occultist theories,[7] and geopolitical and Eurasianist conceptions.[8] One might expect this ideological diversity to reflect a lengthy evolution in Dugin's intellectual life. Quite to the contrary, however, all these topics did not emerge in succession but have coexisted in his writings since the beginning of the 1990s. Though Eurasianism and geo-politics are his most classic and best-known "business cards" for public opinion and the political authorities, his philosophical, religious, and political doctrines are much more complex and deserve careful consideration. The diversity of his work is little known, and his ideas are therefore often characterized in a rash and incomplete way. We therefore ought to look for his intellectual lineage and try to understand his striving to combine diverse ideological sources. Dugin is one of the few thinkers to consider that the doctrinal stock of Russian nationalism has depreciated and must be revitalized with the help of Western input. He is thus "anchoring" Russian nationalism in more global theories and acting as a mediator of Western thought. It is this aspect of his work that mainly interests me here.

Dugin's Social Trajectory and Its Significance

It is particularly important to understand Dugin's complex place within Neo-Eurasianism, because, to a certain extent, his position is representative of certain more general phenomena and thus helps trace the evolution of Russian nationalist ideas over the past twenty years. Between 1985 and 1990, Dugin was clearly in favor of a "right-wing" Neo-Eurasianism and was close to conservative or even monarchist circles. In 1988, he joined Pamiat', but he did not feel intellectually at home there, because his ideas for a doctrinal renewal of the right were out of place in this fundamentally conservative organization. He therefore left Pamiat' the following year, condemning its nostalgic monarchism and vulgar anti-Semitism. In 1990–91, he founded several institutions of his own: the Arctogaia Association, a publishing house of the same name, and the Center for Meta-Strategic Studies. During this period, he drew closer to Gennady Ziuganov's Communist Party and became one of the most prolific contributors to the prominent patriotic newspaper *Den'* (later renamed *Zavtra*), which was at that time at the height of its influence. His articles published in this newspaper contributed to the dissemination of Eurasianist theories in Russian nationalist circles. At first he was supported by the nationalist thinker Aleksandr Prokhanov, who, just like Vadim Kozhinov, thought that only Eurasianism could unify the patriots, who were still divided into "Whites" and "Reds," but quickly turned away and condemned Eurasianism for being too Turkocentric.

From 1993 to 1994, Dugin moved away from the Communist spectrum and became the ideologist for the new National Bolshevik Party (NBP). Born of a convergence between the old Soviet counterculture and patriotic groups, the NBP successfully established its ideology among the young. Dugin's Arctogaia then served as a think tank for the political activities of the NBP's leader, Eduard Limonov.[9] The two men shared a desire to develop close ties with the countercultural sphere, in particular with nationalistically minded rock and punk musicians, such as Yegor Letov, Sergei Troitskii, Roman Neumoev, and Sergei Kurekhin.[10] In 1995, Dugin even ran in the Duma elections under the banner of the NBP in a suburban constituency near Saint Petersburg, but he received less than 1 percent of the votes.[11] However, this electoral failure did not harm him, because he was simultaneously busy writing numerous philosophical and esoteric works to develop what he considered to be the Neo-Eurasianist "orthodoxy." Limonov would thereafter describe Dugin as "the Cyril and Methodius of fascism, because he brought Faith and knowledge about it to our country from the West."[12] He left the NBP in 1998 following numerous disagreements with Limonov, seeking instead to enter more influential structures.

Dugin hoped to become a "counsel to the prince" and presented himself as a one-man think tank for the authorities. He appeared to exert a certain influence on Vladimir Zhirinovsky and Ziuganov as well as on Aleksandr Rutskoi of the Social Democratic Party. He has been especially keen on getting in touch with acting military officers; coming from a military family, he regularly asserts that only the army and the secret services have a real sense of patriotism. Thus, in 1992, the first issue of *Elementy* carried texts by three generals who were then heads of departments at the Academy of the General Staff.[13] His entry into parliamentary structures was largely made possible by the publication (in 1997) of the first version of his most influential work, *The Foundations of Geopolitics: Russia's Geopolitical*

Future,[14] which seems to have been written with the support of General Igor' Rodionov, who was minister of defense in 1996–97.[15] It is considered to be a major study of geopolitics, and it is often presented as the founding work of the contemporary Russian school of geopolitics. By 2000, the book had already been reissued four times, and it became a major political tract, enjoying a large readership in academic and political circles. Thanks to this book, Dugin has been invited to teach at the Academy of the General Staff as well as at the Institute for Strategic Research in Moscow. He has offered them a certain vision of international politics colored by an "isolationism that only serves to disguise a project of expansion and conquest."[16] Following this bestseller, Dugin considerably expanded his presence in the main Russian media; to some, he became a respectable personality of public life.

Thus, the years 1998 to 2000 saw the transformation of Dugin's political leanings into a specific current that employs multiple strategies of entryism, targeting both youth counterculture and parliamentary structures. He succeeded in establishing himself as an adviser to the Duma's spokesman, the Communist Gennady Seleznev, and, in 1999, he became chairman of the geopolitical section of the Duma's Advisory Council on National Security, dominated by Zhirinovsky's Liberal-Democratic Party (LDPR). He has stated that "the Center for Geopolitical Expertise, which works simultaneously with the Presidential Administration, the Government of the Russian Federation, the Council of the Federation and the State Duma, could become the Eurasian platform's analytical tool."[17] Dugin also regularly publishes in *Krasnaya Zvezda,* the army newspaper, and on Russian official Web sites.[18] The success of his book on geopolitics, now used as a textbook by numerous institutions of higher education, as well as his lectures at the Academy of the General Staff and at the so-called New University, satisfy his desire to reach the political and intellectual elites. As a result, he has moved away from opposition parties such as the Communist Party of the Russian Federation (CPRF) and the LDPR and closer to centrist groups, lending his support to the then–prime minister, Yevgeny Primakov. In 2000, he briefly participated in the Rossiia movement led by Seleznev and wrote its manifesto, before leaving due to disagreements with its leadership.

Vladimir Putin's election as president in March 2000 caused an even stronger shift in Dugin's political attitudes, as he began to move closer to the country's new strongman. On April 21, 2001, he resolved to put his cards on the table and created a movement named Evraziia, of which he was elected president. During its founding convention, Evraziia—often described as a brainchild of presidential counsel Gleb Pavlovsky—officially rallied to Putin and proposed to participate in the next elections as part of a governmental coalition. The movement's goal, according to Dugin's declarations, is to formulate the "national idea" that Russia needs: "Our aim is not to achieve power, nor to fight for power, but to fight for influence on it. Those are different things."[19] On May 30, 2002, Evraziia was transformed into a political party that Dugin defines as "radically centrist," an ambiguous formulation that springs from his Traditionalist attitude. Dugin accepts the combination of "patriotism and liberalism" that he says Putin is proposing, on the condition that the liberal element remains subservient to state interests and to the imperatives of national security. As he affirms, "our patriotism is not only emotional, it is also scientific, based on geopolitics and its methods,"[20] a classic claim of Neo-Eurasianists. According to its own data, the new party has fifty-nine regional branches and more than 10,000 members. Its creation was publicly welcomed by Aleksandr Voloshin, then the head of the presidential administration, and Aleksandr Kosopkin, chief of the administration's Internal Affairs Department.

Dugin also enlisted the support of another influential figure close to the president, Mikhail Leont'ev, the presenter of *Odnako* (broadcast by the first channel of Russian State Television), who joined the party's Central Committee. Strengthened by his success after these public displays of recognition, Dugin hoped to acquire influence within a promising new electoral formation, the Rodina bloc, and to use it as a platform for a candidacy in the parliamentary elections in December 2003. This alliance, however, was tactically short-lived, and questionable in its ideological import. Thus, Dugin never concealed his disdain for the monarchist nostalgia and the politicized orthodoxy embodied by Rodina leaders such as Dmitry Rogozin and Natalia Narochnitskaia. Indeed, it seems that Sergei Glaz'ev was the one who was responsible for the rapprochement with Dugin.[21] Although Glaz'ev cannot be considered a Neo-Eurasianist, he did participate in the founding convention of Evraziia in 2002. The two men share an interest in economic policies leaning toward socialism, and Dugin acknowledged his sympathy for Glaz'ev's economic ideas (which he calls "healthy") even after the latter left Rodina in March 2004.

Dugin and Glaz'ev met as early as February 2003 to form a party they defined as "left-patriotic." In July, Evraziia declared itself ready to support the creation of this electoral bloc. However, internal arguments over personalities ensued: the bloc needed to choose three leaders who would be sure to become deputies if it gained power and would benefit most from the campaign's publicity. Dugin hoped to be chosen but was hampered by his political marginality linked to his reputation as an extravagant theoretician whose ideas are too complex to inform an electoral strategy.[22] At the end of September, the disappointed Dugin left the Rodina bloc, explaining at a press conference that Rodina's nationalism was too radical for him—a statement that must draw a smile from those familiar with his work. This nationalist setting had not disturbed him until then. Nor did he move closer to Rodina when certain overly virulent nationalists such as V. I. Davidenko, the leader of the small Spas Party, were expelled from Rodina's list of candidates under pressure from the Kremlin.

Dugin's accusations against Rodina fall into two categories. He condemns the bloc for being too close to the CPRF and its oligarchy, and he criticizes its "irresponsible populism." He also takes to task those he calls "right-wing chauvinists": Sergei Baburin and the Spas movement.[23] By contrast, Dugin insists on the conciliatory and multinational mission of his Evraziia Party, which is "a political instrument that expresses not only the Russians' interests but also those of the small peoples of Russia and its traditional confessions and communities."[24] Dugin has also accused some Rodina members of racism and anti-Semitism, stressing the fact that the party includes former members of Russian National Unity as well as Andrei Savel'ev, who translated *Mein Kampf* into Russian.[25] The first set of criticisms is justified by Dugin's own convictions: He has never hidden his disdain for the present Communist Party, does not appreciate the emotional attitude of the Orthodox in matters of international politics, rejects all Tsarist nostalgia, has always denounced the racialism of Aleksandr Barkashov's theories, and condemns electoral populism. The second set of criticisms seems more opportunistic; a close reading of Dugin's works clearly reveals his fascination with the National Socialist experience and his ambiguous anti-Semitism. Today, he is attempting to play down these aspects of his thought in order to present himself as a "politically correct" thinker waiting to be recognized by the regime.

In return, instances of Dugin borrowing ideologically from Rodina seem rather rare. His Traditionalist, National Bolshevik, and esoteric ideas, which constitute an important part of his thinking, are not appreciated by Rodina and have not exercised any influence on the bloc's conceptions. Indeed, Rodina is more conservative than revolutionary, and it cannot take up Dugin's provocative suggestions, which often aim to break the social order. The strictly Neo-Eurasianist aspect of Dugin's ideas—his best-known "trademark" in Russian society today—is in tune with some of Rodina's geopolitical conceptions, but this concurrence is actually founded on the anti-Westernism that is common to both, not on a shared vision of Russia as a Eurasian power. For this reason, despite their attempted alliance, Rodina may not be said to have adopted elements of Neo-Eurasianist thought in the strict sense of the term. Nevertheless, these difficult relations did not stop Dugin from being delighted with the results of the December 2003 elections, which carried four nationalist parties (the presidential party United Russia, the CPRF, the LDPR, and Rodina) into the Duma. Dugin has connections with every one of them, and some members of each of these parties openly acknowledge having been inspired by his theories.

After this personal failure in Rodina, Dugin reoriented his strategies away from the electoral sphere and toward the expert community. Hence the transformation of his party into an "International Eurasianist Movement," formalized on November 20, 2003. The new movement includes members from some twenty countries, and its main support seems to come from Kazakhstan and Turkey. Whereas the original organization founded in 2001 comprised mainly figures from civil society,[26] the Supreme Council of the new Eurasianist Movement includes representatives of the government and parliament: Mikhail Margelov, head of the Committee for International Relations of the Federation Council (the Parliament's Upper House); Albert Chernyshev, Russia's ambassador to India; Viktor Kaliuzhny, vice minister of foreign affairs; Aleksey Zhafiarov, chief of the Department of Political Parties and Social Organizations in the Justice Ministry; and so on. The International Eurasianist Movement even officially asked Putin and Nursultan Nazarbaev to head the movement's Supreme Council.

Dugin congratulates himself on having moved beyond a mere political party to an international organization. He now cultivates his image in neighboring countries, heavily publicizing his trips to Turkey, but also to Kazakhstan and Belarus. He has become a zealous supporter of the Eurasian Economic Union and is pleased to think that he has influenced Aleksandr Lukashenko's and Nazarbaev's decisions in favor of a tighter integration of their countries with Russia. After having criticized the Kazakh president for many years,[27] in 2004 Dugin devoted an entire book to him, titled *The Eurasian Mission of Nursultan Nazarbaev,* expressing his joy that "for the first time in the history of Eurasianist thought, such a top politician exists," incarnating nothing less than "Eurasianism in action."[28] His Web site also presents the different Eurasianist groups in Western countries. Italy is particularly well represented, with numerous translations of Dugin's texts, several Eurasianist-inspired Web sites, and a journal, *Eurasia: Rivista di studi geopolitici.* France is represented by the "Paris-Berlin-Moscow" association, while Britain has long had a Eurasianist movement of its own. Austrian, Finnish, Serbian, and Bulgarian associations, and of course organizations in other post-Soviet republics, especially in Ukraine and Kazakhstan, are presented as "fraternal parties."

Having at first enthusiastically welcomed Putin as a "Eurasian man,"[29] since early 2005 Dugin appears to have become deeply disappointed by the president. According to him, Putin hesitates to adopt a definitively Eurasianist stance and has an entourage dominated by Atlanticist and overly liberal figures. In current affairs, Dugin is trying to play on the wave of anti-Westernism that swept part of the Russian political scene after the revolutions in Georgia in 2003, Ukraine in 2004, and Kyrgyzstan in 2005. He thus set up a Eurasianist Youth Union, led by Pavel Zarifullin, which became highly visible in September 2005 with the heavily publicized creation of an "anti-orange front" and the organization of the first "Russian Marsh" in November the same year. Dugin is thus pursuing, with relative success, his objective of building up a global cultural hegemony; he is trying to gain a foothold in alter-globalization movements and to participate in international ideological regroupings, for example, by participating in the alter-globalization Indymedia network.[30] This right, which Dugin modernizes and profoundly renews in his theories, seems therefore to succeed in its Gramscian strategy of entering left-wing structures that are badly informed and looking for allies—of any kind—in their struggle against American domination.

Thus Dugin's regular but always temporary presence in the political field cannot, it seems, be considered a new phase of his life that would build on an already completed body of doctrine. Although Dugin currently seems to be concentrating on his involvement in the Eurasianist movement and publications on the topic of Eurasianism, one should not forget that a similar combination had been in place from 1994 to 1998, when his membership in the NBP went hand in hand with publications on the concept of National Bolshevism. Dugin thus seems to adjust his strategy in accordance with the available opportunities to influence public opinion. Moreover, he continues even today to disseminate the Traditionalist ideas that have been his mainstay since the beginning, displaying a high degree of doctrinal consistency. What has evolved is his public status, marked by his desire no longer to be considered an original and marginal intellectual but rather to be recognized as a respectable political personality close to the ruling circles.

A Russian Version of Antiglobalism:
Dugin's Geopolitical Theories

All the Neo-Eurasianist currents that emerged in the 1990s share an imperial conception of Russia, but they are all based on different presuppositions.
Dugin occupies a particular position inside this group, and he is sometimes
criticized virulently by the other Neo-Eurasianists. Indeed, Dugin "distorts"
the idea of Eurasia by combining it with elements borrowed from other intellectual traditions, such as theories of conservative revolution, the German
geopolitics of the 1920s and 1930s, René Guénon's Traditionalism, and the
Western New Right. Nevertheless, Dugin has enjoyed the greatest public
success of all the Neo-Eurasianists, and he most directly influences certain
political circles looking for a new geopolitics for post-Soviet Russia. He
thus largely outweighs small intellectual groups that pursue their own Neo-
Eurasianist reflections without having any direct access to a larger public.
He can be considered today as the principal theoretician of Neo-Eurasianism, even though he shared this role with Aleksandr Panarin in the 1990s.

Dugin's attraction to the early Eurasianism developed by Russian émigrés in the 1920s and 1930s is not a belated addition to his doctrines. At the
end of the 1980s, while he was still close to certain monarchist groups, he
had already become the apostle of a Eurasianist conception of Russia and
had contributed to its spread among the patriotic circles linked to *Den'*. Today, he continues to be a dominant influence among those trying to rehabilitate the founding fathers of Eurasianism; he has edited compilations of
the principal texts of the movement's main theoreticians—Pëtr N. Savitsky,
Nikolay S. Trubetzkoy, Nikolay N. Alekseev, L. Karsavin, and the like—at
Agraf, and later at Arctogaia.[31] In his introductions to these compilations,
he systematically tries to link the interwar Eurasianist teachings as closely
as possible with his contemporary definition of Neo-Eurasianism. He does
not, however, appropriate the highly elaborate theories of the founding fathers concerning the historical, geographical, or religious legitimacy of the
Russian Empire. He is content with trying to establish a geopolitics for post-
Soviet Russia, helping the country to become aware of its particular eschatological sensibility.

Dugin even criticizes the founding fathers for having been overly philosophical and poetic and above all too "intuitive";[32] according to him, Eurasianism had the right intuitions (e.g., the idea of a "third continent" and the
importance of the Mongol period in the formation of Russian identity) but

was unsuccessful in formalizing them theoretically. "In Eurasianism we are confronted with a double indeterminacy: the indeterminacy characteristic of Russian thought itself, and an attempt to systematize this indetermination into a new indeterminate conception."[33] His attitude toward the other Neo-Eurasianists is even more negative; apart from Gumilev, many of whose ethnicist conceptions he shares, Dugin considers his ideological competitors worthless, and he affirms that their Neo-Eurasianist conceptions are "less coherent, being an adaptation to a changing political reality of the whole complex of ideas already mentioned."[34]

Dugin's Eurasianism involves a great interest in geopolitics, the main discipline on which he bases his theories. For him, geopolitics by definition serves the state in which it is elaborated. Thus, Russian geopolitics could only be Eurasianist, because it is responsible for restoring Russia's great-power status. It is also intended exclusively for the elites; according to Dugin, geopolitics is opposed to the democratic principle because the ability to know the meaning of things is unavoidably restricted to the leaders.[35] It is to this end that Dugin refers to the big names of the discipline, such as the Germans Friedrich Ratzel (1844–1904), Karl Haushofer (1869–1946), and Friedrich Naumann (1860–1919); the Swede Rudolf Kjellen (1864–1922); and the Briton Sir Halford Mackinder (1861–1947). Indeed, there is little that is Russian in Dugin's intellectual baggage. Apart from Konstantin Leont'ev,[36] whom Dugin sometimes mentions, he is far more inspired by Western authors than by Russians. For example, he speaks with admiration of the German organicists, such as Ernst Jünger (1895–1998), Oswald Spengler (1880–1936), Arthur Moeller van den Bruck (1876–1925), Ernst Niekisch (1889–1967), and Carl Schmitt (1888–1985). From Schmitt, he borrows his conception of the *nomos,* the general form of organization of the objective and subjective factors of a given territory, and the theory of Großraum, "large spaces."

Dugin attaches great value to this German heritage, and he wishes to be viewed as a continental geopolitician on a par with Schmitt and Haushofer; Russia's centrality and continental expanse, to him, are comparable to those of Germany in the 1920s and 1930s. He thus develops his own bipolar interpretation of the world, opposing the "Heartland," which tends toward authoritarian regimes, to the "World Island," the incarnation of the democratic and commercial system. He combines the classic Eurasianist theories with this bipolar division of the world into sea-based and land-based powers, or "thalassocracies" and "tellurocracies," and links them to various classic couples of concepts from "Russian thought" (Western Christianity / Orthodoxy,

West/East, democracy/ideocracy, individualism/collectivism, societies marked by change / societies marked by continuity). The opposition between capitalism and socialism is seen as just one particular historical clash destined to continue in other forms. "The two primordial concepts of geopolitics are land and sea. . . . They are outside Man, in all that is solid or liquid. They are also within him: body and blood. . . . As the two main terms of geopolitics, they are significant both for civilizations of the traditional kind and for wholly modern states, peoples and ideological blocs. . . . Any state, any empire draws its strength from a preferential development of one of these two categories."[37]

Dugin then divides the world into four civilizational zones: the American zone, the Afro-European zone, the Asian-Pacific zone, and the Eurasian zone. Russia must strive to establish various geopolitical alliances organized as concentric circles. In Europe, Russia must of course ally itself with Germany, to which Dugin pays particular attention. Presented as the heart of Europe, Germany should dominate all of Central Europe as well as Italy, in accordance with the theories of "centrality" developed by nineteenth-century Prussian militarism as well as the Nazi geopoliticians. In Asia, Russia should ally itself with Japan, appreciated for its pan-Asian ideology and the Berlin-Rome-Tokyo axis during World War II. Within the Muslim world, Dugin chooses Islamic Iran, admired for its moral rigor. He presents Iran as one of the few real forces of opposition against American globalization, and he invites it to unify the entire Arab world, as well as Pakistan and Afghanistan, under its leadership. Dugin characterizes this quadruple alliance of Russia-Germany-Japan-Iran, which would react against the thalassocracies (the United States, Britain in Europe, China in Asia, and Turkey in the Muslim world), as a "confederation of large spaces,"[38] because each ally is itself an empire that dominates the corresponding civilizational area. Unlike the Eurasianists of the 1920s, Dugin does not talk of an irreducible and romantic opposition between East and West; in his theories, both Asia and Europe are destined to come under Russian-Eurasian domination.

Because the maritime and democratic enemy allegedly has a "fifth column" in Russia, Dugin calls for a restoration of the Soviet Union and a reorganization of the Russian Federation and reminds his readers that "the battle for the integration of the post-Soviet space is a battle for Kiev."[39] He is the only Neo-Eurasianist to include in his political project not only the Baltic States but also the whole former socialist bloc.[40] His Eurasia must even expand beyond Soviet space, for he proposes incorporating Manchuria, Xinjiang, Tibet, and Mongolia, as well as the Orthodox world of the Balkans;

118
CHAPTER 4

Eurasia would only reach its limits with "geopolitical expansion right up to
the shores of the Indian Ocean,"[41] an idea that was taken up and popularized by Zhirinovsky. Dugin also proposes a general repartition of the Russian Federation, and especially of Siberia, which he considers to have been
on the verge of implosion for quite some time. He calls for the abolition of
the "national republics," to be replaced by purely administrative regions
subservient to Moscow. In *The Foundations of Geopolitics,* he acknowledges his hopes for the breakup of Yakutia, Tatarstan, Bashkortostan, and
Buryatia, condemned for their separatism and their capacity to form Buddhist or pan-Turkic anti-Russian axes with the neighboring regions. He
wishes to unify them with industrialized regions that have a Russian majority, such as the Urals or the Pacific shore (*Primorskii krai*).[42]

As in the Eurasianism of the 1920s and 1930s, the non-Russian peoples,
and particularly the Turko-Muslim minorities, are treated ambiguously.
They are appreciated as key elements confirming the distinctiveness of Russia's Eurasian identity but are also presented as potential competitors or
even enemies if they were to decide to no longer go along with a Russian-
dominated multinational Eurasia. The international events of the past few
years—especially the terrorist attacks of September 11, 2001, the second
war in Chechnya, and the ensuing terrorist acts that covered Russia with
blood—forced Dugin to fine-tune his conception of Islam and to be more
cautious in his positive appreciation of a certain type of Islamic radicalism.
At a symposium called "Islamic Threat or Threat against Islam?" organized
by Evraziia on June 28, 2001, the party officials disavowed fundamentalism, presented as a danger to traditional Islam, and asserted a wish to create
a Eurasian Committee for Russian-Muslim Strategic Partnership. According to Evraziia, traditional Islam, Sufism, Shi'ism, and Orthodox Christianity are spontaneously Eurasian, whereas Catholicism and Protestantism, but
also U.S.-sponsored radical Islamism, represent Atlanticism. Dugin thus
tries to distinguish between Shi'ite fundamentalism, which he considers
positive, and Sunni fundamentalism, which he disparages.

Dugin's wish to dissociate a "good" traditional Islam from the more radical branches of Islam, all of which he equates with Wahhabism, is shared
by numerous contemporary Russian nationalist movements, which aim to
woo official Russian Islam. This kind of talk permitted Dugin to recruit the
leaders of the Central Spiritual Board of Russian Muslims into his Evraziia
movement. Dugin tries to preclude any competition with Turkic Eurasianism on the question of the country's religious and national minorities. He
has managed brilliantly to present his movement not only as a tool for up-

holding Russian power but also as a pragmatic solution to Russia's internal tensions. Thus, from its creation in 2001, Evraziia includes representatives of sensitive regions such as Yakutia-Sakha, the North Caucasus, and Tatarstan, and he was pleased to bring together all of Russia's confessions; many muftis from the Central Spiritual Board of Muslims, including their leader, Talgat Tadzhuddin, but also Buddhists (Dordzhi-Lama, the coordinator of the Union of Kalmyk Buddhists) and members of the Radical Zionist Movement, adhered to the party and stated their desire to fight the rise of religious extremism using the integration strategy implicit in the Eurasian idea.

However, Dugin does not limit himself to bringing Eurasianism's geopolitical view of Russia up to date. He also seeks to anchor it in a global vision and to present it as a relevant mode of analysis that would help explain the entire evolution of the post-bipolar world. Once again, Dugin is playing the "guide," using the innumerable Western texts he is familiar with to adapt classic ideas from the history of Russian thought to contemporary debates. Thus, for several years, he has centered his argument about the Eurasian nature of Russia entirely on the topic of globalization. According to him, globalization presents as an obvious truth what is actually an ideology: representative democracy as the end of the history of human development, the primacy of the individual over any community, the impossibility of escaping the logic of the liberal economy, and so on.[43] Rejecting the current alternative between globalization and preserving the nation-state, Dugin calls for a creation of regional empires and, in this framework, presents Eurasia as a "collective imperial sovereignty" (*kollektivnyi imperskii suverenitet*).[44] He argues that only the Eurasianist solution of a multipolar world made up of several "regional empires offers a viable alternative with a strong theoretical potential that could face up to the current globalization processes instituted by the United States. Russia is the incarnation of the search for a historical alternative to Atlanticism. Therein lies her global mission."[45]

Like all Neo-Eurasianists, Dugin subscribes to Samuel Huntington's "clash of civilizations" theory, which is fashionable in Russia. Huntington's theory allows Dugin to affirm the necessity of maintaining the Russian imperial structure and to reject any prospect of a global equilibrium. According to him, the Russian people need to be prepared to defend "their national Truth not only against their foes but also against their allies."[46] Indeed, Dugin's geopolitical doctrine cannot function without creating enemies. He bases his ideology on conspiracy theories, presenting the new world order as a "spider web" in which globalized actors hide in order to better accomplish their mission. Dugin even dedicated a whole book (published in 1993 and republished in a revised version in 2005) to what he calls conspirology. The ideas expressed in it are contradictory. He harshly criticizes the presuppositions about the Jewish, freemason, Marxist, and other conspiracies held by numerous left- and right-wing political groups, but he also shares some of their ideas.[47] For example, he recounts a secret history of the Soviet Union in which a Eurasianist order opposes its Atlanticist counterpart. The putsch of August 1991 is described as the culmination of the occult war between these two orders. According to Dugin, however, the alternatives to globalization remain limited: either left-wing ideologies worked out in the West, or the stagnation typical of non-Western countries. Dugin also notes that these two alternatives are opposed to each other even though they share a common enemy. He therefore proposes that Russia elaborate a fertile combination, because "all antiglobalization tendencies are potentially 'Eurasianist.'"[48]

Dugin does not play the autarky card at any cost; he is convinced that the Eurasian model of resistance to American domination is exportable to the rest of the planet. He presents it as the most appropriate way of resisting the so-called New World Order. One of the aims of his thinking is therefore, as he describes it, "to transform Russian distinctiveness into a universal model of culture, into a vision of the world that is alternative to Atlanticist globalism but also global in its own way."[49] Thus Russia is called upon to participate in world affairs while constructing a certain Eurasian cultural autarky. Much more than, for example, Pëtr Savitsky and Prince Trubetzkoy, Dugin seems to have completely internalized the contradiction between, on the one hand, an exaltation of national distinctiveness and a passionate rejection of any borrowing that would risk "warping" Russia and, on the other hand, a desire for geopolitical and ideological expansionism and a new messianism. Far from being just a "successor" to the first Eurasianists, he is a theoretician who has multiple or even contradictory facets; many other doctrines have influenced his intellectual evolution at least as much as, if not more than, Eurasianism.

Traditionalism as the Foundation of Dugin's Thought

Traditionalism is a comparatively little studied strand of thought, although many twentieth-century thinkers were more or less discreetly inspired by it.[50] In the 1920s, René Guénon (1886–1951) formalized the main concepts of Traditionalism in five books.[51] He went through a Catholic phase, followed by a spiritualist stage (first in a theosophist lodge, then in the Martinist Order), during which he discovered the oriental religions and became disappointed with the West, which he thought incapable of restoring a mystical bond with faith. He left France for Cairo, where he joined an Egyptian order and tried to put his Traditionalist precepts into practice in Sufism. During the 1930s, his ideas were developed in Italy, Germany, and Romania, and Traditionalism became one of the main catchwords for fascist-minded spiritualist groups. The work of Guénon's main disciple, Julius Evola (1896–1974), an Italian painter close to the Dadaists, should be mentioned here. One of his books, *Revolt against the Modern World* (1934), had a deep influence on German and Italian neo-pagan movements. Traditionalism gained a new impetus in the 1960s, in particular in the Muslim world and, to a lesser extent, in Russia.

  Traditionalists believe in the Tradition, that is, in the existence of a world that was steady in its religious, philosophical, and social principles and started disappearing with the advent of modernity in the sixteenth century. Modernity is considered to be harmful in that it destroys the preestablished hierarchical order that is natural to the world: the hierarchical ordering of human beings is believed to be of transcendent origin and to have a mystical value. The Tradition is better preserved in non-Western civilizations, but through the colonial experience, the reassessment of the past begun in the West during Renaissance spread to other cultural spaces. Guénon gives this view—which, in its political aspects, is a typical example of counterrevolutionary thought (e.g., Joseph de Maistre, Louis de Bonald)—a religious coloring that makes Traditionalism stand out among conservative currents. For him, all religions and esoteric traditions—regardless of their concrete practice—reveal the existence of a now-extinct original sacred Tradition. Dubbed the "primordial Tradition," it is seen as the secret essence of all religions. Guénon then urges the modern world to regain an awareness of this unity in the face of the desacralization and secularization of the modern world. Through this appeal, he has influenced numerous Gnostic and Masonic currents, as well as several Sufi orders.

  Some Traditionalist texts seem to have been known in the USSR since the 1960s thanks to the poet Yevgeny Golovin and his discovery of Louis Pauwels's *The Morning of the Magicians*. From the end of the 1970s, Dugin participated in Golovin's circle of occultist intellectuals, which included, among others, the Muslim thinker Geydar Dzhemal', and had earlier been inspired by the writer Yuri Mamleev, who emigrated to the United States in 1974. The intellectual unity of this circle was based on a simultaneous

rejection of the Soviet experience, the West, and Slavophilism. These clan-
destine activities, as well as the possession of forbidden books, caused
Dugin to be expelled from the Moscow Aviation Institute where he had been
studying. Introduced to Traditionalism at a very young age, Dugin translated the 1933 version of Evola's *Pagan Imperialism* into Russian in 1981
and distributed it in samizdat. Choosing among the various currents of Traditionalism, Dugin did not content himself with the search for an individual inner spiritual way—such as that, for example, of A. K. Coomaraswamy
(1877–1947), which concentrates on the aesthetic aspect of Traditionalism.
Dugin is closer to Evola, who developed a politicized vision of Traditionalism, and he does not hesitate to affirm a sacrificial conception of politics:
"We need a NEW PARTY. A party of Death. A party of the total vertical. A
Party of God, a Russian equivalent to Hizbollah that would act according
to wholly different rules and pursue entirely different projects. For the System, death is indeed the end. For a normal person it is only a beginning."[52]

The influence of Traditionalism on Dugin seems to be fundamental; it
constitutes his main intellectual reference point and the basis of his political attitudes as well as his Eurasianism. He has made considerable efforts
to disseminate Traditionalist thought in Russia. He regularly translates extracts from the works of the great Traditionalist theoreticians, René Guénon
and Julius Evola, but also from so-called soft Traditionalist authors like
Mircea Eliade and Carl Jung, so-called hard Traditionalists like Titus Bur-
ckhardt, converts to Sufism like Frithjof Schuon, and converts to Islamism
like Claudio Mutti. The journals *Elementy,* and especially *Milyi angel,*
whose full subtitle is "Metaphysics, Angelology, Cosmic Cycles, Eschatology, and Tradition," are dedicated to the diffusion of Traditionalist thought.
They include articles on specifically Russian apocalyptic traditions, aiming
to facilitate the acceptance of Traditionalism in Russia by proving that elements of it were present in old popular conceptions (the mystical currents
of Orthodoxy, the myth about the submerged city of Kitezh, hesychasm,[53]
and the teachings of Gregory Palamas).

Dugin also lectured on Traditionalism at the New University in 2002, and
he published his lectures in *The Philosophy of Traditionalism* in the same
year. He believes that the contemporary period, being profoundly eschatological, allows him to disseminate the Traditionalist message much more
broadly than before and to reveal the radical and revolutionary character of
Guénon by teaching what Dugin calls Guénon's "eschatological humanism."[54] "Tradition, according to Rene Guénon's definition, is the totality of
divinely revealed non-human Knowledge, which determined the make-up
of all sacral civilizations—from the paradisiacal empires of the Golden Age,

which disappeared many millennia ago, to the Medieval Civilization which, in its various forms (Christian, Islamic, Buddhist, Confucian, etc.) largely reproduced the fundamental parameters of the Sacred Order."[55] According to Dugin, the mission of soteriological Traditionalism has three stages: The first, or individual stage, is to contribute to the development of the Tradition as such (i.e., of esotericism); the second, political and exoteric stage, is to reaffirm the superiority of the laws of the church (or, e.g., of the Shari'a); and the third, or social stage, is to assist in the restoration of a hierarchy of medieval orders.

Dugin is never, however, a simple ideological "reproducer." He hopes to "Russify" the doctrines that inspire him and to adapt them to what he calls the traditional concepts of the Russian world. Thus, he defines himself as a "post-Guénonist,"[56] seeking to deepen Guénon's basic ideas, which implies acknowledging certain points of disagreement with the founding father. His main criticism of the Western Traditionalists, and in particular of Guénon, concerns their vision of Orthodoxy. In *The Metaphysics of the Gospel* (1996), Dugin asserts that Guénon, who held that Christianity became exoteric after the great ecumenical councils, was actually targeting the two Western confessions, but not Orthodoxy, which has retained its initial character and esoteric foundations to this day.[57] He also affirms that metaphysics and ontology, which Traditionalism attempts to rehabilitate, have been particularly well preserved in Orthodoxy, which has never rejected an eschatological approach: "We are the Church of the End Times . . . the history of the terrestrial church is probably nearing its end."[58]

Concerning the divisions between neo-pagans and Christians that shook the Western Traditionalist movement, Dugin remains in an ambiguous position that is revelatory of his own hesitations on this matter. He appreciates the rehabilitation of paganism as Tradition proposed by Evola. Like him, he believes that Christianity has remained the most pagan monotheism (through the figure of the Trinity), and he admires the importance of entropy and eschatology in the pagan religions. He remains, however, deeply anchored in Christianity and, like Guénon, sees it (but only in its Eastern variety) as the repository of Tradition. Dugin affirms that the "developmental stages of metaphysical constructions [evolve] from orthodox Traditionalism in the Guénonian sense to a definitive assertion of Trinitarian Orthodox metaphysics in which all the most valuable insights have found their complete and accomplished expression."[59]

However, Dugin is attracted to neo-pagan conceptions, which exalt the body and harmony with nature, although he remains embedded in Orthodoxy as the founding institution of Russian distinctiveness. His position on this question is therefore revolutionary in its break with Christianity, and fundamentally conservative in its respect for the religious institution and its hierarchy. Dugin links an esoteric account of the world to Orthodoxy, which he sees as having preserved an initiatic character, a ritualism where each gesture has a symbolic meaning. He thus calls for the restoration of an Orthodox vision of the world, for a "clericalization [otserkovlenie] of everything."[60] This opposition, however, which had divided the German National Socialists and later the New Right, may seem less relevant for Russia: Orthodoxy, unlike Catholicism or Protestantism, is more easily instrumentalized as a specifically national rather than universal faith. This is indeed how Dugin interprets it: he regularly participates in the various nationalist movements launched by official Russian Orthodoxy.[61] His adherence, since 1999, to the Old Believers allows him to uphold a strictly national faith without having to make the difficult choice of converting to paganism and rejecting official Orthodoxy.[62]

Dugin tries to present the Russian schism of the seventeenth century as the archetype of Traditionalist thought, born of the rejection of the secularization of Orthodoxy, which he dates at around the same time as that given by Guénon for the end of Tradition in the West (after the end of the Thirty Years' War in 1648). Thus, "Eurasianism will only be entirely logical if it is based on a return to the Old Belief."[63] According to Dugin, the schismatic church is simultaneously conservative and revolutionary, espousing a cult of the earth (like paganism), free of an institutionalized conception of faith, and driven by a fundamentally apocalyptic vision of the fate of humanity. This view is ideologically convenient because it enables Dugin to avoid making a choice between a national paganism and a universal faith. Thus, Orthodoxy, and in particular the Old Believers, can incorporate neo-paganism's nationalist force, which anchors it in the Russian soil and separates it from the two other major Christian confessions.

Dugin fully agrees with the Traditionalist criticism of spiritualism. Guénon already considered spiritualism to be a "counter-initiation," a reconstruction of pseudo-traditions actually born of modernity, which must be condemned for wanting to usurp the real Tradition. For Dugin too, theosophism, cosmism, and the New Age religions are a spiritualist version of postindustrial modernity and a veiled cult of technology.[64] He condemns their populism and lack of coherent spiritual conceptions, whereas he sees Traditionalism as intended for a restricted elite, which alone is able to understand its requirements.[65] Dugin views religion as being at the foundation of societies as well as modes of analyzing societies. This implies a reinterpretation of modern Western intellectual life, and especially of its scientific attitudes. Following the Traditionalist precept that rationality is a mental construct and progress is a notion that bears no relation to reality, Dugin argues that the positivist foundation of contemporary science must be questioned in its very principle.[66] Since the Renaissance, the separation between sacred and profane, like that between art and science, has opened the way to a distorted vision of the human ability to understand the universe.

Dugin therefore calls for a rehabilitation of esoteric knowledge as part of scientific research, and he appreciates Romantic *Naturphilosophie* because of its intention to recreate a holistic knowledge of the world. Likewise, he believes in the imminent end of positivist science and in the rebirth of synthetic sciences that would be full of meaning and reveal humanity's place in the world. Dugin formulates this idea by trying to theorize so-called sacred sciences (*sakral'nye nauki*). According to him, their sacredness expresses itself not in a specific methodology but rather in the functions and goals attributed to the discipline. Like the modern sciences, thus, these sacred sciences have a specific object of research, but they do not lose their ties with ontological and gnoseological knowledge.[67] One of the fields capable of fusing objective data and philosophical background is geopolitics. Dugin systematically presents it not as a simple scientific discipline but as a Weltanschauung, a metascience that encompasses all the other sciences, thereby endowing them with meaning. According to him, "Geopolitics is a vision of the world. It is therefore better to compare it not to sciences, but to systems of sciences. It is situated on the same level as Marxism, liberalism, and so on—that is, systems of interpretation of society and history."[68]

Dugin does not limit himself to a spiritual or intellectual understanding of Traditionalism. He asserts that it is in itself "an ideology or meta-ideology that is in many ways totalitarian and requires that those who adopt it accept its stringent requirements."[69] Among these requirements, political commitment seems fundamental to Dugin. According to him, Traditionalism is the metaphysical root of numerous political ideologies, in particular those known as the theories of the third way. He thus outlines three types of doctrines that are simultaneously philosophical, religious, and political, and that govern the entire history of the world. The first, which he calls the polar-paradisiacal one, expressed itself on the religious level as esotericism or Gnosticism; on the historical level as the medieval civilization of the Ghibellines, and then as German National Socialism; and on the political level as eschatological totalitarianism. The second ideology, called the creation-creator one, is religiously exoteric; its historical incarnation is Catholicism or classical Sunnism. On the political level, it blends theocracy, clericalism, and conservatism. The third ideology, defined as mystical materialism, is a form of absolutist pantheism embodied in the militant atheism of the liberal West.[70] Dugin thus formalizes two "rights," a revolutionary and a conservative one (the third ideology represents the "left"), and he displays a distinct preference for these former visions of the world.

Dugin also proposes another Traditionalist terminology with which to define the political spectrum, which he sees as always being divided into three groups. The right stands for "History as Decadence, the necessity of instantaneous restoration, the primacy of eschatology." The center stands for "History as Constancy, the necessity to preserve the balance between the spiritual and the material." The left stands for "History as Progress, the necessity to contribute to its advancement and acceleration in every way possible."[71] In this second account, conservatism seems to be classified as being in the center, thereby reserving the right exclusively for the revolutionary movement, of which Dugin considers himself a representative. This reveals the ambiguous political place he attributes to Traditionalism:

> From the point of view of Integral Traditionalism, the only adequate position for implementing the principles of the Sacred Tradition to contemporary political reality is, under normal conditions, the position that is often called "extreme right." . . . But social history advances in a direction which is strictly opposed to this ideal—from theocracy to secularism, from monarchism to egalitarianism, and from spiritual and empire-building discipline to an apology of comfort and individual well-being. . . . This is why the extreme right on a political level is too far on the left for the genuine Traditionalist. . . . Some Traditionalists may pass from an extreme-right position to an extreme-left, revolutionary, and even socialist or communist wing, while remaining fully consistent and logical in their actions.[72]

This idea of the interchangeability of left and right is reminiscent of certain ideas of the Western New Right.

The Russian Proponent of the New Right?

Dugin has often been compared to Alain de Benoist (born 1943), the principal theoretician of the French movement called "New Right." This school of thought emerged in the second half of the 1970s, going back to the Groupe d'Études et de Recherche sur la Civilisation Européenne (GRECE) and the magazine *Nouvelle École*.[73] The two men met during Dugin's stay in Paris at the end of the 1980s, and they remained close collaborators for a few years. In 1992, for example, the patriotic newspaper *Den'* published the transcript of a roundtable discussion with Dugin, Aleksandr Prokhanov, Sergei Baburin, and de Benoist.[74] When Dugin launched his own journal the same year, he called it *Elementy* and presented it as the Russian version of *Éléments,* the magazine of the European New Right. This publication made the split between Dugin and the more classical nationalists of *Den'* (the future *Zavtra*) official but did not prevent disagreements with de Benoist. Thus, in 1993, de Benoist strove to clear himself of associations with Dugin after a virulent French and German press campaign against the "red-and-brown threat" in Russia. In an interview, he acknowledged that he had become aware of a number of ideological divergences with Dugin, concerning politics—for example, on the concept of Eurasia and Russian imperialistic tendencies[75]—but also theory. Indeed, de Benoist makes only partial use of Traditionalism, whereas Dugin draws on the whole body of that doctrine. Conversely, de Benoist is strongly attracted to Heidegger's philosophy, whereas Dugin does not find it congenial.

Nevertheless, the careers of both men have many features in common. For example, it is impossible to classify either using predefined ideological patterns or to pin down their political sympathies precisely in the classical right-left spectrum. Both reject populism and, in spite of a few fruitless attempts, neither of them has been able to find a political party capable of reflecting their complex thought. Since the early 1990s, de Benoist has never hidden his contempt for Jean-Marie Le Pen's National Front,[76] while Dugin condemns the famous figures of Russian nationalism, such as Eduard Limonov, Gennady Ziuganov, or Vladimir Zhirinovsky, despite having more or less directly inspired them. Like the French thinker, he subjects the entire right-wing spectrum in his country to fierce criticism, denies the relevance of the distinction between right and left, and cannot accept the electoral populism of those groups, in particular their most xenophobic statements. In the diversity of his sources of inspiration and in his striving to find an alternative way of thinking, Dugin seems as alienated from traditional Russian nationalism as de Benoist is from the classic French nationalism of Charles Maurras or Maurice Barrès.

Both Dugin and de Benoist have therefore regularly had to explain their stance, and they have been considered as "traitors" by other factions of the

128

radical right. Dugin, for example, provided a lengthy explanation of his dismissal of ethnonationalism. According to him, the Russian nationalist milieu is divided into two groups. On the one hand are the Pan-Slavists and monarchists, who have an ethnocentric and politically outdated vision of Russia; on the other hand are the Eurasianists, Communists, and pro-statists, who give priority to great state power over ethnic feeling and who are above all focused on the future.[77] Indeed, like de Benoist, Dugin attempts to "dissociate the question of identity affirmation from the question of nationalism";[78] he extols nonxenophobic nationalism, criticizes Pan-Slavist sentimentalism such as it manifested itself in Russia during the Balkan wars of the 1990s, and rejects the popular anti-Caucasian phobia instrumentalized by politicians such as Ziuganov, or, even more strongly, Zhirinovsky.

Dugin thus calls for a rational, dispassionate nationalism, one that would acknowledge its borrowings from alternative projects such as religious fundamentalism, third-worldism, or left-wing environmentalism. Since the 1980s, Dugin and de Benoist have been the main proponents, in their respective countries, of a doctrinal revitalization of right-wing thought. Both also presuppose that the conquest of political power requires first gaining cultural power. For more than a decade, de Benoist's aim has been to disseminate his doctrines in French intellectual circles, in particular through the journal *Krisis,* which offers a space for critical discussion between the foremost right-wing and left-wing thinkers. This preference for culture also explains Dugin's choice of public strategy over the past few years.

In spite of their break, Dugin continues to make regular references to de Benoist, and shares his hope for a continental destiny for Europe, built along overtly anti-Atlanticist lines. He borrows many conceptions from the Jeune Europe movement, as well as from the Belgian Jean Thiriart (1922–92), who had striven for a Euro-Soviet empire to be brought about by a movement he called "national communitarianism." What is common to all these trends is a striving for what they call organic democracy, which would place the state at the service of the national community. This kind of democracy would express itself in political unanimity as well as in a return to a "natural hierarchy" of social castes, and in a (professional, regional, or confessional) corporatism that would leave no room for the individual outside the collectivity. Thus, Dugin distinguishes himself from other figures in the Russian nationalist movements precisely through his militant Europeanism, his exaltation of the Western Middle Ages, and his admiration for Germany. All these ideological features contrast strongly with the ethnocentrism of his competitors and a Soviet tradition of equating Germany with "fascism."

This is why Dugin has often been criticized, in particular by the Communists, for whom the Russian "antifascist" tradition rules out the recognition of any German, and more generally Western, cultural influence on Russian nationalism.

Even more than de Benoist, Dugin has an ambiguous position on the racial question. GRECE has largely abandoned the theme of "biological realism," which was very present in Jeune Europe and other radical nationalist factions, and has preferred to insist on a cultural and nonracial differentialism. De Benoist was the main driving force behind this evolution, and, since the end of the 1960s, he has condemned all racial ideas, which he presents as an application of the Judeo-Christian presuppositions he criticizes. Nevertheless, racial arguments remain important in other Western radical right-wing circles. On this point, Dugin does not go as far as de Benoist: He remains more influenced by racialist currents as well as by those Traditionalists who, like Evola and unlike Guénon, were also sensitive to racial topics. Thus, Dugin condemns racialism in its Nazi version for having led to the Holocaust but also for having crystallized around a German-centered vision of the world instead of a European one. Dugin supports Evola's criticism of the racial and anti-Semitic determinism of Third Reich Germany but shares his vision of race as the "soul" of peoples.[79]

He systematically constructs an opposition between race and geopolitics, between nationalism and loyalty to the state, and systematically takes a stand in favor of the latter. Nevertheless, he regularly uses the term "race" to clarify what he calls "civilizational" differences. For instance, Eurasia to him is a racial synthesis between "whites" (the Indo-European Slavs) and "yellows" (the Finno-Turkic peoples); according to the Evolian principle of "spiritual racism," each of these "races" is endowed with innate qualities revelatory of certain philosophical principles,[80] which Dugin, borrowing from the Slavophile A. S. Khomiakov[81] (1804–60), calls the Frisian and the Finnish principles. The former, the principles of the "whites," are associated with internal freedom and esotericism; the latter, those of the "yellows," correspond to tyranny and exotericism. The hybrid nature of Eurasia, which is simultaneously white and yellow, gives it a global role to play because "the Turkic peoples of Siberia have often perceived the Russians as 'continuing' or 'resuming' the mission of Genghis Khan himself. . . . Aristocratic marriages did not only serve to establish family or ethnic ties between the Russians and the Turkic peoples, but secretly presupposed a transfer of the sacral geographic doctrine of the Turks to the Slavic elite, which in its turn had preserved the memory of its Nordic origins."[82]

Dugin's texts abound in references to Aryanism and neo-paganism, a classic corollary of the racial ideology and of the idea of the original superiority of the whites. Here again, his inspiration comes from the New Right, which since the 1950s has tried to transcend traditional nationalism by refocusing on the European idea, and from the doctrines of Europe-Action. These proponents of the idea of an ethnic and cultural unity of European peoples no longer wish to express their identity in an insular or chauvinistic manner, remembering the obstacles that divided the European nationalists during World War II. Thus Dugin accepts the theory of a "defense of the West," if this term is understood in its ancient racial and Aryan sense, not in terms of contemporary Western culture. In his works, he regularly refers to Guido von List (1848–1919) and Jörg Lanz von Liebenfels (1874–1954), the famous theorists of Germanic Aryanism, and presents himself as one of the founders of Ariosophy, or the science of Aryan wisdom.

There are even more frequent references to Hermann Wirth (1885–1981), one of Dugin's favorite authors, and to his occultist theories on the Arctic homeland of the original Aryan peoples. "Thousands of years ago, our land welcomed the descendants of the Arctic [meaning a hypothetical Atlantis-like Arctic continent], the founders of the Hindu and Iranian civilizations. We (especially as Orthodox believers) are direct heirs of the Arctic, of its ancient tradition."[83] Guénon allegedly affirmed that the Hyperborean civilization was not in Scandinavia but more to the east, a theory that Dugin has discussed at length, in particular in *The Mysteries of Eurasia* (1991). In this book, he presents Siberia and its enormous Nordic continental mass as the original cradle of the Aryans, as well as the magical center of the world, following the idea that "the continents have a symbolic significance."[84] In *The Hyperborean Theory* (1993) and *The Philosophy of Traditionalism* (2002), he also professes his belief in runic writing, a kind of Aryan Grail written in a universal proto-language, supposedly discovered and published by Wirth in 1933 under the name of *Chronicle of Ura-Linda*.[85]

Dugin's occultist leanings are also apparent in his striving to create a metaphysics of the cardinal points, which he perceives as absolutes that are sources of identity. The North and the East are at the heart of his esoteric concerns. The North confirms Russia's Nordic identity, a fundamental element of the discourse of racial identity inspired by Nazism. The East is the expression of Russia-Eurasia's inner Oriental nature. "The *Drang nach Osten und Norden* constitutes the natural geopolitical process of Russian history."[86] Russia's global role then appears distinctly, because only Russia combines the symbolic distinctions of being racially Northern, Eastern by its cultural and religious choices, and economically Southern, an ally of a developing world resisting Westernization. In a blend of the Nazi and Eurasianist traditions, Dugin sees Siberia as destined to play a major role in the new Russian identity. He thus elaborates a cosmogony of the world in order to make Siberia, the last "empire of paradise"[87] after Thule, the instrument of his geopolitical desire for a domination of the world, justified by Russia's "cosmic destiny."[88]

Dugin advances various occultist lines of reasoning in favor of this Hyperborean theory, drawing on the mystique of the alphabets, sounds, numbers, and geometric symbols; references to the kabbalah; alchemy, Hermeticism, Gnosticism, and the law of astrological correspondences; parallels with Iranian and Indian culture; and so on. Dugin defines this set of theories as sacred geography (*sakral'naia geografiia*), that is to say, the science of the secrets of world history, of the enigmas of ancient civilizations and continents, and of the origin of races, religions, and old mythologies.[89] All these elements of occultist culture are not specific to the New Right; they have their roots in the esoteric ideas of the founding fathers of Traditionalism, and they were explored by mystical currents of the 1920s and 1930s that were close to fascism.

Fascism, Conservative Revolution, and National Bolshevism

The connections between Dugin's ideas and fascism have been a subject of much debate.[90] However, the terms of the debate stand in need of definition. Fascism is a historically circumscribed phenomenon that was politically and intellectually liquidated with the end of World War II, though it left some traces with small Neo-Fascist groups that reappeared, above all in Europe and in Latin America, in the second half of the twentieth century. Fascism can also be chronologically and ideologically divided into fascist movements and fascist regimes (in Italy and Germany). Only the first interest us here. To classify a body of thought as "fascist" does not, then, mean to predict that it will take power and endanger human lives, nor to categorize it in a discriminatory manner that would deny it the right to be analyzed. This terminology merely points to an adherence to a specific intellectual tradition. Intellectual fascism shares with the other currents of the "extreme right" a Romantic heroism (a cult of the leader, the army, and physical effort, and the indoctrination of the young) but distinguishes itself from them by its revolutionary and prosocialist aspects, as well as by its attraction to futurism and esotericism. Dugin's ideas share many features of this original fascism, as he is expecting a cultural revolution aiming to create a "New Man." It cannot, however, be equated with fascism if that is understood to designate the contemporary racist extreme right—a designation that is, moreover, historically and conceptually incorrect.

On economics, Dugin unapologetically stands "on the left," even if this Western European classification is not necessarily applicable to the Russian political spectrum. Dugin repeatedly asserts that he has borrowed from certain socialist theories, in particular those on economics, because he is in favor of giving the state a crucial role in production structures. Economics was not at all addressed in his first works, but it seems to have taken on an increasing importance since 2001. Dugin even hopes to establish the "theoretical sources of a new socialism,"[91] based largely on a paternalistic version of Keynesian economics. He has also appropriated some Marxian ideas; for him, the opposition between labor and capital, Continentalism and Atlanticism, and East and West, are parallel.[92] These left-wing conceptions played a role in Dugin's rapprochement with the socialist-leaning economist Sergei Glaz'ev and their brief alliance in 2003 within the Rodina bloc, which presented itself as a left-wing alternative to the Communist Party.

Dugin never plays the communist card. He has only negative things to say about Marxism-Leninism such as it existed in the USSR, and has, for several years, been a condescending critic of the Communist Party. He appreciates Ziuganov's borrowings from his geopolitical theories but condemns his electoral exploitation of Soviet nostalgia and most of all regrets his ideological inconsistency. According to Dugin, the CPRF no longer has a claim to the heritage of the Communist Party of the Soviet Union and cannot even present itself as a left-wing party, because it advances a series of arguments that Dugin classifies as right wing, such as social conservatism, racism, anti-Semitism, monarchism, calls for tax cuts, and the like. Dugin therefore believes that the Communist Party can be defined as an unacknowledged Eurasianist movement, whose function is to express social discontent but not to take power.[93]

This combination of economic socialism and conservatism regarding values is typical of currents espousing the so-called third way. Dugin acknowledges his fundamental attraction to revolutionary ideas; he has never been a partisan of any return to the past, which explains his gradual break with so many other nationalist figures. He does not play the card of Tsarist or Soviet nostalgia and sees himself as resolutely turned toward the future. For example, he is a militant proponent of the introduction of modern technologies in Russia, cultivating a strong presence of his own on the Internet and calling for a "modernization without Westernization"; Eurasianism must be "a combination of openness and dynamism with tradition and conservatism."[94] He is thus fully in accordance with the doctrines of so-called National Bolshevism, whose theoreticians he admires, whether they are Russian exiles, members of the Soviet party apparatus, German Communists, or left-wing Nazis. During his dissident years, Dugin seems to have opposed this strand of thought, which he did not identify as "Traditionalist."[95] But in the 1990s, he changed his mind and attempted a synthesis between his Guénonian philosophical conceptions and the political ideas of the National Bolsheviks. Like many dissidents, Dugin only took a positive view of the Soviet experience after two events: a trip to the West in 1989, and the disappearance of the Soviet regime in 1991.

Dugin then developed the distinction proposed by Mikhail Agursky—between "National Bolshevism," a messianic ideology that has a national basis but a universal vocation, and "national communism," the Soviet newspeak term that designated the separatism of the Russian Empire's ethnic margins.[96] Basing himself on Karl Popper,[97] Dugin defines National Bolshevism as a "meta-ideology common to all enemies of the open society."[98] Indeed, what is most important for him is that right-wing and left-wing totalitarian ideologies are united in their refusal to accord a central role to the individual and to place it above the collectivity, be it social or national. The phenomenon of National Bolshevism, then, is not a specific moment of history but a philosophical conception of the world that has lost none of its relevance, bracketing together all nonconformist thinkers seeking an alternative to liberalism and communism.

Dugin's view of National Bolshevism rests largely on mystical foundations, which once more reminds one of the original Fascists. He stresses the parallels between esotericism and political commitment, be it Fascist, Nazi, or Bolshevik; National Bolshevism is thus to him merely a politicized version of Traditionalism, the modernized expression of the messianic hopes that have existed in Russia since the fall of Constantinople in 1453. According to Dugin, it heralds "the Last Revolution—the work of an acephalous, headless bearer of cross, hammer, and sickle, crowned by the eternal swastika of the sun."[99] Thus, for him, the most complete incarnation of the third way was German National Socialism, much more so than Mussolini's Italy or the interwar Russian exiles. He then points out parallels between "Third

Rome, the Third Reich, the Third International,"[100] and he attempts to prove their common eschatological basis. For Dugin, the original triad of Father, Son, and Holy Spirit reveal to the initiated that the Third Reich, just like Third Rome, will be the kingdom of the Holy Spirit. Thus, examining the fear that the term "fascism" still causes today, even though the phenomenon no longer exists as such, Dugin explains: "By 'fascism' we do not mean a concrete political phenomenon, but our deep-seated secret fear that brings together the nationalist, the liberal, the communist, and the democrat. This fear does not have a political or ideological nature; it expresses a more general, more deep-seated feeling which is common to all people irrespectively of their political orientation. This is 'magical fascism.' "[101]

Dugin therefore advances a positive reading of fascism and does not denounce Nazism, even though he condemns its racism. He is content with regretting that Adolf Hitler attacked the USSR and made mistakes in his application of the theories of conservative revolution, which were better preserved by left-wing Nazis who called for an alliance between Germany and the Soviet Union. He especially appreciates the Waffen-SS[102] and, even more, the cultural organization Ahnenerbe. In his publications of the 1990s, particularly in periodicals and on his Web sites, his ideological arsenal borrows from another typical component of the original fascism: the ideologization of sex. According to him, men and women respond to different philosophical principles (active and passive), and men's superiority is proven etymologically because, in numerous languages, a single term designates both male persons and human beings in general.[103] Thus, the liberalization of sex, pornography, feminism, homosexuality, and the fashion for Freudianism and psychoanalysis are part of the process of the forced Westernization of the world. This "era of gynecocracy"[104] heralds the "castration" of men and, along with it, the disappearance of traditional society. Dugin calls for a revindication of eroticism in a phallocentric and patriarchal way, and he hopes to develop a "patriotic conscience" of the sexual act because "the empire-building urge is the highest form of planetary eroticism, of macrocosmic sexuality."[105]

Like the original fascists, Dugin admires the Romantic taste for death and combat; shares a contempt for contemporary society, which he believes to be bourgeois and decadent; and aspires to form young, purified generations: "The ideal Eurasian is a strong, healthy, and beautiful person who had passionarity and passion and is ready to take responsibility and perform heroic deeds and feats, is prepared for trials and victories, great love and happy family life, ready to continue his line and lead a fulfilled and simultaneously pious life. . . . Our ideal is to make good physical and moral health, strength, valor, fidelity and pride honorable goals."[106] The journals *Elementy* and *Milyi Angel,* as well as the Web sites linked to Dugin, are therefore filled with a strong military symbolism and sometimes exhibit muscular, weapon-laden, and khaki-clad bodies. The back cover of one of his latest books, *The Philosophy of War* (2004), is particularly explicit: "The value of peoples, cultures, and societies is proved in war and through it. . . . The beautiful is what has as its foundation the accomplishment of self-affirmation. War renews Man, and the price to pay for this gigantic personal effort confirms his adherence to the community. War has always been a collective business, having as its goal the conservation of the people and the state, the increase of their power, of their space, and of their life regions. Herein lies the social and national significance of war."[107]

A Veiled Anti-Semitism

Dugin's exaltation of this warlike spirit, combined with numerous references to fascist ideas, prompts questions on the place of the "Jewish question" in his thought. As with the other Eurasianist thinkers, this question is particularly complex because they all combine philo-Semitic and anti-Semitic arguments. Dugin proposes his own version of that conjunction in the form of a paradoxical Judaeophobic philo-Zionism.

In *The Conservative Revolution* (1994), Dugin recognizes that the state of Israel has realized a kind of Traditionalism: "The only state that has partly managed to implement certain aspects of the Conservative Revolution is the state of Israel."[108] This prompted him to establish close links with some ultranationalist Israeli currents. Thus, since 1998, Dugin has sought to develop contacts with that part of the Israeli right that upholds the belief that all Jews must live in Israel. This militant Zionism agrees with him because it is in accordance with the principle of ethnopluralism: All peoples should live in peace, but "at home." The Eurasianist movement is linked with two radical Zionist groups: Be'ad Artzeinu, controlled by Rabbi Avram Shmulevich, and Vladimir Boukharsky's MAOF Analytical Group. These two groups, situated to the right of the right-wing Israeli Likud Party, are led by two former Soviet citizens of Jewish origin who emigrated to Israel and are now committed to politicizing Israeli Russians. Both of them participated in the founding convention of Evraziia and occupy important positions in the party hierarchy.[109] The Web site of the International Eurasianist Movement also mentions a link with Avigdor Eskin, a former Soviet Jew who took refuge in Israel and is now fighting the "liberal oligarchy" that he says is running the country.[110] Some radical currents of Judaism (most often Zionist, but also Chassidic and mystical) are also represented in Evraziia by Rabbis still living in Russia, for example, Adol'f Shaevich. They are all united by the idea that Jewish tradition, like Orthodoxy and Islam, is a target of unceasing attacks by secularization, a kind of religious globalization; only the unification of the traditionalists of all religions will allow them to develop strategies of resistance.[111]

Dugin's objective of an alliance with Israel derives from the idea of a distinction between "good" and "bad" Judaism, which had already been developed by the first Eurasianists, in particular in Iakov Bromberg's texts on the Jewish question. Dugin borrows from Bromberg the distinction between a Eurasian and an Atlanticist Jewishness. For Bromberg, the goal was to involve the Jews of the Russian Empire in the construction of Eurasia and to invite them to cultivate their specificities without trying to assimilate to the Russians. However, he belittled the West European Jews, whom he saw as bearers of political and economic modernity, of capitalism and communism, and as being excessively assimilated to the Romano-Germanic world. In Dugin's texts, the distinction is different. The "good" Jews are the citizens of Israel, as well as those who choose to leave for Israel, because this act signals their awareness of their irreducible Jewish specificity. The "bad" Jews are those who continue to live in the diaspora and try to be assimilated by the surrounding cultures, be it in the Atlanticist or the post-Soviet world. Thus, unlike the original Eurasianists, Dugin does not attempt to attract East European Jews, whom he presents as historical enemies of Russian nationalism.[112]

Dugin thus demonstrates a complex philo-Zionism combined with anti-Semitic statements, another combination typical of a part of the Western New Right. Though he regularly criticizes the vulgar anti-Semitism espoused by most currents of Russian nationalism, he does expound a more sophisticated and euphemized version of anti-Semitism, centered on more subtle religious and philosophical arguments. For example, he disagrees with Guénon, who considered the kabbalah to be authentic esotericism; for Dugin, the sense of the universal—an indispensable element of any real Traditionalism—is absent from the kabbalah, which, like the Talmud, is founded on the Jewish ethnic consciousness.[113] He also argues that Traditionalism views history as cyclical, whereas Judaism, because of its pessimism, regards it as linear.[114] For Dugin, the idea of God's incarnation as a man fundamentally changed the metaphysical cosmogony of Christianity. Thus, "from the point of view of Orthodox esotericism, Judaism and the kabbalah are without doubt the counter-initiation."[115] Dugin then considers the term "Judeo-Christianity" to be an incorrect formula, in particular for Orthodoxy, which he argues is even more distant from Judaism than is Catholicism.[116]

This argument illustrates Dugin's version of anti-Semitism. He attempts to efface the common historical roots that link Judaism to the two other monotheistic religions, and he accuses the Jewish world of having inspired a biological conception of itself. This inversion, a classical feature of anti-Semitism, is found in many of his texts, where he rejects, but also partly admires, the Jews' alleged capacity for conceiving of themselves as a race. Thus, according to Dugin, Israel is the archetypal example of a state founded on an ethnic or racial principle, born of the Holocaust, of course, but also having contributed to the creation of this drama to which the Jews fell victim. Dugin argues that German racism and Jewish messianism are two forms of "ethnic eschatologism," an ideological couple in which it is difficult to know which caused the other; their polarity is a sign of their intimate correlation.[117]

Dugin also repeatedly asserts that the Jews consider themselves to be a chosen people, which squarely opposes them to Russian Messianism, another ideology of national exceptionalism. Another consistent opposition between Judaism and Russianness concerns the relation to territory. According to Dugin, life in the diaspora has desacralized in the Jewish mind the territories on which the Jews have lived for two millennia, and only the long-inaccessible land of Israel has kept its sacred character. Their lack of emotion toward nature and their theological rejection of redemption by the earth—embodied by Jesus in Christianity—reveal their incompatibility with the Eurasian idea, for which territory is laden with meaning, as well as with Russian identity, marked by the cult of the nurturing soil. The famous "Jewish nomadism" found its most sophisticated expression in the maritime character of the thalassocracies.[118] This is why only the traditionalist Jews returning to live in Israel can be in agreement with the Eurasianist idea, all others being (possibly unconscious) bearers of an Atlanticist identity marked by affective indifference toward soil.

In his interpretation of Jewishness, Dugin also employs the esoteric elements that he develops in his theory of peoples. According to him, the world is divided into two types of cultures: Finnish (Judaism and Sunnism) and Aryan (Christianity, Aryan paganism, Shiism). The parallel is also sexual;

Dugin argues that masochism is Jewish, whereas sadism is Aryan.[119] The fundamental difference between them resides in their vision of the universe. For the Jews, the cosmos is God's place of exile, whereas in Christianity, it is the place willed by God. Dugin's anti-Semitism appears in full here; the identity of the Jews, the "Finnish" culture par excellence, is not just different from that of the Aryans, it is unassimilable to it. This irreducibility foreshadows, according to him, the coming metaphysical war between the Aryan and Semitic worlds: "The world of Judaica is a world that is hostile to us. But a sense of Aryan justice and the gravity of our geopolitical situation require us to comprehend its laws and its interests. Today, the Indo-European elite is facing a titanic task: to understand those who are different from us not only culturally, nationally, and politically, but also metaphysically. And in this case to understand does not mean to forgive, but to vanquish."[120] This paradoxical combination of a classic anti-Semitism and a politically committed philo-Zionism can partly be explained by Dugin's differentialist theories.

Ethno-Differentialism and the
Idea of Russian Distinctiveness

As was noted above, Dugin followed the theoretical turn of the New Right, which moved from a biological view of the differences between peoples to a primarily cultural one. This fashion for ethnopluralism, transferred from the "left" to the "right" in the 1980s, catches on particularly well in Russia, where it fits into a conception of national distinctiveness that was already highly ethnicized. This differentialist neoracism (in Taguieff's formula) and the exaltation of the "right to be different" are neither a new idea nor a mere import from the West. Throughout the nineteenth century, the principal thinkers of "Russian national distinctiveness" had upheld a culturalist approach, and, unlike their Western colleagues, accorded only very little importance to racial determinism.[121] Slavophile and Pan-Slavist thought remained under the influence of Hegel and Herder, and perceived the factual dimension of reality as a hidden fight between ideas. Thus, for over a century, it has been "normal" for Russian intellectuals sensitive to the national question to affirm, in Dugin's phrase, that "every people moves through History according to its own trajectory, upholding its own understanding of the world. That is why what is good for some peoples cannot be applied to others."[122]

Dugin, however, deploys an ambiguous culturalist and biological terminology with regard to this question; he uses the term *ethnos* with a positive meaning, seeing it as the primary point of collective reference ("the whole, the *ethnos*, is, according to the Eurasianists, higher than the part, the individual"[123]) but at the same time remains critical of ethnonationalism. According to Dugin, the superiority of the collectivity over the individual must be expressed in the political field as "political ethnism." This differential pluralism would be based on a corporatist system that would institutionalize intermediate echelons between the individual and the state. It would reveal Russia's true imperial nature. Unlike the Russians, who are "the empire's constitutive nation" (*imperoobrazuiushchaia natsiia*), the non-Russian peoples may benefit from cultural autonomy but not from sovereignty, contrary to what was proclaimed during perestroika.[124] No nationality should be recognized territorially, because "the Russians will exist as the only national community within a supranational imperial complex."[125] Dugin argues that the negotiations between the federal center and the subjects of the federation started by Boris Yeltsin fostered separatism in the Caucasus and in the Volga-Urals region. This ethnocentrism should, on the contrary, be condemned, because it stands in the way of a supraethnic unification of the Eurasian nation. Dugin's strength is in his capacity for playing with concepts; for example, he proposes to "meet these identification tendencies of the peoples and regions of the Federation halfway,"[126] but it in a controlled way that would subject them to the center.

Whether he bases himself on Eurasianist or New Right arguments, Dugin condemns nationalism in its ethnic and "chauvinist" variety, which he considers dangerous and obsolete. The idea of an ethnic miscegenation of peoples, celebrated by Western newspeak, appears to him as disastrous as was the theory of racial purity, because both lead to ethnocide. On the contrary, "the Eurasianist attitude toward the ethnos remains conservative, based on the principle of the absolute necessity of protecting each ethnic group from the prospect of historical disappearance."[127] This terminology remains paradoxical; not only does Dugin refrain from rejecting the idea of race, he also seems confused in his understanding of ethnicity, because he gives it an eminently culturalist and civilizationist meaning while at the same time using the terminology of the *ethnos*, which, following the Soviet tradition, remains very much tied to nature and even biology. This contradiction can be explained by his "postmodern" approach: He says he wishes to restore all the ideas, both religious and ethnic, that have been thrown out by modernity, which is why he addresses the ethnic question in both a positive and a negative way—positive when he uses it against the globalized liberalism that he views as destructive of the differences between peoples, and negative when he sees ethnic nationalism as preventing the affirmation of Eurasian unity.

Reacting to the increase in xenophobic violence perpetrated by skinhead movements, he attempts to distinguish between two categories of nationalism:

Russian statehood must recognize the value of every people while singling out the special role of the Russian ethnos. . . . Recognizing the centrality of the Russian people will put an end to the painful feeling of humiliation triggered by the series of historic misfortunes the Russians have experienced over the past decades. But along with an appropriate acknowledgment of the Russians' merits, we must specially stress the openness of Russian culture and the Russian ethnos, which has always been aware of bearing a cultural and civilizational mission for the benefit of all the other peoples of Russia. In this case, a "nationalism of love" should be opposed to the "nationalism of hatred."[128]

Thus Dugin's main activity, for several years, has been to speak out for a new interpretation of the idea of human rights. He is convinced that they constitute, through their claim to universality, a "new form of totalitarianism." He proposes to develop a theory of the "rights of peoples,"[129] appropriating third-worldist discourse as the right has been doing for some time. According to Dugin, this theory will first be put into practice in Russia, because, due to its natural federalism, that country advocates ethnocultural autonomy in exchange for unitarianism in state affairs. "The concept of 'people' [narod] must be recognized as the fundamental legal category, as the main subject of international and civil law."[130] Individuals will be legally identified by their ethnic, religious, or cultural affiliation. A similar theory had already been proposed a long time ago by Panarin, who put forward a "civilizational" rather than political pluralism, which he saw as typical of Eurasia.

Dugin's absolutization of the ethnic collectivity implies a difficult attitude toward the idea of cultural transfer. As Pierre-André Taguieff has justly and repeatedly noted, the cult of difference implies a phobia of intermingling; it celebrates heterogeneity but fears the mixing of peoples and traditions. Dugin considers the possibility of miscegenation between populations, or the transfer of cultural or political elements from one "civilization" to another, as dangerous. Indeed, he claims he has a "tolerant attitude toward ethnic miscegenation on the level of the elites, but a cautious attitude on the level of the masses."[131] Here he is once more in tune with the tradition of Soviet ethnology, which, following the theories of Iulian Bromlei and Lev Gumilëv, had regularly called for the development of endogamous traditions to preserve the "genetic pool" (*genofond*) of each ethnic entity. Once again, Dugin succeeds with aplomb in fitting old conceptions based on Russian or Soviet stereotypes into global intellectual debates. He adapts the Russian case to a more global theory on the current recomposition of collective identities under conditions of globalization, anchoring his ideas in alter-globalization movements, many of which have turned differentialism into one of their main dogmas.

Conclusions

A survey of Dugin's ideas naturally prompts questions about the extent to which he is representative, about his strategies, and about the networks through which his ideas are spread. In many senses, especially regarding his career, he can be considered to represent the general evolution of the Russian nationalist milieus over the past two decades. In the first half of the 1990s, these currents, then presented as "red-and-brown," were united in their opposition to the liberal reforms of the Yeltsin era. A change in their attitude toward the establishment set in during Yevgeny Primakov's term as prime minister and gained momentum when Putin came to power, an event that recomposed and narrowed down the political spectrum. Numerous nationalist figures came to support the authorities while preserving their political structures, resulting in a kind of vociferous but fictitious opposition. This was the case with Ziuganov's Communist Party, as well as with Zhirinovsky's LDPR and the Rodina bloc. Dugin also followed this path from radical opposition to public professions of loyalty. This is why he likes to classify himself as being in the "radical center" of the public spectrum: radical in his political and philosophical doctrines, but centrist by virtue of his support for the current president.[132] He thus embodies one of the main tendencies of the European radical right, which virulently attempts to differentiate itself from the centrist discourse of the powers that be on an ideological level, while developing a public strategy for gaining respectability. As he acknowledges, "to have any potential, a nationalist project must be intellectual, correct, and presentable: an enlightened nationalism."[133]

Paradoxically, Dugin is isolated within the nationalist currents in Russia. He is one of their few substantial thinkers, and his theories inspire numerous public figures and movements. At the same time, his theoretical position is too complex for any party to follow him entirely and turn him into its official thinker. He is also disturbing for the entire camp of Russian nationalism on several points: He condemns populism, which is central to the strategies of the main figures—Ziuganov, Zhirinovsky, and Limonov. The various nationalist currents do not recognize him as their ideologist; thus, while he makes numerous Aryanist statements and adopts an ambiguous anti-Semitism, he is seldom quoted by Aryanist authors, because he does not refer to the main neo-pagan reference work, the *Book of Vles*.[134] He is also strongly criticized by anti-Semitic circles for condemning theories of a Jewish plot, rejecting revisionism, and apparently denying the authenticity of the *Protocols of the Elders of Zion*. This elitist position, which he refuses to compromise in exchange for electoral success, is reminiscent of Alain de Benoist. However, Dugin cannot be entirely equated with the New Right; his stance is also informed by Traditionalism and fascism (in the sense outlined above). Thus he does not go as far as de Benoist on third-worldism, and he uses racist arguments in a more pronounced way.

Dugin's intellectual eclecticism assures him a certain degree of success among the young generation, revealing post-Soviet Russia's lack of foundations of identity. His attractive points include his occultist leanings, his exacerbated religious sensibility, and his rejection of communist ideology but not of the Soviet experience, as well as his ahistorical discourse about Russian grandeur. Not only do his geopolitical theories restore to Russia the role of a global superpower; he also modernizes a certain variety of political fundamentalism, exalts a sense of hierarchy and war, resurrects the mythical triangle between Germany, Russia, and Japan, and argues that cultures are incommensurable and unavoidably come into conflict with one another.

Taguieff proposes classifying radical right-wing thinkers into three very distinct, and too often confused, ideological traditions: counterrevolutionary traditionalists, conservative revolutionary Europeanists, and liberal neo-conservatives.[135] Dugin is profoundly opposed to the third group, but he combines elements from the first two to varying degrees; depending on the time and place, he may combine Guénonian esotericism with the search for a revolutionary third way. Attempts to classify such a doctrine and personality inevitably remain guesswork: Dugin is above all in search of himself, and his inner quest, particular the religious one, probably constitutes one of the matrixes of his political doctrines. His strategies are therefore tailored to fit his personal evolution and the institutional position he hopes to reach. These strategies are organized along several lines; he understands that the Eurasianist and geopolitical part of his theories is best suited to be widely spread in contemporary Russian society. In the same way, the idea of a unification of the patriotic scene and the creation of a kind of "union of nationalists without borders," which the International Eurasianist Movement hopes to become, strike a chord with numerous Russian political circles. Traditionalism, eschatologism, and esotericism are relegated to the background of his public activities and are reserved for a more restricted circle of initiated followers, for example, in the framework of the New University.

Dugin thus seems to have succeeded, at least with regard to this aspect of his thought, in his entryism into official structures. Indeed, as was observed very justly in the weekly *Obshchaia gazeta,* "Dugin is no longer considered to be the preacher of an ideological sect, but rather as an officially recognized specialist on geopolitical questions."[136] Dugin thus attempts to pursue a multiform strategy on the fringe of the classical electoral political spectrum. He develops a geopolitical discourse aimed at a large public, a concept of Eurasia as the basis for a new ideology of Russian great power for the Putin establishment, and Traditionalism and other philosophical and religious doctrines restricted to small but influential and consciously elitist intellectual circles. Even if his institutional presence, in Russia and abroad, is based on groupuscules, the influence of his personality and his works must not be underestimated. In spite of his rhetorical radicalism, which few people are prepared to follow in all its philosophical and political consequences, he has become one of the most fashionable thinkers of the day. Using networks that are difficult to trace, he is disseminating the myth of Russian great power, accompanied by imperialist, racialist, Aryanist, and occultist beliefs that are expressed in a euphemistic way and whose scope remains unclear, but that cannot remain without consequences.

Dugin's role as an ideological mediator will probably be an important point to consider in any long-term historical assessment; he is one of the few thinkers to engage in a profound renewal of Russian nationalist doctrines, which had been repetitive in their Slavophilism and their Tsarist and/or Soviet nostalgia. His originality lies precisely in his attempt to create a revolutionary nationalism refreshed by the achievements of twentieth-century Western thought, fully accepting the political role these ideas played between the two world wars. Therefore, in his opposition to American globalization, Dugin unintentionally contributes to the internationalization of identity discourse and to the uniformization of those theories that attempt to resist globalization. He illustrates that, although aiming for universality, these doctrines are still largely elaborated in the West. This is a paradoxical destiny for a Russian nationalist, whose self-defined and conscious "mission" is to anchor a profoundly Western intellectual heritage in Russia, and to use it to enrich his fellow citizens.

Chapter 5

The View from "Within": Non-Russian Neo-Eurasianism and Islam

The interwar Eurasianists always struggled to reconcile their Russian nationalism with their positive view of ethnic diversity. The Russian Neo-Eurasianists of the 1990s and 2000s have attempted to redefine national identity, arguing that Russia's closeness to the "East" is the basis of its distinctive, non-European identity, and that becoming aware of this fact is a precondition for rebuilding Russia's empire. This change of outlook would have been impossible without a reappraisal of the ethnic and religious diversity in the Russian Federation, that is, without the acknowledgment that the Turkic peoples and Islam are constituent parts of Russia. Clearly, the groups concerned could not remain indifferent to the reemergence of Eurasianism in Russia. The so-called Oriental peoples refuse to be mere passive objects serving the cause of Russian imperialism. A number of non-Russian intellectuals have denounced Eurasianism as an expression of Russian nationalism, and they have reclaimed the status of their peoples as subjects in their own right. The mere fact that there were national minorities in the USSR, and now in the Russian Federation, they argue, does not mean that all the peoples of the country must be fused into a single entity. Quoting the famous nineteenth-century Kazakh ethnographer Chokan Valikhanov, the Kazakhstani historian A. Nysanbaev points out that "Eurasia is not synonymous with Russia."[1]

Starting in the second half of the 1980s, intellectuals in Tatarstan and Kazakhstan used the newfound liberties of perestroika to demand a fairer recognition of the Turkic aspect of Soviet identity. Throughout the 1990s, part of the elites in the two republics—one a region of the Russian Federation and the other independent—used references to Eurasia to support the idea that a Turkic and Muslim national identity is compatible with the Rus-

145

sian cultural heritage. In the latter half of the 1990s and especially since 2000, new social milieus have started using the term "Eurasia" in new ways. The new proponents of Eurasianism are not intellectuals in the strict sense; they hold positions in political and administrative bodies or associations representing various ethnic and religious groups. Eurasianism, thus profoundly transformed to serve a Turkic or Muslim cause, has found new supporters within Islamic representative bodies in Russia, as well as in the presidential administrations of Tatarstan and Kazakhstan. It also seems to be spreading to Turkey.

The Emergence of Muslim Eurasianist Political Parties

The ongoing politicization of the Eurasianist idea, which Aleksandr Dugin had been anticipating for several years, reached a new stage in the spring of 2001 with the creation of two Eurasianist political parties: Dugin's Evraziia and Abdul-Vakhed V. Niiazov's Eurasianist Party of Russia. There was bitter competition between these two parties, which stood for completely different conceptions of Eurasianism, revealing some of the underlying political tensions that had beset Eurasianism in the 1920s and have become even more evident in the 1990s and 2000s. Dugin's Evraziia is the most radical embodiment of the nationalism that was always present in the original Eurasianism. By contrast, a view of Eurasia as something like a pre- or post-Soviet version of Soviet "peoples' friendship" predominates within Niiazov's Eurasianist Party.[2]

However, his was not the first party to try to combine a more or less Eurasianist program with an overt commitment to Islam. The earliest such attempt was made by the Islamic Party of Rebirth (Islamskaia Partiia Vozrozhdeniia), which was created in June 1990 in Astrakhan. This party, which was made up essentially of Tajiks and Dagestanis, managed to register in two different places: Moscow and Dagestan. Its chairman was the Avar Akhmed-Kadi Akhtaev; his deputy was the philosopher Geidar Dzhemal', a former dissident of Azeri origin who has become one of the most original post-Soviet Russian Islamic thinkers. The only regional conference the party ever organized took place in 1992 in Saratov with the help of Mufti Mukaddas Bibarsov. The movement has been profoundly divided ever since its foundation, because its third leader, Vali Sadur, an Oriental scholar of Tatar origin, has been in constant conflict with the other two.[3] Sadur quickly left the Islamic Party of Rebirth and subsequently created the small Islamic

Congress of Russia (Islamskii Kongress Rossii). Despite his departure, the Party of Rebirth remained split into several apparently irreconcilable movements, inspired, respectively, by Saudi Wahhabism (especially among Dagestani members), the Islamic Brotherhood (e.g., Akhtaev), Khomeini's Iran (e.g., Dzhemal'), and Turkish Islamism. As early as 1991–92, faced with the disintegration of the USSR, the Tajik branch of the Islamic Party of Rebirth broke off to become an autonomous Tajik party and took part in the civil war that ravaged Tajikistan until the peace agreement of June 1997.

The Islamic Party of Rebirth saw itself as a pan-Soviet movement: It wanted to preserve the unity of the Soviet Union, 40 percent of whose population was defined as Muslim, hoping it would one day become a Muslim state. It therefore firmly condemned the federal and autonomous republics' demands for sovereignty, any form of pan-Turkism or ethnocentrism, and the traditional Sufism that is widespread among the Muslims of the former Russian Empire.[4] In terms of geopolitics, it called for an anti-Western alliance between Russia and the Muslim states. Thus Akhtaev explained that "Orthodoxy and Islam feel an equal need to oppose Americanism and the 'new world order' it is imposing upon countries with traditional ways of life."[5] The Islamic Party of Rebirth strove for not only political but also cultural and religious rapprochement between Russia and Islam. Dzhemal', for instance, states that "Russia's only chance to avoid geopolitical disappearance is to become an Islamic state."[6] Thus the movement was situated at the borderline of Eurasianism, because it talked of conversion rather than cultural symbiosis; it considered that Russia's Muslims are more important than the Russians in shaping the country's destiny, because only Islam is the spiritual heart of the Eurasian continent. Although the Spiritual Board of Muslims explicitly condemned it for what it saw as fundamentalism, the Islamic Party of Rebirth set a precedent in Soviet and Russian society by founding a political identity on Islam and obtaining legal recognition.

New organizations emerged after the disappearance of the Islamic Party of Rebirth in 1994. Three small parties claimed to represent Russia's Muslims: the Union of Muslims of Russia (Soiuz Musul'man Rossii); the Nur movement; and the Islamic Committee of Russia (Islamskii Komitet Rossii), led by Dzhemal', which, however, quickly merged with other parties with broader aims and disappeared from the electoral scene. Nur, directed by Khalit Iakhin and later by Vafa Iarullin and Maksud Sadikov, was the only party registered at the legislative elections of 1995. Though its overall share of the vote was less than 1 percent, it achieved impressive results in several regions: over 5 percent in Tatarstan, where it was supported by the Tatar nationalist movement Ittifak; 23 percent in Ingushetia; and 12 percent in Chechnya.[7] Nevertheless, it too quickly disappeared from the public scene. Once more, this did not mean that the issue of political Islam was no longer on the agenda; on the contrary, Nur's demise led to several new attempts to institute a stable organization that would be able to politicize Russia's Muslims. In the summer of 1999, a new coalition named Medzhlis brought together several Islamic organizations, including Nur, the Islamic Congress, the Muslims of Russia, and the Refakh movement. But this coalition came apart due to the personal rivalries of its leaders, who ended up by joining other political parties. Indeed, their aims were often contradictory: Mufti Bibarsov supported Iabloko for its opposition to the Second Chechen War, whereas Dzhemal' was a member of the Movement in Support of the Army, directed by Al'bert Makashov, a former general of Cossack origin.

The creation, in 1998, of the Refakh-Blagodenstvie (Welfare) movement, directed by A.-V. Niiazov, brought some institutional stabilization. Niiazov quickly left the Medzhlis coalition and made it known that he supported the propresidential party in the 1999 Duma election. He and three other members of his movement won Duma seats on the Unity (Edinstvo) ticket. It was the first time since 1906 that politicians campaigning on an Islamic platform were elected to the Duma. As Niiazov explained, "We can count on at least five seats. This goes to prove that the Unity movement really reflects the unity of the peoples of Russia. But apart from us, there will also be Muslim single-mandate deputies and Muslims who are members of other parliamentary groups. On our count there will be approximately 35 Muslims all in all."[8] However, Unity spoke out against Niiazov's idea of creating a Muslim parliamentary group in the Duma. Refakh tried to boost its position by presenting itself as the party of all the national minorities, collaborating with Ramazan Abdulatipov, the leader of the Assembly of the Peoples of Russia. In 2001, the leaders of Refakh decided to secede from Unity; Niiazov was in conflict with the propresidential parliamentary group because of his radical statements on Palestine, but also because he hoped to go it alone.

However, he stated that Refakh "does not intend to oppose President Vladimir Putin. And what is more, many of the president's actions, especially in foreign policy, may be seen as expressing Eurasianist ideas."[9] Moreover, new legislation was passed banning associations that are not political parties from running in elections and outlawing parties based on religion, forcing Refakh to change tack. At its fifth congress in 2001, the movement transformed itself into a full-fledged political party, the Eurasianist Party of Russia (EPR), which also included several other small parties and religious groups. The EPR was registered by the Ministry of Justice in June 2001. One hundred and fifty delegates from sixty-seven regions of the Russian Federation took part in its founding congress. Initially, it was made up of seven organizations: Refakh (Welfare) or the Union of Muslims of Russia, Orthodox Unity (Pravoslavnoe Edinstvo), Chechen Solidarity (Chechenskaia Solidarnost'), the Congress of Buddhist Peoples (Kongress Buddistskikh Narodov), the Saint Petersburg Patriots (Patrioty Sankt-Peterburga), Young Moscow (Molodaia Moskva), and the Party of Justice and Order (Partiia Spravedlivosti i Poriadka). In May 2001, Niiazov also founded a multipartisan union called "Eurasia" within the Duma, which included over twenty deputies.

￼The EPR's social base remained essentially Muslim; in ethnic terms, its members were mainly Caucasians, Tatars, and Bashkirs.[10] Though only one-fourth of the members of its governing board presented themselves as Muslims, the party received substantial funding from Muslim public figures and entrepreneurs. Several muftis who held administrative positions joined the party: Usman Iskhakov, Akhmet Shamaev, and Shafig Pshikhachëv, respectively the heads of the Spiritual Boards of the Muslims of Tatarstan, Ichkeria (Chechnya), and Kabardino-Balkaria, as well as the plenipotentiary representative of the Coordination Center of the Muslims of the North Caucasus, Kharun Bacharov, and the Duma deputy for Chechnya, Aslambek Aslakhanov. The entire leadership of the EPR was very young (around thirty years of age), and with the exception of a few journalists and entrepreneurs, all were also holding positions in regional administrations. The EPR's chairman, A.-V. Niiazov, had been less active as a Eurasianist than Dugin but was no newcomer to politics. Indeed, his career has been rather dazzling: In 1990, he was the head of the Islamic Cultural Center in Moscow; in 1992, he became the director of the Islamic Cultural Center of Russia; in 1995, he was made cochairman of the Union of Muslims of Russia; from 1997, he was the head of the Spiritual Board of the Muslims of the Asian Part of Russia; and in 1999, he founded his own movement, Refakh.

With its numerous regional branches,[11] the EPR hoped to cross the 5 percent threshold in the 2003 legislative elections and sit in the Duma as an independent parliamentary group rather than as part of United Russia (Edinaia Rossiia). The party officially had 8,000 members but claimed it would have 100,000 by the end of 2003. Its ultimate aim was obviously to attract the Muslim vote, staking its bets on the future; because birthrates are higher among Muslims than among other Russian citizens, they will have a key role to play in ensuring Russia's stability in a few decades. More generally, the party hoped to represent all national minorities (just under 20 percent of Russia's population) by calling for the "creation of a new system of Eurasian spiritual values."[12] In the December 2003 legislative elections, the EPR tried to target a large range of non-Muslim voters, courting Pavel Borodin, the secretary of the Russian-Belarusian Union, to tap into his political networks.

The EPR in fact decided to play the integrationist card to woo those nostalgic for the Soviet Union; no longer counting on Russia's Muslims alone, it tried to attract all citizens who are in favor of creating post-Soviet supranational bodies. However, Borodin's decision to create an electoral alliance with the EPR, titled the Great Russia—Eurasian Union (Velikaia Rossiia—Evraziiskii Soiuz), prompted much controversy in the Russian press. The Union of Orthodox Citizens, for example, strongly condemned Borodin, saying that the Russian-Belarusian Union, being partly based on the two countries' common Orthodox identity, could not be chaired by someone who was "associated" with Islam.[13] Whatever was behind this political alliance, the coalition suffered a crushing defeat in the legislative elections, coming in sixteenth with only 0.28 percent of the vote. After this setback, the EPR vanished from the political scene. However, its main leaders, such as Niiazov, continue to look for an electoral "niche" and try to politicize Russia's Muslim community. Thus we are likely to see new institutions appearing in coming years.

Unlike the other Neo-Eurasianist movements, which are rooted in intellectual milieus, the EPR was theoretically unsophisticated. It presented itself as an "instrument for translating Eurasianist issues into the sphere of practical politics."[14] Though it did not directly mention other contemporary currents of Neo-Eurasianism, it did make it clear that it preferred the original 1920s Eurasianist movement as well as Turkic versions of Eurasianism: "The Party's ideological platform is the Eurasianist ideology: a consistent system of views and ideas whose foundations were laid in the works of N. Trubetzkoy, P. Savitsky, and L. Gumilëv. It has blossomed again since it was infused with new content in the works of O. Suleimenov, N. Nazarbaev, and many others."[15] At its founding congress, the EPR even received support from two famous writers, the Kazakh Olzhas Suleimenov (who agreed to chair the party's supervisory board) and the Kyrgyz Chingiz Aitmatov.

The EPR's writings on identity were classic expressions of Eurasianism; it tried to articulate Russia's intermediate position not only on a political level but also on economic, social, and cultural levels. The Eurasians, the

EPR claimed, are people of "togetherness" (*sobornost'*), but this has nothing to do with Soviet-era collectivism. For example, the party welcomed the return of the two-headed eagle as Russia's coat of arms; symbolically looking both eastward and westward, it stands for the dialogue between Orthodoxy and Islam—two religions that the EPR maintained are close in their fundamental principles—but also between Slavic and Turkic peoples. In economics, the EPR advocated both the advancement of a market economy and state support for small enterprises and disadvantaged social classes through some kind of neocorporatism. Unlike Dugin's movement, which pays less attention to economics than to things spiritual, the EPR took a positive view of small business. In politics, it called for "healthy conservatism" and supported President Putin's reforms.

All the Neo-Eurasianist movements are sensitive to religious issues and believe that the revival of public spirituality is a solution to Russia's problems. Whereas all the other currents are profoundly Orthodox, the EPR stated that Islam also has the potential to pull Russia out of "moral degeneration" in close collaboration with Orthodoxy. It also differed from its competitors in its moderate stance on Mikhail Gorbachev's reforms. Whereas the other Neo-Eurasianists are often very critical of the liberalization of the Soviet regime, the EPR did regret that Gorbachev ended a state as well as an ideology, but it appreciated him for having allowed freedom of speech. Its ideal would have been a Soviet Union in its old borders yet freed from the ideology of socialism. The EPR's statements have none of Dugin's rhetorical redundancy or his virulent messianism, but its leaders held a similarly essentialist view of Russia, considering it to be self-evidently true: "For Eurasianism is not a question but the Answer, not a negation but an Affirmation, not a disease but the Cure. Thus it is exactly what is needed today for Russia and the entire community of peoples living between the Baltic Sea and the Pacific Ocean, from within the Arctic Circle to the Pamir Mountains and the Hindu Kush."[16]

Like many Neo-Eurasianists, Niiazov tries to bestow scientific legitimacy upon his political aims. Of course, he cannot compete with the other Neo-Eurasianist theorists, because none of the EPR's leaders have published theoretical works on Eurasianism or hold academic positions. However, during its short existence, the EPR participated in numerous conferences on Eurasianism, probably hoping to become identified with a particular sector of the ideological field. Niiazov also tried to invent a family history that would provide a posteriori justification for his choices. It is well known that Niiazov (whose real name is Vadim Medvedev) is an "ethnic" Russian convert to Islam; yet he claims that he was born in Omsk, in a traditionally Kazakh region, and is a descendant of the Siberian Khan Kuchum,[17] and that his great grandfather, Rashid Qadi Ibrahim, was a famous Muslim theologian and one of the founders of the first Union of the Muslims of Russia in 1905.

The EPR's political program boiled down to two main points: in domestic politics, it called for a new balance in center-periphery relations; internationally, it wanted to rebuild links between the post-Soviet republics. On the latter issue, the EPR overtly acknowledged a Eurasianist influence; its aim was to "create on post-Soviet territory, using legal political means, a Federative Eurasian Union, whose core would be a democratic and economically strong Russian state."[18] Its members hoped that the state would officially propagate a new ideology based on the principles of patriotism and a community of fate between the peoples of the Commonwealth of Independent States. In consequence, the EPR firmly supported the project of a Eurasian Economic Community and spoke out in favor of pragmatic Eurasianism, following the model that the Kazakh president Nursultan Nazarbaev has been advocating for more than a decade. The EPR also called for the creation of a Eurasianist party in Kazakhstan and was supported in this by Beibit Sarapaly, the leader of the small People's Patriotic Movement of Kazakhstan. Also in keeping with the traditional Eurasianist model, the EPR tried to reinforce Russia's links with the Muslim world. Party delegates visited Iran, Libya, Pakistan, Malaysia, and Indonesia, and Niiazov personally met with Yassir Arafat and Mu'ammar al-Gadhafi.

In domestic politics, the EPR wanted to overcome the separatist and centrifugal tendencies that endanger the Russian Federation, while granting the "national" regions greater autonomy. It therefore advocated reorganizing the country's regional makeup and reducing the number of republics or "national" regions where the ethnic minorities represent a small percentage of the population. In return, it proposed to create cultural autonomies in regions with compact clusters of "small peoples" and to guarantee them proportionate representation in state bodies. The EPR was among the few parties that called for a political, rather than military, solution to the Second Chechen War, and it condemned the widespread "physiognomic" discrimination of Caucasians. It also organized demonstrations against the pogrom in Tsaritsyno and repeatedly denounced what it called the "national fascism" of Russian extremist groupuscules.[19]

Of course, the two Eurasianist parties—Dugin's and Niiazov's—never collaborated; even beyond their political disagreements, the clans and personal interests they stood for were difficult to reconcile. They also had different conceptions of their political role: Niiazov wanted to be present on the public scene in order to tap into the hypothetical Muslim vote, whereas Dugin prefers to exercise an ideological influence over those in power. He therefore accused the EPR of being a Kremlin puppet, virulently criticizing its "perversion" of the idea of Eurasia. For him, the competing party was just a "crude attempt by Islamic radicals to reverse the centralistic tendencies of the state" supported by Eurasianism.[20] Despite these attacks, Niiazov remains nuanced; for example, he recognizes that "Dugin has a somewhat esoteric, and even exotic, understanding of Eurasianist ideas, but he also has sound thoughts."[21] He even seems to have been influenced by Dugin's terminology, announcing that the EPR occupies "a sacral place between the old and the new political system" and that the world today is "on the threshold of the age of Aquarius"[22]—esoteric statements that are at least surprising coming from a Muslim.

Part of the Russian (especially nationalist) press equated the two parties. Some saw them as mere creatures of the Kremlin or even the former KGB (now FSB). This utter confusion demonstrates the extent to which some perceive the idea of Eurasia as fundamentally Muslim and anti-Russian; even Dugin's Evraziia Party, which makes no secret of its Great Russian nationalism, has been accused of propagating Islamism. The EPR has been particularly criticized for its alleged proposal to create an independent Chechen Republic in the framework of the Russian-Belarusian Union. It has also been denounced as a primarily commercial enterprise serving the interests of its leaders. Indeed, the party created an association that advances its members' business activities, which in turn fund the party. It wished to "promote intraparty corporatism, expressed in the preferential treatment of party members, in active support for the advancement and defense of their economic interests and social rights, and in the development of entrepreneurial initiatives."[23] Niiazov's personality and biography have also been subjected to critical scrutiny: Some highlighted his late conversion to Islam (suggesting self-interested motives); others mentioned his attempted "coup" against Mufti Ravil' Gainutdin at the Islamic Cultural Center in 1991 and recalled that the minister for emergency situations, Sergei Shoigu, speaking at a Unity congress in 2000, publicly accused him of supporting "Turkish Wahhabites" and using his position to enrich himself.

Thus the politicization of the idea of Eurasia contributed to bringing out divergences that had remained indistinct as long as the movement had remained exclusively intellectual. Evraziia and the EPR offer very different, if not to say strictly opposing, interpretations of Eurasianism. They are united only in their loyalty to the presidential administration and in their geopolitical conceptions: Russian great-power politics, rapprochement with part of the Muslim world, and reinforcement of intra–Commonwealth of Independent States relations. However, the EPR turned out to be much less anti-Western than Dugin's party, whose fundamental tenet is the rejection of "Atlanticism." In domestic politics, the EPR saw itself above all as representing and expressing the interests of the Russian Federations' minorities, whereas Dugin's *Evraziia* consistently upholds a Great Russian view of Russia. Whereas the former hoped to become political "identity lobbyists" by capturing the Muslim vote, the latter, despite its politicization, remains more of an intellectual enterprise that does not measure its success in quantitative terms.

In spite of these divergences, and although Muslim politicians refuse to be publicly associated with Russian varieties of Eurasianism, the personal relations between several Islamic leaders and Russian nationalist movements provide food for thought. Thus, for a long time, the important patriotic weekly *Den'* (later, *Zavtra*) published articles by members of the Islamic Party of Rebirth, documenting the sympathy that some in the Russian nationalist movement feel for radical Islam. In the 1995 legislative elections, the leader of the Union of Muslims of Russia, Akhmet Khalitov, was second on the list of candidates of Vladimir Zhirinovsky's Liberal-Democratic Party. Khalitov was a long-standing comrade-in-arms of Zhirinovsky, and he had edited small newspapers such as *Sokol Zhirinovskogo* and *Pravda Zhirinovskogo*. Nur's leader, Khalid Iakhin, was an aide and adviser to the same party's chief ideologist, Aleksei Mitrofanov.

Recent "ethnic" Russian converts to Islam also have extremely ambiguous links with Russian nationalism. Thus the main association of ("ethnically") Russian Muslims, the National Organization of Russian Muslims (Natsional'naia Organizatsiia Rossiiskikh Musul'man, or NORM), founded in June 2004, tries to reconcile a Russian identity with conversion to Islam. According to Ali Polosin—a former Orthodox priest who converted to Islam in 1999 and became director of the Department of Relations with the State at the Council of Muftis of Russia (Sovet Muftiev Rossii, SMR) in addition to teaching comparative religious studies at Moscow Islamic University—Christianity is an alien religion with Jewish origins that was forcibly imposed upon the Russian people. Polosin claims that Russian paganism was a natural monotheism that was close to Islam and even influenced it. The Muslim converts share this hostility toward Christianity with the neo-pagans, who are the—culturally and politically—most radical wing of the Russian nationalist movement.[24]

The creation of NORM met the expectations of certain Muslim ideologists, and particularly Geidar Dzhemal', one of Russia's best-known Islamic thinkers. Dzhemal' "godfathered" the organization and took part in its founding congress. In 1992–96, he anchored the Muslim part of a television broadcast called *Now* (Nyne), making enthusiastic comments about the success of the Iranian regime and Western intellectuals converting to Islam. During perestroika, Dzhemal' had close links with the nationalist Pamiat' movement, frequently wrote for *Den'*, and was partly influenced by Dugin, being in a sense his Islamic equivalent. Today, however, Dugin and Dzhemal' have drifted apart; they differ on Islam and especially on the issue of proselytism. Nevertheless, Dzhemal' comes from the same Traditionalist milieu as Dugin, was a member of a "Black SS Order" that purportedly existed in the USSR in the 1970s, and tried to introduce fascist ideas into Islam to give a clearer focus to Islamism. Thus he regularly draws parallels between Orthodox nationalism and Islamic renewal, and he recognizes that the "Red-Brown" and "Green" movements have common objectives.[25] Nevertheless, his conception of Islamism remains influenced by Traditionalist precepts, and his theories are little appreciated by other Islamists, who see them as inspired by Yevgeny Golovin and Dugin and thus incompatible with their own view of Islam.

The politicization of Russia's Muslims has been largely unsuccessful. Yet the phenomenon itself remains significant, because it signals the emergence of a political elite seeking to revive a Muslim parliamentary group in the Duma such as had existed in late imperial Russia. For the time being, this elite remains isolated from the bulk of the population, and its political potential is hard to gauge. But theoretically it could come to play an increasing role, given the rapid growth of nominally Muslim population groups in Russia. Eurasianist slogans enable these politicians to play the card of religious (Islamic) or ethnic (Turkic) distinctiveness in the hope of securing a stable electoral niche while remaining strictly loyal to the Russian state. The bodies representing the Muslims of the Russian Federation, who are also trying to appropriate Eurasianist themes, are playing a similar game.

The Eurasianist Games of the Russian Muftiates

Islamic representative bodies in Russia explicitly reject any form of religiously based political extremism and stress their loyalty to the secular authorities, hoping to gain influence over their decisions. But because these institutions remain subordinated to the powers that be and are riven by personal rivalries, they encourage the emergence of more radical and less governable movements on their fringes. This damages the public image of Islam in Russia and strongly encourages confusion between religion and politics. The leaders of these institutions claim that they are above political squabbles because their objectives are spiritual; yet they try to gain advantages by lending their theological support to competing political parties.[26]

This is true of Talgat Tadzhuddin, the chairman of the Central Spiritual Board of Muslims (Tsentral'noe Dukhovnoe Upravlenie Musul'man, or Ts-DUM), and Ravil' Gainutdin, who chairs the SMR, a rival institution created in 1996. Both regularly state that they do not support the creation of religiously based political parties, which in any case are prohibited under Russian legislation. In practice, however, both institutions interfere in politics, not only by their almost unflinching support for the president but also by backing partisan organizations. Many muftis are members of political parties. They officially join them as simple citizens, but their membership really signifies an acknowledgment of the ideological links between their institution and a party. More marginal movements, such as the Islamic Congress of Russia, accuse the two main leaders, as well as their rivals and fellow muftis N. Ashirov and M. Bibarsov and younger figures who lack theological training, for example, Abdul-Vakhed Niiazov, of being puppets of the regime. The president of the Islamic Congress, M. Saliakhetdinov, argues that instead of representing the *umma*, these people pursue the narrow and self-interested agendas of their own institutions, which are subordinated to the secular authorities on the model of the Orthodox Church, strongly contributing to the bureaucratization of the muftis and their transformation into a clergy that serves the state rather than Islam.[27]

* Tadzhuddin and Gainutdin, as well as the institutions they represent, are divided on several points, especially concerning the relationship of Islam with Orthodoxy. Although the Russian state is officially secular, there are numerous signs—some subtle, some less so—indicating that Orthodox Christianity enjoys a higher status than other religions. Tadzhuddin has never made a secret of his friendship with Alexis II and his support for the Orthodox Church. He considers the patriarch to be "the country's supreme spiritual leader"[28] and regularly states that "our motherland is Holy Rus'."[29] He also supported the Orthodox Church when it opposed plans for Pope John Paul II's visit to Russia.[30] He shares its wariness of Catholic and Protestant proselytism, and denounces all non-Orthodox Christian confessions as dangerous "sects."[31] For several years, he has been semiofficially

referring to the TsDUM as "Spiritual Board of the Muslims of Holy Rus' " (Islamskoe DUM Sviatoi Rusi).

Tadzhuddin profits from the historical prestige of the Spiritual Assembly of Orenburg, created by Catherine II in 1788. He is the only representative of Russian Islam at the Organization of the Islamic Conference and at UNESCO.[32] His Central Spiritual Board of Muslims at least officially oversees the Muslim communities of the Baltic States and Ukraine. Although, during the breakup of the USSR, he proved unable to preserve a single unified organization representing all the Muslims of Russia, he remains an important figure; even his opponents find it hard to deny his competency in theological matters, which contrast with most other Muslim clerics' lack of proper training. He also played a major role in bringing Islam back to the public scene: In 1989, he orchestrated the thousandth anniversary of the Volga and Ural peoples' Islamization, following the model of the anniversary of the Christianization of Kievan Rus' the year before.

In 2003, a project to introduce a course in "foundations of Orthodox culture" at Russian schools sparked heated debate. Once more, Tadzhuddin sided with Orthodoxy. He expressed his hope that the project, once implemented, would eventually turn into a course on all of Russia's so-called traditional religions.[33] Thus he accepts Orthodoxy's claim to the status of "first among equals" and is content with playing a loyal second fiddle. His militant ecumenism makes him an original personality; he regularly states that there are different religions yet all worship the same God, and he encourages the construction of ecumenical mosques, for example, the "friendship mosque" (*mechet' druzhby*), which uses symbols of the three great monotheistic religions and is open for prayer to all believers. This ecumenical openness to the other monotheistic religions (which, however, excludes the other Christian confessions, on the Orthodox model) is rounded off with a highly conciliatory vision of the pre-Islamic past. As early as 1992, Tadzhuddin was criticized by the other Muslim organizations for his statements on Tengrism,[34] which he presents as an early form of monotheism, and for his claim that the ancestors of the Tatars were already praying to Allah under the name of Tengri, well before the first prophets. His recurrent attempts to have the Tatar site of Bulgary (where the Volga Bulgars adopted Islam in 922) recognized as the fourth holy site of Islam have enraged Gainutdin and the other Russian muftis.[35]

Because of his political activities, Tadzhuddin has often been called a "Soviet man" who continues to play the game of ideological subordination to the authorities, accepts various fashionable yet speculative nationalist theories (e.g., on Tengrism), and is overcautious in relations with the other Muslim countries. Movements such as the Islamic Congress of Russia vehemently criticize his rejection of the unity of the *umma* in favor of a strictly state-centered and Russified conception of Islam.[36] Indeed, his ostentatious and carefully cultivated closeness to Orthodoxy and his rehabilitation of the pre-Islamic faith of the Turkic and Mongol peoples have alienated foreign theologians, who are used to more rigorous conceptions of Islam.[37] He was also much criticized for his virulent strictures upon Russian Muslims going to study abroad and his demand that the Russian state be exclusively responsible for training future imams—statements that further offended foreign countries wishing to create links with Russian Islam. Finally, he is opposed to the Euro-Islam advocated by Tatarstan's president, Mintimer Shaimiev, criticizing it as a secret form of Wahhabism and claiming that the republic lets fundamentalist missionaries preach in Russia and disseminate anti-Christian writings.[38]

The Kremlin has consistently remained neutral in the dispute between the TsDUM and the SMR, probably because it is pleased with the way these divisions complicate the representation of Islam in Russia. Yet under the veneer of official neutrality, and despite Tadzhuddin's closeness to the authorities via his Orthodox friends, the presidential administration seems to favor Gainutdin.[39] The respective positions of the two men and their institutions in their struggle for official favors changed dramatically in 2003, when the United States launched its war in Iraq. During a meeting of United Russia in Ufa on April 4, Tadzhuddin issued a thunderous call for jihad (saying, "It is not I who express this criticism, but God speaking through me"[40]) and identified the United States, the United Kingdom, and their allies as direct enemies. The Ministry of Justice and the Office of the Public Prosecutor seem to have discreetly threatened the TsDUM with closure in response to these statements, which legally count as calls for religious hatred. What prompted Tadzhuddin to make such an unexpectedly radical speech remains mysterious, especially considering that he has always accused foreign fundamentalists of calling for a "clash of civilizations." The SMR profited from this incident by asking the rival institution to be excluded from several associations and representative bodies.[41]

Gainutdin's public statements are unlike Tadzhuddin's. The SMR also constantly denounces "Wahhabism" as alien to Russian Islam; but it is more militantly Muslim and less close to Orthodoxy. It often stresses two facts it says will have a serious impact in the long term: that Islam is Russia's second-largest religion, and that Russia has many Muslim neighbors.[42] Gainutdin openly states that he is worried about Orthodox attempts to question the secular status of the Russian state and its schools. Many articles published on the SMR's Web site oppose Orthodox desires to obtain recognition of Russia's fundamentally Christian character, saying that this would endanger the fragile religious balance in the country.[43] The authors are troubled by the renewal of an ethnocentric Russian nationalism that supports the discrimination of ethnic minorities, and they argue that this may in turn radicalize the Muslims.[44]

After the publication of the "Foundations of the Social Conception of the Orthodox Church" in August 2000, the SMR decided to issue a document titled "The Main Points of the Social Program of the Muslims of Russia" (Osnovnye polozheniia sotsial'noi programmy rossiiskikh musul'man). Published on March 25, 2001, this program reaffirms the secular status of the state and its institutions and calls for a tripartite agreement between the state, the Orthodox Church, and the SMR to regulate the presence of clergy in schools, hospitals, prisons, and the army.[45] Gainutdin's institution has also made successful contributions to theological training. Russian imams' much-criticized lack of background in Islamic studies is especially worrying to state officials, who fear that clerics may slide into extremism. The SMR initiated the creation of two prestigious institutions: Moscow Islamic University, founded in 1999, and the Islamic University of Russia, created in 1998 in Kazan and managed by the SMR, the Spiritual Board of Tatarstan, and the Institute of History of Tatarstan's Academy of Sciences.[46]

Despite this more insistent Islamic militancy, Gainutdin also makes Eurasianist statements highlighting Russia's multireligious character and insisting on the diversity of the Russian Federation. If Russia is not exclusively European or Slavic, then it cannot be considered exclusively Christian: "Our [Eurasianist] idea is based on the principle that representatives of dozens of nationalities and religions are living together. It must draw on centuries of Russian history, on Russia's historical experience of coexistence between peoples and religions, and on the distinctiveness of Russia's civilization."[47] Muslim officials want to turn Islam into a cornerstone of Eurasia: "The economic and cultural links between Europe and Asia are rooted deep in past centuries, and since the Middle Ages Islamic culture has had a stake in the great civilization of Eurasia. Without recognizing this, one cannot understand the essence of Eurasian culture."[48]

Tadzhuddin's and Gainutdin's divergent statements highlight the opposition between two possible Eurasianist views of Islam's place in contemporary Russia. The first, represented by Tadzhuddin and the TsDUM, sees

Islam as a minority faith in a country with an Orthodox majority and accepts the symbolic or even legal primacy of the Moscow Patriarchate. It does not hesitate to adopt the rhetoric of the most traditional forms of Russian nationalism, and it presents Russia's Muslims as conscious of Russo-Orthodox supremacy. The second current, embodied by Gainutdin and the SMR, more openly advocates equality between Orthodoxy and Islam, implying an official recognition of the country's multinational and multiconfessional character. Its objectives are less ideological than Tadzhuddin's, and it is more closely involved in current social realities, as demonstrated by Gainutdin's involvement in theological training and his participation in the debate about the place of Muslims in the Russian army.

The rivalry between the two men also affects their personal commitment to the idea of Eurasia. Tadzhuddin was long reluctant to accept the emergence of Muslim parties, but he finally agreed to head Nur,[49] and he later joined Dugin's Evraziia. In the first half of the 1990s, he already wrote for Eduard Bagramov's journal *Evraziia: Narody, kul'tury, religii.* He later became a member of Evraziia's Central Committee and took part in three key events: the movement's founding congress on April 21, 2001; the congress on May 30, 2002, at which Evraziia was transformed into a political party; and the conference that announced the creation of the International Eurasianist Movement on November 20, 2003. At the interconfessional forum marking the 2,000th anniversary of the birth of Christ, he said: "It was not an accident that the Almighty predestined Europe and Asia to be together. They are joined at the Urals as if by a mighty welding seam. And let me add: The distinction between two continents—Europe and Asia—is artificial; it leads us away from the truth. Objectively there is a single continent, Eurasia. It can be said with certainty to be the cradle of all mankind. Not only do the cultures of West and East come into contact here; all the messengers of the Almighty have come from the East."[50] This is Tadzhuddin's version of the main culturalist ideas of Eurasianism on the unity of peoples at the juncture between Europe and Asia. At the first Congress of Evraziia, he also affirmed that "Eurasianism is the most harmonious and sincere Russian patriotism" and the only ideology that will be able to save Russia and help it recover its global influence.[51]

According to Tadzhuddin, the Russian Eurasianists, despite being rooted in the Orthodox tradition, have much in common with Islam: "We are faced with similar threats, we have common enemies, we have the same ethical and spiritual ideal."[52] The mufti does not seem embarrassed by Dugin's radicalism; indeed, Dugin's references to mystical Orthodoxy and pre-

Christian Slavic paganism follow the same logic as the rediscovery of Tengrism for the Turkic peoples. Thus, in an interview, Tadzhuddin states: "We are convinced that the aims and tasks of the Evraziia party, its philosophy and ideology, ideally respond to the interests of Russia's Muslims."[53] Elsewhere he adds: "This is how we representatives of Russia's non-Slavic peoples, we Russian Muslims, perceive this eastward movement, this state-building impulse."[54] Tadzhuddin even seeks a religious justification for his political alliances, and he has no qualms about linking this ideology to his faith, for "God himself has destined the peoples of Russia for Eurasianism."[55]

By contrast, his rival Gainutdin supports Dugin's opponent Niiazov and his Eurasianist Party of Russia. Thus the group around Refakh, the EPR, and Damir Serazhetdinov's Civic Party (Grazhdanskaia partiia Rossii) is closely linked to the SMR and therefore strongly opposed to Tadzhuddin. The group enjoys the patronage of the mufti of Siberia, N. Ashirov, even more than Gainutdin's, although Niiazov has been reconciled with Gainutdin for several years. Tadzhuddin does not hide his sense of rivalry with Niiazov and his exasperation at the idea that the two are fighting not only for the spiritual and institutional leadership of Russia's Muslims but also for political control over the idea of Eurasianism. Niiazov's Eurasianist Party, he claims, is "not only [marked by] adventurism, but also represents sabotage by those foreign forces to whom the flowering and consolidation of great Russia . . . means death."[56] He can count on Dugin's support on this point, because the leader of Evraziia is just as disconcerted at this unexpected competition over the Eurasianist theme; according to Dugin, Mufti Ashirov is overtly Wahhabi and has supporters among the Taliban and Chechen separatist fighters.

Once more, these divisions reveal Eurasianist ideological continuities that run deeper than rival personal strategies. Tadzhuddin's membership in Dugin's party parallels his support for the Orthodox hierarchy and his attachment to the concept of "Holy Russia," showing that he perceives the Russian Federation as primarily the country of the "ethnic" Russians (*russkie*). By contrast, Gainutdin's and other SMR officials' support for Niiazov's party corresponds to their more autonomist views of Islam, their more militant attitudes about religious and ethnic matters, and their view of Russian identity as primarily civic (*rossiiskii*). Tadzhuddin and Gainutdin embody the two poles of traditional Russian Eurasianism: on the one hand, Russian nationalism and Orthodox messianism; and on the other hand, a more secular patriotism, which combines great-power ambitions with an acknowledgment of Russia's multiethnic and multireligious character. Thus

Eurasianism has become one of the crystallization points for the opposition between the various Islamic representative bodies, which use the two Eurasianist parties to translate their competition into politics. The same is true, to an extent, of yet another religious conception, Tatar Euro-Islam, which also, albeit with specific nuances, uses the Eurasianist idea of a synthesis between Western and Eastern religious principles.[57]

Tatarstan: The Pragmatic Eurasianism of Russia's "Ethnic" Regions

Tatarstan may be considered the first non-Russian bearer of Eurasianism: It supports a substantive variety of federalism and was at the helm of the ethnic republics' autonomist revolt during discussions on a new constitution in 1993. The period of head-on opposition to Moscow ended with the bilateral treaty of February 15, 1994, which gave Tatarstan the (unconstitutional) status of an "associated state."[58] Nevertheless, Tatarstan continues to stress its distinctive—loyal yet autonomous—status, for example, by directly joining the Organization of the Islamic Conference. Thus Tatarstan is the locomotive of non-Russian Eurasianism: There is a large and economically active Tatar diaspora both in Russia and abroad; and the republic is geographically located at the heart of the Russian Federation, close to Moscow, but also to the great industrial regions in the Urals, and to the now-independent Central Asian republics.[59] Tatarstan thinks of itself as the first among equals in the Russian Federation, and it cements this position of an "internal stranger" by playing the Eurasianist card.

Tatarstan's paradoxically loyalist position within the Russian Federation is reflected in the equally ambivalent political biography of its president, Mintimer Shaimiev: He ran on the ticket of the pro-Yeltsin party Our Home Is Russia (Nash dom—Rossiia) in the 1995 legislative elections; toyed with dissent as a member of Fatherland—All Russia (Otechestvo—Vsia Rossiia), the party of the regional *nomenklatura* led by Yevgeny Primakov; and ended up by joining Unity, the party that supported Vladimir Putin's bid in 1999–2000. This loyalty was rewarded by the Constitutional Court, which ultimately validated several regional presidents' moves to remain in power for a third term, enabling Shaimiev, Murtaza Rakhimov in Bashkortostan, and Kirsan Iliumzhinov in Kalmykia to hold on to their mandate. Thus, on March 25, 2005, Tatarstan's Council of State granted presidential powers to Shaimiev for the third mandate.

 Ever since perestroika, Shaimiev has stressed the ethnically mixed character of his state. He has sought to turn Tatarstan into a symbol of Russia's awareness of its religious and ethnic diversity. For him, the path to sovereignty implies perfecting the Soviet system of federalism rather than trying to restore a lost Tatar state. Like many Neo-Eurasianists, he remains "Sovietically correct," praising the merits of internationalism and refusing to institutionalize ethnic differences. As early as the beginning of the 1990s, Shaimiev very symbolically announced the reconstruction of the Orthodox Cathedral of Annunciation as well as the Kul-Sharif Mosque (both inside the Kazan Kremlin), and he established religious parity by conferring public status upon both Orthodox and Islamic holidays.[60]

 The republic also rehabilitated Sultan Galiev (1880–1941?), a Tatar forerunner of third-worldism and symbol of 1920s national communism. On a rhetorical level, Sultan-Galievism allows the authorities to combine a Turkic and Muslim Tatar national identity with European-style modernity and a strong loyalty toward the Russian state.[61] Sultan Galiev's belief that membership in the (then-Bolshevik) Russian state was compatible with a unification of the Turkic peoples is attractive to contemporary Tatar intellectuals and politicians, who have always seen themselves as the elite of the Turkic world. Thus, for Tatar supporters of Eurasianism, that ideology fits "naturally" and almost seamlessly into the history of thinking about the Tatars' identity and place in Russia. Eurasianism subtly draws on the paradoxes of Russianness: The Tatars, they argue, have been "internal" to Russian identity for centuries; they have been a part of everyday life in Russia for five hundred years; and, indeed, the state ruled from Moscow could not exist without the Turkic and Muslim peoples.

   The Eurasianist card was also played by Vassili N. Likhachev, a close collaborator of President Shaimiev's who presented himself as the very incarnation of Tatar Eurasianism. He was the only Russian to have held a top position in Tatarstan's administration,[62] and for a long time he was vice president of the Federation Council, the upper chamber of the Russian parliament, where he was in charge of nationalities issues. Supporting Nazarbaev's project of a Union of Eurasian States, he proposed turning Kazan into the capital of the future Eurasian institutions, presenting his country as the "bridge" between Russia and Central Asia.[63] Tatarstan's presidential administration consistently upholds a Eurasian image of the republic: On the occasion of the 1,000th anniversary of the city of Kazan, celebrated with pomp on August 30, 2005, the city administration unveiled a statue of Lev Gumilëv in one of the main streets. Engraved under the statue is one of the historian's most famous sentences: "I am a Russian who throughout his life has defended the Tatars from calumny." The decision to erect the statue had been made after the project of a bust of Peter the Great met with criticism from Tatar nationalists. The Kazan city administration explained this last-minute change by claiming that "the inhabitants of Kazan feel closer to Gumilëv than to Peter I."[64]

In the early 1990s, the All-Tatar Public Center (Vsetatarskii Obshchestvennyi Tsentr, or VTOTs), which at the time served as an institutional framework for the portion of the Tatar political elite, saw itself as an enlightened, fundamentally secular oligarchy interested in preserving the republic's ethnic and religious diversity. The VTOTs sought to uphold a strong national identity that would, however, be compatible with Russian political realities.[65] The formation of this "new" identity signified the rehabilitation of Islam as a defining element of national identity, and the development of a modern faith that would respect official secularism and the other religions. This provided the framework that has, until today, shaped the proposals for reconceptualizing Islam spearheaded by Rafael' Khakimov, who is theorizing the pragmatic policies of Tatarstan's authorities. As a political adviser to President Shaimiev, Khakimov heads the ideological section of the Tatarstan–New Century Party (Tatarstan's version of the pro-Putin United Russia Party) and directs the Institute of History of the Academy of Sciences of Tatarstan. However, this hegemonic position does not secure him a monopoly on public statements on Islam; he merely voices the official position of the Tatarstani administration on religious matters.[66]

Khakimov is trying to elaborate a subtle theological position; he condemns the traditionalist, antimodern, and communitarian form of Islam as ethnocentric, but he also opposes the idea of a universal unity of Islam. He argues that Islam in its historical development was rooted in national cultures, which the Koran itself recognizes as legitimate. Thus Islam is not at all essentially monolithic; on the contrary, it is fundamentally pluralistic. Khakimov's aim is to enhance the status of Hanafism as a pragmatic theological school that, in addition to the Shari'a, recognizes the value of common law, that is, adjusts Islamic principles to different contexts. Khakimov advocates a flexible approach to dogma and, using the traditional expression, wants to reopen the gates of *ijtihad* that were closed in the ninth century.[67] In a famous pamphlet titled *Where Is Our Mecca? (A Manifesto of Euro-Islam)*, he insists on dissociating Islam from Arab culture; one can be Muslim, he argues, without having any cultural links with the classical Middle East.[68]

Khakimov obviously draws on the reformist ideas of jadidism, which emerged among Tatar Muslims in the late nineteenth century and spread to all of Russian Turkistan.[69] Jadidism also wanted to rehabilitate individual judgment against community opinion and the local *madhhab* in cases where they were wrong. The ideas of Ismail Gaspraly are easy to adapt to contemporary Euro-Islam: The profoundly Russified jadidist elite sought to reconcile Islam with Western liberal and progressivist thought and give the Turkic Muslims an active role in Russia. Although the jadidists believed in the future political unity of the Turkic world, in contemporary Tatarstan they are presented as strictly Tatar national heroes, bracketing out the pan-Turkist and pan-Islamic aspects of their theories, which are perceived as disruptive from the point of view of contemporary political realities.[70]

Khakimov acknowledges the intimate links between jadidism and communism; in the 1920s, before they were liquidated, many jadidists tried to elaborate an "Islamic socialism" that could be squared with the atheist context of communism. According to him, "jadidism is the source of all contemporary Tatar culture."[71] He considers jadidism to have been a direct precursor of the Euro-Islam he is trying to develop. He believes there is an intrinsic link between the national and the religious questions; for him, Tatar identity, or "Tatarness," largely draws its meaning from jadidism, and vice versa. They are the two cultural factors that will determine the people's future: "First, the status of Tatar as the key language in the Turkic group. Second, jadidism as one of the most highly developed forms of Islam."[72]

Thus Khakimov's ideas are not at all free of nationalist implications. He has publicized his national convictions in several texts, including *Who Are You, Tatar?* published in Russian in 2002. In particular, he accuses the Russian authorities (both Tsarist and Soviet) of having divided the Tatars into several ethnic groups by institutionalizing the Tatars of Crimea, Astrakhan, and Siberia, but also the Nogais and Bashkirs.[73] For him, the Bashkir nation is an artificial construct created by the Bolsheviks, and the claims of the contemporary Kriashens[74] and Bulgars to the status of separate peoples are similarly unfounded. He also virulently criticizes Tatar society's lack of commitment to the adoption of the Latin alphabet, a project that had been voted in 2002 by the Second World Congress of Tatars but deemed unconstitutional by the Russian State Duma.

More generally, Khakimov condemns Russian historiography and its discriminatory view of the Tatars as barbarous sons of the Mongol Empire; for him, they are "descendants of the Turkic genius."[75] He even claims they played a key role in the constitution of the Russian Empire, because this was born of the seizure of Kazan and Astrakhan in 1552 and 1556, respectively. He argues that the Tatars, having been the first Russified Muslims, joined the Muscovite aristocracy, fought to expand the empire, "opened up" Siberia and Central Asia, and remained Russia's key mediator in relations with the Muslim world. Having the longest tradition of coexistence with the Russians, Khakimov maintains, the Tatars have thus for five centuries contributed to Russia's Eurasian identity. Although Khakimov's ideas are Eurasianist, they also have a pan-Turkist aspect because he sees the Tatars as the unifiers of the Turkic peoples. According to him, Turkic unity is inevitable, even against opposition from Moscow, and in the long term it will strengthen Russia, because the Turkic peoples are the "natural" allies of the Slavs.[76]

Tatar Euro-Islam shares Eurasianism's positive conception of modernity. According to Khakimov, the Tatars understand the need for a secular state, a democratic and liberal political system, and mastery of cutting-edge technologies. Islam must serve to modernize society, not to (re)traditionalize it; since the late nineteenth century, the arrival of capitalism in Russia has "fundamentally changed the functions of Islam; from being an institution of ethnic preservation, it had to become a factor of development."[77] Thus Khakimov accepts or even applauds the paradoxical behavior of a vast majority of Tatars, who consider themselves Muslims although only a tiny minority frequents mosques. Khakimov takes these sociological data to confirm his concept of Euro-Islam, understood as the "contemporary form of jadidism—a neo-jadidism that better reflects Islam's culturological aspect than its ritual side."[78] He wants to root Islam in modernity: Being the religion of free human beings, it must result from free choice. There can be no intermediary between God and humanity; and there can be no Islamic justice without equality among men, and between men and women. *Ijtihad* is the only way to introduce liberal thought into Islam, enabling it to avoid a "clash of civilizations" and to respond to the growth of Islamophobia in Russia.

However, Khakimov's theories garner little popular support in Tatarstan: They are not appreciated among the *ulema,* who interpret them as a form of forcible modernization through covert secularization; they are too intellectual and elitist for the masses; and they are seen above all as an expression of official opinion on religious matters. Indeed, Tatarstan's strategy inside the Russian Federation is precisely a combination (ideologically legitimated wherever possible) of emphasized cultural (national, linguistic, religious) distinctiveness and acceptance of modernization: "The fates have decreed for the Tatars to become the northern outpost of Islam; they are situated on the border between West and East, not only geographically, but culturally as well."[79]

Khakimov's theories may be understood as an original version of Tatar-style "liberation theology"; yet they are firmly embedded in Eurasianism: Although, unlike the EPR or the Spiritual Boards, Khakimov is not directly inspired by theorists such as Dugin, he declares Tatarstan to be a "bridge between civilizations" or a cultural crossroads. Thus "we need jadidism because it draws on the values of the West and the East in equal measure."[80] This entirely rhetorical claim about the possibility of combining "Eastern" and "Western" elements, defined (if at all) from an essentialist perspective, is fully in line with the Eurasianist tradition of combining an acceptance of technological modernity with strong nationalism. Moreover, Khakimov has repeatedly referred to Gumilëv and seems to accept his terminology, for example, when he writes that "the ethnos carries a biological energy and obeys different laws than social processes."[81]

Nevertheless, the Russian Eurasianists vehemently criticize Tatarstan's Eurasianist strategy. Dugin in particular believes that President Shaimiev actually seeks to weaken the Russian state, hoping that Tatarstan will gain independence in the long term. Dugin thinks that Tatarstan would not hesitate to support U.S. geopolitics against a Eurasian great power. The Tatar political game is indeed ambiguous, and Shaimiev has never concealed that the long-term interests of his republic are more important to him than those of the Russian Federation. In the first half of the 1990s, he was faced with an outspoken nationalist movement recruited among Tatar intellectuals; but today the nationalists are marginalized in public life in Tatarstan and have partly adopted Islamic slogans.[82] The president's intermediate position seems to have been politically more successful over the past fifteen years. It has secured Tatarstan a privileged status and a stable international reputation. Eurasianism is a useful narrative means for highlighting the purported national distinctiveness of the Tatars, although in fact they are sociologically indistinguishable from other Russian citizens.

In the first half of the 1990s, non-Russian Eurasianism had other supporters; the Congress of the Turkic Peoples of Russia, for example, chose it as its main ideology, arguing that, with 14 million Russian and 40 million former Soviet citizens, the Turkic peoples had to be the Russians' first-choice partner.[83] The Congress called for Turkic unity and proposed thinking about the role Turkic politicians could one day play in Russia: "The Congress of Turkic Peoples is called upon to play a substantial positive role

. . . in preserving the unity of the Russian state."[84] Moreover, Tatarstan is not the only ethnic republic of the Russian Federation that is able to draw on the simultaneously external and internal positions with regard to Russian identity that finds its expression in non-Russian Eurasianism. The same goes for Bashkortostan, which, in 2000, hosted one of the big annual Eurasianist conferences.[85] There are also local versions of Eurasianism in the republics of Altai, Tuva, Buriatia, Kalmykia, and Yakutia-Sakha, each of which sees itself as being at the "center" of Eurasia and at the "juncture" of Slavic and Asian culture, while at the same time referring to specific motifs of regional history and to the heroes of national eposes.[86]

For example, Mikhail E. Nikolaev, president of Yakutia-Sakha from 1992 to 2002, claims that the Sakha people belonged to the Uighur Khanate, which he maintains was the cradle of the first Eurasian empire, extending from Manchuria to the Bosphorus well before the time of Genghis Khan.[87] This type of argument, where a historical legitimation is combined with a geographic definition, seems to be a typical feature of Eurasianism. Yakut Eurasianism has survived Nikolaev's departure. In 2004, the minister of culture, Andrei Borisov, a member of the Supreme Council of Dugin's International Eurasianist Movement, was instrumental in adapting Dugin's Eurasianism to a Yakutian context. He is the rector of the Institute of Arctic Studies (Arkticheskii Gosudarstvennyi Institut Kul'tury i Iskusstva), created in 2000, which, as he explains, "does not study geography or the climate. It studies the arctic spirit, the subtle energies of the High North,"[88] Yakutia being the centerpiece of the hyperborean continent called Arctogaia. In November 2004, Borisov organized Dugin's visit to Iakutsk, where he was officially welcomed by Prime Minister E. Borisov and Vice President A. Akimov.

Yakutian Eurasianism has two tasks: to show Moscow that reinforcing the Russian state requires respect for the regions; and to present Yakutia-Sakha as a locomotive for Siberia and the Russian Far East. Yakutia-Sakha is the region's largest republic; it is rich in mineral resources; and it symbolizes the junction between the economic interests of Siberia's Russians and the northern peoples' striving for autonomy. Yakutia-Sakha, the argument goes, represents Russia's presence in the world's economically most dynamic area, the Asia-Pacific zone. This non-Russian Eurasianist strategy uses narrative techniques and virtual economic stimuli to present itself as part of regions such as the Far East, whose geographical distance from Moscow is seen as a guarantee of autonomy: Siberia could well do without Moscow, but not vice versa. Thus Andrei Krivoshapkin and Sviatoslav Mikhailov,

Dugin's local disciples, call upon Russia to become aware of its Eurasian-ist heritage in Siberia: "Therefore, if Russia wants to heed Trubetzkoy's precept and rebuild Genghis Khan's empire, then it will obtain the full support of common people in Yakutia. This would signify a return to time-proven traditions dating back thousands of years, when the people lived in harmony not only with themselves but also with their natural environment."[89]

Conclusions

Non-Russian Eurasianism differs from the Russian version on several points. It naturally gives pride of place to the Turkic and/or Muslim peoples, presented as the pivot of Eurasia. In this view, the Russian people are European and partly alien to Eurasia, as opposed to the Turkic peoples, who are considered to better illustrate the great meeting between Europe and Asia. Russia is no longer understood as a great power but as the most backward part of Europe, by contrast with the dynamism of the Far East and China, with whom Turkic speakers are said to have closer links *by essence.* This opens the door to a kind of blackmail inside the Russian Federation: Russia will only regain its geopolitical position by becoming a Eurasian power, but it will only gain access to Eurasia by acknowledging the Turkic peoples and emphasizing their role. Russia is thus asked to represent itself, at least in part, as a Turkic and Muslim state, if it wants to avoid implosion, preserve its hold on the "near abroad," and be recognized as the leader of the Asian and Middle Eastern countries that, to all Eurasianists, are natural allies against Europe.

Thus non-Russian Eurasianism skillfully exploits Russia's stereotypical fears of losing its great-power status and seeing its national identity destroyed by the dynamic demographic development of Muslims. Unlike Russian Eurasianism, the pivotal role claimed by the Turkic Muslims has not, at least so far, been coupled with messianic or universalist ambitions; their Eurasianism is intended for domestic consumption, perhaps destined to become one of the ideological frameworks allowing non-Russians to express themselves in the Russian Federation or even to "take power" within regional administrations.

The proponents of this form of Eurasianism have two objectives: to assert themselves against Moscow; and to occupy a hegemonic position in their own respective regions: Tatarstan in the Volga-Ural zone, Yakutia-Sakha in Siberia and the Far East, the Turkic speakers as a whole as Russia's only organized national minority, and the like. The Eurasianist idea is just what all these actors "need"; it allows them to develop an identity that, on the one hand, upholds the right to differ, Islam, national traditions, and therefore autonomy, and that, on the other hand, implies no political risks. In being very loyal toward Russia, the adherents of non-Russian Eurasianism are not separatist (at least for the time being); they are merely trying to create a conscious minority identity inside Russia. Unlike the intellectual and sometimes mystical Eurasianism of Gumilëv, Panarin, or Dugin, this is a less theoretical and more pragmatic Eurasianism, centered on the search for a political, economic, and symbolic balance between center and periphery.

Chapter 6

Neo-Eurasianism in Kazakhstan and Turkey

The Russian Eurasianists often perceive non-Russian Eurasianism as a form of disloyal competition. They are unwilling to abandon "their" discourse to others and lose control over its long-term implications. From being an exclusively Russocentric ideology, Eurasianism has turned into a mode of expression for non-Russians, including newly independent nationalities such as the Kazakhs. The concept of "Eurasia" has outgrown its original intellectual framework, informing new and more general geopolitical conceptions as far afield as Turkey, as documented by the emergence of Turkish Eurasianism. The minorities of the former Russian Empire use the term "Eurasia" to envision an *internal* transformation of the country. Classical pan-Turkism, by contrast, implied Russia's all-out retreat from, or at least loss of standing in, Turkic lands. The reemergence of Eurasianism in Russia and the increasing use of the term "Avrasya" in Turkey, however, establish a new ideological balance. The implication is that Russia and Turkey are no longer competing for the mythical territory of Inner Asia—which both Eurasianists and pan-Turkists claim as their people's ancestral homeland—but are Eurasian allies. Only Eurasia, the argument goes, can bring the two countries together and transform their status as Europe's "periphery" into an identity-building and political framework that would allow them to triumph over the West and control the Turkic-speaking world.

Kazakhstan: Eurasianism in Power

Non-Russian Eurasianism exhibits great ideological diversity. Tatarstan's Eurasianism is only one of the existing types. The case of Kazakhstan il-

171

lustrates a second kind of non-Russian Eurasianism, one that is more ideological and more nationalist and emulates the Russian model. The case of
Kazakhstan is special among attempts to reclaim Eurasianism for non-
Russians—first of all because Kazakhstan is an independent republic rather
than a region of the Russian Federation, but also because it is the only Central Asian state to have paid attention to this issue, which leaves, for example, Uzbekistan or Tajikistan indifferent. Despite repeatedly criticizing
Russian Eurasianism for its nationalist implications, Kazakh Eurasianism
has also gradually come to resemble traditional Kazakh nationalism as the
state and its leader, Nursultan Nazarbaev, have embraced more radical views
on national identity. "Eurasianist" Kazakh nationalism has several embodiments: a literary tradition introduced by Olzhas Suleimenov; a highly
pragmatic variety used by the presidential administration; and a type of Eurasianist rhetoric that merely masks a much more traditional view of the nation and its right to exist, and mentions Russia only in the negative.[1]

The Literary Tradition: Olzhas Suleimenov

Independent Kazakhstan prides itself on having produced the first non-
Russian variety of Eurasianism in the work of the great Kazakh poet Olzhas
Suleimenov, who offered a positive reading of the Turkic peoples' role in
Russian history. Born in 1936, Suleimenov was one of the main representatives of Soviet Kazakh culture from the 1960s onward. A Russian-
language writer and poet, but also a historian, he expressed Kazakh nationalism within the framework then set by "peoples' friendship," which
implied the superiority of the Russian "big brother." As a member of the
Communist Party, Suleimenov joined his republic's Central Committee in
the 1970s and was named president of the Union of Writers of Kazakhstan
in 1983. He was an important public figure in Soviet academic life.

In 1989, Suleimenov was elected deputy of the Supreme Soviet of the
USSR and started a political career as leader of the Nevada-Semipalatinsk
ecological movement, which was instrumental in bringing about the closure
of the nuclear testing ground in Kazakhstan. After 1991, he kept his status
as an official representative of Kazakh culture, but he was marginalized
politically; having been a potential competitor to President Nazarbaev in
the first years of independence, when he directed the People's Congress
(Narodnyi Kongress Kazakhstana), he was discreetly removed from the political elite by being appointed ambassador to Rome and permanent representative to UNESCO. In the 2000s, he has continued to seek shelter in a

diplomatic and cultural role, which enables him to remain a popular figure without having to stand up against Nazarbaev's authoritarianism. However, he is not unequivocally resigned to this role, and continues to elaborate new ideological guidelines for contemporary Kazakh nationalism.

As early as the 1970s, Suleimenov tried to rehabilitate Turkic nationalism in the Soviet Union; his book *Az i Ia,* published in 60,000 copies in 1975, unleashed a heated debate. First, in December 1975, the book was vehemently criticized by the Russian nationalist journal *Molodaia Gvardiia.* The author of the article, Apollon Kuz'min, who had also spoken out against Lev Gumilëv, accused the author of hostility toward the Russians, Turkic nationalism, and pro-Zionism. After another attack in a different nationalist journal, *Russkaia literatura,* the debate reached the culture subdepartment of the Central Committee's ideology department. In February 1976, it forced Suleimenov to explain himself to the Academy of Sciences, which condemned his writings. The director of the publishing house was fired, and Suleimenov's publications as well as books that quoted him were withdrawn from bookstores and libraries. For several years, he could only publish poetry. He was instructed to write a self-critical letter, published in *Kazakhstanskaia pravda* on March 19, 1977, in which he acknowledged his errors and historical inaccuracies, but refused to repudiate his conclusions. Remaining in a semidissident position until perestroika, *Az i Ia* was a refutation of the official view of the Turkic peoples' place in history. One of its aims was to denounce Soviet Orientalism and, more generally, Russian historiography, much of which, Suleimenov argues, is based on a denial of antiquity to those peoples.[2] *Az i Ia* was the first instance of "inverted" Eurasianism. It no longer aimed to demonstrate Russia's mastery over its fate and its openness toward the East. On the contrary, it argued that Russia culturally became part of the steppe, and that in order to survive it had no historical choice but to become more Turkic.

In the 1970s, both supporters and opponents perceived the book as a work of historiography, even though Suleimenov's adversaries questioned its scientific worth. Yet it clearly seems to have been influenced by the linguist Nikolai Marr (1864–1934) and the poet Velimir Khlebnikov (1885–1922). An aesthetic reading of this prima facie historical work thus seems to be called for. The literary historian Harsha Ram has even proposed interpreting the book as a work of literature, suggesting that the confusion of genres—poetry, history, and linguistics—was intentional: Suleimenov needed the metaphor of *Az i Ia* in order to elaborate a new science of language. The title of the book may be read as the Russian term for "Asia"

(*Aziia*), but it also stands for the first letter of the Old Slavonic alphabet and the last letter of the modern Russian alphabet, which, in addition, mean "I," respectively, in the two languages. This pun introduces the two chapters of the book, the first of which is devoted to the Russian/Slavic world and the second, directed against Indo-European linguistics. Thus, for Harsha Ram, the book's title signifies both "the Slavs and the Turks" and "me and I" and is a subtle synonym for "Eurasia."[3]

The first part of the book is devoted to the famous *Lay of Igor's Host,* a medieval Russian text supposed to have been written in the twelfth century that recounts the defeat of Prince Igor of Novgorod at the hands of the Polovtsians, and contains numerous appeals for political unity addressed to the Russian principalities of the time. The original manuscript, discovered at the end of the eighteenth century, perished in the Burning of Moscow in 1812, and hence could not be dated using modern techniques. Although its authenticity was corroborated by Soviet historiography, it remains highly contested; in fact, the document is very probably a forgery, perhaps written in the fourteenth century. Because of its appeals for Russian unity, the *Lay of Igor's Host* remains central to Russian nationalism. This is why Suleime-nov mounts a frontal attack on this monument of literature to support his case against Russia and his acculturation thesis. Though he does believe in the manuscript's historical authenticity, he proposes an iconoclastic inter-pretation that stands in stark contrast with the Russian nationalist reading. The text's numerous stylistic and lexical borrowings from Turkic lan-guages, Suleimenov argues, show that the political and economic elites of the time were bilingual and that there was an ethnic and cultural symbiosis between the Slavs and the Turkic peoples.[4] He considers this as proof of an early fusion between Kievan Rus' and the Steppe; the Turks, he argues, built the political and military structure of the first Russian state. The famous Polovtsian incursions into Kievan territory, though much decried in me-dieval Slavic chronicles, had merely been a response to a demand from the Russian princes. Only the peoples of the steppe could defend Russia, and, indirectly, Europe, from the Mongol invasion and the onslaught of Islam.

The second part of the book is a more poetic reflection on the Turkic peo-ples' place in the world and their universality. Once more, it is through lin-guistics, and more precisely etymology, that Suleimenov seeks to rehabili-tate Turkology by endowing the Turkic peoples with a prestigious ancestry. They are presented as worthy heirs to the ancient Eastern civilizations, who belonged to the magnificent culture of Sumer and, because of their cultural closeness to the Scythians, were some of the first "state-builders" on Eurasian territory. Since Kazakhstan's independence, Suleimenov has pursued the Sumerian line of argument he first elaborated in the 1970s. His latest books, *The Language of Writing* (1998), *The Turks in Prehistory* (2002), and *Intersecting Parallel Lines* (2002), advance new etymological arguments in support of the claim that Sumerian and Etruscan were Turkic languages.[5]

Suleimenov denounces the Eurocentrism of Soviet scholarship, but he seems to be entirely ignorant of structuralism and unaware of any links between languages other than genetic ones. Thus the Kazakh writer contributes to a rehabilitation of linguistic theories that date back to the early nineteenth century, drawing on a current of Romanticism that sought to appropriate the prestige of the ancient languages through philology and the study of sonorities. Yet despite his fervent Kazakh nationalism, Suleimenov does not share other Eurasianist authors' fascination for the original Altaic cradle of the Turks and their links with the Mongols. Imbued as he is with classical culture, his historical writings are focused on the Mediterranean; for him, Turkic grandeur can only be confirmed by Mesopotamian civilizations whose legacy is also important for the West.

Thus Suleimenov's Eurasianism is a poetic and intimate one, reflecting his literary talent and style. Though it does have distinctive aspects, it also shares a number of features with traditional Russian forms of Eurasianism: a predilection for remote periods of history, an interest in the Ancient East in preference to the Greco-Roman world, special attention to etymology and similarities of sound, a study of the past aimed at finding portents of a glorious and universal future, the use of biological metaphors, and the idea that peoples are living persons. On this last point, Suleimenov has obviously been influenced by Gumilëv. The Kazakh writer has always been candid about his admiration for Gumilëv's role in the milieu of the *shestidesiatniki*, the 1960s liberals who, in the wake of de-Stalinization, challenged the Soviet ideological stranglehold on arts and letters.[6] This awareness of Gumilëv's original contribution to Soviet scholarship seems to go back to a friendship between Gumilëv and Suleimenov's father formed in the labor camps.[7]

Today, Suleimenov believes that independent Kazakhstan illustrates the principles of multiethnicity, tolerance, and diversity that are characteristic of Eurasia; the country has become such an intercultural blend of Kazakhs, Russians, and other minorities, Suleimenov argues, that the titular Kazakhs can no longer define their identity without taking into account the European borrowings that gave them access to the world at large.[8] The tradition started by Suleimenov is being used by both the political authorities and also by intellectuals. Whereas in Tatarstan, Eurasianism is presented as a mode of

176 CHAPTER 6

Orthodox-Muslim relations, the religious syncretism of Kazakh Eurasian-ism has a larger scope, embracing all the religions that have ever (co)ex-isted in the steppe. For example, the Kazakh Eurasianists make a great deal of archaeological traces of Nestorian Christianity, Zoroastrianism, Bud-dhism, and Shamanism, trying to go beyond the classic Orthodox-Islamic dualism.

Murat Auezov, the son of the famous Kazakh writer Mukhtar Auezov (1897–1961),[9] is one of the representatives of this current. For him, Eura-sia is the axis of world history, the cradle of the greatest religions born in the first millennium BCE—Confucianism and Taoism, Buddhism, and Zoroastrianism—and has even influenced Ancient Greece and the pre-Christian Semites. The nomadic tribes of Central Asia thus played a special role in awakening the consciousness of sedentary peoples, and an aware-ness of that fact must "become our national pride."[10] Thus many Kaza-khstani texts on Eurasia diverge from the classical definition of the concept as given by the interwar Eurasianists, turning it into a form of universality. Revealingly, B. Tashenov claims that "Eurasianism was not born in the 1920s or during the colonial period; it was born with humanity. . . . Eurasianism helped humanity to become aware of itself as one whole."[11]

This religious syncretism is an affirmation of the supposed universalism of Kazakh Eurasianism, presented as a philosophy of the world. In this view, Eurasianism is no longer a geographic notion but a way of life, a mode of meeting between the peoples and religions of the Old Continent. It is no longer limited to the search for a dialogue between West and East but paves the way for humankind's development in the postmodern age. This is clearly expressed by Beibut Mamraev, former vice president of the Institute of Literature of the Academy of Sciences: "It seems to me that contempo-rary Eurasianism must not define itself merely as the unity of Eurasian space itself. The idea of Eurasianism is supraethnic and suprapolitical; it is fully in tune with the idea of the unity of all cultures of the world, where each culture, independent of how many people belong to it and how it expresses itself concretely and spiritually, is part of the global mosaic."[12]

Eurasianism as a State Ideology

Beyond this literary tradition, which has great symbolic importance but a limited social impact, Eurasianism, in Kazakhstan, is entirely associated with President Nazarbaev's regime. Even when Eurasianism first reemerged immediately after the disappearance of the USSR, it did not meet with unanimous acceptance. Some intellectuals denounced it as a rhetorical illusion intended to mask the country's ethnic polarization. The opposition intellectual and politician Nurbulat Masanov (1954–2006) called Kazakhstan a "state of ethnic apartheid,"[13] which continues the Soviet system of ethnic classification, using a segregationist nomenclature to fix identities. Indeed, Eurasianism may be considered the newspeak of independent Kazakhstan in terms of nationalities policy, and the country's main Eurasianist publications are very clearly in the hands of people close to the president.

Nazarbaev proposed a Union of Eurasian States as early as 1994. It was to have supranational bodies and replace the ineffective Commonwealth of Independent States with a new post-Soviet economic and political space, free of communist ideology. Nazarbaev's project spelled out the union's mode of functioning in detail: a referendum on membership of the union in every candidate country; Russian as the working language; a consultative council for each of various sectors of the economy; simplified procedures for changes of citizenship between member states; a rotating presidency; supranational bodies, including a consultative parliament; a new common currency; a capital (Nazarbaev proposed Kazan or Samara); and the like.[14] The project was of course never implemented; at the time, it met with a rather disapproving response both in Boris Yeltsin's Russia and in neighboring countries, which were then busy trying to build new alliances and move away from their former Soviet compatriots.

Nevertheless, throughout the 1990s, Kazakhstan and its president constantly stood out on the post-Soviet scene by dint of their commitment to rapprochement between the Soviet successor states. Several economic and customs treaties were signed, mainly between Russia, Belarus, Ukraine, and Kazakhstan; but Nazarbaev's greatest victory was the creation, on October 10, 2000, of the Eurasian Economic Community (Evraziiskoe Ekonomicheskoe Soobshchestvo, or EvrazES), including Russia, Belarus, Kazakhstan, Kyrgyzstan, and Tajikistan, which were later joined by Uzbekistan.[15] The EvrazES plans to establish a customs union between its members and, in the long run, to build a common market.[16] Thus Nazarbaev embodies a pragmatic, economically based Eurasianism, whose integrationist ideas are popular among those who have suffered from the breakdown of links between the former Soviet republics. He is supported by several associations for the advancement of the Eurasian idea and by some economic circles.[17] The Kazakhstan Year in Russia in 2003 and the Russia Year in Kazakhstan in 2004 spawned a plethora of official publications in Almaty and Astana on the reinforcement of relations between the two countries and their commitment to a common destiny.

Nazarbaev also regularly makes Eurasianist speeches at the Lev N. Gumilëv Eurasianist University in Astana, brandished as an example of Kazakhstan's integrationist goodwill, but also of the institutionalization of Eurasianism as the official ideology of independent Kazakhstan. This new university, founded in 1996 by presidential decree, is in fact the city's former Pedagogical Institute, now rebranded as an elite institution. The president gave his blessing to the proposal to name the new university after Gumilëv; just as in Tatarstan, the Kazakhstani authorities fully subscribe to a positive view of Gumilëv's legacy. During celebrations of ten years of independence held at the university in 2001, the great Kyrgyz writer Chingiz Aitmatov welcomed Kazakhstan's Eurasianism and the choice of name for the university, which he said was a confirmation of Kazakhstan's status as the epicenter of Eurasia.[18]

Nazarbaev created a Eurasianist Center at the university from scratch, charging it with formulating the distinctive features of Kazakhstan's ideology and differentiating it from its Russian "competitors." The center organizes several annual conferences on Eurasianism, and the president of the republic opens the plenary sessions in person. Each year the fall semester starts with lectures on Eurasianism and Gumilëv's work. The university's rector, Sarsengali Abdymanapov, sees himself as one of the main champions of Eurasianism (as well as Tengrism). On September 27, 2004, he created an Institute for Scholarly Research on Eurasianism at the university. The founding decree stipulates that the institute's goal is "to define a conception of Eurasianism that would respond to Kazakhstan's national interests; to develop a geopolitical methodology for the historical, socioeconomic, and ideological interpretation of the development of contemporary civilization; and to advise state, educational, and academic organizations on Eurasianism."[19]

Although Gumilëv University theoretically has a regional ambition, its stated objectives reveal the strictly national scope of this variety of Kazakh Eurasianism. Its activities are divided into several branches: the first branch, humanities and social sciences, is limited to a folkloristic study of national traditions; the second branch covers economic topics (energy strategy, transportation networks, and the unification of customs and financial systems); the third branch concerns security; the fourth branch focuses on the study of religions; and the fifth branch covers political studies, with several key topics, such as globalization and the analysis of the ideas of President Nazarbaev. The university's clear Kazakhcentrism and lack of interest in other so-called Eurasian peoples indicate that the Kazakh Eurasianists seek to elaborate an ideology that would be peculiar to their own country or at least to the Turkic world and allow them to avoid taking a stand on Russia.

The vast majority of Kazakh Eurasianists reject the Russocentric ideas of 1920s Eurasianism and, for some, what they call "Soviet Eurasianism," that is, Moscow's nationalities policy, which, they argue, was aimed at leveling national differences. They all condemn the fascistic tendencies of Neo-Eurasianists such as Aleksandr Dugin, and several critical articles in Kazakhstani academic periodicals criticize this "revival of Russian messianism and imperialism."[20] However, though Dugin was openly criticized by the Eurasianist Center in Astana in the late 1990s, perceptions have evolved rapidly since 2002. His increasing public respectability, the creation of the Evraziia Party, and his own support for Kazakhstani-style pragmatic economic Eurasianism seem to have facilitated a reconciliation with the Kazakh Eurasianists, or more precisely made them aware of a number of common interests.

In 2004, Dugin published a book glorifying President Nazarbaev; naturally, this contributed to his rehabilitation in the Kazakhstani media. He organized a tour to present his book in several Kazakhstani cities and at the Academy of Sciences; was invited to air his views in a show on the Rakhat television channel (which belongs to Nazarbaev's daughter Dariga Nazarbaeva); and widely publicized his meeting with the Kazakh members of the International Eurasianist Movement, including Gani Kasymov, the leader of the small Party of Patriots of Kazakhstan. On April 2, 2004, Dugin was even received, with great pomp, at a conference organized at Gumilëv University by the Ministry of Education and the presidential administration, along with many high-ranking officials. In the mid-1990s, President Nazarbaev was funding Eduard Bagramov's journal *Evraziia;* now he seems to have found common ground with Dugin. Not only has Dugin managed to establish himself on the Kazakhstani scene as he did in Russia by monopolizing Eurasianism; he has also succeeded in seducing the Kazakhstani administration by bracketing out his esoteric and Traditionalist ideas and giving prominence to a view of Eurasianism as an economic model for post-Soviet integration.[21]

Despite Dugin's success in Astana, many official documents very clearly state that Nazarbaev's Eurasianism must be considered the third and final stage in the development of that ideology; after the interwar movement and

180

Gumilëv, the Kazakh president, they say, has established a definitive understanding of Eurasia, finally abandoning political philosophy to start implementing Eurasianist ideas in practice.[22] Nevertheless, official Kazakhstani Eurasianism cannot be interpreted exclusively as a foreign policy strategy and a doctrine of economic realism favorable to the preservation of privileged relations with the former Soviet republics and especially with Russia.

Kazakhstani Eurasianism also has a domestic aspect, which concerns the ethnic balance within the country. Nazarbaev was overtly nostalgic for the USSR in the first years of independence, curtailing any strong expression of Kazakh nationalism; yet in the second half of the 1990s, he clarified his previously ambiguous stance on this question. Indeed, Nazarbaev could not leave the issue of Kazakhness to his nationalist political opponents. He was therefore forced to tone down his statements on the country's civic identity and the importance of the Russian language; to avoid losing political clout, he had to present himself both as the president of all Kazakhstanis *and* that of the Kazakhs only.[23] Thus Kazakhstani Eurasianism changed considerably during the 1990s, particularly in its stance toward the local Russians. It originally took a positive view of colonization as an intensive interaction bringing European culture to the Kazakhs through the Russians and thereby giving meaning to the idea of Eurasia. Since the end of the 1990s, however, Kazakh Eurasianism has abandoned this rhetoric, instead taking up the most classic arguments of Kazakh nationalism. Thus the historical works on the country's place in Eurasia published in Kazakhstan have very little to say about colonization, except to denounce it as a "colonial takeover,"[24] and prefer to dwell on the existence of numerous Kazakh proto-states several centuries before the Russian conquest.

The authors of these books make a number of claims about the Russian impact on Kazakhstan: the Russian presence shattered Kazakh unity by reinforcing the Horde system; Tsarism offered no assistance to the Kazakhs in their struggle against the Jungars; Russia destabilized all of Eurasia by obliterating its centerpiece, the Kazakh state; the Russian peasants who settled in the steppes learned everything from the nomads without giving anything in return except for the destruction of traditional lifestyles. A key notion in this denunciation of Russian colonization is the classic nationalist idea that historians need to reveal "true" dates and borders. Thus, to highlight the long Kazakh resistance to the Russian invasion, the Eurasianist historians try to extend their people's history back in time, and its virtual territory into Siberia. According to them, the Kazakhs' centuries-old struggle for independence began not in the eighteenth century but in 1585, with the clashes between the Cossack Yermak and the khan of Siberia, Kuchum, along the River Irtysh: "With Kuchum begins the Kazakh people's struggle for liberation against Russian conquest."[25] Thus Kazakh Eurasianism fully fits into the current post-Soviet fashion for nationalist historiography, and it seems incapable of proposing a different interpretation of colonial history, one that would be less centered on conflict and victimhood.

The popular reception of the ruling circles' Eurasianist ideology is difficult to gauge because of a lack of serious sociological studies. A fraction of the population seems to be favorable to a Kazakhization of the state and opposed to the idea of a civic Kazakhstani identity, where the Kazakh nation would be an element among others. Nor does the Russian minority (one-third of the population, according to the 1999 census) seem to be very receptive to Nazarbaev's official Eurasianism, though for exactly opposite reasons: The Slavs react as minorities in a now-alien state and perceive Eurasianism as the newspeak of a regime that otherwise discreetly supports the country's Kazakhization.[26] By contrast, the political and cultural representatives of the other minorities often speak out in favor of official Eurasianism, endorsing officially sanctioned multiculturalism. This difference in attitudes between the Russians and the other minority groups is partly due to their different treatment by the state.

The most revealing example of this differentiated policy and Eurasianism's ambiguous implementation seems to be the Assembly of Peoples (Assambleia Narodov Kazakhstana), often presented, in very Soviet terms, as the "laboratory of peoples' friendship." Gumilëv University's Eurasianist Center is dubbed "the scientific base of the Assembly,"[27] which in turn is charged with fleshing out the official ideological directives coming from Astana. The relationship between these two institutions could of course be seen the other way round; the Eurasianist Center would then appear to provide theoretical legitimacy to the Assembly and to the new state's nationalities policy. Created by decree on March 1, 1995, and not mentioned in the constitution, the Assembly is directed by the president of the republic on the basis of a supposed "people's will." Although it is merely a consultative body, the Assembly has initiated two referendums, one on extending the presidential term of office and the other on the new constitution.

In fact, this official body aims to drown the Russian problem in a folkloristic and apolitical view of all the nationalities living in Kazakhstan. Its 300 members, appointed by the president, are supposed to represent all the national minorities' republican-level cultural centers. However, the representation of the various nationalities is not proportional to their share in the population. The Assembly includes 26 percent Kazakhs; 15 percent Russians; 6.5 percent each Koreans, Germans, and Tatars; and smaller proportions of the other minorities. The overrepresentation of the minorities, including those who number only a few thousand, in this body as well as in regional assemblies may be interpreted as an official attempt to avoid Russian-Kazakh polarization. Kazakhstan's legislation grants priority to the titular nationality and recognizes numerous specific minority rights (preferential quotas in universities and the administration, etc.). The Russians, however, fit none of these categories; they are not considered "titular," yet they are too numerous to be a simple minority among others. Whereas the minorities ask for, and receive, cultural and linguistic rights, the Russians demand more political concessions and meet with refusal.

The Assembly's propaganda work *The Warmth of the Kazakhstani Soil,* written by the deputy Oleg Dymov, acknowledges that the Assembly "supports . . . Nazarbaev's nationalities policy."[28] As a representative of official Eurasianism, Dymov highlights the great generosity of the Kazakhs who, despite their suffering, have always cordially welcomed other peoples on their soil: "The propensity for human concord lives in the blood of each people, but it is more highly developed among the Kazakhstanis. This is due to the generosity of the Kazakh land and to the very character of the Kazakh people."[29] Both the Assembly of Peoples and Nazarbaev constantly blur the distinction between "Kazakh" and "Kazakhstani." Dymov's book, which is intended to present all the country's nationalities, has almost nothing to say about the Russians. At the end of the book, the author speaks bluntly of "the Russian question, which does not really exist."[30] Thus Nazarbaev's statements on the nationalities question and their implementation through the Assembly of Peoples are a far cry from the Russophilia one might expect from a "Eurasianist" ideology.

Is Eurasianism a Variety of Kazakh Nationalism?

The presidential administration's version of Eurasianism is ambivalent on Russia and the Russians: Diplomatic, political, and economic relations with Russia are welcomed as a confirmation of Kazakhstan's "Eurasian" status, but this positive assessment does not extend to Russians living in Kazakhstan. Kazakh Eurasianism is Janus-faced; it presents a modernized version of old Soviet internationalism to the outside world, yet domestically it occupies the rhetorical niche of nationalism. This ambivalence, which it shares with Russian Eurasianism because it is rooted in the internal contradictions of the founding fathers' ideas, plays a fundamental role in the elaboration of post-Soviet Kazakh nationalism.

Although the idea of being at the "crossroads" of several worlds remains important in official Kazakhstani pronouncements, it becomes increasingly difficult to grasp who is at the crossroads of what. "The Kazakh steppe and towns were a crossroads of dialogue between the great cultures of the South and the East, the North and the West. . . . Kazakh culture, like that of our Turkic ancestors, has always been syncretic."[31] The idea is that the nomads, rather than the caravans traveling between sedentary cultures, linked the cultures of the old continent and transmitted ideas, knowledge, and products. Whereas in 1994, Nazarbaev meant all the post-Soviet republics when he wrote about "Eurasia," his programmatic text *Kazakhstan 2030,* published in 1997, focuses on his own nation. In his book *In the Stream of History,* published in 1999, the concept of a "bridge" between cultures is applied simultaneously to the Turkic world as a whole, the Kazakhstani state, and the Kazakh people. So is the Eurasianist idea meant to be implemented in a supranational union, separately in republics such as Russia or Kazakhstan, or in Kazakhstan as the sole embodiment of the Eurasian multicultural principle?

The president seems to favor the third solution in most of his statements. The Eurasian idea, he suggests, will come to fruition not from a meeting between different post-Soviet cultures but inside Kazakhstan: "Kazakhstan is a unique state in Asia where European and Asian roots are intertwined. . . . The combination of different cultures and traditions allows us to absorb what is best in European and Asian culture."[32] Thus, if post-Soviet Eurasia is slow in the making, Kazakhstan will have to build it on its own; because of its past and its national diversity, it is even more "predestined" than Russia to become the center of Eurasia. The former director of the Eurasianist Center in Astana, Seit Kaskabasov, buttresses the president's vision with more elaborate historical arguments. For example, he states that there are three Eurasianist states: Russia, Kazakhstan (both heirs to Genghis Khan's legacy), and Turkey (with its Byzantine and Ottoman heritage), which must jointly constitute a new trans-Eurasian axis. However, according to this logic, Kazakhstan gets pride of place because it is at the center of the center, a meeting place for the two other states. The "median people" the original Eurasianists struggled so much to find are not the Russians but the Turks. Islam has a better claim than Orthodoxy to representing Eurasian spirituality, because, Kaskabasov explained, it is the only really universalistic religion, having proven its ability to adapt to a diverse range of cultures.[33]

Moreover, even though Nazarbaev continues to present his country as multiethnic, he does not hesitate to define Kazakhstani identity as specifically Kazakh: "The culture of the Kazakhs must be seriously assimilated by the representatives of the other *ethnoi,* just as the Kazakhs, in their own time, earnestly studied Russian culture."[34] He thus holds on to the principle of one people being more equal than the others: "The Kazakhs must become a new big brother and a model for the minorities. Official Eurasianism does not really accept a republican identity, or rather reserves it for the Kazakh people. A legal, constitutional, and international basis has been given to the fact that all of Kazakhstan is the historic and ancestral territory of the Kazakh nation."[35] This desire to claim all of a territory for one's own nationality, based on a restrictive interpretation of the Western idea of the nation-state, also finds a linguistic expression; Nazarbaev affirms that knowledge of the titular language is the key element in national consolidation. The widespread use of Russian, he writes, is merely "the trace of a bygone linguistic era."[36]

Thus official discourse is enmeshed in its own contradictions: How can one call for the consolidation of the Kazakhstani political nation if this is based exclusively on Kazakh culture? Many Kazakh Eurasianists are content to equate Kazakhness with Kazakhstani identity, often using ethnicistic language, just as their Russian rivals regularly blur the distinctions between *russkii, rossiiskii,* and *evraziiskii.* Several scholars, especially V. Inushin, claim, for example, that the biophysicists have proven the existence "of a psycho-bio-energetic space or mental field created by the long coexistence and generational communication between the main *ethnoi* of Kazakhstan. The unity of the state is preserved thanks to the unconscious unity of numerous *ethnoi.*"[37] Similar ethnicistic pronouncements were made by the great man of official historiography, Manash E. Kozybaev (1931–2002), who claimed that there is a "Eurasian racial type," which he presented as having all the cultural features of Kazakhness.[38]

These authors also argue that the Kazakhs are the only ones to have a specifically Eurasian legitimacy that goes back to the first centuries CE. Thus, Kazakhstan, they say, is heir to the ninth-century Khazar Khaganate, which in turn was the capital of the first "Old Eurasia." Kazakh identity is said to be characterized by a spirit of tolerance and a rejection of extremism, as demonstrated historically by the conversion of the Khazar elites to

Judaism and the presence of Nestorian Christians.[39] The local Eurasianists also claim that Kazakhs were the first to have given a modern expression to the Eurasianist ideology; the Russified elites of the nineteenth century[40] and early-twentieth-century Kazakh symbolist poets first formulated the principles of Eurasianism, well before the Russians appropriated them in the 1920s. In the Soviet period, this idea only survived in the works of Suleimenov and Auezov, and thus the Kazakhs owe nothing to their Russian colleagues, who only rediscovered the term after the collapse of the USSR.

The increasing nationalist radicalism of Kazakh Eurasianism is even more evident among historians. The classic Eurasianist tradition, they argue, calls for a reassessment of the steppe and its nomadic culture; thus Kazakhstan carries "the destiny of the first nomadic continent at the center of Eurasia."[41] These views on the nomads, inspired by a *Naturphilosophie* that postulates the harmony of the whole and its parts, serve to affirm the existence of a national culture that lived in symbiosis with nature. However, the Kazakh Eurasianists reject theories from the history of migration according to which the Kazakhs only arrived in what is now Kazakhstan in the fifteenth century, although the idea of peoples migrating from East to West was one of the great Romantic themes of the original Eurasianism. Like their nationalist colleagues, they prefer to think that the nation has been living on its current territory throughout its long history: "The Kazakh *ethnos* has been taking shape for centuries. It did not arrive on this territory as a result of colonization or conquest. The Kazakhs' historical horizon goes back a very long time, well beyond the emergence of the first Kazakh khanate."[42]

Not only do these authors very clearly reject the Russian legacy; they also diverge from the original presuppositions on the common destiny of the Turkic peoples: "Contemporary Kazakhstan encapsulates the entire historical experience of the Turkic peoples, from the Iakuts to the Bulgars, from the Seljuks to the Ottomans."[43] This Kazakhcentric pan-Turkism allows them to insist on a supposed continuity of the Kazakh state since ancient times: the Eastern Scythians (Sakha), the Huns around Lake Balkhash, the Turkic Khaganate, feudal urban life in Semirech'e in the tenth and eleventh centuries, and the Desht-i-Kypchak, said to have extended from Korea to the Black Sea and from the Yenisei to the Iranian borders. This Turkic legacy, they maintain, has come to definitive bloom in post-1991 independent Kazakhstan: "The Kazakh people may be seen as heir to the historico-cultural legacy of all the Eurasian spaces."[44] The rationale is that "the Kazakhs, known as a people under the name of Kipchaks, were the core of all the Turkic tribes."[45]

This nationalist rhetoric borrows directly from Murad Adzhi, a best-selling essayist from Russia who has been regularly invited to Kazakhstan. Adzhi may be considered the main Turkic representative of the nativist theories that have developed across the former Soviet Union. Nazarbaev himself seems to like this kind of historical writing and regularly refers to Adzhi's books. In his book *In the Stream of History,* he maintains, following Adzhi, that the Scythians' Aryan culture developed in the Kazakh steppes, fostering agriculture, cattle breeding, and urban development. It was only with the arrival of the Mongols in the thirteenth century that the country turned nomadic, and the Kazakhs, until then belonging to the Indo-European type, acquired Mongoloid features.[46] In their search for an Aryan past, the Kazakh Eurasianists attach great value to the Iranic legacy of the steppes, associated with the Andronov culture, the Scythians, and the Alans. The Kazakh Eurasianists value sedentary cultures over nomadic ones; Kazakhstan, they claim, had a unique system of "steppe cities" such as Otrar, Taraz, and Turkistan. They consequently deny any Mongol influence and, a fortiori, the theory that the Kazakhs and Uzbeks only arrived in the region in the fifteenth century.

As a corollary of this special interest in the sedentary past, Kazakh Eurasianism stresses the country's Muslim character and its links with the sedentary culture of Turkistan, now incarnated by neighboring Uzbekistan. For example, Nazarbaev likes to recall the global significance of Al-Farabi, Al-Khorezmi, Al-Biruni, Mahmud Kashgari, and Yusuf Balasaguni,[47] and especially of Ahmed Yassavi, the "prophet of the Muslim religion in Kazakhstan,"[48] whose 1,500th anniversary was officially celebrated in the city of Turkistan in 2000. Finally, the Kazakh Eurasianists try to reclaim moments in national history that are difficult to square with the original Eurasianist ideals; for example, they see themselves as heirs to the early-twentieth-century nationalist historians who were members of Alash Orda, bracketing out their pan-Turkism and pan-Islamism.[49] Thus they seem to leave behind Eurasianism's traditional Russocentrism; though Valikhanov and Abai are still celebrated for their openness to European cultures, the emerging national pantheon also includes new, more clearly Central Asian and Muslim figures. This view of Kazakh identity partly conflicts with the traditional Eurasianist principles: Islam and sedentariness are valued over nomadism and shamanism; Russian colonization is virulently criticized and no longer understood as an openness to the European world but as a dark era of violence and "genocide"; and the Eurasianist idea is seen as having found its sole expression in the Kazakh people, rather than in its interaction with Russia. The Kazakh Eurasianists' historical nationalism thus makes them hard to distinguish from their other nationalist colleagues, whom one should expect they would oppose. This blurred distinction indicates the extent to which Eurasianism is above all a means to bolster the standing of one's own nation.

For more than a decade, non-Russians in the Russian Federation have been criticizing the revival of Russian Eurasianism as a new form of imperialism and an attempt to turn Russia's national diversity exclusively to the profit of the "ethnic" Russians. However, since the late 1990s, Kazakh Eurasianism, which shares this critical view, has become as nationalistic as its Russian equivalent, despite an initially more ecumenical approach, for example, in the writings of Olzhas Suleimenov. Its advocates, including both President Nazarbaev and academics trying to legitimate Eurasianism as official Kazakhstani thinking, have, in a sense, adopted the form but not the content of Eurasianism and continue to advance arguments derived from vintage Kazakh nationalism. Though Kazakh Eurasianism is less known than its Russian equivalent, it offers an unexpected insight into the fundamental ambiguities of Eurasianism; Eurasianism always speaks of a large "civilizational area" spanning the center of the Old Continent (with borders that may be more or less precise, and indeed often deliberately imprecise), but its objectives in fact remain inherently national in both the Russian and the Kazakh cases.

Thus Eurasianism seems to be a specific form of nationalism. It rejects any strictly ethnic definition of the nation and construes large regions with common cultural traits. Yet it nevertheless sees the people it represents as the first among equals, a view that is often tainted with messianism. For the time being, despite their disagreements, the non-Russian Neo-Eurasianists restrict themselves to a post-Soviet framework and are not attracted to pan-Turkism in the strict sense. On the contrary, Turkey is very often presented as a threat and a more bothersome and alien "big brother" than familiar Russia. Although the Turkish model is often ignored by the Eurasianists studied here, they will at some point need to take a stand on Turkish views of the entire Turkic world as a meeting place between East and West. The battle for the status of a crossroads between "Western" and "Eastern" culture thus no longer boils down to the old historical duel between Russia and Turkey. The forgotten Turkic and Central Asian Muslims, who had long remained passive objects of other people's theories, have entered the stage and made the picture more complex.

The Turkish Case: On the Confusion between Turkism, pan-Turkism, and Eurasianism

Just like the Russians, the Turks long defined themselves through their empire. The centrifugal tendencies of the turn of the twentieth century, when the old multiethnic empires were disintegrating into new nation-states, forced them to find a new national identity of their own, something that was often perceived as a constraint or defeat. The tensions between partisans of a restricted but ethnically homogeneous national identity and a more imperial model remained visible throughout the twentieth century, and the collapse of the Soviet Union rekindled the debate, both in Russia and in Turkey. Thus, in Turkey, no distinction is made between Turkic and Turkish "Turks,"[50] just as in Russian there is terminological confusion between the two words for "Russian," *russkii* and *rossiiskii,* in addition to *evraziiskii* in Eurasianist writings.

Common Ideological Roots: Romanticism and "Pan-" Ideologies

Eurasianism and Turkism both strive to reclaim Western discourse about their own group. The implicit aim is to transform theories that are often depreciatory into positive elements of collective identity. The two ideologies have common ideological roots: Johann Gottfried von Herder, German Romanticism, and *Naturphilosophie.* Together, these intellectual sources gave rise to two main archetypes: an affirmation of national distinctiveness aimed at creating a nation-state, and a desire for regional integration of all those one considers to be "one's own" (pan-Americanism, pan-Arabism, pan-Islamism, pan-Europeanism, etc.). The Slavophile idea that was at the origin of Eurasianism emerged in response to pan-Germanism; Turkism also originated from a complex relationship with Slavophilism, which was both a model and a competitor, and with the ambivalent views of Western Romantic Turkology.[51] Both Slavophiles and Turkists wanted to establish a nation-state, but they were also looking for a larger cultural unity. In different times and places and espoused by different writers, the two projects could either compete with or reinforce each other.

Hence the national questions that occupied Pan-Slavist, Crimean, Turkestani, and Ottoman intellectuals, especially after the Young Turk revolution of 1908, may not only be compared but also studied in their interaction and ideological interlacement. There were also personal links. The Tatar Ismail

Gaspraly or Gasprinskii, the founder of jadidism, was very heavily influenced by the Pan-Slavist theories that dominated the intellectual scene at the time of his studies at Kazan Pedagogical Institute and the Military Academy in Moscow.[52] He strove to transpose these Slavophile doctrines into a Muslim framework, arguing that the Turkic peoples must finally unite to renew Islam through contact with the West. Jadidism then spread to the Ottoman Empire: Gaspraly's newspaper *Tercüman* and all other jadidist publications were disseminated in Istanbul. Moreover, since the eighteenth century, the Ottoman capital regularly absorbed waves of Turkic émigrés fleeing from Russia, who contributed to enriching cultural contacts and transfers between the two empires.[53]

Thus Turkish nationalism emerged in the early twentieth century, at a time when that of Russia's Turkic peoples, especially the Tatars, was already much more pronounced. In the Ottoman Empire, identity was based solely on religion. The word "Turk" was pejorative, applied only to the peasant or nomadic masses of Anatolia. However, during Tanzimat (1839–78), the term "fatherland" (*vatan*) began to denote more than one's local homeland and came to span the entire empire. The elites of the time tried to foster a new patriotic feeling—Ottomanism—and the term "Turk" took on additional meanings.[54] However, the loss of the Balkan territories and the development of Arab and Kurdish nationalism presented a challenge to Ottomanism and contributed to spreading the idea that only the Turks were really loyal to the empire. Many Tatar or Azeri nationalists made significant contributions to the emergence of (pan-)Turkism, especially Ahmed Ağaoğlu (1869–1939) and Yusuf Akçura (1876–1935). The former, an Azeri by origin, played an important role in the creation of the journal of the Turkish Hearths, *Türk Yurdu,* and became a historian of the nationalist movement. The latter, a Tatar from Kazan, emigrated to the Ottoman Empire in 1904, advocated a political form of Turkish nationalism, and became one of the founders of the Turkish History Society (Türk Tarih Kurumu).

In 1921, the Tenth Congress of the (Bolshevik) Communist Party denounced pan-Turkism and pan-Islamism as "bourgeois."[55] The memory of jadidism, prohibited in the USSR from 1928, remained alive among Muslim émigrés in the Soviet Union's neighboring countries, such as Romania, Manchuria, Korea, and of course Turkey. Exile crystallized their pan-Turkism, and they founded several journals and organizations to express their hope of creating a supranational Turkic entity one day. These émigré organizations were also driven by anti-Sovietism, and some compromised themselves by collaborating with Nazi Germany in the hope of toppling the

Soviet regime, as was the case, for example, of the journal *Prométhée*, published in Poland from 1926 to 1938 with the support of Marshal Józef Piłsudski.[56]

Turkism, Turanism, Pan-Turkism, and Kemalism: Discursive Layers of Turkish Identity

Jadidist influence only really made itself felt in Turkey after the 1908 revolution brought the Committee of Union and Progress to power. The first nationalist organizations—the Association of the Turkish Homeland (Türk Yurdu Cemiyeti) and the Turkish Hearth (Türk Ocağı)—were founded, respectively, in 1911 and 1912.[57] The Young Turks' Turkism did not really aim to unify all the Turkophones; it merely wanted to create an ethnically homogeneous Turkish state, an idea already advanced by Yusuf Akçura as early as 1904. During World War I, the Hearths' interest in the "External Turks" (Dış Türkler) grew, and they combined their nationalism with Turanism, a vague and mythical view of Inner Asia that borrowed many of its Romantic features from nineteenth-century Turkology, especially in its Hungarian variety. However, these two currents quickly drifted apart and became antagonistic: Turanists sought to include Central Asia in the new Turkish identity in the making, while Anatolists wanted to exclude it, based on a more realistic view of politics. The border between these two conceptions was not watertight; for example, Ziya Gökalp (1875–1924), one of the most important literary nationalists, was both Ottomanist and pan-Turkist, while remaining attached to a conception of the nation derived from the Islamic *umma*.[58]

Yusuf Akçura developed a political variety of nationalism and strove for a kind of pan-Turkism that would be at the service of the state rather than opposing it. His pragmatic Turanism was limited to hopes for an alliance between the former Ottomans and the Tatars, and his paternalistic conceptions anticipated what was to become Kemalism.[59] Indeed, once the failure of Ottomanism's civic ideology had become evident, the nation could only be unified along linguistic and ethnic lines.[60] After Mustafa Kemal Atatürk came to power, the ideological construction of Kemalism only reinforced the areligious definition of the Turkish nation, proclaiming a kind of nationalism whose scope was limited to the territory of the Turkish Republic. Thus, after 1923, pan-Turkism was officially condemned, and nationalism became a state ideology, which concentrated on Turkicizing the minorities (Armenians, Greeks, and Kurds). The Hearths were forced to limit their activities to Turkey, and information about the "external Turks" gradually disappeared from their journal, *Türk Yurdu*.[61] The problem of ethnic affiliation was finally resolved in a subjective definition based on an attachment to Turkishness, without reference to language or religion.[62]

Thus interwar pan-Turkism remained profoundly marked by the Kemalist reforms. A the time, Turkey cultivated good relations with the USSR and, in consequence, curbed the Hearths' pan-Turkist ambitions, which Moscow perceived as a threat to the Soviet Union's socialist legitimacy.[63] Nevertheless, even while Kemalist Turkey was on good terms with Moscow, the pan-Turkist background of official historiography never disappeared, informing the idea that the new Turkish state was not the accomplishment but a point of departure for the liberation of all the Turkic peoples. Moreover, Atatürk wanted the state to be the prime producer of discourse on the nation, and he sought to silence all those who elaborated alternative histories. The Hearths were made to submit to the hardening political stance; in 1924, they were forced to abandon politics, and they declared their support for the new regime and Atatürk's Westernizing reforms. Nevertheless, they were subjected to party and state control in 1927 and were finally abolished (along with all other independent associations) in 1931. The preceding year, the Turkish Hearths' Commission for Historical Research published a 600-page book titled *An Outline of Turkish History*, carrying out what Étienne Copeaux has defined as a "coup d'état in history": the famous historical theses of Mustafa Kemal, which exalted the ancient past of the Turks in Inner Asia and the genius of the Turkish race, which he claimed had brought civilization to the other peoples, were rapidly raised to the rank of official historiography, and disseminated in history textbooks from 1931 onward.[64]

Although preference was given to a linguistic and ethnic definition of the nation, in the 1930s and 1940s this was supplemented with a racialist discourse that had not existed before, among either Tatars or Turkistanis.[65] After the Kemalist takeover of Turkism and its ambiguous references to physical anthropology, pan-Turkism swerved radically rightward, and the nationalists took over the topic of the Central Asian past. This racialist approach to the nation was especially popular among extreme right-wing milieus that advocated rapprochement with Nazi Germany. To them, as to many associations of Turkic-speaking émigrés from the former empire, the German attack on the USSR in June 1941 seemed to announce the long-awaited liberation of the "external Turks." However, the main leaders of the pan-Turkist extreme right were arrested in 1944 and faced a large-scale trial organized by the authorities, who were fearful of the Soviet advance in the

Balkans. This movement survived in Alparslan Türkeş's party and the Idealist Hearths (Ülkü Ocakları), for whom Turkishness was a mystic state linked to qualities seen as inherent in the Turkish race.

As Kemalism weakened, religion reemerged as a possible criterion for defining Turkishness. In the 1950s, Turkish nationalism began to highlight the monoreligious character of the Turkish nation, and official secularism was discreetly set aside. The year 1970 saw the creation of the Intellectuals' Hearth (Aydınlar Ocağı), followed by the Foundation for the Study of the Turkish World, two institutions that enabled the nationalists and religious activists to unite around a syncretistic view of identity. At the time, Westernization began to be seen as a threat to the country's identity and stability; these institutions contributed to the elaboration of a new layer of national discourse, called "Turko-Islamic synthesis"; the Turks, they argued, are predestined for Islam, because they have always been monotheists; they must reclaim Muhammad's religion from the Arabs. Thus religion began to be used to prop up the unity of the Turkish world.[66] After the military coup d'état of 1980, the Intellectuals' Hearth contributed to reinforcing the Kemalist cult while introducing the religious factor into political life. The Turko-Islamic synthesis became the country's new ideology and was introduced into history textbooks from 1986 onward.

Ibrahim Kafesoğlu (1914–84), the leader of the Intellectuals' Hearth, contributed to relaunching pan-Turkism as a form of cultural and religious, rather than ethnic or racial, solidarity with Turkic speakers. Pan-Turkism also made a comeback to the political stage. From the 1960s onward, the former army officer Alparslan Türkeş, the leader of the Nationalist Movement Party (Milliyetçi Hareket Partisi), developed the theme of Turkey's solidarity with the "external Turks." Although his party was not a mass movement, Türkeş managed to be appointed deputy prime minister in 1975–77 and to reintroduce pan-Turkism as one of the main currents of political life. Nevertheless, he did not draw unanimous support from those in pan-Turkist circles, who mostly diverted their attention from the Central Asian Turks to defend those living in Cyprus, Greece, Iran, Iraq, and Syria, a long-standing concern of official Turkish policy. In the 1980s, the journal *Türkiye,* which published articles by supporters of the Intellectuals' Hearth and the Foundation for the Study of the Turkish World, was at the forefront of an information campaign about the Central Asian republics.[67] It gradually managed to raise its public profile, although the ideological current it represented was clearly less popular than theories of "synthesis."

Eurasianism and Turkism: Conceptual Differences and Theoretical Common Ground

Eurasianism and Turkism have a number of common features, but there are also serious differences. First of all, Turkism is the official Turkish state discourse on the nation's identity, although it has gone through considerable changes since the early twentieth century. It has a much larger social base than Russian Eurasianism, which has never transcended the limits of a small circle of intellectuals. The ideological impact of official non-Russian varieties of Eurasianism—for example, in Kazakhstan—is incomparably smaller than Turkism's. Furthermore, as Copeaux has shown, historical Kemalism was paradoxical, claiming to Westernize the country while anchoring it in its Asian past, whereas Eurasianism, despite its modernism, never concealed its negative view of the Western experience and its refusal to emulate it.

Like many other ideologies of identity, Turkism mixes up the history of a territory with that of an ethnic group, a confusion that embraces the history of the Turkic peoples as well as that of Turkey, Anatolia, and Islam.[68] Eurasianism, similarly, uses historical, geopolitical, and ethnological arguments to demonstrate the existence of a supranational entity that is in fact inherently intertwined with Russianness: the exaltation of Eurasian diversity is a screen for Russian predominance and the underlying idea that the whole of Eurasian territory is the exclusive "place of expression" of the ethnic Russians. The Turkish historical narrative recounts the past of three geographical areas with which the Turkish citizen is supposed to identify: Inner Asia, the zone of Arab-Muslim expansion, and present-day Anatolia. Eurasianism also attempts a similar sleight of hand, albeit using a somewhat different type of argument. The territorial continuum of the former Russian Empire and/or the Soviet Union enables the Eurasianists to ignore the diversity of the different regions to which they refer and to pass seamlessly from the Kievan cradle to the legacy of Genghis Khan. The Russian political domination of this whole area, although it has now ended, helps affirm the unity of the different so-called Eurasian spaces a posteriori.

Moreover, the sacralization of Anatolia goes hand in hand with an attempt to legitimate national continuity and to prove that the Turks' presence on their current territory goes back a long way. They are said to possess unique qualities that are "naturally" conducive to state building, and the first peoples of Anatolia, especially the Hittites (which are, in different ways, seen as linked to the Sumerians and Etruscans) are retroactively considered

Turks. A similar mode of reclaiming the past is characteristic of Eurasianism; the Russian version indirectly considers the Scythians and other steppic peoples as proto-Russians, whereas non-Russian and especially Kazakh Eurasianism draws on Turkish ideas on the Hittite and Sumerian ancestry of the Turks. The theory of the solar language (according to which Turkish was once the single original language common to all of humankind),[69] which was popular in Turkey in the 1930s, has been disseminated in the former USSR by Murad Adzhi and is now particularly widespread in Kazakhstan. Likewise, the idea of a Turkish warrior race that was part of the prestigious Aryan world, another feature of interwar Turkish nationalism, has spread to the whole of post-Soviet Central Asia, even though, for linguistic reasons, most of its advocates have no access to the relevant Turkish texts and resort to prerevolutionary or Soviet sources.

Russian and non-Russian Eurasianists and Turkists also share a belief in their respective region's centrality and a redundant terminology of "crossroads" or "bridges" between Europe and Asia. However, official Turkish historiography has seriously dwelled on the cartographic aspect of this belief, unlike Neo-Eurasianism, except in Dugin's geopolitical variety. As Copeaux has shown, the maps included in school textbooks show Eurasia dominated by an enormous Turkic zone, which sidelines the other cultures both geographically and culturally: "Europe is cast out into the periphery, crushed by the continental mass; Africa is almost off the map; and the diagonals of the cartographic image cross near the Altai; around that center, a vast quadrilateral, stretching from the Aral Sea to Mongolia, demarcates the *anavatan,* the original hearth and the motherland."[70] All this is very similar to Russian representations of Eurasia, where the great historical centers of civilization, especially Europe, are perceived as being on the periphery of the former Russian Empire's continental mass. The two ideologies thus share a quantitative and territorial logic, which serves to cement tenuous cultural communities, between the Turks and the other Turkic peoples in one case, and the Turkic peoples and Slavs in the other.

On a historical level, both Eurasianism and Turkism have sought to rehabilitate the figures of Genghis Khan and Tamerlane; both have pursued the latter's ideal of an immense empire stretching from China to the Danube; and both have developed an almost mystical view of Turan as a place where humanity is regenerated and great world empires emerge. Both ideologies unconsciously treat Inner Asia as a consolation prize. The pan-Turkists needed a new empire in Central Asia to compensate for the loss of the Mediterranean Ottoman Empire. The émigré Eurasianists of the 1920s and the Neo-Eurasianists are shocked by the swift disappearance of the Tsarist Empire/Soviet Union, and they comfort themselves with the idea that the Russian Empire was natural and may thus be hoped to be reconstituted quickly; this is their way of dealing with the identity crisis that has set in after the loss of empire. Thus interest in things Turkic is a mere extension of Turkish nationalism, just like Eurasianism is but a reformulation of traditional Russian nationalism. Despite the apparent opposition between these theories and certain classic tenets of nationalism, and despite personal rivalries and clashes of ambition and influence between theorists, both pan-Turkism and Eurasianism are extensions (conscious or unconscious) of the national imagination of former imperial powers.

Enter Eurasia (Avrasya): The 1990s

The collapse of the Soviet Union contributed to rekindling Turkish interest in Central Asia beyond the restricted extreme-right pan-Turkist circles to which it had been confined since the age of Kemalism. Turkey's role in NATO has noticeably declined since the end of the Cold War, and its relations with the European Union are bumpy; hence, it has perceived the collapse of the Soviet Union as a chance to enhance its regional role.[71] The rediscovery of Central Asia enabled it to revive an assertive notion of Turkishness but also to highlight Turkey's role as a natural transit point for Central Asian oil and gas destined for the Mediterranean region. Although Ankara's new infatuation with Central Asia developed among politicians with no links to the extreme right, they have (often involuntarily) adopted certain features of pan-Turkist logic in presenting "Turkishness" as the natural link between these countries. Thus the idea of Turkic unity "from the Great Chinese Wall to the Adriatic," in President Süleyman Demirel's phrase, has become a recurrent cliché in Turkish public discourse. Moreover, Alparslan Türkeş accompanied Demirel on his first visit to Central Asia in April 1992; for external observers, this documented the ambiguity of Turkish policy toward the new states.

After the declarations of independence in the latter half of 1991, the Turkish authorities decided to place their policies toward the Central Asian states and Azerbaijan on a cultural footing. Turkey hoped to play an active role in Central Asian state building and export the Turkish model of democracy, secularism, and modernity that has ensured the country's success. However, the naive optimism of the first years led Turkey to commit strategic mistakes that went down very badly with the new Central Asian governments, which soon began to criticize the new "big brother."[72] But Ankara was not solely responsible for the profound deception that beset Turkish–Central Asian relations starting in the mid-1990s. The authoritarian backlash in the Central Asian states and their unwillingness to create effective regional bodies complicated matters a great deal. Pan-Turkism was relegated to dissident circles that were marginalized on the political and cultural scene.[73] Today, any reference to pan-Turkism is perceived in Central Asia as a challenge to the new states' legitimacy. Moreover, the two most authoritarian countries, Uzbekistan and Turkmenistan, have repeatedly limited cooperation with Turkey or even tried to end it altogether, accusing Ankara of welcoming political dissidents from their countries. Moreover, trade between Turkey and its Turkophone neighbors never reached expected levels; Russia remains by far the most important post-Soviet trading partner for the Central Asian states, but also for Turkey.[74]

The inter-Turkic congresses held since 1992 have all more or less failed to meet their objectives. The same goes for Ankara's policies of linguistic integration; proposals to introduce a common alphabet have failed to garner any serious support. The Central Asian countries preferred to preserve the logic of linguistic differentiation inherited from the Soviet era and, in some cases, Romanize their alphabets in their own way.[75] Efforts to translate works of literature between Turkic languages and to reinterpret common holidays such as Navruz have also had little impact in Central Asia. However, Turkey can be credited with several projects that have had a social and political impact. For example, the country introduced large-scale exchange programs for Central Asian students and founded Turkish university and schools in Central Asia;[76] and it has tried to participate in the modernization of telecommunications, used the Türksat satellite to launch two TV channels, Avrasya and TRT International (which actually have a limited audience in Central Asia),[77] and sought to create a platform for the dissemination of the Turkish model and local cooperation through the *Zaman* newspaper, published in Turkish, Russian, and Central Asian languages.

Many of these projects are managed by the Turkish International Cooperation Agency (Türkiye İşbirliği ve Kalkınma Ajansı), created in 1992 under the auspices of the Foreign Ministry and later subordinated directly to the prime minister. [78] This ambitious project, albeit now scaled down, has greatly contributed to spreading the term "Eurasia" on the Turkish public scene, especially through its publications: *Eurasian Files—Avrasya dosyası,* a bulletin created in 1994 that mainly offers economic information;

Eurasian Studies—Avrasya Etüdleri, a historical and geopolitical quarterly; and, since 2002, *Avrasya Bülteni.*[79] Thus the Turkish authorities have tried to link the new integrationist terminology with traditional Kemalist ideas on national identity, although this "return" to Central Asia (and to the Balkans) is in itself contrary to Atatürk's view of Turkish history as constantly moving westward. This type of Eurasianism has been on the rise in state bodies since 1998, when the European Union refused to consider Turkey's candidacy. Thus the political authorities' insistence on Turkey's role in Eurasia is two-pronged: in relations with Brussels, it serves to present Turkey as a bridge to the Middle East and Central Asia, but it may also be used to blackmail the European Union or even take revenge if it should definitively rejects Turkey's membership bid.

Thus the parallels between Turkish Avrasya and Russian Evraziia are tenuous, and there is no direct relationship between them, although many articles in *Avrasya dosyası* and *Avrasya Etüdleri* comment on the existence of the rival Russian term. Russian Eurasianism is often criticized; many authors present it as a new imperialist attempt to negate the identity of the non-Russian peoples of the former Soviet Union. Dugin is denounced as an extreme-right author, and the very idea of a Russian-controlled Eurasia is perceived as an improper form of competition with the Turkish model, presented as being more egalitarian. Nevertheless, while the term "pan-Turkism" still has a pejorative ring in Turkey, and authors who use it are automatically associated with the radical right, the idea of Eurasia has endowed certain pan-Turkist presuppositions with the status of "political correctness." The idea of Eurasia, which does not clearly imply the political unification of the Turkic peoples under Turkish domination, makes it possible to sidestep excessively political connotations and clears those who use it from any suspicion of imperialism toward the "Turkic brothers."[80]

However, this transformation is not simply a harmless terminological change. On the contrary, it expresses Turkish politicians' profound disillusionment with Central Asia.[81] Ankara has failed in its attempt to reclaim the idea of Turkic unity, having proven unable to provide a definition that would be pluralistic enough to spare Central Asian sensibilities in matters of national cultural heritage. But in the course of a decade, Turkey has managed to readjust its policies and objectives to more modest expectations. The term "Avrasya," which is less ambitious than the ideas of classic pan-Turkism, stresses the fact that relations have become more pragmatic and therefore calmer. Indeed, throughout the 1990s, the Avrasyan terminology of official diplomacy was taken up by pragmatic private actors—tourist and transportation firms, multinationals working with one or several former Soviet countries, and the like.

Russia and Turkey: Alliance or Competition for Control over the Concept of "Eurasia"?

In general, the Turkish idea of Avrasya seems less ideologically militant than its Russian equivalent; yet, since the early 2000s, the term has evolved in new directions. On the one hand, attempts are made to turn the two "Eurasias" into allies rather than competitors; on the other hand, there has been a Dugin-style ideologization of the term in response to American ascendancy. The question is whether the concurrence of these two modes of "Russification" of the Turkish Avrasya is incidental or whether they are two sides of the same coin. In the 1990s, articles on the Turkish variety of Avrasya systematically criticized Russian Eurasianism; in the early 2000s, the tone changed noticeably. Several Turkish advocates of a more militant Eurasianism called upon their fellow citizens to emulate Russia in developing a specifically Turkish interpretation of this concept.[82]

The term "Avrasya" first became popular with religious circles that were not previously linked to the pan-Turkist extreme right. Thus the modernizing Islamists around Recep Tayyip Erdoğan have been publishing the newspaper *Avrasya kuşağı* since 2000, and partisans of a Turko-Islamic synthesis edit *Yeni Avrasya*.[83] Fethullah Gülen's movement publishes Russian and Turkish versions of *DA Diyalog Avrasya*,[84] which has already carried several interviews with Dugin; other proponents of this movement include the Ahmed Yassavi Foundation and the Marmara Group Foundation, directed by Akkan Suver, which regularly organizes "Eurasian economic summits." In November 2006, this nongovernmental organization was the first to be accorded an observer member status by the Parliamentary Assembly of the Organization of the Black Sea Economic Cooperation. There are also two social-democratic papers, *Avrasya Etnografya Vakfi* and *Avrasya Dergisi,* as well as the above-mentioned *Zaman*.[85]

Dugin participated in this reorientation in his own way, managing to have his book on geopolitics translated into Turkish (and Arabic). The translation was published in Ankara in 2003 as *Rus Jeopolitiği Avrasyacı Yaklaşım* and seems to have gone down well with part of the Turkish military. There have been several conferences on Eurasianism that called for cooperation with Russia, all with participants from the military. The first visit of the International Eurasianist Movement took place in December 2003. It received quite widespread media coverage in Turkey, due in particular to the presence of the writer and journalist Atilla Ilhan (1925–2005). For many decades, Ilhan consistently wrote on the subject of a Turkish-Russian alliance, even during the Cold War. Through his books, he popularized the idea of a Turkish-Russian alliance preordained by geopolitics and insisted on "Eurasianist" heroes such as Ismail Gasprinsky, Sultan Galiev, and Mulla Nur Vakhidov.[86] This rapprochement between Dugin and Ilhan consequently helped Russian Eurasianism to reach some Turkish political and intellectual elites.

Dugin has been eager to profit as much as he can from these contacts with Turkey; in 2006, he published a book specifically devoted to what he now calls "the Moscow-Ankara axis."[87] The success of his theories in some Turkish circles also enabled him to organize a visit to Turkey in December 2004 to attend a big symposium featuring former president Süleyman Demirel and several high-ranking officers.[88] Demirel is known for his pan-Turkist leanings and his desire to forge closer relations with both Central Asia and Russia, and he seems to welcome the spread of Turkish-style Eurasianism. Dugin has also visited the Turkish Republic of Northern Cyprus to defend the cause of this self-proclaimed state recognized only by Turkey. He was given a high-profile reception; after inaugurating a branch of the International Eurasianist Movement, he met with the president of Northern Cyprus, Rauf Denktash, as well as Prime Minister Mehmet Ali Talat, who has since succeeded Denktash as president.

Although Dugin has made highly critical statements about Turkey as an Atlanticist outpost in the East, he has been systematically looking for allies in Turkey and ended up by finding a partner, the Turkish Workers' Party (Türkiye İşçi Partisi), led by Doğu Perinçek.[89] This small communist-leaning party quickly became attracted to Eurasianism; Perinçek took part in the founding congress of the International Eurasianist Movement in 2003 and was elected into its Supreme Council. The Workers' Party and its associated newspaper, *Aydınlık*,[90] have been supporting rapprochement between Turkey and Russia on the basis of a Eurasian alliance that would be opposed to the American model. Both Dugin and Perinçek believe that the Romanov and Ottoman empires competed for several centuries precisely because they had so much in common; both were situated on the "fault line" between Europe and Asia, between Orthodoxy and Islam. At the end of the nineteenth century, both countries experienced a rift between Westernized, European-oriented elites and traditional, Oriental masses, a division that they believe persists to this day. Only Eurasian conciliation can enable the two countries to overcome this internal and external cleavage and forge an alliance around the idea of the intrinsic unity of the Old Continent's median space and the need to resist "Atlanticist" cultural standardization.

The avowed aim of Dugin's supporters and their Turkish allies is to create an interparliamentary Eurasian assembly, including not only Russians and Turks but also representatives of Iran and the Arab states. This proposal was launched by Abdulkadir Ateş, the representative of the Turkish delegation to the Organization for Security and Cooperation in Europe. In Moscow, it was endorsed by the Turkish ambassador, Kurtuluş Taşkent, who met with Dugin,[91] as well as several officials at the Ministry of Foreign Affairs and the Federation Council. The project was also supported by a Moscow-based think tank, the Society for the Development of Intellectual Contacts between Russia and Turkey. In 2005, this was institutionalized into a Center for Russo-Turkish Research directed by the Russian ambassador to India, Albert Chernyshev, a member of the Supreme Council of the International Eurasianist Movement, and codirected by the director of the prestigious Institute of Asian and African Countries at Lomonossov University, M. S. Meier, who is also a member of the Eurasianist movement.[92] Once more, Dugin has used all the ingredients of his previous successes by combining the political networks of high-ranking officials at the main ministries (defense, interior, and foreign affairs) with the scientific legitimacy provided by academic circles, especially in Oriental studies.

Thus, Dugin is exporting to Turkey the strategy he applied, with some success, in Russia and Kazakhstan, which consists in bracketing out his Traditionalist views and publicly stressing a pragmatic conception of Eurasia, presented as the only plausible strategy of regional economic integration and resistance to the American model. Dugin presents himself as the leader of a respectable think tank serving the economic and political interests of his own country and Turkey. This definition of Eurasia enables him to attract a large spectrum of sympathizers who are unaware of the other ideological ingredients of Dugin's movements: businesspeople seeking to improve conditions for trade between the former USSR and Turkey; army officers deceived by Turkey's loss of clout in NATO and shocked by the way the country has been humiliated since the start of the Iraq war; politicians and intellectuals looking for a notion of Turkishness that would facilitate Ankara's rapprochement with the new Central Asian countries; and, on the other side of the political spectrum, left-wingers intent on converting communism into alter-globalism.

Turkey has developed a very pragmatic and instrumental interpretation of Eurasianism, one that is far less politicized than in Russia. The various types of Turkish Eurasianism sketched here differ on several crucial points: their view of Islam, of course, but also their stance on potential EU membership and actual membership in NATO, the very symbol of Atlanticism—two issues Russia does not need to confront. As Stéphane de Tapia notes, there are five different uses of the term "Avrasya": a purely commercial one among companies working with the post-Soviet states; a pragmatic one at state institutions, such as the Turkish International Cooperation Agency, that want to promote the Turkish model of secular democracy in the post-communist countries; references to Turkic brotherhood both by extreme-right pan-Turkic movements and by advocates of a Turko-Islamic union (with the latter stressing the Muslim background of Turkic unity more than the former); and, as the latest reinterpretation of the idea of Eurasia, an alter-globalist left in search of new allies.[93] Pan-Turkism enjoyed a brief spell of popularity among Turkish politicians in the first half of the 1990s, but afterward withdrew to its traditional social niche, the Turkish nationalist milieu. However, it runs as a consistent thread through official discourse on Turkey's national identity and its links with the ancestral Turkic homeland in Inner Asia. Eurasianism has further growth potential because of its intrinsic polysemy, which distinguishes it from pan-Turkism.

The Kazakhstani example clearly shows how pan-Turkic and Eurasianist ideas are perceived differently; pan-Turkism is seen as a new form of domination and an imposed, alien form of discourse on the Kazakhs, whereas Eurasianism is adapted and reformulated to serve specific nationalist objectives. Moreover, Eurasianism is understood as a symbol of a modern economy and identity (a cult of national diversity, differentialism, etc.), whereas pan-Turkism is criticized as being an outdated conception of the nation, one that has excessive religious implications and is out of tune with early-twenty-first-century economic and political realities. Finally, Eurasianism's appeal to both the left and the right wings of the political spectrum, be it in Russia or Turkey, as well as its flexible stance on economics and its alter- or antiglobalism, might well ensure it a greater life span than pan-Turkism. But this success comes at a price: With every new use, the term "Eurasia" loses more of its internal coherence.

Conclusion: The Evolution of the Eurasian(ist) Idea

The term "Eurasian" was invented in the nineteenth century to refer to children of mixed Euro-Asian couples, and it was later used to highlight the geological unity of the Old Continent. Thus, from the beginning, it stood for different modes of combination, alliance, or fusion between two entities seen as having a substantive reality: "Europe" and/or "the West," on the one hand (the difference has never really mattered to Eurasianist thinkers); and "Eurasia" and/or "Asia," on the other hand. In the interwar period, a group of Russian émigrés transformed the idea of *Eurasia* into an ideology called *Eurasianism:* a complex set of ideas that marshal a range of disciplines (history, linguistics, geography, economics, and ethnology) to demonstrate the naturalness of the entity designated as Eurasia. This intellectual construct has two levels: If Eurasia exists, merely awaiting self-revelation, this means, first, that the peoples inhabiting it have something in common and, second, that they ought to live together in a single state. The Eurasianist ideology is fundamentally statist; it is based on the presupposition that only a polity "conscious" of its own identity may aid the "realization" of the naturalness of Eurasia. In this respect, the culturalist theories of Eurasianism are intrinsically linked to a legitimation of empire and are part of a tradition of movements that, since the Slavophiles of the 1830s and 1840s, have been seeking to define how Russia is a distinctive, non-European civilization.

The ideology of Eurasianism took shape in the 1920s; in the following decade, however, the Eurasianist movement collapsed. The emergence of a bipolar world after 1945 made the idea of Eurasia recede into the background. Superpower rivalry in the Cold War admitted only two geopolitical entities, "East" and "West," which were later supplemented by the "developing world." The idea of Eurasia was smothered by that of the "Eastern bloc." To most people, the political makeup of the Soviet Union sufficed to explain why so many peoples across all of Northern Asia and Eastern Europe were united in a single state. However, this eclipse of the Eurasianist idea did not amount to its total disappearance. In the USSR itself, the discursive confrontation between different nationalisms revolved around the acceptance or explicit rejection of the idea of an intrinsic unity between the peoples of the Soviet Union, although the term "Eurasia" was not used, and the debate was dominated by Nikita Khrushchev's notion of a fusion (*sliianie*) of the Soviet peoples. Thus, in the 1970s and 1980s, both dissident and official academic historians hotly debated the respective contributions of the Russian and Turkic peoples to their common history. Russian nationalists and non-Russian thinkers clashed over whether it was "natural" for the two groups to have been historically part of the same state, and about their respective preeminence in each period of history.

When the Eastern bloc crumbled in 1989 and the Soviet Union fell in 1991, the worldviews of certain intellectual milieus on both sides of the Berlin Wall proved to be fertile ground for a rediscovery of the term "Eurasia." In the states of the former Soviet Union, culturalism quickly became one of the main ways of making sense of the USSR's unexpected collapse. Some academics, whose prestige and living conditions deteriorated in the space of a few years, shifted straight from economic to cultural determinism. This answered the need for new global explanatory schemes that would help in clarifying, accepting, and coming to terms with the changes of the past twenty years. The term "Eurasia" allowed them to transcend the Soviet experience and avoid grappling with its failure. To call the new states that emerged on the international scene in 1991 "post-Soviet" is merely to state the fact that for seventy years they were Soviet, although the term also carries a covert but universally understood reference to their earlier history as part of the Russian Empire, however long or short. To say that they are also "Eurasian" suggests that they are distinctive in a special way, defined by various currents of Eurasianism. Underlying the belief in this distinctiveness is the idea that the current political fragmentation will be short-lived, that it is destined to disappear because of Eurasia's "natural" unity.

The different currents of Russian Neo-Eurasianism that emerged in the 1990s all share a set of convictions: an assertion of the cultural unity and common historical destiny of the Russians and the non-Russian peoples of Russia, the former Soviet Union, or parts of Asia; the idea that the central geographical position of this space at the heart of the Old Continent inevitably entails an imperial form of political organization; a belief in the existence of cultural constants that explain the deeper meaning of contemporary political events; a rhetorical cult of national diversity combined with a dismissal of real autonomy for the minorities; and a rejection of Europe and/or the West and/or capitalism through criticism of "Atlanticist" domination, considered disastrous for the rest of humankind. With its insistence on the purported historical constants of religion and national mentalities, the idea of Eurasia thus makes it possible to dispense with reflection about the Soviet regime and, more generally, about the political and social changes of the twentieth century. It presupposes that the post-Soviet societies have no need for any collective work of memory, and thereby reveals the difficulty of leaving behind an ideology as schematic as that which was dominant in the USSR. The Russian theorists of Neo-Eurasianism perceive the term "Eurasia" only in its Russocentric aspects; for them, the past centuries have proven that Eurasia can only unite around Russia, as the *natural* power in Northern Asia.

The Russian Neo-Eurasianists focus on competing with the West and perceive the other "Eurasian" peoples as mere building blocks that bear out their theories; in the 1990s, however, they faced entirely unexpected competition from swiftly developing non-Russian varieties of Eurasianism. References to the entity of Eurasia became widespread among the so-called Turko-Muslim peoples—those most immediately concerned about the Orientalist rhetoric of Eurasianism—but also, in less theoretical varieties, across all of the former Soviet Union. The reality of "Eurasia" is all the more questionable because, even leaving aside its tumultuous history, this concept has now become a polysemous term with mutually contradictory political, economic, and cultural meanings. Today, the various Neo-Eurasianist doctrines are anything but united; Russian varieties of Eurasianism, with their insistence on the superiority of the Russians, are diametrically opposed to those elaborated in the "Turko-Muslim" states, which are in turn divided and compete with each other. Every group thinks of itself as the *bridge, crossroads,* or *heart* of Eurasia, a symbolic self-definition used to justify specific political, economic, and identity-building choices in a rapidly changing world where everyone scrambles for a "place in the sun."

The Unity of Eurasianism

Although the different currents of Eurasianism share many presuppositions, it is far from obvious that Eurasianism is a united movement. First of all, the original Eurasianism of the 1920s and 1930s must be distinguished from contemporary Neo-Eurasianism. Whatever one may think of the idea of "Eurasia," it is clear that Neo-Eurasianism has not attained the advanced theoretical level of its precursor, nor the recognized intellectual qualities of thinkers such as Prince Trubetzkoy, Roman Jakobson, George Vernadsky, or Pëtr Savitsky. Moreover, the specific historical context of Russian émigré life in the West and the social position of the Eurasianist movement within the émigré community have little in common with the sociological profile of Neo-Eurasianism. Just like "fascism" or "National Bolshevism," Eurasianism is a specific historical phenomenon that belongs to a particular period of the past. Concerning the present day, we can only speak of *Neo*-Eurasianism, and even that term has to be used sparingly, either when we wish to highlight that contemporary thinkers are claiming the Eurasianist heritage or in those cases where the parallels do look convincing. The point is not only to clarify intellectual lineages but also to avoid using an imprecise and pejorative vocabulary that would stand in the way of serious analysis.

Moreover, the Neo-Eurasianists themselves have a paradoxical attitude toward the founding fathers. Lev Gumilëv, Aleksandr Panarin, and Aleksandr Dugin, as well as the theorists of Turkic, Turkish, or Kazakhstani Eurasianism, sometimes speak harshly of the original Eurasianists and certainly do not see themselves as disciples of the old masters. On the contrary, their writings show that they consider them, at best, to have partially anticipated their own, much more accomplished ideas. We should also note several conceptual differences between Neo-Eurasianism and the original Eurasianism. First of all, Russian Neo-Eurasianism does not share the exaltation of the East that was so prominent with the original Eurasianists, who had been strongly marked by the Romantic Orientalism of the nineteenth century: The contemporary authors do not conceal their fear of Islamic fundamentalism; they feel no particular sympathy for the cultures of Central Asia and Mongolia; and they seem to have a preference for the Asia-Pacific region, which they consider a paragon of economic dynamism. Their views on history are less sophisticated than those of the original Eurasianists. Thus, for example, none of them has taken up Vernadsky's idea of "rhythms of Russian history" governing the dialectic between forest and steppe. Savitsky's thinking about Russia's *spatiality* as the primordial justification of Eurasian unity has found no real followers, nor has his interest in the idea of a geographical *symmetry* of empire and a *geometrical* rationality of Eurasian space.

Neo-Eurasianism also radicalized the paradoxical determinism of interwar Eurasianism, upsetting the balance that the founding fathers had struck between fatalism and liberty, between divine will and human choice. Thus every Neo-Eurasianist current has "specialized" the original ideas: Eurasianism has been turned into a current of geopolitics by Dugin, into a theory of humanity and nature by Gumilëv, into a strand of integrationist thinking by Nursultan Nazarbaev, and into a focus on the relations between Russia and its national minorities by the Turkic Eurasianists. The Neo-Eurasianists have thus largely ruined the equilibrium of interwar Eurasianism, which had successfully combined different perspectives on the world and different modes of expression of the Russian imperial cause. They have lost the literary quality of the first Eurasianists and have stressed the "scientific" character of writings on Eurasia. Consequently, Neo-Eurasianism has attracted fiercer criticism, for its proponents are less subtle in their statements of Eurasian unity and more radical in their claims to possessing a demonstrable "truth." Furthermore, Gumilëv has accorded fundamental importance to his theories of the *ethnos,* and Dugin to his "spiritual racism." This shows that Neo-Eurasianism has been profoundly modified by external influences, which have reinforced its ethnic determinism.

But this doctrinal and historical distinction between Eurasianism and Neo-Eurasianism leaves open the question of Neo-Eurasianism's internal unity. Is it a single intellectual current, or several mutually opposed movements? On the one hand, there is a notable lack of communal spirit among the Neo-Eurasianists, who most often present themselves as authors individually developing novel ideas that owe little to their predecessors or contemporaries. Each of them denigrates the other currents and refuses to be associated with them. On the other hand, it seems that since the creation of the Evraziia Party and, later, the International Eurasianist Movement, Dugin has succeeded, on a tactical level, in rallying around himself first Panarin and Eduard Bagramov, then the Kazakh ideologists at Gumilëv University (despite their earlier disagreements), and finally some of the Turkic Eurasianists. This does not mean that all these people share Dugin's theoretical predilections, for example, for Traditionalism or German occultism; but he has managed to discreetly set aside these aspects of his thought, and he publicly underscores a more pragmatic facet of Eurasianism. The call for a political and economic rapprochement between the countries of the former Soviet Union as well as between them and the neighboring Asian powers is Eurasianism's most attractive feature, the smallest common denominator for the highly disparate currents that constitute Neo-Eurasianism.

Nevertheless, the strictly Russian varieties of Neo-Eurasianism must be distinguished from "non-Russian" Neo-Eurasianism, be it *rossiiskii* (pertaining to the whole of Russia), Kazakhstani, or Turkish. Proponents of the latter often criticize the Russian Neo-Eurasianists for their Russocentrism or even imperialism and call their theories biased for failing to give full expression to Eurasia's multicultural character. This opposition between Russian and non-Russian Eurasianism cuts across another important distinction: that between different levels of theoretical sophistication. In this respect, there is a first group of authors (all of them Russian) whose thought cannot be reduced to Eurasianism. Gumilëv, Panarin, and Dugin have each produced a distinctive and complex body of work, supplementing Eurasianism with a so-called science of the *ethnos* (Gumilëv), an alter-globalist philosophy (Panarin), or esoteric doctrines (Dugin). By successfully embedding the Eurasianist theme in a larger set of arguments, they have ensured its success and broadened its spread, for its ideas are now integrated into more general views on the analysis of "ethnic processes," "Orthodox civilization," or Russia's mission in spearheading the rejection of American-type globalization. However, the other currents that call themselves Eurasianist do not necessarily accept all the teachings of these three authors; each draws on the pool of available arguments as it sees fit, leaving aside those layers of theory for which it has no use.

Beyond these highly theorized versions of Eurasianism, each embodied by a single author with a circle of disciples, there is a large breeding ground for Eurasianism that is receptive to highly diverse currents. Many Russian academics have, more or less successfully, picked up the terminology of Eurasianism. The same goes for the non-Russians, including Islamic parties that call themselves Eurasianist to circumvent the difficulties inherent in building a political platform on a religious basis; official Islamic institutions that are seeking to justify their minority status in a country often presented as fundamentally Orthodox; academic and ideological circles in the autonomous republics of the Russian Federation in search of a language that would allow them to praise their ethnic group's distinctiveness while flaunting their loyalty to Russia; official propaganda in multinational countries such as Kazakhstan, which hopes that its position "between empires" might foster rather than destroy its young statehood; and Turkish political circles persuaded that the idea of Avrasya might be a way out of the dilemma between membership in the European Union and an Islamization of Turkish identity.

Thus the diversity of Neo-Eurasianism is not simply ideological; it is also the result of the social and political diversity of its proponents as well as the widely differing contexts of their societies. Eurasianism may be the official stance of the authorities and specifically the presidential administration, as is the case in Nazarbaev's Kazakhstan, Mintimer Shaimiev's Tatarstan, and, to a lesser extent, Yakutia-Sakha and Kyrgyzstan. It may also emerge within official organizations whose relations with the powers that be are ambiguous, such as the representative institutions of the Muslim Turkic peoples, or of Islam more generally, inside the Russian Federation. It may be espoused by academics charged with formulating a new way of talking about the nation, such as Rafael Khakimov in Tatarstan or the scholars at the Eurasianist Center of Astana University, with more or less felicitous results depending on their degree of intellectual autonomy. In Russia in the 1990s, Eurasianism was also a discourse of political opposition, or even a form of dissidence. It was in those terms that Dugin and Panarin articulated their own attitude toward the liberalism and Westernism of Boris Yeltsin's regime. Due to the country's political evolution, the Neo-Eurasianists have now abandoned this dissident mindset, because the new patriotic ideology enables them to feel in tune with the authorities and society, even though their theories are not identical with the official ideology.

Thus, the milieus espousing Neo-Eurasianism—composed of academics and politicians—are socially similar yet claim to be representing different groups: writers and artists (the journals *Literaturnaia Evraziia* and *Evraziia*), think tanks speaking in the name of the ruling elites (Dugin), purportedly independent university circles (Panarin), the official authorities (Nazarbaev and Shaimiev), alter-globalist political parties (in Turkey), and the institutions and constituent regions of the Russian Federation (the Russian muftiates). They may be groupuscules (*Literaturnaia Evraziia* and *Evraziia*), academics of some institutional standing (Gumilëv and Panarin), a politicized intellectual movement (Dugin), or a state bureaucracy serving the Eurasianist ideology, as in Kazakhstan. This polymorphic character of Neo-Eurasianism is due to the variety of the political projects it serves. Thus the movement may assert that the unity of Eurasia will be the work of a single state (Russia, Kazakhstan, or Turkey), achieved through a political rearrangement of the formerly Soviet lands or through an alliance among different Eurasian and Asian countries; it may see either the Russians, the Kazakhs, the Turks, or a combination of them, as the symbolic embodiment of Eurasianness; it may stand for an opening to the Muslim world (for Russia) or signify access to Europe (for Kazakhstan); it may be seen as a path to global domination (for Dugin) or merely as a means of regulating the internal affairs of the Russian Federation (for the Turkic Muslims); and the like.

Organicism at the Service of Authoritarianism: "Revolution" or "Conservatism"?

To understand (Neo-)Eurasianism as a whole, we need to be aware of its organicist background. Much of Russian philosophy has been particularly receptive to the Romantic ideology of the nineteenth century, marked by the emergence of a universal biology studying processes that affect plants and animals as well as humans. The organicist metaphor is no simple rhetorical analogy; it has cognitive and normative functions, because it selects certain phenomena as scientifically relevant. It proposes an essentialist conception according to which every species is characterized by its essence, which is invariable and distinct from all other species. Thus life results from the *coherent* organization of a whole. All the Eurasianist theories likewise exalt totality; the different Eurasian cultures are invested with meaning by a unity that transcends them, just as the sciences are understood as being authentic only if they expose all human destiny in a synthetic manner.

This cult of totality is expressed primarily through what Panarin called "culturological transcendentalism": Because every civilization is the bearer of a parcel of divine truth, its disappearance would impoverish humanity. Gumilëv was the only Neo-Eurasianist to have relegated culture to the realm of the superficial; he openly despised the humanities and seems to have wanted to theorize totality through biology and genetics. The original Eurasianists, like all Romantics, were inspired by a certain form of naturalism; Gumilëv's biologism pushed this search for a total explanation of human nature to an extreme, reducing the history of humankind and its cultural diversity to a combination of biochemical energies. Whether they are biological or culturalist, the Eurasianist theories all submit humanity to a totality that transcends individual persons and to which they belong *by essence*. These theories are therefore conservative in that they teach that people can only fully realize their potential by respecting political, social, and cultural hierarchies. These hierarchies constitute a sort of superstructure where no element may be questioned without destabilizing the whole; for example, rejecting autocracy as the *natural* political system for Russia would be tantamount to negating Russia's national identity and Orthodox religion, and vice versa.

Although it shares these organicist traits with the ideas of the founding fathers, Neo-Eurasianism has none of the futuristic and revolutionary aspects of the original Eurasianism, which had been stimulated by the October Revolution and the idea that humanity can change the face of the Earth merely through the power of its will. Both movements emerged during moments of profound crisis for the Russian Empire (in 1917 and 1991, respectively), but Neo-Eurasianism is much more defeatist than its predecessor. Although both rely on the famous "decline of the West" theory, the original Eurasianism was optimistic in its belief that salvation will come from the non-Western world, whereas Neo-Eurasianism seems more uneasy about the future of humankind, worried as it is about the global situation in relation to ecology and nuclear conflict, and conscious of the divisions among the non-Western countries. Thus, if for the first Eurasianists the eschatological perspective guaranteed humanity's regeneration, for the Neo-Eurasianists it is a confirmation that humankind has developed out of control and may be on the verge of disappearance.

The first and second waves of Eurasianism must also be distinguished on the level of political theory. The first was clearly part of the so-called conservative revolutionary movements that developed in interwar Germany, France, and Italy. It shared fascism's determination to combine "left-wing" economic principles with "right-wing" political ideas and to regard nationalism not as a conservative factor but as the driving force of social modernization and a revolution in human nature. Thus it combined elements of conservatism and revolution that appear at first incompatible, and openly called for "revolutionary reaction," in Suvchinsky's formula.[1] As for Neo-Eurasianism, it does call for a third way, but this call has lost its revolutionary quality, except in Dugin's theories. The new third way is no longer the search for a middle ground between a market economy and interventionism, and between democracy and totalitarianism; instead, it serves to extol an authoritarian, paternalistic, and autocratic state, which would be able to prevent any radical attack on existing social reality and would provide all citizens with a conservative and therefore comforting ideology. Thus Neo-Eurasianism signals a profound disillusionment with modernity, born of the failure of both communism and the reforms of the 1990s, as well as a pessimistic outlook that was alien to the original Eurasianists. Among all the Neo-Eurasianist movements, only Dugin's may be exempted from this description; he is the only one to emulate the revolutionary spirit of the founding fathers, the only one to expect a cultural revolution and the emergence of a "New Man," and the only one to openly cultivate a provocative taste for combat, sex, and esotericism. In these respects, he is close to theories of conservative revolution and fascism, and distant from the other

Neo-Eurasianists with their striving for respectability and acceptable conduct, and their cult of established hierarchies.

Nationalism: Veiled or Openly Espoused?
The Cultural Racism of Eurasianism

Despite its strong conservatism, Neo-Eurasianism looks highly modern against the background of Russian nationalism as a whole. The movement is free of Tsarist leanings, a cult of the bygone peasant world, or excessive Slavophilia. It distances itself from the Soviet nostalgia of Gennady Ziuganov's Communist Party, condemns Vladimir Zhirinovsky's populist antics, and rejects the violent xenophobia of the skinhead movements and the small radical parties that inspire them. On the contrary, Neo-Eurasianism advocates a modernity that would be simultaneously authoritarian and republican, and a form of secularized theocracy. It sees itself as a serene and respectable nationalism: one that is in tune with modern society, technological development, and respect for global cultural and religious diversity, one that espouses a less nervous and more reasoned anti-Westernism than the other nationalist movements. As Dugin himself acknowledges, "to have any potential, a nationalist project must be intellectual, correct, and presentable. It must be an enlightened nationalism."[2]

Thus, in many ways, the Neo-Eurasianists occupy an ambiguous place within the nationalist spectrum. Some accuse them of wanting to sacrifice an exhausted Russia to the Turko-Muslim peoples. However, Russian nationalism is itself multifaceted; it is not limited to ethnocentric currents obsessed with the idea that the Russians had to pay their empire dearly and were robbed by the other peoples of the Soviet Union. There is also a strong current of Russian nationalism that remains loyal to the state, be it imperial or Soviet. Moreover, the distinction between an ethnocentric and an imperial strand of Russian nationalism is ultimately irrelevant, because all existing groups espouse a combination of the two. Thus, despite their apparent cult of diversity and calls for multiculturalism, the Neo-Eurasianists follow the founding fathers in exalting a "Russian Russia," an empire whose central linguistic, cultural, and religious features are those of the ethnic Russians. As Savitsky states, "The history of the expansion of the Russian state is to a large degree the history of the adaptation of the Russian people to its place-development, Eurasia, and of the adaptation of the entire Eurasian space to the economic and historical needs of the Russian people."[3] On this account, the smaller peoples of Eurasia are not mutually connected; they only have unidirectional links with Russia, the true and only matrix of Eurasia. The diversity may be Eurasian, but the totality remains strictly Russian. Thus (Neo-)Eurasianists are relativist in their attitude toward Europe, but universalistic toward their own internal Asia; they condemn nationalism whenever it impedes the assertion of Eurasian unity or Russian superiority, but they defend it whenever it is opposed to a West that, they believe, destroys every people's distinctive features.

The entirely rhetorical illusion of Eurasianism's opposition to nationalism is cultivated by both the movement's proponents and its opponents. It is also reinforced by the sophisticated culturalism of the Eurasianist doctrines, which superficially seem to condemn any feeling of national superiority and uphold the right to differ. Yet while they talk much about a symbiosis of cultures and religions, the theorists of Neo-Eurasianism often support a certain national "purity." Gumilëv openly calls for endogamy, even within each Eurasian people; Dugin classifies peoples by spiritual races; Panarin rejects the possibility of transcivilizational borrowings; and even Kazakhstani Eurasianism strives to develop a Kazakh identity that would be as little Russified as possible. This discursive ambiguity is one of the major features that Neo-Eurasianism shares with Western New Right theories, which call upon every people to preserve something like a national thesaurus and resist any cultural integration. These differentialist arguments are borrowed from ethnopluralist theories originally developed by the Western third-worldist left and appropriated by the New Right in the early 1980s.

This transition from "race" to "culture" made the assertion of differentialism possible. In the course of the nineteenth century and in the first half of the twentieth century, a racialized discourse on national specificity was widespread in all Western countries. In Russia, however, ever since the Slavophiles, thinkers who have tried to answer the so-called Russian question have written about the right to differ primarily in a culturalist vein. Nevertheless, although the Slavophile, Pan-Slavist, and (Neo-)Eurasianist definitions of the Russian nation are not based on racialist presuppositions, this does not mean that they do not uphold an idea of national superiority. Pierre-André Taguieff's analysis of racism sheds light on this ambiguous variety of nonracialist nationalism. According to him, classical racism, as it was formulated by its Western ideologists, gives pride of place to racial heredity in determining "fitness" and proposes a theory and practice of inequality and domination. There is, however, a different and much less known racism, which can be called differentialist. This variety is not interested in classifying races on a value scale; what counts is not their inequality but their incommensurability. Whereas classical racism is heterophobic, differentialist racism is heterophile, because it appreciates other cultures, but it is mixophobic, because it rejects the idea of miscegenation.

Taguieff's terminology, elaborated as part of the search for a definition of the New Right's neoracism, provides an indirect yet fundamental explanation of (Neo-)Eurasianism's distinctive features. Taguieff explains: "I distinguish between two types of racism as a form of ideological thought. One of them is universalist: It postulates the existence of a universal scale of values for the assessment of races and civilizations, which are classified as fit, less fit, or unfit, according to variable sets of criteria. The other is communitarian: It absolutizes group identity and is less focused on inequality than on incommunicability, incommensurability, and incomparability. It follows that mankind is broken up into closed wholes: The differentialist imperative demands that the community be preserved as it is, or purified. Inegalitarian racism is fundamentally obsessed with the loss of rank, the lowering of those who are superior; differentialist racism, by contrast, is obsessed with the loss of the group's own, with the disappearance of what is proper to each group."[4]

Thus, like their Slavophile and Pan-Slavist predecessors, but unlike Gumilëv, who has a distinctive position on this issue, the Eurasianists and Neo-Eurasianists are not racist, do not see cultures as hierarchically divided into "superior" and "inferior" ones, and do not believe that there are relevant genetic differences between people or nations. For them, peoples are not biological entities but cultural, religious, or territorial realities; history is the process of a realization of ideas, in the Hegelian sense, rather than a dark fight for survival between peoples. However, the rejection of cultural assimilation is an integral part of Russian nationalist culture. The love/hate relationship with the West is supplemented, to varying degrees, with a belief in irreducible national specificity, extreme relativism, cultural autarky, a religious or political messianism, and a xenophobic rejection of mixing and borrowing. However, this fear of symbiosis with the West—for all these theories clearly target the West—goes hand in hand with an acclamation of difference. Russian nationalism, and especially (Neo-)Eurasianism, thus seeks to legitimate itself through *heterophilia:* It wants all cultures to remain themselves in their incommensurability. The Romantic, Herderian influence is crucial; universalism emerges out of the concrete diversity of the world, rather than from the abstraction of humanity as being everywhere the same; it is by cultivating their specific features and by inviting others to cultivate theirs that the Russians would find their place in the world.

The strength of this differentialism shared by the Western New Right and (Neo-)Eurasianism lies in its avoidance of the issue of a hierarchy of peoples through the idea that every one of them is unique and must "remain itself." This belief in the impermeable nature of cultures has significant political consequences, because it rejects the logic of human rights in favor of the rights of peoples. In the name of this ethnopluralism, both Panarin and Dugin have adopted an ambiguous stance on the Jews, condemning them for trying to assimilate to the "Western" and "Eurasian" cultures but appreciating displays of Jewish particularism. Because the point, for them, is to avoid any crossover, they praise the most radical form of Zionism for enabling the Jews to put an end to miscegenation. Gumilëv is the only one not to take a nuanced view of this matter, for among Neo-Eurasianists he is the one least favorable to culturalist differentialism and most influenced by particularly rigid ethnicistic conceptions. Thus, for Gumilëv, "race" is replaced by *ethnos,* and for the others, by the notion of *culture,* also thought of as a natural and primordial whole that may not be adulterated. These doctrinal thinkers are thus as indebted to Julius Evola's "spiritual racism" as to certain contemporary alter-globalist theories, whose combination of right- and left-wing ideas suits the Neo-Eurasianists because they no longer believe in the binary left/right distinction and hope for a reshaping of political conflicts.

Science, Political Movement, or Think Tank?

On the basis of their holistic view of societies, the (Neo-)Eurasianists also challenge the democratic system: They believe that political parties split society instead of bonding it; and they believe that parliamentary games are superficial and offer no response to profound collective anxieties. This makes it difficult for them to define the status of their pronouncements. Do they want to be a school of scholarly thought whose objective would be to prove the existence of an entity named "Eurasia"? Do they think of themselves as a political party in search of a constituency? Or are they merely interested in influencing political and economic decisionmakers? All the (Neo-)Eurasianist movements are ambiguous in their attitude toward the "political," if this is understood as a public sphere where different modes of legitimacy are at work, be they electoral or dependent on other forms of social consensus. On several occasions, Eurasianists and Neo-Eurasianists have taken a stand on communism, the USSR, and the Soviet heritage, as well as on the constitutional regime that they believe would be best for their country. They have asserted their wish for public approval; they have claimed to represent their societies; and they often portray themselves as spokespeople for the silent masses who they maintain are in favor of preserving the political unity of the territory they call Eurasian. However, this auto-legitimation is unconvincing: Not only have the (Neo-)Eurasianists enjoyed highly limited organizational support, in the interwar period and since the 1990s; but even their own political ambitions are strongly qualified.

Indeed, they presuppose that the conquest of political power requires that they first capture cultural power. Thus elections are not really crucial. Like the Eurasianists of the 1920s, the Neo-Eurasianists attach less importance to the formal political game, which they see as a Western import of little relevance, than to their ideological entryism into state bodies: those of the Soviet Union and the Communist Party in the case of the earliest Eurasianists, and the presidential administration and central and regional authorities in the strategies of their successors. Thus (Neo-)Eurasianism is very clearly a Weltanschauung and does not, strictly speaking, belong to the domain of politics. It is no accident that it has developed in intellectual milieus who want to be recognized as "counsels to the prince" and within state bodies that care little for electoral representation. Even the two parties that, in 2001–3, claimed to be Eurasianist, developed Gramscian strategies, just as the original Eurasianists had hoped, in their time, to infiltrate the highest decision-making bodies without spreading their convictions more widely. Thus, in a certain way, just how representative (Neo-)Eurasianism is may be irrelevant; official acceptance of Eurasia as an enlarged geopolitical definition of Russia may well develop without any popular support, as long as the authorities espouse it.

The antidemocratic backlash in contemporary Russia seems to bear out this strategy. The institutionalization of various associations and lobbies signals a lack of interest in Western-style electoral games and a preference for a system partly reminiscent of the Soviet Union: Real political and economic issues are debated within state bodies, between different corporations that are more or less linked to the presidential administration, and inside a single party—formerly the Communist Party of the Soviet Union and now, increasingly, United Russia. The more and more monolithic character of the regime does not mean that there are no tensions; they simply no longer surface in public, being more and more restricted to the internal workings of the presidential administration and those institutions that have managed to tap into this body. This perfectly corresponds to the conception of politics espoused by Eurasianism since its inception, and its contemporary proponents are well versed in this mode of operating—much more so than in the unpredictable democratic game. Thus the strength of (Neo-) Eurasianism lies not in its impact on the electoral scene but in its ability to cater to the needs of a regime that seems to be looking for a new ideology.

The (Neo-)Eurasianists' desire to become the Kremlin's (or the new states') ideological gray eminences is linked to their search for scientific legitimacy. They all confuse academic research with political punditry, and they use their academic positions to legitimize pronouncements that actually belong to the domain of personal opinion rather than scholarly discourse validated by a community of peers. Their legitimacy is expressed in the language of religious truth just as much as that of scientific validity. Indeed (Neo-)Eurasianism sees itself as a hermeneutics: It interprets phenomena by considering them as signs, as symbols of something that transcends them. It is persuaded that the sciences necessarily converge and therefore calls for the creation of new disciplines to recover the lost unity of science. This is why both the founding fathers and contemporary writers, namely, Gumilëv, Panarin, and Dugin, try to establish the existence of such new disciplines: personology, geosophy, ethnosophy, and historiosophy in the 1920s, and science of the *ethnos*, geopolitics, global political prognostication, conflictology, culturology, and conspirology today. Herein lies one of the main contradictions of (Neo-)Eurasianism: On the one hand, the movement asserts that the phenomena it studies are natural; on the other hand, it considers it necessary to construct a discourse that would finally reveal Eurasia to itself.

"Eurasia" is rarely used as a neutral term. With a stroke of the pen, the ideological dimension of the *Soviet* past is wiped out, as are the aspects of the political construct known as the "West" that it reflected. If Eurasia is the geographic combination of Europe and Asia, then the "West," China, and all the countries of the Old Continent are also Eurasian; this may well be an interesting perspective, but it is not what is meant by those who use the concept. If Eurasia is only a part of the Old Continent, encompassing the countries at its "heart," then the term is exceedingly imprecise; where are the borders of Eurasia, and how can we define them without entering culturalist ground? If Eurasia is simply the territory of the old Russian Empire and/or the Soviet Union (i.e., the former minus Finland and Poland) and/or that of the current Commonwealth of Independent States (i.e., that minus the Baltic states), why do we need a new term in addition to those just listed?

The (Neo-)Eurasianist movement has constantly exploited these ambiguities: It has permanently oscillated between defining "Eurasia" as either the
space historically dominated by Russia or the whole of the Old Continent.
This subtext has served to discreetly affirm that Russia's calling is to dominate both these Eurasias.

However, despite the ideological commitments of Eurasianist theoreticians, the movement actually sought to deconstruct binary oppositions, like
that between the dynamism of Europe and the backwardness of Asia, and
was led to stop thinking of the West as the norm of development. It enables
theoreticians to decentralize the chief historical narrative, which until then
had been limited to Moscow and Saint Petersburg, and thereby to take into
account the multiplicity of regional identities. It underscores the territorial
factor, emphasizes the continuity of certain social phenomena beyond the
political ruptures of 1917 and 1991, and gives historical depth to contemporary globalization—which, as Marc von Hagen points out, only got under way with the birth of empires. As he explains, the idea of "Eurasia" goes
beyond both the dominant paradigms of Slavic studies, that of "Russia/Ori-
ent" and that of "Soviet Union/modernization"; it reveals that these two
paradigms are complementary rather than contradictory, and it enables theoreticians to take into account the *longue durée* of history and demographic,
economic, and cultural phenomena that are continental in scale.[5]

Is Eurasianism Relevant to Explanations
of Contemporary Geopolitical Change?

This concept of Eurasianism leaves open the question of Eurasia as a geopolitical reality. Many countries feel the need for multipolarity, seen as synonymous with equilibrium. So may Eurasia become a new eastern version
of the European Union, a group of states with equal rights striving for a
regional unity that would allow them to give expression to a specific worldview? This would require that several conditions be fulfilled: The members
of the Commonwealth of Independent States would have to overcome their
current conflicts; they would have to share a single conception of politics;
and this supranational construct would have to be such that the new states
do not perceive it as a return to Russian domination. This virtual Eurasia
would have to overcome two handicaps that the European Community
never faced: an internal colonial past, because all these states have been
dominated by Russia, whereas the Western countries exported their colo-

nialism out of Europe; and an imbalance of power, for whatever Russia's intentions, it would be difficult for it not to "crush" its smaller neighbors if all were to make decisions collectively.

Thus, one of the main challenges facing this virtual geopolitical Eurasia is to find what could unite the disunited post-Soviet states; in the 1990s, the general tendency across the whole region, after Gorbachevian liberalism, was toward tougher political regimes, a reinforcement of paternalistic states, and the emergence of ethnocracies. So the post-Soviet countries' "community of fate" seems questionable: What could they really want to share? Many of these societies are in the grip of nostalgia for the USSR, but this is not tantamount to a desire to turn back. The political elites have no interest in reconstituting any supranational entity. The Georgia-Ukraine-Azerbaijan-Moldova affiliation was the first prototype of an "anti-Russian Eurasia,"[6] and the geopolitical events after the September 11, 2001, terrorist attacks, which allowed the United States to install military bases at the heart of that region, created a breach in post-Soviet political unity. This breach is likely to widen now that the "colored revolutions" have enabled Georgia (in 2003), and Ukraine (in 2004) to move away from the old Russian center and become more openly pro-Western, although this geopolitical reversal did not signal profound political change or a return to the liberal principles prevalent during perestroika.

So what can Eurasia mean on a geopolitical level, if it is not an alliance of states willing to join forces with Russia against "American supremacy"? With the exception of the European Union, all attempts to elaborate a regional identity that rejects "American unipolarity" on the basis of, for example, pan-Asian, Eurasian, or Islamic unity often look like covers for clubs of authoritarian states. These states use the fashionable culturalist "right to differ" to refuse to move toward a democratic system, which they consider to be a covert version of Western neoimperialism. So is Eurasia destined to remain a group of states that wish to preserve a paternalistic hold on their societies, an area where ideocratic and autocratic conceptions of politics are dominant, Vladimir Putin's "vertical of power" being the first concrete implementation?

The solidarity between these authoritarian regimes is not only political but also economic and geopolitical; the reinforcement of strategic and security cooperation between the former Soviet republics, the increasing energy links between Russia and Asia, and the emergence of regional Russo-Chinese bodies such as the Shanghai Cooperation Organization suddenly seem to bear out the Neo-Eurasianist theories. The success of the Eurasian Economic Community, which recently swallowed the Central Asian Cooperation Organization and has facilitated Uzbekistan's return into the Russian-dominated Collective Security Treaty Organization of the Commonwealth of Independent States, seems to delineate a new "Eurasian" hard core encompassing the countries of Central Asia (with the exception of Turkmenistan, which remains isolated), Russia, Belarus, and Armenia. Will the pragmatic aspect of Neo-Eurasianism allow it to become the "politically correct" doctrine in political and military decisionmaking circles and in those sectors of business that seek to develop relations with Asia? In any case, given the attraction of the European Union for the Western margins of the former empire (Ukraine, Moldova, Belarus), the turmoil in the Middle East, and the growing power of China, it is unclear what future any "Eurasian" idea may have in the twenty-first century, because demographic developments are depleting the whole region.

Psychological Compensation or Part of a Global Phenomenon?

The much-invoked entity of Eurasia has remained elusive on a scientific level; in politics, its proponents have espoused authoritarian conceptions; and its geopolitical contours remain hazy at best. So is Eurasia destined to remain an intellectual construct? Indeed, the various Eurasianist doctrines do not correspond to a rational, "objective" logic; they must be studied as elements in the construction of identities and the invention of nations and be viewed in their historical context. As early as the eighteenth and nineteenth centuries, the terms North Asia, Turan or Turania, and Inner or High Asia had enabled Westerners to project their fantasies into this unknown space and endow the peoples inhabiting it with common cultural features. Even at the time, Russia's position with regard to that imaginary space was unclear. Today, across the non-Western world, Orientalist and reificationist theories elaborated in the West have been internalized and transformed by some of those targeted, for example, with the concept of Négritude in Sub-Saharan Africa. Russia has been both a colonial power in Asia and a state that has borrowed its intellectual framework from the West; and it has also seen its Eurasianist theories, which were originally Russocentric, appropriated by the non-Russian peoples of what is called Eurasia.

⁑ The decline of Marxism as a global explanatory scheme and what has been perceived as its political failure have facilitated the return of culturalism. The success of Samuel Huntington's book *The Clash of Civilizations* and the comeback of geopolitics are only the tip of the iceberg; with the intellectual retreat of Marxism, socioeconomic explanations seem to have been supplanted by the idea that only national identities, cultures, and religions can explain the world as it is today.[7] Thus the Balkan wars of the 1990s have been analyzed in a geoculturalist framework (as a resurgence of the historical and religious dividing line between the old Habsburg lands and the Ottoman-dominated part of the Balkans). The conflicts that are ripping the Middle East are often presented as being civilizational or religious wars, a struggle between "the great Satan" and the "axis of Evil." This ethnicist and culturalist interpretation of conflicts that are really about the ideological mastery of the world and about carving up the planet's wealth obviously gives legitimacy to the idea of Eurasia. The Neo-Eurasianists have been assiduous readers of *The Clash of Civilizations,* although they do not share its author's ideas that Eurasia is situated on an intercivilizational fault line and that Russia is directly threatened by the coming clash between the Orthodox and Islamic civilizations. They nevertheless support its two main tenets: that "civilizations" are the matrix of history, and that the new century will witness a confrontation between them. All they need to do is to shift the battle lines out of Eurasia; the clash will not take place between Orthodoxy and Islam, as the United States would have it, but between, on the one hand, a Eurasian civilization uniting Orthodoxy, traditional Islam, and Buddhism, and, on the other hand, a West that is both an ally and a victim of the Islamic fundamentalism it financed for decades.

Thus, in a way, the spread of Eurasianism across the former Soviet Union signals that this region is, albeit unwillingly, taking part in globalization. In both its real and imagined aspects, globalization is "internalized" by different societies and provokes reactions in every country. Never before, it seems, have there been as many identity-based reactions against what is seen as homogenization. The rise of protectionist or at least differentialist theories of identity across the world is also an (involuntary) form of the globalization of reactions against globalization. So is Eurasianism simply the Russian version of the great backlash against eighteenth-century theories of progress that is currently taking place in so many countries? Is it on a par with Islamism, the Christian fundamentalist and creationist worldview of American evangelical movements, and European calls for ethnic and religious communitarianism? Eurasianism uses the same doctrinal schemes as cultural fundamentalism, including the feeling that "culture" and "ethnos" are coextensive. Neo-Eurasianism confirms that the former Soviet Union is fully in tune with the major ideological developments taking place across the planet in the early twenty-first century.

Thus, Neo-Eurasianism is not simply a short-term psychological compensation for the disappearance of the Soviet Union, whose borders were considered to be those of the "real" Russia. By insisting that empire is the natural political form for Eurasia, its adherents hope to demonstrate that any secession is destined to fail, and the new states have no choice but to revert to a unified political entity. In this regard, Neo-Eurasianism, sometimes presented as being on the margins of classical Russian nationalism, is in a certain way at its heart: It claims that the collapse of the communist ideology does not signify the breakup of the country; maintains that Russia must, by nature, be a superpower; and expresses the sentiment of *hypertrophied identity* that the emergence of new borders has triggered among part of the post-Soviet elites. It thus proposes to synthesize all currents of Russian nationalism, bracketing out their disagreements. In refusing to distinguish between what is ethnically Russian, what pertains to Russia as a whole (*rossiiskii*), and what is Eurasian, Neo-Eurasianism openly espouses a position that the other movements merely imply.

In this respect, (Neo-)Eurasianism is a classic example of a flexible ideology. This explains its success, its diversity, and its breadth of coverage: It is a political doctrine in the strict sense of the word, a theory of nation and *ethnos,* an alter-globalist philosophy of history, a new pragmatic formulation of "Sovietism," a substitute for the global explanatory schemes of Marxism-Leninism, a set of expansionist geopolitical principles for Russia, and much else. The lack of a precise definition of "Eurasianism" makes it a catholic ideology, although its concept of "civilization" is only a euphemism for "nation" and "empire." For all the heterogeneity of Eurasianism, it is still possible to pin down its ideological matrix: restoration, a synthesis of anti-Western arguments, and a culturalist defense of political authoritarianism. Thus (Neo-)Eurasianism lives in the virtual world of a Eurasian identity that has always been more complex than the Eurasianists conceived and of a political unity that is no more. However, it is not only a political doctrine; it sees itself as the extension of the Russian imperial imagination, and it awkwardly formulates the "mental atlas" of citizens who consider themselves to have lost out in the changes that have taken place in this part of the world over the past twenty years. So is Eurasia a hyperbolic version of an alternative identity, the dream of a *different* Russia?

Having espoused a form of "spiritual opposition" to the liberal reforms of the 1990s for a decade, Neo-Eurasianism contributed to adjusting the rhetoric of Russia's elites to the expectations of large parts of Russian society. The derogation of parliamentarism and political parties, the brutal inequalities generated by the privatizations and the emergence of a new class of oligarchs, the humiliation due to the loss of superpower status, the disappointment with the West's behavior during the wars in the former Yugoslavia and in Chechnya, and Russians' disillusionment with the market economy following the crisis of the summer of 1998—all contributed to turning Eurasianism into a "politically correct" discourse. Like so many others, the Eurasianists want to put an end to the post-Soviet elites' mimicry of the West. They stress that Russia's interests do not automatically coincide with those of the West and that the failure of communism was the end of a European idea. Thus, Neo-Eurasianism is one of the elements of the nationalist mainstream that dominates the country today, with its tautological idea that Russia's distinctive feature is to be Russian. Neo-Eurasianism has not become the Kremlin's main ideology, but it has found its place within the new patriotic doctrine, whose exceedingly vague theoretical contours highlight the Putin regime's striving for social consensus: Cultural fundamentalism has become a way to avoid politics.

Notes

Notes to the Introduction

1. M. Laruelle, *L'Idéologie eurasiste russe ou comment penser l'empire* (Paris: L'Harmattan, 1999).

2. M. Laruelle, *Mythe aryen et rêve impérial dans la Russie du XIXe siècle,* preface by Pierre-André Taguieff (Paris: CNRS Éditions, 2005).

3. P. A. Chaadaev, "Filosoficheskie pis'ma k g-zhe . . . ," in *Sochineniia* (Moscow: Pravda, 1989), 508. (Here and throughout the book, an effort has been made to translate all Russian quotations from the Russian originals rather than the French translation. However, a few texts were not available to either the author or the translator at the time of translation, and these were translated from the French. Chaadaev's Letters, incidentally, were originally written in French.—translator's note.)

4. F. Dostoevsky, *Sobranie sochinenii v 15-i tomakh: Dnevnik pisatelia, 1881* (Moscow: Nauka, 1995), vol. 14, 509.

5. See S. Layton, *Russian Literature and Empire: Conquest of the Caucasus from Pushkin to Tolstoy* (Cambridge: Cambridge University Press, 1994).

6. See D. Schimmelpenninck van der Oye, *Toward the Rising Sun: Russian Ideologies of Empire and the Path to War with Japan* (Dekalb: Northern Illinois University Press, 2001).

7. His book—*The Three Worlds of the Asian-European Continent* (Tri mira aziisko-evropeiskogo materika), published in *Slavianskii sbornik* in 1892—spelled out the first vision of Russia as "Eur-Asia." He called for a reinterpretation of space, scorned the idea that Europe and Asia are divided by the Urals, and asserted the existence of three radically different spaces in the Old World: Europe, Russia, and Asia.

8. See M. Laruelle, "Existe-t-il des précurseurs au mouvement eurasiste? L'obsession russe pour l'Asie à la fin du XIXe siècle," *Revue des études slaves,* nos. 3–4 (2004): 437–54.

9. The term "Turanian" was especially widespread in the nineteenth century. It designated the Turkic peoples in their entirety, sometimes encompassing the Mongols and various peoples whose languages do not belong either to the Indo-European or the Semitic language families. See M. Laruelle, "La question du 'touranisme' des Russes: Con-

223

tribution à une histoire des échanges intellectuels Allemagne-France-Russie au XIXe siècle," *Cahiers du monde russe*, nos. 1–2 (2004): 241–65.

10. See D. Savelli, "L'Asiatisme dans la littérature et la pensée russes à la fin du XIXe siècle," doctoral dissertation, Université de Lille III, 1994.

11. V. Kozhinov, "Evraziistvo i sovremennost,'" *Liki Rossii*, no. 2 (1992), http://www.patriotica.ru/actual/stol_eurasia.html.

12. On Zhirinovsky, see E. Klepikova and V. Solov'ev, *Zhirinovsky: Russian Fascism and the Making of a Dictator* (Reading, Mass.: Addison-Wesley, 1995); A. J. Motyl, "Vladimir Zhirinovsky: A Man of His Times," *Harriman Review*, nos. 7–9 (1994): 11–18; and G. Frazer and G. Lancelle, *Absolute Zhirinovsky: A Transparent View of the Distinguished Russian Statesman* (New York: Penguin, 1994).

13. On the strategies of the CPRF, see L. March, *The Communist Party in Post-Soviet Russia* (Manchester: Manchester University Press, 2002).

14. G. Ziuganov, *Geografiia pobedy: Osnovy rossiiskoi geopolitiki* (Moscow: N.p., 1999).

15. V. Putin, "Rossiia: Novye vostochnye perspektivy," *Nezavisimaia gazeta*, November 14, 2000; republished by A. Dugin, *Evraziistvo: Teoriia i praktika* (Moscow: Arktogeia, 2001), 3–4.

16. This terminology is used, e.g., in P. Rangsimaporn, "Interpretations of Eurasianism: Justifying Russia's Role in East Asia," *Europe-Asia Studies* 58, no. 3 (2006): 371–89; M. Schmidt, "Is Putin Pursuing a Policy of Eurasianism?" *Demokratizatsiya* 13, no. 1 (2005): 87–99; and L. Tchantouridze, "Awakening of Spirits: Eurasianism and Geopolitics in the Foreign Policy of Russia," Ph.D. dissertation, Queen's University, Kingston, Canada, 2001.

17. Statement by Anatoly Chubais, an important figure in the first Yeltsin governments and current director of United Energy Systems, made in October 2003; http://newsfromrussia.com/main/2003/09/25/50165.html.

18. "Rossiia: zapadnyi put' dlia evroaziatskoi tsivilizatsii?" *Vserossiiskii tsentr izucheniia obshchestvennogo mneniia* (VTsIOM), no. 32 (November 13, 2001), http://www.levada.ru/press/2001111300.html.

19. The new post-Soviet academic discipline called "culturology" thinks of itself as a "science of civilizations" and offers a global explanation of the world that is partly inspired by dialectical materialism but replaces its economic determinism with a culturalist variety. On this, see M. Laruelle, "The Discipline of Culturology: A New 'Ready-Made Thought' for Russia?" *Diogenes*, no. 204 (2004): 21–36; and J. Scherrer, *Kulturologie: Rußland auf der Suche nach einer zivilisatorischen Identität* (Göttingen: Wallstein Verlag, 2003).

20. See the examples cited by V. Shnirel'man, "Lev Gumilëv: ot 'passionarnogo napriazheniia' do 'nesovmestimosti kul'tur,'" *Etnograficheskoe obozrenie*, no. 3 (2006): 8–21.

21. V. Putin, "Vystuplenie prezidenta Rossiiskoi Federatsii V. V. Putina v universitete imeni L. N. Gumileva," in *Programnye dokumenty OPOD "Evraziia"* (Moscow: Arktogeia, 2001), 8.

22. Putin, "Rossiia," 6, 8.

23. A. Akaev, *Kyrgyzskaia gosudarstvennost' i narodnyi epos "Manas"* (Bishkek: Uchkun, 2002), 15–16.

24. D. Trenin, *The End of Eurasia: Russia on the Border between Geopolitics and Globalization* (Washington D.C.: Carnegie Endowment for International Peace, 2002), 35.

25. P. Sériot, "La double vie de Trubetzkoy, ou la clôture des systèmes," *Le gré des langues* (Paris), no. 5 (1993): 113.

26. M. Olender, *Les langues du Paradis: Aryens et Sémites—un couple providentiel* (Paris: Seuil-Gallimard, 1989), 35.

27. P.-A. Taguieff, *Sur la Nouvelle droite: Jalons d'une analyse critique* (Paris: Descartes & Cie, 1994), vii.

28. I researched the topic between 1998 and 2006. During this period, I regularly spent time in Moscow and Saint Petersburg; made field trips to Turkey (2001), Tatarstan (2004), and Kazakhstan (2001, 2003, and 2005); and interviewed all the main Neo-Eurasianist theorists, with the exception of L. G. Gumilëv and Aleksandr Panarin, who died before I had a chance to meet them.

Notes to Chapter 1

1. N. Riasanovsky, "Prince Trubetskoy's *Europe and Mankind*," *Jahrbücher für Geschichte Osteuropas* 12 (1964): 207–20.

2. M. Bassin, "Russia between Europe and Asia: The Ideological Construction of Geographical Space," *Slavic Review* 50, no. 1 (1991): 1–17.

3. For a brief genealogy of the Eurasianist movement, see G. Nivat, "Du panmongolisme au mouvement eurasien: Histoire d'un thème millénaire," *Cahiers du monde russe et soviétique,* no. 3 (1966): 460–78.

4. "Yes, the Russian revolution was not man-made. . . . It was indeed a 'judgment,' but a divine judgment rather than a 'judgment of history.' " G. Florovskii, *Na putiakh: Utverzhdenie evraziitsev* (Prague: Evraziiskoe knigoizdatel'stvo, 1922), 289.

5. For more historical detail, see S. Glebov, "The Challenge of the Modern: The Eurasianist Ideology and Movement, 1920–29," Ph.D. thesis, Rutgers, the State University of New Jersey, 2004; and Otto Böss, *Die Lehre der Eurasier* (Wiesbaden: O. Harrassowitz, 1961).

6. E.g., Savitsky and Vernadsky long remained in contact with N. K. Rerikh (1874–1947), whose futuristic and "Oriental" paintings they influenced.

7. N. V. Riasanovsky, "The Emergence of Eurasianism," *California Slavic Studies,* no. 4 (1967): 39–72.

8. E. E. Litauer, "Soznanie i sovremennost'," *Evraziia,* no. 11 (February 2, 1929): 2.

9. E.g., *Evraziistvo: Opyt sistematicheskogo izlozheniia* (Paris: Evraziiskoe knigoizdatel'stvo, 1926).

10. The Glavnoe politicheskoe upravlenie, or State Political Directorate, was the Soviet secret police and counterintelligence agency in the 1920s. Reacting to the Soviet infiltrations, Savitsky, Alekseev, and Chkheidze published a leaflet to announce the expulsion of several members from the Eurasianist organizations. See P. Huber and D. Kunzi, "Paris dans les années trente: Sur Serge Efron et quelques agents du NKVD," *Cahiers du monde russe et soviétique,* no. 2 (1991): 285–310.

11. N. S. Trubetskoy, "Ideokratiia i proletariat," *Evraziia,* no. 1 (November 14, 1928): 2. Thus the dictatorship of the proletariat is presented as a manifestation of the Eurasianist principle of ideocracy.

12. N. N. Alekseev, V. N. Il'in, and P. N. Savitsky, *O gazete "Evraziia" (Gazeta "Evraziia" ne est' evraziiskii organ)* (Paris: Evraziiskoe knigoizdatel'stvo, 1929).

13. Ibid., 7.

14. Fëdorov was particularly appreciated by the Marxist Eurasianists. According to them, in his book *Filosofiia obshchego dela* he drew the social conclusions from the Russian Orthodox tradition and thereby made the Eurasianists aware of their own philosophy, that of "Russian cosmism."

15. The only publications Trubetzkoy recognizes as Eurasianist are his book *Evropa i chelovechestvo;* his articles in *Rossiia i latinstvo, K probleme russkogo samopoznaniia, Evraziiskii vremennik,* and *Evraziiskaia khronika;* and, in spite of everything, those in the first two issues of *Evraziia.*

16. K. I. S. (pseudonym), "O evraziistve i opasnostiakh evraziistva," *Evraziia,* no. 8 (January 12, 1929): 3.

17. After 1935, he published "Mysli ob avtarkii," "Ob idee-pravitel'nitse ideokraticheskogo gosudarstva," "Upadok tvorchestva," "O rasizme," and "Mysli ob indoevropeiskoi probleme."

18. This was done by, e.g., calling the Clamart schismatics "socialist Eurasianists," and the others "original Eurasianists" or "ideocratic Eurasianists." However, this resolution was not adopted; because the Eurasianist movement did not become a political party, the committee refused to rule on terminological issues. See *Evraziiskie tetradi,* no. 4 (1935).

19. Ibid.

20. P. P. Suvchinsky, "Inobytie russkoi religioznosti," *Evraziiskii vremennik* 3 (1923): 105.

21. M. Baissvenger [Beisswenger], "Konservativnaia revoliutsiia v Germanii i dvizhenie evraziitsev—tochki soprikosnoveniia," *Konservatism v Rossii i v mire,* no. 3 (2004): 49–73; L. Liuks [Luks], "Evraziistvo i konservativnaia revoliutsiia: Soblazn antizapadnichestva v Rossii i Germanii," *Voprosy filosofii,* no. 6 (1996): 57–69.

22. N. S. Trubetzkoy, "Nash otvet," in *Istoriia, kul'tura, iazyk,* by N. S. Trubetzkoy (Moscow: Progress, 1995), 339–48.

23. P. P. Suvchinsky, "K preodoleniiu revoliutsii," *Evraziiskii vremennik* 3 (1923): 38.

24. N. Trubetzkoy, "My i drugie," *Evraziiskii vremennik* 4 (1925): 66–81; republished in *Rossiia mezhdu Evropoi i Aziei: Evraziiskii soblazn* (Moscow: Nauka, 1993), 85.

25. Ibid.

26. The Slavophiles wanted to renew Russia through a reorganization of society (be it using the *mir* or the *zemstvo*). The Eurasianists thus attempted to extenuate their opposition to the Soviet Union's atheist policies by presenting society and religion as intrinsically linked or even identical; if a nation's "symphonic personality" expresses the divine character of its people, then the mode of social organization symbolizes the high spiritual level of the Russian people.

27. "Evraziistvo: Opyt sistematicheskogo izlozheniia," in *Puti Evrazii: Russkaia intelligentsiia i sud'by Rossii* (Moscow: Russkaia kniga, 1992), 388.

28. Suvchinsky, "K preodoleniiu revoliutsii," 33.

29. *Evraziistvo i kommunizm,* a brochure published with no reference, found in the Slavic Department at the Prague National Library.

30. "Evraziiskaia industrializaciia," *Evraziia,* no. 26 (May 18, 1929): 2.

31. Ibid.

32. Thus Alekseev, in his essay "Khristianstvo i ideia monarkhii"—in *Russkii narod i gosudarstvo* (Moscow: Agraf, 1998), 48–67—rejects the idea that the political regime

called for by Christianity is monarchy. He tries to show that the traditional Russian authorities took up multiple religious traditions (Asian despotism, paganism, etc.), and Orthodoxy is therefore compatible with the republican ideocratic regime advocated by Eurasianism.

33. "We believe that the 'people' or the 'nation' are not a random selection of citizens who fulfill the conditions of universal suffrage, but an aggregate of historical generations, past, present, and future, who constitute a unity of culture formalized by the state." N. N. Alekseev, "Evraziitsy i gosudarstvo," in *Rossiia mezhdu Evropoi i Aziei*, 169.

34. P. P. Suvchinsky, "Monarhiia ili sil'naia vlast'?" *Evraziiskaia khronika* 9 (1927): 24.

35. L. Karsavin, "Osnovy politiki," in *Rossiia mezhdu Evropoi i Aziei*, 194.

36. J. Schlanger, *Les métaphores de l'organisme* (Paris: L'Harmattan, 1995).

37. "We want, in other words, to replace the artificially anarchist order of the representation of individuals and parties by an organic order of the representation of needs, knowledge, and ideas. This is why we don't need a political party such as Western-style democracy would require." Alekseev, "Evraziitsy i gosudarstvo," 169.

30. "K otsenke sovremennosti," *Evraziia*, no. 35 (September 7, 1929): 3.

39. F. (pseudonym), "Politicheskie ocherki sovremennoi Italii," *Evraziia*, no. 13 (February 16, 1929): 7.

40. A. P. Antipov, "Novye puti Germanii," in *Novaia epokha: Ideokratiia, Politika, Ekonomika, Obzory* (Narva: Izdanie Evraziitsev, 1933), 35–43.

41. G. Vernadskii, "Mongol'skoe igo v russkoi istorii," *Evraziiskaia khronika* 5 (1927): 155.

42. *Evraziistvo: Opyt sistematicheskogo izlozheniia* (Paris: Evraziiskoe knigoizdatel'stvo, 1926), 32.

43. P. N. Savitsky, "Geograficheskie i geopoliticheskie osnovy evraziistva," in *Kontinent Evraziia*, ed. P. N. Savitsky (Moscow: Agraf, 1997), 300.

44. Iu. Shirinskii-Shikhmatov, "Rossiiskii natsional-maksimalizm i evraziistvo," *Evraziiskii sbornik* 6 (1929): 28.

45. S. Lubenskii (a pseudonym of Savitsky), "L'eurasisme," *Le monde slave* (Paris), January–Mach 1931, 86.

46. P. N. Savitsky, *Rossiia: Osobyi geograficheskii mir* (Paris: Evraziiskoe knigoizdatel'stvo, 1927), 47.

47. "Eurasia is defined as a geographic world that lies to the north of the Tibetan and Iranian plateaus and is based on . . . the desert and steppic area that stretches in an unbroken strip from the Chinese Wall to the borders of Galicia." Ibid.

48. "Evraziistvo: Opyt sistematicheskogo izlozheniia," 378.

49. Savitsky, *Rossiia*, 57.

50. P. N. Savitsky, "Geograficheskie i geopoliticheskie osnovy evraziistva," in *Kontinent Evraziia*, 301.

51. P. N. Savitsky, "Povorot k Vostoku," in *Iskhod k Vostoku: Predchuvstviia i vershenie* (Sofia: Rossiisko-bolgarskoe izdatel'stvo, 1921), 2.

52. N. S. Trubetzkoy, "Verkhi i nizy russkoi kul'tury," in *K probleme russkogo samopoznaniia* (Paris: Evraziiskoe knigoizdatel'stvo, 1927), 31.

53. N. S. Trubetzkoy, "Obshcheslavianskii element v russkoi kul'ture," in ibid., 93.

54. "Thus the Ugro-Finnic-Samoyed (aka 'Uralic'), Turkic, Mongol and Manchu families are united by a whole series of common traits into a single 'union of Uralic-Altaic language families,' despite the fact that modern science denies any genetic rela-

tion between these families." N. S. Trubetzkoy, "Vavilonskaia bashnia i smeshenie iazykov," *Evraziiskii vremennik*, 3 (1923): 116.

55. R. Jakobson, *K kharakteristike evraziiskogo iazykovogo soiuza* (Prague: Izdanie Evraziitsev, 1931).

56. Ibid., 4.

57. R. Jakobson, *Evraziia v svete iazykoznaniia* (Paris: Izdanie Evraziitsev, 1931), 3.

58. P. N. Savitsky, "Introduction" to "L'Eurasie révélée par la linguistique," by R. Jakobson, *Le Monde slave* (Paris, 1931), 367.

59. E. Khara-Davan, *Chingis-khan kak polkovodets i ego nasledie* (Belgrade: N.p., 1929), 55.

60. E. Khara-Davan, "O kochevnom byte," in *Tridtsatye gody* (Paris: N.p., 1931), 83–86.

61. In Trubetzkoy's terminology, "Turanian" stands for five ethno-linguistic groups: Ugric, Samoyed, Turkic, Mongol, and Manchu.

62. N. S. Trubetzkoy, "O turanskom elemente v russkoi kul'ture," in *Rossiia mezhdu Evropoi i Aziei*, 62.

63. Ibid., 142.

64. Ibid., 71.

65. V. P. Nikitin, "My i Vostok," *Evraziia*, no. 1 (November 24, 1928): 8.

66. N. S. Trubetzkoy, "Ob idee-pravitel'nitse ideokraticheskogo gosudarstva," in *Istoriia, kul'tura, iazyk*, 441.

67. Trubetzkoy, "Vavilonskaia bashnia i smeshenie iazykov," 334.

68. Trubetzkoy, "Verkhi i nizy russkoi kul'tury," 135.

69. P. N. Savitsky, "Introduction" to *Nachertanie russkoi istorii,* by G. V. Vernadskii (Prague: Evraziiskoe knigoizdatel'stvo, 1927), 9.

70. "Evraziistvo: Formulirovka 1927 g.," in *Rossiia mezhdu Evropoi i Aziei*, 224.

71. N. S. Trubetzkoy, "Obshcheevraziiskii natsionalizm," in *Istoriia, kul'tura, iazyk,* 417.

72. M. Bassin, "Classical Eurasianism and the Geopolitics of Russian Identity," *Ab Imperio,* no. 2 (2003): 257–68; S. Glebov, "Granitsy imperii kak granitsy moderna: antikolonial'naia ritorika i teoriia kult'urnykh tipov v evraziistve," *Ab Imperio,* no. 2 (2003): 267–92.

73. Roman Jakobson, ed., *N. S. Trubetzkoy's Letters and Notes* (New York: Mouton, 1975), 12.

74. Trubetzkoy, "O turanskom elemente v russkoi kul'ture," 59.

75. C. J. Halperin, "George Vernadsky, Eurasianism, the Mongols, and Russia," *Slavic Review* 41, no. 3 (1982): 477–93; C. J. Halperin, "Russia and the Steppe," *Forschungen zur Osteuropäischen Geschichte* (Wiesbaden) 36 (1985): 55–194.

76. A. Liberman, "N. S. Trubetzkoy and His Works on History and Politics," in *The Legacy of Genghis-Khan*, ed. N. S. Trubetzkoy (Ann Arbor: Michigan Slavic Publications, 1991), 295–375.

77. G. V. Vernadskii, "Protiv solntsa: Rasprostranenie russkogo gosudarstva k Vostoku," *Russkaia mysl'*, no. 1 (1914). In this text, Vernadsky tried to demonstrate that, in Russia, history depends on geography. Russian temporality unfolds on large territories unknown to the West and is therefore a time of repetition, of circularity. Vernadsky went as far as to specify the numerical relation between space and time: a distance of 1,000 versts is equivalent to a one-hundred-year step back in time. Eurasia thus has unique properties, just like the universe as a whole; the further you look, the further you go back

in time. Eurasia is therefore a proper subject of astronomy, and the Eurasian experience is relevant to the rest of the universe.

78. E. Khara-Davan, *Chingis-khan kak polkovodets i ego nasledie* (Belgrade: N.p., 1929), 12.

79. Ibid., 142.

80. "The role of Rome and that of Byzantium, unifier of the cultures of the West and the East, the agricultural, maritime culture and the nomadic, steppic culture—that role passed on to the empire of the Mongols at the beginning of the 13th century, after the fall of the Byzantine empire." G. V. Vernadskii, "Mongol'skoe igo v russkoi istorii," *Evraziiskaia khronika* 5 (1926): 157.

81. P. N. Savitsky, *Šestina sveta: Rusko jako zemepisní a historickí celek* (Prague: Melantrich, 1933), 137.

82. Khara-Davan, *Chingis-khan kak polkovodets i ego nasledie*, 3.

83. N. S. Trubetzkoy, "Nasledie Chingis-khana: Vzgliad na russkuiu istoriiu ne s Zapada, a s Vostoka," in *Istoriia, kul'tura, yazyk*, 248.

84. G. V. Vernadskii, *Opyt istorii Evrazii* (Berlin: Izdanie Evraziitsev, 1934), 15.

85. Savitsky, *Šestina sveta*, 139.

86. P. N. Savitsky, "Step' i osedlost'," in *Rossiia mezhdu Evropoi i Aziei*, 125.

87. B. Shiriaev, "Nadnatsional'noe gosudarstvo na territorii Evrazii," *Evraziiskaia khronika* 7 (1927): 8.

88. P. P. Suvchinsky, "Inobytie russkoi religioznosti," *Evraziiskii vremennik* 3 (1923): 82.

89. N. S. Trubetzkoy, "Religii Indii i khristianstvo," in *Na putiakh: Utverzhdenie Evraziitsev* (Berlin: N.p., 1922), 178.

90. Ibid.

91. Ibid.

92. Ibid., 223.

93. "Buria nad Aziei," *Svoi put'*, no 2 (April 1932): 2.

94. V. P. Nikitin, "Iran, Turan i Rossiia," *Evraziiskii vremennik* 5 (1927): 87.

95. Trubetzkoy, "O turanskom elemente v russkoi kul'ture," 150.

96. F. A. Stepun, "Rossiia mezhdu Evropoi i Aziei," in *Rossiia mezhdu Evropoi i Aziei*, 307–27.

Notes to Chapter 2

1. A. Vodoliagin and S. Danilov, *Metafizicheskaia os' evraziistva* (Tver': N.p., 1994), 84.

2. Quoted in B. Naarden, "*I Am a Genius, but No More Than That:* Lev Gumilëv, Ethnogenesis, the Russian Past and World History," *Jahrbücher für Geschichte Osteuropas* 44, no. 1 (1996): 54.

3. For more biographical details, see A. Titov, "Lev Gumilëv, Ethnogenesis and Eurasianism," PhD thesis, School of Slavonic and East European Studies, University College London, 2005. I would like to thank Alexander Titov for having provided me with a copy of his thesis before it was published.

4. See V. I. Kozlov, "O biologo-geograficheskoi kontseptsii etnicheskoi istorii," *Voprosy istorii,* no. 12 (1974): 72–85.

5. *Vspominaia L. N. Gumilëva: Vospominaniia, publikatsii, issledovaniia* (Saint Petersburg: Rostok, 2003), 237.

6. Ibid., 246.

7. See Y. Brudny, *Reinventing Russia: Russian Nationalism and the Soviet State, 1953–1991* (Cambridge, Mass.: Harvard University Press, 1998), 181–91.

8. "Spravka: Mekhanizm zazhima publikatsii L. N. Gumilëva, doktora istoricheskikh nauk s 1961 g., za period s 1975 po 1985 g.," in *Vspominaia L. N. Gumilëva*, 244–45.

9. See L. Nikolaeva, "Mir—vchera, segodnia, zavtra," *Evraziia*, no. 4 (1996): 65.

10. The book is recommended for pupils from eighth through eleventh grades. *Vspominaia L. N. Gumilëva*, 213.

11. This important site features online versions of most of his books, articles, and interviews: http://gumilevica.kulichki.net/start.html.

12. The publication is now hosted by the Russian Society (Russkoe obshchestvo), a site that belongs to the Patriotic Ring, a network of Russian nationalist Web sites: http://www.rusidea.ru.

13. An earlier version of this section was published as M. Laruelle, "Lev N. Gumilëv (1912–1992): Biologisme et eurasisme en Russie," *Revue des études slaves,* nos. 1–2 (2000): 163–90.

14. L. N. Gumilëv, "Menia nazyvaiut evraziitsem," *Nash sovremennik*, no. 1/1991, p. 132. Another article by Gumilëv is titled "Zametki poslednego evraziitsa," *Nashe nasledie*, no. 3 (1991): 19–34.

15. Savitsky had been one of the few Eurasianists really to have participated in the White movement, where he acted as secretary to P. V. Struve, then foreign affairs minister in General Wrangel's government.

16. I have consulted the letters in P. N. Savitsky's file at the Prague Slavic Library as well as those that have been republished in various editions of Eurasianist works. However, I have not succeeded in obtaining access to the letters kept in the L. N. Gumilëv archive in Saint Petersburg.

17. L. N. Gumilëv, "Skazhu vam po sekretu, chto esli Rossiia budet spasena, to tol'ko kak evraziiskaia derzhava," in *Osnovy evraziistva,* ed. A. Dugin (Moscow: Arktogeia, 2002), 479.

18. Gumilëv had access to these works: N. P. Toll', *Skify i gunny* (Prague: Izd. Evraziitsev, 1928); P. N. Savitsky, *O zadachakh kochevnikovedeniia: Pochemu skify i gunny dolzhny byt' interesny dlia russkogo?* (Prague: Evraziiskoe knigoizdatel'stvo, 1928); and E. Khara-Davan, *Chingis-Khan kak polkovodets i ego nasledie* (Belgrade: N.p., 1929).

19. Letter from P. N. Savitsky to L. N. Gumilëv, dated June 1958. P. N. Savitsky file, Prague Slavic Library. (Yermak was a sixteenth-century Cossack leader whose exploration of Siberia paved the way for Russian expansion.—translator's note.)

20. L. N. Gumilëv, "Menia nazyvaiut evraziitsem," republished in *Ritmy Evrazii: Epokhi i tsivilizatsii* (Moscow: Progress, 1993), 23.

21. For more details on these aspects of the original Eurasianism, see M. Laruelle, *L'Idéologie eurasiste russe ou Comment penser l'empire* (Paris: L'Harmattan, 1999), 116–45.

22. On the definition of Eurasianism as a "geographic ideology," see ibid., 148–72.

23. On this, see P. Sériot, "Jakobson entre l'Est et l'Ouest, 1915–39," *Cahiers de l'ILSL* (Lausanne), no. 9 (1997): 213–36; and G. Nicolas and P. Sériot, "La Russie-Eurasie d'après Savitskii," *Cahiers de géographie du Québec* 42, no. 115 (1998): 67–91.

24. In one of his letters, Gumilëv states that nomadic culture is inferior to the cul-

tures of other peoples. Savitsky finds this unacceptable: "I generally refuse to divide the world into a civilized and an uncivilized part." Savitsky's letter to Gumilëv dated January 1, 1957, was republished in *Ritmy Evrazii,* by Gumilëv, 205.

25. "I do not deny that Timur partly belongs to the Levant (in your sense of the word). But by origin and ideology he is part of the nomadic world. Not only did he use Genghis Khan's military regime; he was also imbued with ideas that go back to Genghis Khan. Timur's strength lay in this link with both the Levantine and the nomadic tradition." Ibid., 206.

26. "Unfortunately, in his subsequent discussion of the need to 'Orthodoxize' Mongol statehood, the author [Trubetzkoy] overlooks the fact that there are many Mongol Christians [Nestorians]." L. N. Gumilëv, "Zametki poslednego evraziitsa," 22.

27. "I lost 55 years of my life trying to understand what is behind the sacramental term 'Orient,' and I know that there is no Orient in general, and will never be. The Orient has been concrete and different in different periods of history." L. N. Gumilëv, "Sila epokhi," *Dekorativnoe iskusstvo SSSR,* no. 7 (1989): 34.

28. For more details on this issue, see M. Laruelle, "Histoire d'une usurpation intellectuelle: Gumilëv, 'le dernier des eurasistes'? Analyse des oppositions entre L. N. Gumilëv et P. N. Savickij," *Revue des études slaves,* nos. 2–3 (2001): 449–59, as well as my reply to critical reactions: M. Laruelle, "L. N. Gumilëv, une oeuvre contestée: Réponse aux critiques de V. Ermolaev et A. Titov," *Revue des études slaves,* no. 4 (2005): 511–18.

29. L. N. Gumilëv, *Chërnaia legenda: Druz'ia i nedrugi Velikoi stepi* (Moscow: Progress, 1994), 322–23.

30. Ibid., 124.

31. L. N. Gumilëv, *Etnogenez i biosfera zemli* (Leningrad: Gidrometeoizdat, 1990), 161; (An abridged English translation of this book, by an unknown translator, was published as Leo Gumilëv, *Ethnogenesis and the Biosphere* [Moscow: Progress, 1990]. In the present chapter, however, quotations from the book have been translated directly from the Russian. In particular, *passionarnost',* a term coined by Gumilëv, is translated as "passionarity" rather than "drive."—translator's note.)

32. L. N. Gumilëv, "Otkuda est' poshla Rus'," *Slovo,* no. 8 (1992): 11.

33. L. N. Gumilëv and K. P. Ivanov, "Etnicheskie protsessy: Dva podkhoda k izucheniiu," *Sotsiologicheskie issledovaniia,* no. 1 (1992): 56.

34. Gumilëv, *Etnogenez i biosfera zemli,* 136.

35. L. N. Gumilëv, "Les fluctuations du niveau de la mer Caspienne," *Cahiers du monde russe et soviétique* 6, no. 3 (1965): 361.

36. L. N. Gumilëv, *Tysiacheletie vokrug Kaspiia* (Moscow: Misel' i K, 1992), 100.

37. On Romanticism's essentialism and striving for synthesis, see G. Gusdorf, *Le Romantisme,* 2 vols. (Paris: Payot, 1993).

38. Letter from L. N. Gumilëv to P. N. Savitsky from the end of 1957, P. N. Savitsky's file at the Prague Slavic Library.

39. Gumilëv regularly criticizes synchronic thinking, i.e., the analysis of things that coexist in the same era yet actually have a different ethnogenetic "age." The diachronic approach, he claims, is better because it is comparative: It allows us to determine the relative "lag" or "advancement" of an *ethnos.* Gumilëv, *Tysiacheletie vokrug Kaspiia,* 53.

40. Gumilëv, *Etnogenez i biosfera zemli,* 30.

41. D. M. Balashov, "V kakoe vremia my zhivem," *Soglasie,* no. 1 (1990), quoted by Gumilëv, *Ritmy Evrazii,* 133.

42. Gumilëv, *Etnogenez i biosfera zemli,* 276.

43. Ibid., 19.

44. Ibid., 348.

45. Ibid., 175.

46. Ibid., 150.

47. L. N. Gumilëv, *Drevniaia Rus' i Velikaia step'* (Moscow: Mysl', 1989), 599–600.

48. Gumilëv tries to establish whether the presence of nomads in that region depends on climate change. He singles out three periods when the steppes dried out (the third, tenth, and sixteenth centuries), each of which corresponded to a decline of the nomadic civilizations along the Caspian shores. Gumilëv thinks that this way he can draw a comparative table to show that climatological data and historical facts coincide. See L. N. Gumilëv, "Izmenenie klimata i migratsii kochevnikov," *Priroda,* no. 4 (1972): 44–52.

49. "Therefore I will put the question differently. I will ask, not only how the geographical milieu affects people, but also in what way people themselves are constitutive parts of that outer layer of the Earth which is now called the biosphere?" Gumilëv, *Etnogenez i biosfera zemli,* 37.

50. L. N. Gumilëv, *V poiskakh vymyshlennogo tsarstva* (Moscow: Klyshnikov, Komarov i Ko., 1992), 264.

51. "It is obvious that, just like some chemical reactions only occur at high temperatures and in the presence of catalysts, so ethnic hybridization proceeds differently depending on the level of passionary tension." Gumilëv, *Drevniaia Rus' i Velikaia step',* 77. Gumilëv even goes so far as to draw technical parallels, presenting humanity as a mechanism among others; the *ethnos,* he writes, emerges out of various substrates, which recall "a simple electric battery, where current requires zinc, copper, and an acid." Gumilëv, *Etnogenez i biosfera zemli,* 322. He also makes frequent use of the organicist metaphor of illness: "The Ismailis were successful in their struggle to simplify the system, thus rendering their *ethnos* defenseless. They were acting like a cancerous growth in an organism, and perished together with the social organism." Gumilëv, *Chërnaia legenda,* 116.

52. L. N. Gumilëv, "Pis'mo v redaktsiiu 'Voprosov filosofii'," *Voprosy filosofii,* no. 5 (1989): 161.

53. Gumilëv, "Menia nazyvaiut evraziitsem," 24.

54. L. N. Gumilëv, "Etnogenez i biosfera zemli," *Priroda i chelovek,* no. 4 (1992): 59.

55. See B. G. Rosenthal, *The Occult in Russian and Soviet Culture* (Ithaca, N.Y.: Cornell University Press, 1997).

56. L. N. Gumilëv and V. Iu. Ermolaev, "Gore ot illiuzii," in *Osnovy evraziistva,* ed. Dugin, 467.

57. L. N. Gumilëv, "Zametki poslednego evraziitsa," in *Ritmy Evrazii,* 36.

58. See V. Shnirelman and S. Panarin, "Lev Gumilëv: His Pretension as a Founder of Ethnology and His Eurasian Theories," *Inner Asia* 3, no. 1 (2001): 1–18.

59. Gumilëv, *Etnogenez i biosfera zemli,* 125.

60. L. N. Gumilëv, *Ot Rusi do Rossii* (Saint Petersburg: Iiuna, 1992), 19.

61. Gumilëv, *Etnogenez i biosfera zemli,* 125.

62. "Zones of passionary thrusts are narrow strips, about 300 km wide if latitudinal, and somewhat larger if meridional, covering roughly 0.5 of the planet's circumference [no unit of measurement is specified in the text]. They resemble geodesic lines. They appear infrequently, about two or three times in a millennium, and almost never twice in the same place." Gumilëv, *Etnogenez i biosfera zemli,* 345.

63. L. N. Gumilëv, "Etnogenez i biosfera zemli," *Priroda i chelovek,* no. 2 (1989): 58.

64. See R. Paradowski, "The Eurasian Idea and Leo Gumilev's Scientific Ideology," *Canadian Slavonic Papers* 41, no. 1 (1999): 19–32.

65. Gumilëv, *Ot Rusi do Rossii,* 20.

66. Gumilëv, "Pis'mo v redaktsiiu 'Voprosov filosofii'," 160.

67. Nikolai Danilevsky, the great theorist of Pan-Slavism, is the author of *Rossiia i Evropa* (1871), a book that was especially celebrated after the Russo-Turkish war of 1877–78. Nikolai Strakhov called it "a catechism or complete code of Slavophilism." Danilevsky completed Slavophilism's transformation into a realist doctrine, a militant, nonmetaphysical nationalism. He converted Christian faith into a belief in Slavic nationalism, and he presented Orthodoxy as a mere cultural feature of the Russian world. Thus he called not for spiritual renewal but for a political construction. Less relativist than Spengler, he nevertheless anticipated the cultural pessimism of the early twentieth century. Inspired by the typologies of Georges Cuvier, Danilevsky classified the different cultural-historical types or civilizations that played a role in history and articulated the "laws" that govern them. Whereas every civilization so far has been one-dimensional—religious (Jewish), cultural (Greek), political (Roman), or technical (Western)—Slavic civilization will be "four-directional" and will therefore become the most complete realization of humankind's potential. See N. Ia. Danilevsky, *Rossiia i Evropa: Vzgliad na kul'turnye i politicheskie otnosheniia slavianskogo mira k germano-romanskomu* (Saint Petersburg: Glagol, 1995).

68. Gumilëv, *Etnogenez i biosfera zemli,* 104.

69. According to Gumilëv, the *sub-ethnos* is a closed group born of a religious schism or a change of landscape (Old Believers, Cossacks, or small Finnic, Siberian, or Turkic peoples), which, however, while it is itself a totality, presents no challenge to the systemic unity of its *ethnos.*

70. A *super-ethnos* is made up of several *ethnoi* linked by a common historical destiny. It is not strictly speaking an ethnic unit; rather, it is a unit of passionary thrust. Gumilëv identifies about twenty of them for all of human history (although he does not name them), a number that is close to Arnold Toynbee's count of civilizations.

71. The *meta-ethnoi* are considered to constitute the highest level of the ethnic hierarchy; they are a group of *ethnoi* and *super-ethnoi* that possess shared cultural features and an awareness of their community. Examples of *meta-ethnoi* include the Soviet people and the Slavs.

72. Gumilëv, *Tysiacheletie vokrug Kaspiia,* 5.

73. Gumilëv, *Ritmy Evrazii,* 77.

74. L. N. Gumilëv, *Khunnu: Stepnaia trilogiia* (Moscow: Kompass, 1993), 8.

75. Gumilëv, *Ot Rusi do Rossii,* 255.

76. Gumilëv, *Chërnaia legenda,* 282.

77. Unlike some of the first Eurasianists, Gumilëv is not attracted to the Old Believers who emerged out of the schism of the seventeenth century. For him, opting for the Greek and universal Orthodox tradition was required in order to rally the other peoples of the Eurasian *super-ethnos* around Orthodoxy, whereas Avvakum's religion was strictly Great Russian and therefore not open to Eurasia. He writes that the schismatics gradually lost their passionarity; from an active *sub-ethnos* they turned into a "relic."

78. Gumilëv offers a new interpretation of the *Lay of Igor's Host* in line with his historical conceptions. According to him, the text was not written in the eleventh century; yet it was no forgery: It was composed by a Russian in the thirteenth century and reveals the Orthodox sense of rivalry with the Nestorian Mongols. Thus, according to Gumilëv, the author was interested in representing the Tatars as hostile Polovtsians and Muslims, whereas in fact they were Christians, too.

79. Gumilëv, *Ot Rusi do Rossii*, 134.

80. Gumilëv, *Ritmy Evrazii*, 129.

81. L. N. Gumilëv, "Skazhu vam po sekretu, chto esli Rossiia budet spasena, to tol'ko kak evraziiskaia derzhava," in *Ritmy Evrazii*, 31.

82. Letter from L. N. Gumilëv to P. N. Savitsky, dated January 1958, P. N. Savitsky's file at the Prague Slavic Library.

83. Gumilëv, *Chërnaia legenda*, 323.

84. Gumilëv, *Ritmy Evrazii*, 65.

85. Gumilëv, *Etnogenez i biosfera zemli*, 80.

86. L. N. Gumilëv, "Kniaz' Sviatoslav Igorevich," *Nash sovremennik*, no. 7 (1991): 143.

87. Gumilëv, *Chërnaia legenda*, 130.

88. Gumilëv, *Tysiacheletie vokrug Kaspiia*, 42.

89. Gumilëv, "Kniaz' Sviatoslav Igorevich," 149.

90. Cf. V. Shnirelman, *Intellektual'nye labirinty: Ocherki ideologii v sovremennoi Rossii* (Moscow: Academia, 2004), 87–122.

91. Letter from L. N. Gumilëv to P. N. Savitsky from late 1958, P. N. Savitsky's file at the Prague Slavic Library.

92. Gumilëv, "Kniaz' Sviatoslav Igorevich," 149.

93. "Two *super-ethnoi* with different ethnogeneses were coexisting in the same natural habitat, interpenetrating as it were. That is the meaning of 'chimera.'" Gumilëv, *Drevniaia Rus' i Velikaia Step'*, 216.

94. Ibid., 137.

95. Ibid., 175.

96. For a history of the anti-Semitic Khazar myth, see V. Shnirelman, *The Myth of the Khazars and Intellectual Antisemitism in Russia, 1970–1990s* (Jerusalem: Vidal Sassoon International Center for the Study of Antisemitism, Hebrew University of Jerusalem, 2002), 44–58.

97. Gumilëv, *Etnogenez i biosfera zemli*, 406.

98. On this, see V. Rossman, *Russian Intellectual Antisemitism in the Post-Communist Era* (Lincoln: University of Nebraska Press and Vidal Sassoon International Center for the Study of Antisemitism, 2002), 72–100.

99. On this, see the articles on Gumilëv in *Etnograficheskoe obozrenie*, no. 3 (2006): V. Shnirel'man, "Uroki Gumilëva: Blesk i nishcheta teorii etnogeneza," 3–7; V. Shnirel'-man, "Lev Gumilëv: Ot *passionarnogo napriazheniia* do *nesovmestimosti kul'tur*," 8–21; and V. Koreniako, "K kritike L. N. Gumilëva," 22–35.

100. N. Mitrokhin, *"Russkaia partiia": Dvizhenie russkikh natsionalistov v SSSR. 1953–1985 gg* (Moscow: NLO, 2003).

101. V. Iu. Ermolaev, quoted by Gumilëv, *Chërnaia legenda*, 23.

102. In his interviews, he reminisces about his military family and his participation in the Battle of Berlin, and often speaks of World War II as the one patriotic bond between all the peoples of the Soviet Union.

103. L. N. Gumilëv, "Etnos, istoriia, kul'tura," *Dekorativnoe iskusstvo SSSR*, no. 4 (1989): 32–33.

104. S. Lavrov, ed., *Lev Gumilëv: sud'ba i idei* (Moscow: Airis Press, 2003), 166.

105. L. N. Gumilëv and V. Iu. Ermolaev, "Gore ot illiuzii," in *Ritmy Evrazii*, 178.

106. Thus, in one of his interviews, Gumilëv regrets having spent fourteen years in camps and endured a publication ban for another fourteen years: "Who did this? Not the authorities. No, the authorities have nothing to do with this. My so-called fellow scholars did it. People sitting in universities, in research institutes, in publishing houses." Gumilëv, *Ritmy Evrazii*, 159.

107. Gumilëv and Ermolaev, "Gore ot illiuzii," 469.

108. In the USSR, "research [in the social sciences] could only be considered scientifically valid if the reality it studied was embedded in a system or structure that determined its functioning. Most frequently scholars did not study a concrete reality; all their efforts targeted the 'underlying structure' or something of the kind." A. Mongili, *La chute de l'URSS et la recherche scientifique* (Paris: L'Harmattan, 1998), 266.

Notes to Chapter 3

1. Alter-globalizationism is to be distinguished from antiglobalizationism: Antiglobalizationists reject globalization as such, uphold the political model of the nation-state and "traditional" nationalist values, and seek to "purge" borrowings from foreign cultures. Alter-globalizationists, by contrast, reject globalization such as they see it developing today, with its underlying economic liberalism, but are not opposed to the "global village" as such. They call for a globalization that would be more concerned with human development, more respectful of the environment and the autonomy of peoples, and synonymous with the search for a new balance between the global North and the global South.

2. The latter published two works: V. Pashchenko, *Ideologiia evraziistva* (Moscow: MGU, 2000); and V. Pashchenko, *Sotsial'naia filosofiia evraziistva* (Moscow: Al'fa, 2003). These books were presented as studies of interwar Eurasianism but were in fact seeking to disseminate that ideology.

3. An earlier version of this chapter was published as M. Laruelle, "L'Empire après l'Empire: Le néo-eurasisme russe," *Cahiers du monde russe* 42, no. 1 (2001): 71–94.

4. Interview with Eduard Bagramov, Moscow, November 2000.

5. The journal was published as a quarterly until 1996, then appears to have ceased publication, reappearing since 2000 as a yearbook. See the tables of contents at http://www.ispr.ru/BIBLIO/JURNAL/Evra/evra.html.

6. A. N. Sakharov, "Osnovnye etapy i osobennosti russkogo natsionalizma," *Evraziia*, no. 4 (1996): 17.

7. Interview with Timur Pulatov, Moscow, November 2000.

8. Anonymous editorial in *Literaturnaia Evraziia*, no. 8 (1999): 5.

9. N. A. Nazarbaev, *Evraziiskii soiuz: Idei, praktika, perspektivy 1994–1997* (Moscow: Fond sodeistviia razvitiiu sotsial'nykh i politicheskikh nauk, 1997), 120.

10. A. S. Panarin, *Filosofiia politiki* (Moscow: Novaia shkola, 1996); A. S. Panarin, *Politologiia: Uchebnoe posobie* (Moscow: Gardariki, 2002).

236   *Notes to Pages 86–89*

11. See the review by V. A. Bazhanov, "A Note on A. S. Panarin's *Revansh Istorii*," *Europe-Asia Studies* 51, no. 4 (1999): 705–8.

12. For a more detailed biography, see A. Tsygankov's fundamental articles: A. Tsygankov, "Aleksandr Panarin kak zerkalo rossiiskoi revoliutsii," *Vestnik MGU: Sotsiologiia i politologiia*, no. 4 (2005): 166–77, and no. 1 (2006): 120–49; and A. Tsygankov, "Natsional'nyi liberalizm Aleksandra Panarina: Uroki porazheniia," *Svobodnaia mysl'*, no. 9 (2005): 100–17.

13. On the relationship between nationalism and foreign policy, see A. Tsygankov, *Whose World Order? Russia's Perception of American Ideas after the Cold War* (Notre Dame, Ind.: University of Notre Dame Press, 2004).

14. A. S. Panarin and B. S. Erasov, eds., *Rossiia i Vostok: Problemy vzaimodeistviia* (Moscow: Rossiiskaia akademiia nauk, 1993); A. S. Panarin and B. S. Erasov, eds., *Rossiia i Vostok: Tsivilizatsionnye otnosheniia*, 3 vols. (Moscow: Rossiiskaia akademiia nauk, 1994–96).

15. A. S. Panarin, *Pravoslavnaia tsivilizatsiia v global'nom mire* (Moscow: Algoritm, 2002), 311.

16. Ibid., 224. Also see B. S. Erasov, "Rossiia v tsentral'noaziatskom geokul'turnom komplekse," *Vostok–Oriens*, no. 6 (1993): 124–31.

17. A physician by training, Leont'ev joined the diplomatic service in 1863 and spent a decade in Crete, Cyprus, and different Ottoman cities as a consul. He rediscovered faith during a serious illness in 1869 and subsequently spent some time on Mount Athos. In the 1880s, unable to support himself by writing, he worked as a censor and editor, living on his estate. He died at the monastery of Sergiev Posad after having taken orders. Leont'ev represented a profound turn in Russian thought and anticipated, in an as yet ambiguous manner, the Eurasianists' turn toward the East, because he favored religious over linguistic and national community and expressed a preference for the Greeks over non-Russian Slavs. Thus, it was by reverting to religious community that Leont'ev turned eastward; his glorification of Byzantium served as a bridge to a partly Asian heritage. His portrayal of Constantinople's role as a window to the Orient introduced a confusion between "the Christian East" and "Asia." Leont'ev was the first to have understood the relevance of the Turanian argument for Russia's desire to assert itself against Europe. See the detailed discussion in M. Laruelle, "Existe-t-il des précurseurs au mouvement eurasiste? L'obsession russe pour l'Asie à la fin du XIXe siècle," *Revue des études slaves*, nos. 3–4 (2004): 437–54.

18. A. S. Panarin, "Pravoslavnaia tsivilizatsiia v global'nom mire," *Evraziiskoe obozrenie*, no. 4 (2001): 4–5, http://eurasia.com.ru/eo/4-5.html; A. S. Panarin, "Ontologiia terrora," in *Geopolitika terrora: Geopoliticheskie posledstviia terroristicheskikh aktov v SShA 11 sentiabria 2001 g.* (Moscow: Arktogeia, 2002), 45–51; A. S. Panarin, "Russkaia pravoslavnaia tserkov' v prostranstve Evrazii," *Materialy VI Vsemirnogo russkogo narodnogo sobora* (Moscow: Arktogeia, 2002), 90–101.

19. A. S. Panarin, *Global'noe politicheskoe prognozirovanie* (Moscow: Algoritm, 2002), 201.

20. A. Umland, *Toward an Uncivil Society? Contextualizing the Recent Decline of Extremely Right-Wing Parties in Russia*, Working Paper 02-03 (Cambridge, Mass.: Weatherhead Center for International Affairs, Harvard University, 2002), http://www.wcfia.harvard.edu/papers/555_Toward_An_Uncivil_Society.pdf.

21. See http://evrazia.org/modules.php?name=News&file=article&sid=1508.

22. B. G. Kapustin, "Rossiia i Zapad: Puti k miru mirov," in *Rossiia i Vostok*, ed. Panarin and Erasov, vol. 1.

23. Panarin, *Pravoslavnaia tsivilizatsiia,* 16.

24. A. S. Panarin, "Slaviano-tiurkskoe edinstvo: Konstruktsiia rossiiskoi gosudar-stvennosti," *Rossiia i musul'manskii mir,* no. 1 (1996): 59.

25. For more detail, see M. Laruelle, *L'Idéologie eurasiste russe ou Comment penser l'empire* (Paris: L'Harmattan, 1999), 148–70.

26. See B. S. Erasov's introduction to *Rossiia i Vostok,* ed. Panarin and Erasov, vol. 1: "Predislovie: O statuse kul'turno-tsivilizatsionnykh issledovanii," 13.

27. B. S. Erasov, "Tsivilizatsiia: Slovo, termin, smysl," in *Rossiia i Vostok,* ed. Panarin and Erasov, vol. 2, 25.

28. Panarin, *Global'noe politicheskoe prognozirovanie,* 46.

29. The *Annales* school is named after the French journal that has published the work of these scholars since World War I.

30. Erasov, "Predislovie: O statuse kul'turno-tsivilizatsionnykh issledovanii," 10.

31. A. S. Panarin, *Rossiia v tsiklakh mirovoi istorii* (Moscow: MGU, 1999), 225.

32. Panarin, *Pravoslavnaia tsivilizatsiia,* 13.

33. Panarin, *Global'noe politicheskoe prognozirovanie,* 8.

34. Panarin, *Pravoslavnaia tsivilizatsiia,* 148.

35. A. S. Panarin, "Predely faustovskoi kul'tury i puti rossiiskoi tsivilizatsii," in *Rossiia i Vostok,* ed. Panarin and Erasov, vol. 3, 40.

36. Panarin, *Rossiia v tsiklakh mirovoi istorii,* 66.

37. Samuel P. Huntington, *The Clash of Civilizations and the Remaking of World Order* (New York: Simon & Schuster, 1996).

38. A. S. Panarin and B. B. Il'in, eds., *Rossiia: Opyt natsional'no-gosudarstvennoi ideologii* (Moscow: MGU, 1994), 139.

39. Panarin, *Pravoslavnaia tsivilizatsiia,* 188.

40. A. S. Panarin, *Revansh istorii: Rossiiskaia strategicheskaia initsiativa* (Moscow: Logos, 1998), 372.

41. A. S. Panarin, *Rossiia v tsivilizatsionnom protsesse* (Moscow: IFRAN, 1995), 2.

42. Ibid., 19.

43. Panarin, *Rossiia v tsiklakh mirovoi istorii,* 19.

44. Panarin, *Rossiia v tsivilizatsionnom protsesse,* 113.

45. Ibid., 72.

46. A. Iugai, "Evraziiskii put' rossiiskoi tsivilizatsii," in *Rossiia i Vostok,* ed. Panarin and Erasov, vol. 3, 145.

47. B. S. Erasov, "Etnicheskoe, natsional'noe, tsivilizatsionnoe v prostranstve Evrazii," in *Rossiia i Vostok,* ed. Panarin and Erasov, vol. 2, 90.

48. B. S. Erasov, "Vybor Rossii v evraziiskom prostranstve," in *Rossiia i Vostok,* ed. Panarin and Erasov, vol. 1, 48.

49. A. S. Panarin, "Vybor Rossii: Mezhdu atlantizmom i evraziistvom," in *Rossiia i Vostok,* ed. Panarin and Erasov, vol. 2, 46.

50. Kapustin, "Rossiia i Zapad," 32.

51. Panarin, "Predely faustovskoi kul'tury i puti rossiiskoi tsivilizatsii," 49.

52. Panarin, *Rossiia v tsivilizatsionnom protsesse,* 197.

53. Panarin and Il'in, *Rossiia,* 128.

54. B. S. Erasov, "O geopoliticheskom i tsivilizatsionnom ustroenii Evrazii," *Evraziia,* no. 5 (1996): 30.

55. Panarin and Il'in, *Rossiia,* 162.

56. Ibid., 163.

57. Panarin, *Rossiia v tsivilizatsionnom protsesse,* 236.

58. Panarin, *Rossiia v tsiklakh mirovoi istorii,* 122.

59. A. S. Panarin, "Rossiia na pereput'e: Raskoly zapadnichestva i sintezy evrazi-istva," *Rossiia i musul'manskii mir,* no. 8 (1995): 7.

60. Panarin and Il'in, *Rossiia,* 185.

61. Ibid., 216.

62. Ibid., 161.

63. A. S. Panarin, "O derzhavnike-Ottse i liberal'nykh nositeliakh edipova kompleksa: K 50-letiiu so dnia smerti I.V. Stalina," *Moskva,* no. 3 (2003), http://www.moskvam.ru/2003/03/panarin.htm.

64. A. S. Panarin, *Iskushenie globalizmom* (Moscow: Algoritm, 2000).

65. Panarin, *Pravoslavnaia tsivilizatsiia,* 406.

66. Panarin, *Rossiia v tsiklakh mirovoi istorii,* 173.

67. Panarin, *Pravoslavnaia tsivilizatsiia,* 404.

68. Ibid., 491.

69. Panarin, *Rossiia v tsiklakh mirovoi istorii,* 275.

70. Panarin, "Vybor Rossii," 38.

71. K. S. Gadzhiev, "Natsional'no-territorial'nye perspektivy rossiiskoi gosudarstvennosti," in *Rossiia i Vostok,* ed. Panarin and Erasov, vol. 2, 74.

72. Panarin sometimes condemns Peter the Great for having wanted to build a European power, but he also thinks that his Empire pursued a real foreign policy toward Asia and his reign remains a constitutive period for Russia because of the empire's eastward advance. Panarin and Il'in, *Rossiia,* 153.

73. A. S. Panarin, "Rossiia na rubezhe tysiacheletii," *Rossiia i musul'manskii mir,* no. 4 (1997): 10.

74. Ibid., 7.

75. Panarin, "Slaviano-tiurkskoe edinstvo," 62.

76. A. S. Panarin, "Paradoksy evropeizma v sovremennoi Rossii," *Rossiia i musul'-manskii mir,* no. 3 (1997): 16.

77. Ibid., 12.

78. Panarin, *Rossiia v tsivilizatsionnom protsesse,* 37.

79. Panarin and Il'in, *Rossiia,* 198.

80. Panarin, *Global'noe politicheskoe prognozirovanie,* 346.

81. On this, see M. Laruelle, *Mythe aryen et rêve impérial dans la Russie du XIXe siècle* (Paris: CNRS Éditions, 2005), 179–91.

82. Panarin, *Rossiia v tsivilizatsionnom protsesse,* 216–17.

83. Panarin, *Pravoslavnaia tsivilizatsiia,* 426.

84. Ibid., 353.

85. Panarin, *Global'noe politicheskoe prognozirovanie,* 133.

Notes to Chapter 4

1. For further details on the distribution of his publications (print runs, re-editions), see A. Umland, "Kulturhegemoniale Strategien der russischen extremen Rechten: Die Verbindung von faschistischer ideologie und metapolitischer Taktik im Neoeurasismus des Aleksandr Dugin," *Österreichische Zeitschrift für Politikwissenschaft* 33, no. 2 (2004): 437–54.

2. V. Likhachëv, *Natsizm v Rossii* (Moscow: Panorama, 2002), 103.

3. The title of this show is not neutral. It refers to a famous collection of articles from 1909 called *Vekhi*, considered a manifesto against the ideology of the radical intelligentsia. The authors of *Vekhi* upheld the primacy of things spiritual and appealed to the revolutionary intelligentsia to recognize the spiritual source of human life; to them, only concrete idealism, manifested in Russia in the form of religious philosophy, allows one to objectify traditional mysticism and to fuse knowledge and faith.

4. All of Dugin's publications are available on the Web. His two Web sites, Arctogaia (http://www.arcto.ru) and Evraziia (http://www.evrazia.org), also feature links to a nationalist network that includes Web sites such as Novoe soprotivlenie (New Resistance), as well as to Web-based magazines such as *Lenin.*

5. A. Dugin, *The Ways of the Absolute* (Puti absoliuta), written in 1989 and published in 1991; A. Dugin, *The Conservative Revolution* (Konservativnaia revoliutsiia, 1994); A. Dugin, *Goals and Tasks of Our Revolution* (Tseli i zadachi nashei revoliutsii, 1995); A. Dugin, *Templars of the Proletariat* (Tampliery proletariata, 1997); A. Dugin, *The Philosophy of Traditionalism* (Filosofiia traditsionalizma, 2002); A. Dugin, *The Evolution of the Paradigmatic Foundations of Science* (Evoliutsiia paradigmal'nykh osnovanii nauki, 2002); A. Dugin, *The Philosophy of Politics* (Filosofiia politiki, 2004); A. Dugin, *The Philosophy of War* (Filosofiia voiny, 2004). See the bibliography for complete citations of these works, listed by their Russian titles.

6. A. Dugin, *The Metaphysics of the Gospel: Orthodox Esotericism* (Metafizika Blagoi Vesti: Pravoslavnyi ezoterizm, 1996); A. Dugin, *The End of the World: Eschatology and Tradition* (Konets sveta: Eskhatologiia i traditsiia, 1997). See the bibliography for complete citations of these works, listed by their Russian titles.

7. A. Dugin, *The Mysteries of Eurasia* (Misterii Evrazii, 1993); A. Dugin, *The Hyperborean Theory* (Giperboreiskaia teoriia, 1993). See the bibliography for complete citations of these works, listed by their Russian titles.

8. A. Dugin, *Conspirology* (Konspirologiia); A. Dugin, *The Foundations of Geopolitics* (Osnovy geopolitiki, 1996; and four revised editions); A. Dugin, *Our Way: Strategic Prospects for Russia's Development in the 21st Century* (Nash put': Strategicheskie perspektivy razvitiia Rossii v XXI veke, 1998); A. Dugin, *The Russian Thing: Essays in National Philosophy* (Russkaia veshch': Ocherki natsional'noi filosofii, 2001); A. Dugin, *The Foundations of Eurasianism* (Osnovy evraziistva, 2002); A. Dugin, *The Eurasianist Path* (Evraziiskii put', 2002); A. Dugin, *The Eurasian Path as National Idea* (Evraziiskii put' kak natsional'naia ideia, 2002). See the bibliography for complete citations of these works, listed by their Russian titles.

9. See A. Rogachevskii, *A Biographical and Critical Study of Russian Writer Eduard Limonov,* Studies in Slavic Language and Literature 20 (Lewiston, N.Y.: Edward Mellen Press, 2003).

10. M. Mathyl, "The National-Bolshevik Party and Arctogaia: Two Neo-fascist Groupuscules in the Post-Soviet Political Space," *Patterns of Prejudice* 36, no. 3 (2003): 62–76.

11. S. Shenfield, *Russian Fascism: Traditions, Tendencies, Movements* (London: M. E. Sharpe, 2001), 194.

12. E. Limonov, *Moia politicheskaia biografiia* (Saint Petersburg: Amfora, 2002), 64.

13. W. Allensworth, "The Eurasian Project: Russia-3, Dugin and Putin's Kremlin," paper presented at the National Convention of the American Association for the Advancement of Slavic Studies, Salt Lake City, November 4–6, 2005.

14. A. Dugin, *Osnovy geopolitiki: Geopoliticheskoe budushchee Rossii* (Moscow: Arktogeia, 1997). On this book, see J. B. Dunlop, "Aleksandr Dugin's 'Neo-Eurasian' Textbook and Dmitrii Trenin's Ambivalent Response," *Harvard Ukrainian Studies* 25, nos. 1–2 (2001): 91–127.

15. For further details on Dugin's connections with military circles, see Dunlop, "Aleksandr Dugin's 'Neo-Eurasian' Textbook," 94, 102.

16. F. Thom, "Eurasisme et néo-eurasisme," *Commentaires,* no. 66 (1994): 304.

17. A. Dugin, "Evraziiskaia platforma," *Zavtra,* January 18, 2000, http://www.zavtra .ru/cgi//veil//data/zavtra/00/320/81.html.

18. These Russian official Web sites include, e.g., http://www.strana.ru.

19. "Evraziistvo: ot filosofii k politike," Dugin's paper prepared for the founding congress of the Evraziia movement, April 21, 2001, http://www.evrazia.org/modules .php?name=News&file=article&sid=734.

20. A. Dugin, "My—partiia natsional'noi idei," paper for the conference preparing the transformation of Evraziia from a movement into a political party, March 1, 2002, http://www.evrazia.org/modules.php?name=News&file=article&sid=736.

21. An economist by training, Glaz'ev was known after the collapse of the Soviet Union as a partisan of economic reforms. In 1991, he was named vice minister and, in December 1992, minister of foreign economic relations in Egor Gaidar's government. He resigned from it after the October 1993 events, when he refused to support Boris Yeltsin in his struggle against the White House. Between 1993 and 1995, he was a Duma deputy, chairing the parliament's committee on economic policies. Between 1995 and 1999, he worked at the Federation Council and moved closer to Aleksandr Lebed'. During these years, Glaz'ev changed his mind on his liberal economic principles and moved closer to the Communists. Today he is an interventionist and statist in economic matters, although he does not advocate a return to the Soviet model. In 1999, he was elected deputy on the CPRF list. Within Rodina, Glaz'ev embodied the left wing. In spite of his hasty departure from the electoral bloc, he succeeded in standing as candidate in the presidential elections of March 2004 and garnered 4.1 percent of the votes.

22. Dunlop, "Aleksandr Dugin's 'Neo-Eurasian' Textbook," 104.

23. A. Dugin, "Partiia 'Evraziia' vykhodit iz bloka Glaz'eva," Km.Ru, September 19, 2003, http://www.km.ru/news/view.asp?id=7DD7770F40434412B24FDB116 DB19000.

24. See http://glazev.evrazia.org/news/190903-1.html.

25. Aleksandr Barkashov's Russian National Unity (RNU) was one of the first groups to emerge after Pamiat' split up. Barkashov, who rejects the Orthodox and Tsarist nostalgia of Pamiat' leaders, founded his own movement as well as the party newspaper *Russkii poriadok.* The RNU borrowed a significant part of its symbols from Nazism: the swastika, the Roman salute, paramilitary clothes, and parts of the Nationalsozialistische Deutsche Arbeiterpartei's program, including a mixed economy and eugenic theories. The RNU contends that the USSR implemented a program of racial miscegenation between Slavs and non-Aryan peoples in order to make the Slavs disappear. The RNU differed from numerous others post-Soviet nationalist groups in its racialist definition of the Russian nation. The movement imploded in 2000 and is now split into numerous small groups.

26. The main exception was Dmitry Riurikov, one of Boris Yeltsin's counselors on international politics. In 2001, he became a member of the central board of Evraziia while he was Russia's ambassador to Uzbekistan (he was later transferred to Denmark).

27. Dugin, *Osnovy geopolitiki,* 159.

28. Ibid., 7.

29. In Russian, it is impossible to distinguish between "Eurasian" and "Eurasianist" (*evraziiskii chelovek*).

30. The Russian Indymedia Web site is http://www.russia.indymedia.org.

31. He also republished Iakov Bromberg's *Evrei i Evraziia* (Moscow: Agraf, 2002) and E. Khara-Davan's *Rus' mongol'skaia* (Moscow: Agraf, 2002).

32. Dugin, *Evraziiskaia missiia Nursultana Nazarbaeva*, 191.

33. As quoted in "Evraziiskii triumf," *Kontinent Evraziia*, ed. P. Savitsky (Moscow: Agraf, 1997), 434.

34. Dugin, *Osnovy geopolitiki*, 159.

35. See the editorial in *Elementy* no. 1 (1992), 2.

36. Leont'ev stood for a far-reaching turn in Russian thought. He argued that Russians are not really Slavs but above all a people mixed with Turkic groups. Leont'ev was the first to understand the potential of the "Turanian argument" to help Russia assert its identity against Europe. See M. Laruelle, "Existe-t-il des précurseurs au mouvement eurasiste? L'obsession russe pour l'Asie à la fin du XIXe siècle," *Revue des études slaves*, nos. 3–4 (2004): 437–54.

37. A. Dugin, "Ot sakral'noi geografii k geopolitike," *Elementy*, no. 1 (1992), http://arcto.ru/modules.php?name=News&file=article&sid=407.

38. Dugin, *Osnovy geopolitiki*, 247.

39. Dugin wants Ukraine to return to Russia's fold and to rearrange its territory in accordance with what he calls the ethnocultural facts, that is, a division between the West and East of Ukraine. For a more detailed analysis of Dugin's view of Ukraine, see Dunlop, "Aleksandr Dugin's 'Neo-Eurasian' Textbook," 109–12.

40. However, Dugin accepts the separatism of those areas that he considers non-Russian (he proposes to return the Kuril Islands to Japan and Kaliningrad to Germany), provided they remain under the control of allies of Eurasia and Continentalism.

41. Dugin, *Osnovy geopolitiki*, 341.

42. For further details, see Dunlop, "Aleksandr Dugin's 'Neo-Eurasian' Textbook," 109–12.

43. A. Dugin, "Evraziiskii otvet na vyzovy globalizatsii," in *Osnovy evraziistva*, 541–63.

44. Dugin, *Evraziiskaia missiia Nursultana Nazarbaeva*, 100.

45. Dugin, *Nash put'*, 47.

46. Dugin, *Osnovy geopolitiki*, 261. See Samuel P. Huntington, *The Clash of Civilizations and the Remaking of World Order* (New York: Simon & Schuster, 1996).

47. Dugin, *Konspirologiia;* also online at http://www.arctogaia.com/public/consp.

48. Dugin, *Evraziia prevyshe vsego. Programmye dokumenty OPOD Evraziia* (Moscow: Artogeia, 2002).

49. Dugin, *Osnovy evraziistva*, 762.

50. The standard reference on Traditionalism is M. Sedgwick, *Against the Modern World: Traditionalism and the Secret Intellectual History of the Twentieth Century* (Oxford: Oxford University Press, 2004).

51. These five books are *Introduction générale à l'étude des doctrines hindoues*, 1921; *Le théosophisme, histoire d'une pseudo-religion*, 1921; *L'erreur spirite*, 1923; *Orient et Occident*, 1924; and *La crise du monde moderne*, 1927.

52. Dugin, *Tampliery proletariata,* 128.

53. Hesychasm is a spiritual school founded by the Desert Fathers in the fourth century CE. It advocates contemplation, the repeated invocation of the name of Jesus and striving for tranquillity. Later, it developed mainly within the Greek Church. Its main proponent was Gregory Palamas (c. 1296–1359).

54. Dugin, *Filosofiia traditsionalizma,* 11.

55. A. Dugin, "O nashem zhurnale," *Milyi Angel,* no. 1 (1991), available at http://www.angel.com.ru.

56. Dugin, *Filosofiia traditsionalizma,* 11.

57. Dugin, *Puti absoliuta;* republished as Dugin, *Absoliutnaia rodina* (Moscow: Arktogeia, 1999), 174.

58. Dugin, *Metafizika blagoi vesti;* republished in Dugin, *Absoliutnaia rodina,* 510.

59. Dugin, *Puti absoliuta,* 152–53.

60. Dugin, *Osnovy geopolitiki,* 255.

61. E.g., see the papers he gave at the Sixth World Russian People's Congress in *Osnovy evraziistva,* 704–15.

62. The Old Believers are a current of Orthodoxy born from the Schism (Raskol), i.e., the separation, in the seventeenth century, of a significant portion of the Orthodox population from the official Russian Church. They rejected Patriarch Nikon's reforms of the orthodox ritual and liturgy. They were repeatedly persecuted in Tsarist times and were at the origin of numerous religious and social revolts against the central authorities. Dugin sees himself as one of the so-called united believers who follow the Old Believers' rites while recognizing the authority of the Patriarch. Other Old Believers, who refuse to acknowledge the Patriarchate in exchange for tolerance of their specific practice of worship, are in a minority today.

63. A. Dugin, *Russkaia veshch,* vol. 1, 568.

64. A. Dugin, "Kontrinitsiatsiia," *Milyi Angel,* no. 3 (1996).

65. A. Dugin, "Russkoe pravoslavie i initsiatsiia," *Milyi Angel,* no. 2 (1996).

66. See A. Dugin, "Evoliutsiia paradigmal'nykh osnovanii nauki," his candidate of sciences thesis defended in 2000 at Rostov-on-the-Don University.

67. Ibid., 66.

68. Dugin, *Osnovy geopolitiki,* 12.

69. Dugin, *Puti absoliuta,* 5.

70. Dugin, *Konservativnaia revoliutsiia,* 85–97.

71. Ibid., 99.

72. Ibid., 4–5.

73. See P.-A. Taguieff, *Sur la nouvelle droite: Jalons d'une analyse critique* (Paris: Descartes & Cie, 1994), 148–296.

74. In *Den'* nos. 2, 22, 34, 37 (1992) and no. 3 (1993).

75. "I have a lot of reservations about a 'Eurasian' construction, which seems to me to be mainly phantasmagorical"; Taguieff, *Sur la nouvelle droite,* 311.

76. Ibid., 254–65.

77. Dugin, *Konservativnaia revoliutsiia,* 131–6.

78. Taguieff, *Sur la nouvelle droite,* 259.

79. Dugin, *Filosofiia traditsionalizma,* 135–91.

80. See, e.g., the chapter "Races, Runes, and Worships" in *Misterii Evrazii,* 673–736, or *Nash put',* 21.

81. The Slavophile philosopher A. Khomiakov (1804–60) saw two philosophical

principles at work in the world: Iranian and Cushite. He borrowed this idea from Friedrich Schlegel's philosophy of history. For more information, see M. Laruelle, *Mythe aryen et rêve impérial dans la Russie du XIXe siècle* (Paris: CNRS Éditions, 2005), 78–87.

82. A. Dugin, *Misterii Evrazii;* republished in Dugin, *Absoliutnaia rodina,* 642. On this topic, see also A. Dugin, *Giperboreiskaia teoriia: Opyt ariosofskogo issledovaniia* (Moscow: Arktogeia, 1993).

83. Dugin, *Filosofiia traditsionalizma,* 176.

84. A. Dugin, *Misterii Evrazii;* republished in Dugin, *Absoliutnaia rodina,* 575.

85. Dugin, *Metafizika blagoi vesti,* 482.

86. Dugin, *Osnovy geopolitiki,* 190.

87. Dugin, *Misterii Evrazii,* 78.

88. Ibid., 26.

89. "Ot sakral'noi geografii k geopolitike."

90. E.g., in *Erwägen Wissen Ethik* 15, no. 3 (2004) between Roger Griffin, Andreas Umland, and A. James Gregor.

91. Dugin, *Osnovy evraziistva,* 638–56.

92. Dugin, *Russkaia veshch,* vol. 1, chap. 2: "The Social Idea," 251–500.

93. A. Dugin, *Programma politicheskoi partii "Evraziia": Materialy uchreditel'nogo s"ezda* (Moscow: Arktogeia, 2002), 112; and Dugin, *Osnovy evraziistva,* 579–88.

94. Dugin, *Evraziiskaia missiia Nursultana Nazarbaeva,* 51.

95. Dugin, *Osnovy evraziistva,* 585.

96. M. Agursky, *Ideologiia natsional-bol'shevizma* (Paris: YMCA Press, 1980). See also E. van Ree, "The Concept of National Bolshevism: An Interpretative Essay," *Journal of Political Ideologies,* no. 3 (2001): 289–307; and D. Shlapentokh, "Bolshevism, Nationalism, and Statism: Soviet Ideology in Formation," *Cahiers du monde russe,* no. 4 (1996): 429–66.

97. K. Popper, *The Open Society and Its Enemies* (London, 1945).

98. Dugin, *Tampliery proletariata,* 8.

99. Ibid., 26.

100. Ibid., 25.

101. Ibid., 188.

102. Dugin, *Konservativnaia revoliutsiia,* 54.

103. Dugin, *Filosofiia traditsionalizma,* 353.

104. A. Dugin, "Eroticheskii idealizm," *Elementy,* no. 6 (1995): 18.

105. Dugin, *Konservativnaia revoliutsiia,* 217.

106. Dugin, *Evraziia prevyshe vsego,* 5.

107. Dugin, *Filosofiia voiny,* back cover.

108. Dugin, *Konservativnaia revoliutsiia,* 27.

109. M. Sedgwick, *Against the Modern World: Traditionalism and the Secret Intellectual History of the Twentieth Century* (Oxford: Oxford University Press, 2004), 237–40.

110. See http://avigdor-eskin.com/index.shtml.

111. Dugin, *Osnovy evraziistva,* 600.

112. Dugin, *Konservativnaia revoliutsiia,* 245–82.

113. Dugin, *Puti absoliuta,* 175.

114. A. Dugin, "Messiantsvo kabbaly," *Milyi angel,* no. 3 (1996), available at http://www.angel.com.ru.

115. Dugin, *Konets sveta,* 348.

116. Dugin, *Metafizika blagoi vesti*, 248.

117. Dugin, *Russkaia veshch'*, vol. 1, 45–46.

118. A. Dugin, "Apokalipsis stikhii," *Elementy*, no. 8 (1997): 56.

119. "Ad-Marginem: Sacher-Masoch," *Elementy*, no. 6 (1995): 64.

120. Dugin, *Konservativnaia revoliutsiia*, 248.

121. See, e.g., M. Laruelle, "Regards sur la réception du racialisme allemand chez les panslavistes et les eurasistes russes," in *L'Allemagne des linguistes russes: Revue germanique internationale*, ed. C. Trautmann-Waller (Paris: CNRS Éditions, 2005), 145–56.

122. Dugin, *Nash put'*, 3.

123. Dugin, *Programma politicheskoi partii "Evraziia,"* 25.

124. A. Dugin, *Evraziiskii vzgliad: Mirovozzrencheskaia platforma OPOD "Evraziia"* (Moscow: Arktogeia, 2002), 62.

125. Dugin, *Osnovy geopolitiki*, 251.

126. Ibid., 593.

127. Dugin, *Nash put'*, 135.

128. A. Dugin, "Edinstvennyi vozmozhnyi natsionalizm dlia Rossii—natsionalizm liubvi," Spas Television Web site, http://spastv.ru/comment/1.

129. Dugin, *Evraziia prevyshe vsego*, 22.

130. Dugin, *Nash put'*, 124.

131. Dugin, *Evraziia prevyshe vsego*, 19.

132. Ibid., 4.

133. Dugin, *Evrazijskaia missiia Nursultana Nazarbaeva*, 144.

134. The *Book of Vles* was proclaimed to be an authentic manuscript by émigré Russian and Ukrainian nationalists as early as the 1950s and 1960s. It was claimed to have been discovered during the Civil War by a White Army officer, but the original wooden plates on which the text was inscribed were supposedly lost during World War II. Although no original is available for dating, neo-pagan circles present it as an unquestionable historical source on the Old Slavs, but also as a book of hymns and prayers to the old gods that may be put to "practical" use.

135. Taguieff, *Sur la nouvelle droite*, 65. This classification should be distinguished from that used by René Rémond (conservatism, liberalism, Bonapartism) to identify political, not just intellectual, currents. Rémond's terms apply to the entire right, not just to its radical fringe.

136. A. Maksimov and O. Karabaagi, "Oni v svoikh koridorakh," *Obshchaia gazeta*, May 31, 2001.

Notes to Chapter 5

1. A. Nysanbaev and E. Kurmanbaev, "Evraziiskaia ideia Chokana Valikhanova," *Evraziiskoe soobshchestvo*, no. 2 (1999): 26–31; the quotation is on 26.

2. An earlier version of this section was published as M. Laruelle, "Le 'Dédoublement' d'une idéologie: Deux partis politiques eurasistes en Russie," *La roulette russe: Outre-terre—Revue française de géopolitique*, no. 4 (2003): 227–40.

3. A. Malashenko, *Islamskoe vozrozhdenie v sovremennoi Rossii* (Moscow: Carnegie Endowment for International Peace, 1998), 121.

4. G. Dzhemal', "Blagodaria IPV SSSR mog stat' 'vostochnym soiuzom' Rossii,"

Rossiia i musul'manskii mir, no. 8 (2000): 28–32; V. Sadur, "IPV—partiia sokhraneniia balansa," *Rossiia i musul'manskii mir,* no. 8 (2000): 32–35; M. Salakheddin, "IPV— partiia integratsii islama v sovremennoe obshchestvo," *Rossiia i musul'manskii mir,* no. 8 (2000): 35–38.

5. A. Aktaev, "Eto vopros very," *Elementy* (Moscow), no. 1 (1992): 12.

6. G. Dzhemal', *Nezavisimaia gazeta,* January 31, 1992, 4.

7. Malashenko, *Islamskoe vozrozhdenie v sovremennoi Rossii,* 141.

8. "Musul'mane v Dume poluchili kostiak," *Nezavisimaia gazeta,* December 20, 1999.

9. A. Lampsi, "Dvizhenie 'Refakh' vyshlo iz 'Edinstva'," *NG—Religii,* March 28, 2001, http://religion.ng.ru/printed/facts/2001-03-28/3_movement.html.

10. The EPR claims to have 40 percent "ethnic" Russian, 30 percent "Turkic," and 10 percent Caucasian members. It includes very few representatives of the small Siberian peoples.

11. The new legislation requires every party to have at least fifty regional branches in order to obtain registration and run for elections.

12. Declaration of the Second Congress, April 27, 2002, consulted in the fall of 2003 on EPR's Web site, http://www.eurasianparty.ru (which ceased to exist in 2005).

13. Declaration of April 4, 2002, *Edinoe otechestvo,* available at http://www .otechestvo.org.

14. Party program consulted in the fall of 2003 at the EPR's Web site, http:// www.eurasianparty.ru.

15. Ibid.

16. Ibid.

17. Khan Kuchum was the defender of one of the last Siberian khanates. He was defeated by the Cossack Ermak on Irtysh River in 1585.

18. Declaration of the Second Congress, April 27, 2002.

19. The infamous Tsaritsyno pogrom took place on October 30, 2001, at a Moscow market near the Tsaritsyno metro station. Four foreign nationals were killed, and 80 people were injured. It was the first such event to have been largely discussed in the media, prompting the Moscow city government to set up a special department to fight youth extremism. Of the 300 skinheads who took part in the pogrom, only 5 were ultimately sentenced (each to several years in prison).

20. A. Dugin, "Evraziiskii proekt ot islama," in *Osnovy evraziistva* (Moscow: Arktogeia, 2002), 619.

21. A.-V. V. Niiazov, "Evraziistvo—ne proekt Kremlia," interview by Anna Zakatnova, *Nezavisimaia gazeta,* July 31, 2001.

22. This is from the first sentence of the EPR's program; the Web site (http:// www.eurasianparty.ru) was consulted in the fall of 2003.

23. Ibid.

24. On Russian neopaganism, see E. Moroz, "Le Védisme, version païenne de l'idée russe," *Revue d'études comparatives Est-Ouest,* nos. 3–4 (1993): 183–97.

25. For the details, see E. Moroz, *"L'Islam habite notre avenir!* Le prosélytisme musulman en Russie, conversions, institutionnalisation et stratégies politiques," in *Islam et politique en ex-URSS (Russie d'Europe et Asie centrale),* ed. M. Laruelle and S. Peyrouse (Paris: L'Harmattan, 2005), 117–34.

26. An earlier version of this section was published as M. Laruelle, "L'appartenance à l'islam comme critère politique? La politisation des directions spirituelles et la con-

stitution de partis musulmans en Russie," in *Islam et politique en ex-URSS*, ed. Laruelle and Peyrouse, 85–115.

27. M. Saliakhetdinov, "Musul'mane Rossii pod kryshei gosudarstva," *Rossiia i musul'manskii mir*, no. 7 (2001): 18–21.

28. N. K. Gvosdev, "The New Party Card? Orthodoxy and the Search for Post-Soviet Russian Identity," *Problems of Post-Communism*, no. 6 (2000): 34.

29. T. Tadzhuddin, "Nasha rodina—sviataia Rus'," in *Programnye dokumenty OPOD "Evraziia"* (Moscow: Arktogeia, 2001), 9.

30. T. Tadzhuddin, "Islam v Rossii," *Rossiia i musul'manskii mir*, no. 7 (2002): 27–31.

31. For a discussion of these issues, see S. Gradirovskii, ed., *Preodolevaia gosudarstvenno-konfessional'nye otnosheniia* (Nizhnii Novgorod: N.p., 2003).

32. Malashenko, *Islamskoe vozrozhdenie v sovremennoi Rossii*, 123.

33. T. Tadzhuddin, "Iz interv'iu s verkhovnym muftiem Rossii Talgatom Tadzhuddinom," *Rossiia i musul'manskii mir*, no. 7 (2003): 32–36.

34. Some Turkic nationalists portray Islam as an alien creed and rehabilitate the old animistic cult of the god Tengri by presenting it as a progressive form of monotheism whose cosmogony is perfectly adapted to the contemporary world. M. Laruelle, "Religious Revival, Nationalism, and the "Invention of Tradition": Political Tengrism in Central Asia and Tatarstan," *Central Asian Survey* 26, no. 2 (2007): 203–16.

35. T. Tadzhuddin, "Lidery rossiiskikh musul'man o prichinakh konflikta v islamskoi obshchine Rossii," *Rossiia i musul'manskii mir*, no. 3 (2001): 30.

36. M. Bidzhi-ulu, "O neobkhodimosti sozdaniia edinoi dukhovnoi struktury dlia rossiiskoi ummy," *Rossiia i musul'manskii mir*, no. 10 (2000): 44–48.

37. A. Maksimov, "Lidery musul'manskogo raskola," *Rossiia i musul'manskii mir*, no. 9 (2001): 58.

38. T. Tadzhuddin, "Nas nel'zia possorit': Iz interv'iu zhurnalista P. Zarifullina s verkhovnym muftiem Rossii T. Tadzhuddinom," 24.

39. A. Shtal'man, "Musul'manskie lidery Rossii obviniaiut drug druga v podderzhke vakhkhabizma," *Rossiia i musul'manskii mir*, no. 8 (2002): 28–30.

40. This was quoted at http://www.izvestiia.ru on April 4, 2003.

41. I. Kviatkovskaia and A. Kliuev, "Verkhovnyi muftii Rossii spriatal sabliu v nozhny," *Rossiia i musul'manskii mir*, no. 6 (2003): 35–36.

42. R. Gainutdin, "Rossiiskie musul'mane—patrioty svoego otechestva: Iz interv'iu zhurnalista L. Mironova s predsedatelem SMR Ravilem Gainutdinom," *Rossiia i musul'manskii mir*, no. 12 (2001): 30–33.

43. The SMR's Web site is http://www.muslim.ru.

44. The journalist Valerii Emelianov's interview with the deputy Fandas Saifullin in *Vse ob islame*, no. 6 (2002), at the Web site of the Council of Muftis of Russia, www.muslim.ru/razde.cgi?id=162&rid0=81&rid1=162&rid2=.

45. V. Pribylovskii, "Rossiiskie patrioty pod znamenem islama," *Rossiia i musul'manskii mir*, no. 2 (2004): 31–38.

46. N. Riazhapov, "Islamskie uchebnye zavedeniia v Rossii," *Rossiia i musul'manskii mir*, no. 10 (2001): 28–33.

47. R. Gainutdin, "Rossiiskaia Federatsiia—eto ee narody, ispoveduiushchie raznye religii," *Rossiia i musul'manskii mir*, no. 3 (1997): 4–5.

48. G. Kerimov, "Islamskaia kul'tura i evraziiskaia tsivilizatsiia," *Evraziia*, no. 3 (1995): 74.

49. Pribylovskii, "Rossiiskie patrioty pod znamenem islama," 31.

50. Tadzhuddin, "Nasha rodina—Sviataia Rus'," 9.

51. T. Tadzhuddin, "Evraziistvo est' samyi garmonichnyi i iskrennii rossiiskii patriotizm," Founding Congress of the Evraziia Party, May 30, 2002, in *Osnovy evraziistva*, 66.

52. Ibid., 67.

53. This quotation is at http://www.evrazia.org/modules.php?name=News&file=article&sid=1033.

54. T. Tadzhuddin, "Russkie stroili ne imperiiu, no Evraziiu, nash obshchii dom," speech given in December 2001 at the Sixth Global Council of the Russian People, in *Osnovy evraziistva*, 611.

55. Tadzhuddin, "Nas nel'zia possorit'," 20.

56. Tadzhuddin, "Russkie stroili ne imperiiu," 614.

57. A. Vorontsova and S. Filatov, "Tatarstanskoe evraziistvo: Evroislam plius evropravoslavie," *Rossiia i musul'manskii mir*, no. 11 (1998): 32–39, and no. 12 (1998): 29–32.

58. See J.-R. Raviot, "Identité régionale et identité nationale: L'émancipation politique du Tatarstan de juin 1988 au 21 mars 1992," *Revue d'études comparatives Est-Ouest*, no. 1 (1993): 101–30.

59. The distance between Bashkortostan and the independent state of Kazakhstan is only 80 kilometers, and another 80 between Kazakhstan and Mongolia—enough to make Russian nationalists tremble with fear of a Turkic-Mongol axis at the very heart of Eurasia.

60. M. Shaimev, "Tatarstan: Dialog religii, dialog kul'tur," *Rossiia i musul'manskii mir*, no. 1 (1996): 44–46.

61. See A. Bennigsen and C. Lemercier-Quelquejay, *Sultan Galiev: Le père de la révolution tiers-mondiste* (Paris: Fayard, 1986).

62. Vasilii Likhachev was vice president of the republic from 1991 to 1995 and president of the State Council of Tatarstan. From 1998 to 2003, he served as Russia's representative to the European Union in Brussels. Since March 2004, he has been representing Ingushetia at the Federation Council and as president of the council.

63. N. A. Nazarbaev, *Evraziiskii soiuz: Idei, praktika, perspektivy 1994–1997* (Moscow: Fond sodeistviia razvitiiu sotsial'nykh i politicheskikh nauk, 1997), 111–4.

64. See http://www.polit-nn.ru/?pt=news&view=single&id=10507.

65. See R. Mukhametchin, "Les composants islamiques de la politique confessionnelle en république du Tatarstan," in *Islam et politique en ex-URSS*, ed. Laruelle and Peyrouse, 41–59.

66. An earlier version of this section was published as Laruelle, "Nouvelles formulations idéologiques et théologiques de l'islam post-soviétique," in *Islam et politique en ex-URSS*, ed. Laruelle and Peyrouse, 273–95.

67. R. Khakimov, *Islam v Povolzh'e*, http://www.kazanfed.ru/dokladi/islam_in_volga_region.pdf.

68. R. Khakimov, *Gde nasha Mekka? Manifest evroislama* (Kazan: Magarif, 2003).

69. A. Khalid, *The Politics of Muslim Cultural Reform: Jadidism in Central Asia* (Berkeley: University of California Press, 1998).

70. On historical Jadidism, see S. A. Dudoignon, "Le Réformisme musulman en Asie centrale: Du 'premier renouveau' à la soviétisation, 1788–1937," *Cahiers du monde*

russe 37, nos. 1–2 (1996); and S. A. Dudoignon, D. Is'haqov, and R. Mohämmätshin, eds., *L'Islam de Russie: Conscience communautaire et autonomie politique chez les Tatars de la Volga et de l'Oural, depuis le XVIIIᵉ siècle* (Paris: Maisonneuve & Larose, 1997).

71. R. Khakimov, "Kriticheskoe myshlenie i obnovlenie islama," *Islam, identichnost' i politika v postsovetskom prostranstve: Kazanskii federalist* (Kazan Institute of Federalism) 13, no. 1 (2005): 28–35, http://www.kazanfed.ru/authors/kKhakimov/publ7/.

72. R. Khakimov, "Kto ty, tatarin?" http://miraska.narod.ru/tatars/hakim2.htm.

73. R. Khakimov, "Ia—samyi tatarstanskii natsionalist," *Komsomol'skaia pravda,* March 21, 2002, http://www.tatar.ru/?DNSID=b11935a40a8d2f2beae0e77066037228&node_id=1563.

74. The Kriashens are a group of Tatar speakers that has been Orthodox for several centuries. Kriashen nationalist intellectuals want the Kriashens to be recognized as a distinct "nationality." In the 2002 census, "Kriashen" was included in the multiple-choice list of "nationalities," something the Tatars perceived as a provocation staged by Moscow to weaken Tatar identity and challenge the Tatars' status as the titular nationality in Tatarstan. However, the final result (about 23,000 Kriashens were counted) did not have any particular repercussions.

75. R. Khakimov, "Kto ty, tatarin?" *Vostochnyi ekspress,* nos. 17–18 (April 26–May 2, 2002): 3.

76. Interview with Rafael K. Khakimov, Institute of Federalism, Kazan, April 2004.

77. R. Khakimov, "Vostok i Zapad sblizhaet idzhtihad—svobodomyslie," *Respublika Tatarstan,* October 7, 2004, http://www.tatar.ru/?DNSID=b11935a40a8d2f2beae0e 77066037228&node_id=2863.

78. Khakimov, "Kriticheskoe myshlenie i obnovlenie islama," 33.

79. Ibid.

80. R. Khakimov, "Evroislam v mezhtsivilizatsionnykh otnosheniiakh," *Nezavisimaia gazeta,* October 26, 1998.

81. R. Khakimov, *Sumerki imperii: K voprosu o natsii i gosudarstve* (Kazan: Tatknigoizdat, 1993), 19.

82. Mukhametchin, "Les composants islamiques," 41–59.

83. R. Salikov and L. Kaliadin, "Vo imia vozrozhdeniia," *Evraziia,* no. 4 (1996): 23–27.

84. Ibid., 27.

85. *Evraziistvo: Istoriko-kul'turnoe nasledie i perspektivy razvitiia, Mezhdunarodnaia nauchnaia konferentsiia—Tezisy dokladov,* December 14–15, 2000 (Ufa: Vostochnyi universitet, 2000).

86. On these examples and specifically on the Kalmyk case, see C. Humphrey, " 'Eurasia,' ideology and the political imagination in provincial Russia," in *Postsocialism. Ideals, Ideologies and Practices in Eurasia,* ed. C. M. Hann (New York: Routledge, 2002), 258–76.

87. M. E. Nikolaev, "Ideia, ob"ediniaiushchaia Rossiiu: Tiurkskii kaganat—pervoe evraziiskoe gosudarstvo," *Nezavisimaia gazeta,* March 5, 1996.

88. See http://www.evrazia.org/modules.php?name=News&file=article&sid=2023. Information on the Iakutsk-based Arctic Institute is available at http://www.universiteti .ru/baza/info-2365.html.

89. A. Krivoshapkin and S. Mikhailov, "Evraziiskii put' razvitiia—eto edinstvennyi put' dlia naroda Sakha," interview with members of the Sakha branch of the Inter-

national Eurasianist Movement, http://evrazia.org/modules.php?name=News&file=article&sid=2015.

Notes to Chapter 6

1. An earlier version of this section was published as: M. Laruelle, "Jeux de miroir: L'idéologie eurasiste et les allogènes de l'Empire russe," *Cahiers d'études sur la Méditerranée orientale et le monde turco-iranien (CEMOTI)* (CERI, Paris), no. 28 (1999): 207–30; and M. Laruelle, "Les ambiguïtés de l'eurasisme kazakh: Ouverture sur le monde russe ou fermeture nationaliste?" *Cahiers d'études sur la Méditerranée orientale et le monde turco-iranien (CEMOTI)*, no. 34 (2002): 119–34.

2. See F. Diat, "Olzhas Sulejmenov: *Az i Ia*," *Central Asian Survey*, no. 1 (1984): 101–21.

3. See H. Ram, "Imagining Eurasia: The Poetics and Ideology of Olzhas Suleimenov's *Az i Ia*," *Slavic Review* 60, no. 2 (2001): 289–311. Khlebnikov was also, in the early twentieth century, trying to reconceptualize relations between the empire's center and its southern periphery. In addition, he wanted to fuse historiography and literature in order to link time and space. Incidentally, in his poetic works of 1919–20, he drew attention to the similarity between the two Russian words for "I" (*az* and *ia*) and the word "Asia."

4. "The nineteenth-century Russians could not be racist: too close were their ties of blood, culture, and politics with the Turkic peoples. Russia formed a bond with the Steppe. Attempts to destroy those very close and indeed political ties have led to the dramatic events unfolding before our eyes." O. Suleimenov, *Az i Ia* (Alma-Ata: Zhazushy, 1975), 102.

5. O. Suleimenov, *Iazyk pis'ma: Vzgliad v doistoriiu—O proiskhozhdenii pis'mennosti i iazyka malogo chelovechestva* (Almaty: Rim, 1998); O. Suleimenov, *Peresekaiushchiesia paralleli* (Almaty: Dauir, 2002); O. Suleimenov, *Tiurki v doistorii: O proiskhozhdenii drevnetiurkskikh iazykov i pis'mennosti* (Almaty: Amatura, 2002).

6. This did not prevent Gumilëv from expressing his disdain for *Az i Ia*. In his article "Spor s poetom" (*Molodaia gvardiia*, no. 12, 1975), he wrote that "the number of factual blunders in Suleimenov's book exceeds the number of pages." The text is online at http://www.gumilevica.kulichki.net/articles/Article02.htm.

7. O. Suleimenov, "Krasota spaset mir . . . Da, esli my spasem krasotu!" *Evraziia*, no. 1 (1993): 45.

8. Ibid., 43–44.

9. Mukhtar Auezov is considered one of the greatest Kazakh writers of the twentieth century. His most famous book, *Abai's Path*, published in the 1950s, highlighted the work of Abai Kunanbaev (1845–1904) as part of the Kazakh national heritage and secured Auezov's fame in Soviet letters.

10. M. Auezov, "Evraziiskaia dukhovnaia traditsiia i preemstvennost' kazakhskoi kul'tury," in *Kul'tura Kazakhstana: Traditsii, real'nosti, poiski* (Almaty, N.p., 1998), 34.

11. B. Tashenov, *Evraziistvo v etnokul'turnoi istorii Kazakhstana* (Almaty: Arys, 2000), 187–88.

12. B. Mamraev, "Les idées eurasistes dans le contexte socio-culturel du Kaza-

250   *Notes to Pages 177–82*

khstan: Les filiations de la tradition et de la modernité," in *L'idée d'Eurasie*, ed. W. Dressler (Paris, forthcoming).

13. N. Masanov, "Natsional' no-gosudarstvennoe stroitel'stvo v Kazakhstane: analiz i prognoz," *Vestnik Evrazii* (Moscow), no. 1 (1995): 120.

14. N. Nazarbaev, *Evraziiskii soiuz: Idei, praktika, perspektivy 1994–1997* (Moscow: Fond sodeistviia razvitiiu sotsial'nykh i politicheskikh nauk, 1997), 38–50.

15. The Central Asian Cooperation Organization (CACO) was created in 2001 on the basis of the earlier Central Asian Economic Community, founded in 1998 by Kazakhstan, Kyrgyzstan, Tajikistan, and Uzbekistan. In October 2005, CACO announced that it was merging in the Eurasian Economic Community, which in turn was boosted with the accession of Uzbekistan, announced in late 2005 and confirmed in January 2006. With the exception of Turkmenistan, which remains isolated, the Central Asian countries now share a common economic space partly integrated with Russia and Belarus, and can be considered to be taking part in Russian-driven processes of post-Soviet integration.

16. A Commonwealth of Independent States Customs Union had been created in 1995, anticipating the Eurasian Community.

17. E.g., the "Red bosses" (directors of big enterprises in the Russian regions), high-ranking military officers, the military-industrial complex, the agricultural lobbies, as well as the institutions of the Commonwealth of Independent States and, more generally, institutions overseeing cooperation between the former Soviet republics.

18. Ch. Aitmatov, "Drevnetiurkskaia tsivilizatsiia: Pamiatniki pis'mennosti," *Kazakhstan: XXI vek*, no. 3 (2001).

19. This is as quoted at http://www.emu.kz/research/eurasia/mission.html.

20. M. Shaikhutdinov, "A. Dugin i imperskaia modifikatsiia evraziiskoi idei," *Evraziiskoe soobshchestvo*, no. 2 (2002): 26–32; M. Shaikhutdinov, "Imperskie proekty geopoliticheskoi identichnosti Rossii," *Evraziiskoe soobshchestvo*, no. 2 (2003): 5–14.

21. However, not everyone falls for Dugin's stratagem. In September 2003, during a press conference-cum-debate between Dugin and the Kazakh nationalist scholar Azimbai Gali, the latter stated that Nazarbaev could not be considered a Eurasianist in Dugin's sense, because he is not anti-Atlanticist, not anti-Semitic, and not antiliberal— three features Gali said are defining of Dugin's thought. See A. Dugin, *Evraziiskaia missiia Nursultana Nazarbaeva* (Moscow: Arktogeia, 2004), 158.

22. S. Bulekbaev and E. Unnarbaev, "Evraziistvo kak ideologiia gosudarstvennosti," *Evraziiskoe soobshchestvo*, no. 3 (2001): 5–12; E. Saudanbekova, "Evraziistvo Gumileva i klassicheskoe russkoe evraziistvo," *Mysl'*, no. 8 (1997): 30–34.

23. "The president is personally responsible for not letting the nation disappear in the coming century or two." N. Nazarbaev, *V potoke istorii* (Almaty: Atamura, 1999), 5.

24. B. Tashenov, *Evraziistvo v etnokul'turnoi istorii Kazakhstana*, 154.

25. K. A. Berdenova, ed., *Evraziistvo v ekonomicheskoi i etnopoliticheskoi istorii Kazakhstana* (Almaty: Ekonomica, 1997), 132.

26. On this, see M. Laruelle and S. Peyrouse, *Les Russes du Kazakhstan: Identités nationales et nouveaux États dans l'espace post-soviétique* (Paris: Maisonneuve & Larose —IFEAC, 2004).

27. O. Dymov, *Teplo kazakhstanskoi zemli* (Almaty: Arys, 1999), 39.

28. Ibid., 8.

29. Ibid., 12.

30. Ibid., 70.

31. Nazarbaev, *V potoke istorii*, 18.

32. Nazarbaev, *Evraziiskii soiuz*, 27.

33. Interview with Seit Kaskabasov, then director of the Eurasianist Center at Lev Gumilëv University, Astana, February 16, 2000.

34. Nazarbaev, *V potoke istorii*, 124.

35. Ibid., 195.

36. Ibid., 62.

37. V. Inushin, *Teoriia i praktika mezhetnicheskogo i mezhkul'turnogo vzaimodeistviia v sovremennom Kazakhstane* (Almaty: Natsional'naia komissiia respubliki Kazakhstan po delam UNESKO, 1998), 64.

38. M. K. Kozybaev, "Uroki otechestvennoi istorii i vozrozhdenie kazakhstanskogo obshchestva," *Stolichnoe obozrenie*, July 10, 1998, 3.

39. S. R. Eleukenov, ed., *Evraziiskii talisman* (Almaty: Bilim, 1996).

40. These elites especially gathered around a famous trio: the ethnographer Chokan Valikhanov (1835–65), the poet and translator Abai Kunanbaev (1845–1904), and the educator Ibrahim Altynsarin (1841–89).

41. Nazarbaev, *V potoke istorii*, 6.

42. Ibid., 24.

43. Ibid., 81. Also see M. Barbankulov, *Zolotaia baba (evraziistvo vo vsem i vsegda)* (Almaty: Rauan, 1998).

44. S. Akatai, "Evraziistvo v kontekste kul'turnoi obshchnosti," in *Kul'tura Kazakhstana: Traditsii, real'nosti, poiski* (Almaty: N.p., 1998), 45.

45. Berdenova, ed., *Evraziistvo v ekonomicheskoi*, 105.

46. Nazarbaev, *V potoke istorii*, 79.

47. All these important figures of medieval Islamic culture were born in Central Asia. They have become key symbols of Central Asia within the Muslim world, and their legacy is being claimed by several countries of the region. Al-Khorezmi (780–850) is famous for having given algebra its name; Al-Farabi (870–950) is known for his Neo-Platonism; Al-Biruni (973–1050?) was versed in mathematics, astronomy, and physics; Mahmud al-Kashgari was the author of an Arabic-Turkish dictionary published in Xinjiang in 1071; and the poet Balasaguni wrote the earliest surviving Turkic poem, *Kuttu Bilim*, during the reign of the Karakhanids (in 1070).

48. Nazarbaev, *V potoke istorii*, 105. The poet Ahmed Yassavi (died 1146) lived in Turkistan. A Sufi sheikh, he founded the Yassaviyya order. Tamerlane decided to build a mausoleum for him in 1394, when the city of Yasi was already a great Sufi center.

49. "Having assimilated the ideas of European democracy without losing their national roots, the leaders of Alash were bearers of the Eurasianist idea." Berdenova, *Evraziistvo v ekonomicheskoi*, 189.

50. Turkish has two different terms, *türk* and *türki*, but this distinction is hardly ever observed; the former term is used indiscriminately to refer to Turkish citizens as well as to the Turkic peoples living outside Turkey.

51. See especially L. Cahun, *Introduction à l'histoire de l'Asie: Turcs et Mongols des origines à 1405* (Paris: Armand Colin, 1896).

52. G. Imart, *Islamic and Slavic Fundamentalism: Foes or Allies?* (Bloomington, Ind.: Research Institute for Inner Asian Studies, 1987).

53. These waves came after the annexation of the Crimea in 1873; after the Crimean War (1853–55); after the Russo-Turkish war of 1878; after the Stolypin Reaction, when many post-1905 political activists were persecuted; after World War I; and, of course,

after the October Revolution and the civil war. See É. Copeaux, "De la mer Noire à la mer Baltique: La circulation des idées dans le triangle Istanbul-Crimée-Pologne," *Cahiers d'études sur la Méditerranée orientale et le monde turco-iranien (CEMOTI)*, no. 15 (1993): 107–20.

54. See F. Georgeon, *Des Ottomans aux Turcs: Naissance d'une nation*, Analecta Isisiana 16 (Istanbul: Isis, 1995).

55. See S. A. Zenkovsky, *Pan-Turkism and Islam in Russia* (Cambridge, Mass.: Harvard University Press, 1960).

56. See É. Copeaux, "Le Mouvement prométhéen," *Cahiers d'études sur la Méditerranée orientale et le monde turco-iranien (CEMOTI)*, no. 16 (1993): 9–46.

57. See F. Üstel, "Les Foyers turcs et les Turcs de l'extérieur," *Cahiers d'études sur la Méditerranée orientale et le monde turco-iranien (CEMOTI)*, no. 16 (1993): 47–62.

58. Z. Gökalp, *Turkish Nationalism and Western Civilization*, trans. and ed. N. Berkes (London: George Allen & Unwin, 1959); and Z. Gökalp, *The Principles of Turkism*, trans. R. Devereux (Leiden: E. J. Brill, 1968).

59. See F. Georgeon, *Aux origines du nationalisme turc: Yusuf Akçura (1876–1935)* (Paris: Institut d'Études Anatoliennes, 1980).

60. See D. Kushner, *The Rise of Turkish Nationalism, 1876–1908* (London: Frank Cass, 1977).

61. See P. Dumont, "La revue *Türk Yurdu* et les Musulmans de l'Empire russe, 1911–1914," *Cahiers du monde russe et soviétique*, nos. 3–4 (1974): 215–331.

62. See J. M. Landau, *Panturkism in Turkey: From Irredentism to Cooperation* (London: Hurst, 1981).

63. See P. Dumont, "La Fascination du bolchevisme: Enver Pacha et le parti des Soviets populaires, 1919–1922," *Cahiers du monde russe et soviétique*, no. 2 (1975): 141–66.

64. See É. Copeaux, "L'Invention de l'histoire," *Les Turcs, Orient et Occident, Islam et laïcité* (Autrement Monde HS), no. 76 (1994): 160–76.

65. E.g., see A. Inan, *L'Anatolie, le pays de la "race" turque: Recherches sur les caractères anthropologiques des populations de la Turquie* (Geneva: Georg, 1941).

66. See É. Copeaux, "Ahmed Arvasi, un idéologue de la synthèse turco-islamique," *Turcica*, no. 30 (1998) : 211–33.

67. See É. Copeaux, "Les 'Turcs de l'extérieur' dans *Türkiye:* Un aspect du discours nationaliste turc," *Cahiers d'études sur la Méditerranée orientale et le monde turco-iranien (CEMOTI)*, no. 14 (1992): 31–52.

68. See É. Copeaux, *Espace et temps de la nation turque: Analyse d'une historiographie nationale, 1931–1993* (Paris: CNRS Éditions, 1997).

69. On this, see J. P. Laut, *Das Türkische als Ursprache? Sprachwissenschaftliche Theorien in der Zeit des erwachenden türkischen Nationalismus* (Wiesbaden: Harrassowitz Verlag, 2000).

70. See É. Copeaux, *Une vision turque du monde à travers les cartes* (Paris: CNRS Éditions, 2000), 61.

71. See V. Mastny and R. Craig Nation, eds., *Turkey between East and West: New Challenges for a Rising Regional Power* (Boulder, Colo.: Westview Press, 1996); and A. Gökalp, ed., *La Turquie en transition* (Paris, Maisonneuve & Larose, 1986).

72. See G. E. Fuller and I. O. Lesser, *Turkey's New Geopolitics: From the Balkans to Western China* (Oxford: Westview Press, 1993).

73. These include the journal *Turkiston Torikhi* and opposition circles in Erk and Birlik (Uzbekistan), Zheltoksan (Kazakhstan), Türkmen ili (Turkmenistan), etc.

74. See G. Winrow, *Turkey in Post-Soviet Central Asia* (London: Royal Institute of International Affairs, 1995).

75. See *La Turquie en Asie centrale: La conversion au réalisme (1991–2000)*, Dossiers de l'IFEA, no. 5 (Istanbul; IFEA, 2001).

76. For details, see B. Balci, *Missionnaires de l'Islam en Asie centrale: Les écoles turques de Fethullah Gülen*, IFEA Series (Paris: Maisonneuve & Larose, 2003).

77. See S. De Tapia, "Türksat et les républiques turcophones de l'ex-URSS," *Cahiers d'études sur la Méditerranée orientale et le monde turco-iranien (CEMOTI)*, no. 20 (1995): 399–413.

78. See www.tika.gov.tr

79. For online access to these publications, see http://www.tika.gov.tr/avdos.asp and http://www.tika.gov.tr/turkdb.asp.

80. See B. Ersanli and V. Korkmaz, "Russian Eurasianism: Model for Iran and Turkey?" *Turkish Review of Eurasian Studies*, no. 4 (2004): 99–133.

81. See L. Bazin, S. Kançal, R. Perez, and J. Thobie, *La Turquie entre trois mondes*, Actes du colloque international de Montpellier, October 5–7, 1995, Varia Turcica XXXII (Istanbul: IFEA–L'Harmattan, 1998).

82. E.g., see the dossier on Russian identity, *Rusya Özel*, in *Avrasya Dosyası*, no. 4 (2001): 16–94.

83. See http://www.yeniavrasya.net/ara.asp.

84. See http://www.da.com.tr.

85. These publications are mentioned by S. De Tapia, "*Avrasya:* Les versions turques de l'Eurasie," in *L'idée d'Eurasie*, ed. Dressler.

86. S. Akturk, "Counter-Hegemonic Visions and Reconciliation through the Past: The Case of Turkish Eurasianism," *Ab Imperio*, no. 4 (2004): 207–38.

87. These extracts are online at http://www.evrazia.org/modules.php?name=News&file=article&sid=2093.

88. See a report on the trip at http://www.evrazia.org/modules.php?name=News&file=article& sid=2116.

89. See his Web site, http://www.doguperincek.com.

90. See http://www.aydinlik.com.tr.

91. See http://evrazia.org/modules.php?name=News&file=article&sid=2407.

92. The center's Web site is at http://allturkey.narod.ru/rutam.htm.

93. De Tapia, "*Avrasya.*"

Notes to the Conclusion

1. P. P. Suvchinsky, "Inobytie russkoi religioznosti," *Evraziiskii vremennik* 3 (1923): 105.

2. A. Dugin, *Evraziiskaia missiia Nursultana Nazarbaeva* (Moscow: Arktogeia, 2004), 144.

3. P. N. Savitsky, "Introduction to G. V. Vernadskii," in *Nachertanie russkoi istorii* (Prague: Evraziiskoe knigoizdatel'stvo, 1927), 9.

4. P.-A. Taguieff, *Sur la nouvelle droite: Jalons d'une analyse critique* (Paris: Descartes & Cie, 1994), 96.

5. M. von Hagen, "Imperii, okrainy i diaspory: Evraziia kak antiparadigma dlia postsovetskogo perioda," *Ab Imperio*, no. 1 (2004): 127–70.

6. This organization, known as GUAM, which was created in 1996, now includes Georgia, Ukraine, Azerbaijan, and Moldova; Uzbekistan also belonged to it from 1999 to 2002. It aims to coordinate the strategic and economic policies of those post-Soviet countries most interested in shaking off Russian influence.

7. See Samuel P. Huntington, *The Clash of Civilizations and the Remaking of World Order* (New York: Simon & Schuster, 1996).

Bibliography

Primary Sources

Monographs and Articles

Akaev, A. *Kyrgyzskaia gosudarstvennost' i narodnyi epos "Manas."* Bishkek: Uchkun, 2002.

Akatai, S. "Evraziistvo v kontekste kul'turnoi obshchnosti." In *Kul'tura Kazakhstana: Traditsii, real'nosti, poiski.* Almaty: N.p., 1998.

Alekseev, N. N. *Na putiakh k budushchei Rossii: Sovetskii stroi i ego politicheskie vozmozhnosti.* Paris: Evraziiskoe knigoizdatel'stvo, n.d.

———. *Russkii narod i gosudarstvo.* Moscow: Agraf, 1998.

Alekseev, N. N., V. N. Il'in, and P. N. Savitskii. *O gazete Evraziia (Gazeta Evraziia ne est' evraziiskii organ).* Paris: Evraziiskoe knigoizdatel'stvo, 1929.

Auezov, M. "Evraziiskaia dukhovnaia traditsiia i preemstvennost' kazakhskoi kul'tury." In *Kul'tura Kazakhstana: Traditsii, real'nosti, poiski.* Almaty: N.p., 1998.

Barbankulov, M. *Zolotaia baba (evraziistvo vo vsem i vsegda).* Almaty: Rauan, 1998.

Berdenova, K. A., ed. *Evraziistvo v ekonomicheskoi i etnopoliticheskoi istorii Kazakhstana.* Almaty: Ekonomica, 1997.

Bromberg, Ia. A. *Evrei i Evrazija.* Moscow: Agraf, 2002.

———. *Rossiia, Zapad i evreistvo: Opyt peresmotra evreiskogo voprosa.* Prague: Izdanie Evraziitsev, 1931.

Dugin, A. *Absoliutnaia rodina.* Moscow: Arktogeia, 1999.

———. *Evoliutsiia paradigmal'nykh osnovanii nauk.* Moscow: Arktogeia, 2002.

———. *Evraziia prevyshe vsego: Programmnye dokumenty OPOD "Evraziia."* Moscow: Arktogeia, 2002.

———. *Evraziiskaia missiia Nursultana Nazarbaeva.* Moscow: Arktogeia, 2004.

———. *Evraziiskii vzgliad: Mirovozzrencheskaia platforma OPOD "Evraziia."* Moscow: Arktogeia, 2002.

———. *Evraziistvo: Teoriia i praktika.* Moscow: Arktogeia, 2001.

———. *Filosofiia traditsionalizma.* Moscow: Arktogeia, 2002.

———. *Filosofiia voiny.* Moscow: Arktogeia, 2004.

————. *Giperboreiskaia teoriia: Opyt ariosofskogo issledovaniia.* Moscow: Arktogeia, 1993.

————. *Konservativnaia revoliutsiia.* Moscow: Arktogeia, 1994.

————. *Konspirologiia.* Moscow: Arktogeia, 1993. Republished in 2005.

————. *Metafizika blagoi vesti: Pravoslavnyi ezoterizm.* Moscow: Arktogeia, 1996.

————. *Misterii Evrazii.* Moscow: Arktogeia, 1991.

————. *Nash put': Strategicheskie perspektivy razvitiia Rossii v XXI veke.* Moscow: Arktogeia, 1999.

————. *Osnovy evraziistva.* Moscow: Arktogeia, 2002.

————. *Osnovy geopolitiki: Geopoliticheskoe budushchee Rossii.* Moscow: Arktogeia, 1997.

————. *Programma politicheskoi partii "Evraziia": Materialy uchreditel'nogo s"ezda.* Moscow: Arktogeia, 2002.

————. *Russkaia veshch': Ocherki natsional'noi filosofii.,* Moscow: Arktogeia, 2001.

————. *Tampliery proletariata: Natsional-bol'shevizm i initsiatsiia.* Moscow: Arktogeia, 1997.

Eleukenov, S. R., ed. *Evraziiskii talisman,* Almaty: Bilim, 1996.

Evraziia: Istoricheskie vzgliady russkikh emigrantov. Moscow: RAN, 1992.

Evraziia v svete iazykoznaniia. Paris: Izdanie Evraziitsev, 1931.

Evraziiskaia perspektiva: Vtoroi mezhdunarodnyi kongress "Kul'tura i budushchee Rossii." Moscow, 1994.

Evraziiskii vremennik III. Berlin: Evraziiskoe izdatel'stvo, 1923.

Evraziiskii vremennik IV. Berlin: Evraziiskoe izdatel'stvo, 1925.

Evraziiskii vremennik V. Berlin: Evraziiskoe izdatel'stvo, 1927.

Evraziiskii sbornik: Politika, filosofiia, rossievedenie. Prague: Evraziiskoe izdatel'stvo, 1929.

Evraziistvo: Deklaratsiia, formulirovka, tezisy. Paris: Izdanie Evraziitsev, 1932.

Evraziistvo: Istoriko-kul'turnoe nasledie i perspektivy razvitiia, Mezhdunarodnaia nauchnaia konferentsiia—Tezisy dokladov. Ufa: Vostochnyi universitet, 2000.

Evraziistvo: Formulirovka 1927 g. Paris: Izdanie Evraziitsev, 1927.

Evraziistvo: Opyt sistematicheskogo izlozheniia. Paris: Evraziiskoe knigoizdatel'stvo, 1926.

Gatsev, G. *Natsional'nye obrazy mira: Evraziia—Kosmos kochevnika, zemledel'tsa i gortsa.* Moscow: Institut DI-DIK, 1999.

Girenok, F. I., ed. *Global'nye problemy i perspektivy tsivilizatsii (fenomen evraziistva).* Moscow, 1993.

Gumilëv, L. N. *Chërnaia legenda: Druz'ia i nedrugi Velikoi stepi.* Moscow: Progress, 1994.

————. *Drevniaia Rus' i Velikaia step'.* Moscow: Mysl', 1989.

————. *Drevnie tiurki.* Moscow: Klyshnikov, Komarov i K, 1993.

————. *Etnogenez i biosfera zemli.* Leningrad: Gidrometeoizdat, 1990.

————. "Etnogenez i biosfera zemli." *Priroda i chelovek,* no. 12 (1988): 56–60; no. 1 (1989): 59–62; no. 2 (1989): 56–61; no. 3 (1989): 58–62; no. 4 (1989): 54–59.

————. "Etnos, istoriia, kul'tura." *Dekorativnoe iskusstvo SSSR,* no. 4 (1989); 32–33.

————. "Les fluctuations du niveau de la mer Caspienne." *Cahiers du monde russe et soviétique* 6, no. 3 (1965): 331–66.

————. *Khunnu: Stepnaia trilogiia.* Moscow: Kompass, 1993.

————. *Iz istorii Evrazii.* Moscow: Iskusstvo, 1992.

————. "Menia nazyvaiut evraziitsem." *Nash sovremennik,* no. 1 (1991): 132–41.

————. "Les Mongols du XIIIe siècle et le *Slovo o polku Igore.*" *Cahiers du monde russe et soviétique* 7, no. 1 (1966): 37–57.

————. *Ot Rusi do Rossii.* Saint Petersburg: Iyuna, 1992.

————. "Otkuda est' poshla Rus.' " *Slovo,* no. 8 (1992): 6–11.

————. "Pis'mo v redaktsiiu '*Voprosov filosofii.*'" *Voprosy filosofii,* no. 5 (1989): 157–60.

————. *Ritmy Evrazii. Epokhi i tsivilizatsii.* Moscow: Progress, 1993.

————. "Sila epokhi." *Dekorativnoe iskusstvo SSSR,* no. 7 (1989): 34–35.

————. *Tysiacheletie vokrug Kaspiia.* Moscow: Misel' i K, 1993.

————. *V poiskakh vymyshlennogo tsarstva.* Moscow: Klyshnikov, Komarov i K, 1992.

————. "Vremia strastei." *Nauka i religiia,* no. 6 (1996): 16–21.

————. "Zametki poslednego evraziitsa." *Nashe nasledie,* no. 3 (1991): 19–26.

Idei i real'nost' evraziistva. Almaty: Daik-press, 1999.

Iskhod k Vostoku: Predchuvstviia i vershenie. Sofia: Rossiisko-bolgarskoe izdatel'stvo, 1921.

Jakobson, R. O. *K kharakteristike Evraziiskogo iazykogo soiuza.* Prague: Izdanie Evraziitsev, 1931.

Karel'skaia, L. P. *L. N. Gumilëv. Otechestvennaia filosofiia.* Moscow: Amrita-Rus', 2005.

Karsavin, L. P. *Sochineniia.* Moscow: Raritet, 1993.

Kaskabasov, S. A., ed. *Problemy evraziistva.* Astana: Evraziiskii universitet, 1998.

Khakimov, R. *Gde nasha Mekka? Manifest evroislama.* Kazan: Magarif, 2003. http://www.kazanfed.ru/authors/khakimov.

————. *Islam v Povolzh'e.* http://www.kazanfed.ru/authors/khakimov.

————. "Kriticheskoe myshlenie i obnovlenie islama." In *Islam, identichnost' i politika v postsovetskom prostranstve: Kazanskii federalist* (Institute of Federalism, Kazan) 13, no. 1 (2005): 28–35.

————. "Kto ty, tatarin?" *Vostochnyi ekspress,* nos. 17–18 (April 26–May 2, 2002). http://www.tatarica.narod.ru/world/politic/unity/who2.htm.

————. *Sumerki imperii. K voprosu o natsii i gosudarstve.* Kazan: Tatknigoizdat, 1993.

————. "Vostok i Zapad sblizhaet idzhtikhad—svobodomyslie." *Respublika Tatarstan,* October 7, 2004.

Khara-Davan, E. *Chingis-Khan kak polkovodets i ego nasledie.* Belgrade: N.p., 1929.

Lavrov, S., ed. *Lev Gumilëv: Sud'ba i idei.* Moscow: Airys-Progress, 2003.

Mir Rossii-Evrazii: Antologiia. Moscow: Vysshaia shkola, 1995.

Na putiax: Utverzhdenie Evraziitsev. Berlin: Gelikon, 1922.

Nazarbaev, N. *Evraziiskii soiuz: Idei, praktika, perspektivy 1994–1997.* Moscow: Fond sodeistviia razvitiiu sotsial'nykh i politicheskikh nauk, 1997.

————. *V potoke istorii.* Almaty: Atamura, 1999.

Nikolaev, M. E. "Ideia, ob''ediniaiushchaia Rossiiu: Tiurkskii kaganat—pervoe evraziiskoe gosudarstvo," *Nezavisimaia gazeta,* March 5, 1996.

Orlov, I. B. *Evraziiskaia tsivilizatsiia.* Moscow: Norma, 1998.

Panarin, A. S. *Global'noe politicheskoe prognozirovanie v usloviiakh strategicheskoi nestabil'nosti.* Moscow: Algoritm, 2002.

————. *Iskushenie globalizmom.* Moscow: Algoritm, 2000.

————. "O derzhavnike-Ottse i liberal'nykh nositeliakh edipova kompleksa: K 50–letiiu so dnia smerti I. V. Stalina." *Moskva,* no. 3 (2003), http://www.moskvam.ru/2003/03/panarin.htm.

————. "Ontologiia terrora." In *Geopolitika terrora: Geopoliticheskie posledstviia terroristicheskikh aktov v SShA 11 sentiabria 2001 g.* Moscow: Arktogeia, 2002.

————. *Politologiia: uchebnik.* Moscow: Prospekt, 1998.

————. *Pravoslavnaia tsivilizatsiia v global'nom mire.* Moscow: Algoritm, 2002.

————. *Revansh istorii: Rossiiskaia strategicheskaia initsiativa v XXI veke.* Moscow: Logos, 1998.

————. *Rossiia v tsiklakh mirovoi istorii.* Moscow: MGU, 1999.

————. *Rossiia v tsivilizatsionnom protsesse.* Moscow: IFRAN, 1995.

————. "Russkaia pravoslavnaia tserkov' v prostranstve Evrazii." In *Materialy VI Vsemirnogo russkogo narodnogo sobora.* Moscow: Arktogeia, 2002.

————. *Strategicheskaia nestabil'nost' v XXI veke.* Moscow: Algoritm, 2003.

————. *Vtoraia Evropa ili Tretii Rim: Izbrannaia sotsial'no-filosofskaia publitsistika.* Moscow: IFRAN, 1996.

Panarin, A. S., and B. B. Il'in, eds. *Rossiia: Opyt natsional'no-gosudarstvennoi ideologii.* Moscow: MGU, 1994.

Panarin, A. S., and B. S. Erasov, eds. *Rossiia i Vostok: Problemy vzaimodeistviia.* Moscow: Rossiiskaia akademiia nauk, 1993.

————. *Rossiia i Vostok: Tsivilizatsionnye otnosheniia,* 3 vols. Moscow: Rossiiskaia akademiia nauk, 1994–96.

Peil', V. A., ed. *Novaia epokha: Ideokratiia, Politika, Ekonomika, Obzory.* Narva: Izdanie Evraziitsev, 1933.

Polkovnikov, G. N. *Dialektika istorii.* Paris: Izdanie Evraziitsev, 1931.

Puti Evrazii: Russkaia intelligentsiia i sud'by Rossii. Moscow: Russkaia kniga, 1992.

Pashchenko, V. *Ideologiia evraziistva.* Moscow: MGU, 2000.

————. *Sotsial'naia filosofiia evraziistva.* Moscow: Al'fa, 2003.

Rossiia i latinstvo. Berlin: N.p., 1923.

Rossiia mezhdu Evropoi i Aziei: Evraziiskii soblazn. Moscow: Nauka, 1993.

Russkii uzel evraziistva: Vostok v russkoi mysl'. Moscow: Belovod'e, 1997.

Samubaldin, S. S. *Drakony i tigry Azii: Smozhet li kazakhstanskii bars proiti ikh tropami?* Almaty, 1998.

Savitskii, P. N. *V bor'be za evraziistvo.* Paris: Izdanie Evraziitsev, 1931.

————. *Kontinent Evraziia.* Moscow: Agraf, 1997.

————. *Rossiia—osobyi geograficheskii mir.* Paris: Evraziiskoe knigoizdatel'stvo, 1927.

————. *Šestina sveta: Rusko jako zemepisnı a historickı celek.* Prague, Melantrich, n.d.

————. *O zadachakh kochevnikovedeniia: Pochemu skify i gunny dolzhny byt' interesny dlia russkogo?* Prague: Evraziiskoe knigoizdatel'stvo, 1928.

Suleimenov, O. *Az i Ia.* Alma-Ata, Zhazushy, 1975.

————. *Iazyk pis'ma: Vzgliady v doistorii—O proiskhozhdenii pis'mennosti i iazyka malogo chelovechestva.* Almaty: Rim, 1998.

————. *Peresekaiushchiesia paralleli.* Almaty: Dauir, 2002.

————. *Tiurki v doistorii: O proiskhozhdenii drevnetiurkskikh iazykov i pis'mennosti.* Almaty: Amatura, 2002.

Tashenov, B. *Evraziistvo v etnokul'turnoi istorii Kazakhstana.* Almaty: Arys, 2000.

Toll', N. P. *Skify i gunny.* Prague: Izdanie Evraziitsev, 1928.

Tridtsatye gody. Paris: Evrazijskoe izdatel'stvo, 1931.

Trubetzkoy, N. S. *L'Europe et l'humanité: Ecrits linguistiques et para-linguistiques.* Trans. Patrick Sériot. Liège: Mardaga, 1996.

————. *Evropa i chelovechestvo.* Sofia: Rossiisko-bolgarskoe knigoizdatel'stvo, 1920.

————. *Istoriia: Kul'tura, Iazyk.* Moscow: Progress, 1995.

————. *Letters and Notes,* ed. R. Jakobson. Berlin: Mouton, 1975.

————. *K probleme russkogo samopoznaniia.* Paris: Evraziiskoe knigoizdatel'stvo, 1927.

————. *Nasledie Chingis-Xana: Vzgliad na russkuiu istoriiu ne s Zapada, a s Vostoka.* Berlin: Evraziiskoe knigoizdatel'stvo, 1925.

Vernadsky, G. V. *Drevniaia Rus'.* Moscow: Agraf, 1997.

————. *Mongoly i Rus'.* Moscow: Agraf, 1997.

————. *Nachertanie russkoi istorii.* Prague: Evraziiskoe knigoizdatel'stvo, 1927.

————. *Ocherk istorii prava russkogo gosudarstva.* Prague: N.p., 1924.

————. *Opyt istorii Evrazii.* Berlin: Izdanie Evraziitsev, 1934.

Vodologin, A., and S. Danilov. *Metafizicheskaia os' evraziistva.* Tver, 1994.

————. "Protiv solntsa: Rasprostranenie russkogo gosudarstva k Vostoku." *Russkaia mysl'*, no. 1 (1914).

Vspominaia L. N. Gumilëva. Vospominaniia, publikatsii, issledovaniia. Saint Petersburg: Rostok, 2003.

Journals Systematically Examined by the Author

Elementy, Moscow, 1992–98.

Evraziia: Ezhenedel'nik po voprosam kul'tury i politiki, Paris, 1928–29.

Evraziia: Narody, kul'tury, religii, Moscow, 1994–.

Evraziia: Obshchestvenno-politicheskii i literaturno-khudozhestvennyi zhurnal, Almaty, 2001–.

Evraziiskaia khronika, Prague and Berlin, 1925–37.

Evraziiskie tetradi, Paris, 1934–36.

Evraziiskii vestnik, Moscow, 2001–.

Evraziiskoe obozrenie, Moscow, 2001–4.

Evraziiskoe soobshchestvo, Almaty, 1992–.

Evraziitsev, Brussels, 1928–34.

Kazakhstan i mirovoe soobshchestvo, and *Kazakhstan-spektr*, Almaty, 1994–.

Literaturnaia Evraziia, Moscow, 1998–.

Milyi Angel, Moscow, 1991–99.

Rossiia i musul'manskii mir, Moscow, 1994–.

Svoi put': Ezhemesiachnaia gazeta, Tallinn, 1931.

Vestnik Evrazii, Moscow, 1993–.

Vtorzhenie, Moscow, 1999–2000.

Secondary Sources
Eurasianism and Neo-Eurasianism

Akturk, S. "Counter-Hegemonic Visions and Reconciliation through the Past: The Case of Turkish Eurasianism." *Ab Imperio*, no. 4 (2004): 207–38.

Alevras, N. N. "Problema Rossii i Evropy v traditsiiakh evraziiskoi shkoly." In *Rossiia i Zapad: Dialog kul'tur.* Moscow: MGU, 1996.

Bassin, M. "Classical Eurasianism and the Geopolitics of Russian Identity." *Ab Imperio,* no. 2 (2003): 257–68.

————. "Russia between Europe and Asia, the Ideological Construction of Geographical Space." *Slavic Review* 50, no. 1 (1991): 1–17.

Bazhanov, V. A. "A Note on A. S. Panarin's *Revansh istorii.*" *Europe-Asia Studies* 51, no. 4 (1999): 705–8.

Beisswenger, M. "Konservativnaia revoliutsiia v Germanii i dvizhenie evraziitsev— tochki soprikosnoveniia." *Konservatism v Rossii i v mire,* no. 3 (2004): 49–73.

Bilenkin, V., "The ideology of Russia's Rulers in 1995: Westernizers and Eurasians." *Monthly Review,* no. 5 (1995): 24–36.

Böss, O. *Die Lehre der Eurasier.* Wiesbaden: O. Harrassowitz, 1961.

Clover, C. "Dreams of the Eurasian Heartland." *Foreign Affairs* 78, no. 1 (1999): 9–13.

De Tapia, S. "*Avrasya:* Les versions turques de l'Eurasie." In *L'Idée d'Eurasie,* ed. W. Dressler. Paris, forthcoming.

Désert, M., and D. Paillard. "Les Eurasiens revisités." *Revue des études slaves* 66, no. 1 (1994): 73–86.

Diat, F. "Olzhas Sulejmenov: *Az i Ia.*" *Central Asian Survey,* no. 1 (1984): 101–21.

Duncan, P. J. S. "Contemporary Russian Identity between East and West." *Historical Journal* 48 (2005): 277–94.

Dunlop, J. B. "Aleksandr Dugin's 'Neo-Eurasian' Textbook and Dmitrii Trenin's Ambivalent Response." *Harvard Ukrainian Studies* 25, no. 1–2 (2001): 91–127.

Ersanli, B., and V. Korkmaz. "Russian Eurasianism: Model for Iran and Turkey?" *Turkish Review of Eurasian Studies,* no. 4 (2004): 99–133.

Glebov, S. "The Challenge of the Modern: The Eurasianist Ideology and Movement, 1920–29." Ph.D. thesis, Rutgers, the State University of New Jersey, 2004.

————. "Granitsy imperii kak granitsy moderna: Antikolonial'naia ritorika i teoriia kult'urnykh tipov v evraziistve." *Ab Imperio,* no. 2 (2003): 267–92.

Fischer, J. *Eurasismus: Eine Option russischer Außenpolitik?* Berlin: Berlin Verlag Spitz, 1998.

Hahn, G. "The Rebirth of Eurasianism." *CDI Russia Weekly,* July 12–18, 2002. http://www.cdi.org/russia/215–14–pr.cfm.

Halperin, C. J. "George Vernadsky, Eurasianism, the Mongols and Russia." *Slavic Review* 41, no. 3 (1982): 477–93.

————. "Russia and the Steppe." *Forschungen zur Osteuropäischen Geschichte* (Wiesbaden) 36 (1985): 55–194.

Hamant, Y. "Le Néo-eurasisme dans la Russie contemporaine." In *L'Idée d'Eurasie,* ed. W. Dressler. Paris, forthcoming.

Humphrey, C. " 'Eurasia,' Ideology and the Political Imagination in Provincial Russia." In *Postsocialism: Ideals, Ideologies and Practices in Eurasia,* ed. C. M. Hann. New York: Routledge, 2002.

Ingram, A. "Alexander Dugin: Geopolitics and Neo-Fascism in Post-Soviet Russia." *Political Geography,* no. 20 (2001): 1029–51.

Kerr, D. "The New Eurasianism: The Rise of Geopolitics in Russia's Foreign Policy." *Europe-Asia Studies* 47, no. 6 (1995): 977–89.

Koreniako, V. "Etnonatsionalizm, kvaziistoriia i akademicheskaia nauka." In *Real'nost' etnicheskikh mifov,* ed. A. Malashenko and M. B. Olcott. Moscow: Carnegie Endowment for International Peace, 2000.

————. "K kritike L. N. Gumilëva." *Etnograficheskoe obozrenie,* no. 3 (2006): 22–35.

Laruelle, M. "Alexandre Dugin: Esquisse d'un eurasisme d'extrême droite en Russie post-soviétique." *Revue d'études comparatives Est-Ouest,* no. 3 (2001): 59–78.

———. "Les ambiguïtés de l'eurasisme kazakh: Ouverture sur le monde russe ou fermeture nationaliste?" *Cahiers d'études sur la Méditerranée orientale et le monde turco-iranien,* no. 34 (2002): 119–34.

———. "L'Empire après l'Empire: le néo-eurasisme russe." *Cahiers du monde russe* 42, no. 1 (2001): 71–94.

———. "Existe-t-il des précurseurs au mouvement eurasiste? L'obsession russe pour l'Asie à la fin du XIXᵉ siècle." *Revue des études slaves,* nos. 3–4 (2004) : 437–54.

———. "Histoire d'une usurpation intellectuelle: Gumilev, 'le dernier des eurasistes'? Analyse des oppositions entre L. N. Gumilev et P. N. Savickij." *Revue des études slaves,* nos. 2–3 (2001): 449–59.

———. *L'Idéologie eurasiste russe ou comment penser l'empire.* Paris: L'Harmattan, 1999.

———. "Jeux de miroir: L'idéologie eurasiste et les allogènes de l'Empire russe." *Cahiers d'études sur la Méditerranée orientale et le monde turco-iranien,* no. 28 (1999): 207–30.

———. "Lev N. Gumilev (1912–1992): Biologisme et eurasisme en Russie." *Revue des études slaves,* nos. 1–2 (2000): 63–90.

———. "Religious Revival, Nationalism and the 'Invention of Tradition': Political Tengrism in Central Asia and Tatarstan." *Central Asian Survey* 26, no. 2 (2007): 203–16.

Liberman, A. "N. S. Trubetzkoy and His Works on History and Politics." In *The Legacy of Genghis-Khan,* ed. N. S. Trubetzkoy. Ann Arbor: Michigan Slavic Publications, 1991.

Liuks, L. "Evraziistvo i konservativnaia revoliutsiia: Soblazn antizapadnichestva v Rossii i Germanii." *Voprosy filosofii,* no. 6 (1996): 57–69.

Luks, L. "Der 'Dritte Weg' der 'Neo-Eurasischen' Zeitschrift 'Elementy'—zurück ins Dritte Reich?" *Studies in East European Thought* 52 (2000): 49–71.

———. "Die Ideologie der Eurasier im zeitgeschichtlichen Zusammenhang." *Jahrbücher für Geschichte Osteuropas* 34 (1986): 374–95.

Mathyl, M. "The National-Bolshevik Party and Arctogaia: Two Neo-Fascist Groupuscules in the Post-Soviet Political Space." *Patterns of Prejudice* 36, no. 3 (2003): 62–76.

Naarden, B. "*I Am a Genius, but No More Than That:* Lev Gumilev, Ethnogenesis, the Russian Past and World History." *Jahrbücher für Geschichte Osteuropas* 44, no. 1 (1996): 54–82.

Nivat, G. "Du panmongolisme au mouvement eurasien: Histoire d'un thème millénaire." *Cahiers du monde russe et soviétique* 7, no. 3 (1966): 460–78.

———. "Russie: Le deuil de l'empire." In *Le déchirement des nations,* ed. J. Rupnik. Paris: Seuil, 1995.

Paradowski, R. "The Eurasian idea and Leo Gumilev's Scientific Ideology." *Canadian Slavonic Papers* 41, no. 1 (1999): 19–32.

Ram, H. "Imagining Eurasia: Olzhas Suleimenov's *Az i Ia.*" *Slavic Review* 60, no. 1 (2001): 289–311.

Rangsimaporn, P. "Interpretations of Eurasianism: Justifying Russia's Role in East Asia." *Europe-Asia Studies* 58, no. 3 (2006): 371–89.

Riasanovsky, N. V. "The Emergence of Eurasianism." *California Slavic Studies,* no. 4 (1967): 39–72.

———. "Prince Trubetskoy's *Europe and Mankind.*" *Jahrbücher für Geschichte Osteuropas* 12 (1964): 207–20.

Sarkisyanz, E. "Russian Attitudes toward Asia." *Russian Review,* no. 13 (1954): 245–54.

———. *Russland und der Messianismus des Orients, Sendungsbewusstsein und politischer Chiliasmus des Ostens.* Tübingen: J. C. B. Mohr, 1955.

Schmidt, M. "Is Putin Pursuing a Policy of Eurasianism?" *Demokratizatsiya* 13, no. 1 (2005): 87–99.

Sériot, P. *Structure et totalité: Les origines intellectuelles du structuralisme en Europe centrale et orientale.* Paris: PUF, 1999.

Shlapentokh, D. V. "Eurasianism: Past and Present." *Communist and Post-Communist Studies* 30, no. 1 (1997): 129–51.

———. "Russian Nationalism Today: The Views of Alexander Dugin." *Contemporary Review* 279, no. 1626 (2001): 29–38.

Shnirel'man, V. "Lev Gumilëv: Ot *passionarnogo napriazheniia* do *nesovmestimosti kul'tur.*" *Etnograficheskoe obozrenie,* no. 3 (2006): 8–21.

Shnirelman, V., and S. Panarin. "Lev Gumilev: His Pretension as a Founder of Ethnology and His Eurasian Theories." *Inner Asia* 3, no. 1 (2001): 1–18.

Thom, F. "Eurasisme et néo-eurasisme." *Commentaires,* no. 66 (1994): 303–10.

Titov, A. "Lev Gumilev, Ethnogenesis and Eurasianism." Ph.D. thesis, School of Slavonic and Eastern European Studies, University College London, 2005.

Torbakov, I. "The Statists and the Ideology of Russian Imperial Nationalism." *RFE/RL* 1, no. 49 (1992): 10–16.

Tsygankov, A. "Aleksandr Panarin kak zerkalo rossiiskoi revoliutsii." *Vestnik MGU: Sotsiologiia i Politologiia,* no. 4 (2005): 166–77; and no. 1 (2006): 120–49.

———. "Hard-Line Eurasianism and Russia's Contending Geopolitical Perspectives." *East European Quarterly* 32, no. 1 (1998): 315–34.

———. "Mastering Space in Eurasia: Russia's Geopolitical Thinking after the Soviet Break-Up." *Communist and Post-Communist Studies* 36 (2003): 101–27.

———. "Natsional'nyi liberalizm Aleksandra Panarina." *Svobodnaia mysl',* no. 9 (2005): 100–17.

Tsymburskii, V. "Dve Evrazii: Omonimiia kak kliuch k ideologii rannego evraziistva." In *Evraziia, liudi i mify,* ed. S. Panarin. Moscow: Natalis-Press, 2003.

Umland, A. "Formirovanie fashistskogo 'neoevraziiskogo' dvizheniia v Rossii: Put' Aleksandra Dugina ot marginal'nogo ekstremista do ideologa postsovetskoi akademicheskoi i politicheskoi elity, 1989–2001 gg." *Ab Imperio,* no. 3 (2003): 289–304.

———. "Kulturhegemoniale Strategien der russischen extremen Rechten: Die Verbindung von faschistischer Ideologie und metapolitischer Taktik im Neoeurasismus des Alexandr Dugin." *Österreichische Zeitschrift für Politikwissenschaft* 33, no. 1 (2004): 437–54.

Vandalkovskaia, M. G. *Istoricheskaia nauka rossiiskoi emigratsii: "Evraziiskii soblazn."* Moscow: Rossiiskaia akademiia nauk, 1997.

Von Hagen, M. "Imperii, okrainy i diaspory: Evraziia kak antiparadigma dlia postsovetskogo perioda." *Ab Imperio,* no. 1 (2004): 127–70.

Russian Nationalism in General

Agursky, M. *Ideologiia natsional-bol'shevizma.* Paris: YMCA Press, 1980.

Allensworth, W. *The Russian Question: Nationalism, Modernization, and Post-Communist Russia.* Lanham, Md.: Rowman & Littlefield, 1998.

Bassin, M. *Imperial Visions: Nationalist Imagination and Geographical Expansion in the Russian Far East, 1840–1865.* Cambridge: Cambridge University Press, 1999.

Besançon, A. *Les origines intellectuelles du léninisme.* Paris: Calmann-Lévy, 1977.

———. *Présent soviétique et passé russe.* Paris: Pluriel, 1980.

Billington, J. H. *Russia in Search of Itself.* Washington and Baltimore: Woodrow Wilson Center Press and Johns Hopkins University Press, 2004.

Brudny, Y. *Reinventing Russia: Russian Nationalism and the Soviet State, 1953–1991.* Cambridge, Mass.: Harvard University Press, 1998.

Devlin, J. *Slavophiles and Commissars: Enemies of Democracy in Modern Russia.* Basingstoke, U.K.: Macmillan, 1999.

Duncan, P. J. S. *Russian Messianism: Third Rome, Revolution, Communism and After.* London: Routledge, 2000.

Dunlop, J. B. *The Faces of Contemporary Russian Nationalism.* Princeton, N.J.: Princeton University Press, 1983.

———. *The New Russian Nationalism.* New York: Praeger, 1985.

———. *The New Russian Revolutionaries.* Belmont, Mass.: Nordland, 1976.

———. *The Rise and Fall of the Soviet Union.* Princeton, N.J.: Princeton University Press, 1993.

Fish, M. S. *Democracy from Scratch: Opposition and Regime in the New Russian Revolution.* Princeton, N.J.: Princeton University Press, 1995.

Franklin, S., and E. Widdis, eds. *National Identity in Russian Culture.* Cambridge: Cambridge University Press, 2004.

Frazer, G., and G. Lancelle. *Absolute Zhirinovsky: A Transparent View of the Distinguished Russian Statesman.* New York: Penguin, 1994.

Gregor, A. J. "Fascism and the New Russian Nationalism." *Communist and Post-Communist Studies* 31, no. 1 (1998): 1–15.

Gvosdev, N. K. "The New Party Card? Orthodoxy and the Search for Post-Soviet Russian Identity." *Problems of Post-Communism,* no. 6 (2000): 29–38.

Hardeman, H. *Coming to Terms with the Soviet Regime: The "Changing Signposts" Movement among Russian Émigrés in the Early 1920s.* Dekalb: Northern Illinois University Press, 1994.

Hauner, M. *What Is Asia to Us? Russia's Asian Heartland Yesterday and Today.* New York: Routledge, 1992.

Hosking, G., and R. Service. *Russian Nationalism: Past and Present,* New York: Macmillan, 1998.

Kaiser, R. *The Geography of Nationalism in Russia and in the USSR.* Princeton, N.J.: Princeton University Press, 1994.

Klepikova, E., and V. Solov'ev. *Zhirinovsky: Russian Fascism and the Making of a Dictator.* Reading, Mass.: Addison-Wesley, 1995.

Korey, W. *Russian Antisemitism, Pamyat and the Demonology of Zionism.* Chur and Jerusalem: Harwood Academic Publishers for Vidal Sassoon International Center for the Study of Anti-Semitism and Hebrew University of Jerusalem, 1995.

Laqueur, W. *Black Hundred: The Rise of the Extreme Right in Russia.* New York: HarperCollins, 1993.

Laruelle, M. "The Discipline of Culturology: A New 'Ready-Made Thought' for Russia?" *Diogenes,* no. 204 (2004): 21–36.

———. *Mythe aryen et rêve impérial dans la Russie du XIXe siècle.* Paris: CNRS Éditions, 2005.

Likhachev, V. *Natsizm v Rossii.* Moscow: Panorama, 2002.

———. *Politicheskii antisemitizm v sovremennoi Rossii.* Moscow: Academia, 2003.

Likhachev, V., and V. Pribylovskii, eds. *Russkoe Natsional'noe Edinstvo: Istoriia, politika, ideologiia.* Moscow: Panorama, 1997.

March, L. *The Communist Party in Post-Soviet Russia.* Manchester: Manchester University Press, 2002.

McDaniels, T. *The Agony of the Russian Idea.* Princeton, N.J.: Princeton University Press, 1996.

Mitrokhin, N. *"Russkaia partiia": Dvizhenie russkikh natsionalistov v SSSR 1953–1985 gg.* Moscow: NLO, 2003.

Moroz, E. "Le Védisme, version païenne de l'idée russe." *Revue d'études comparatives Est-Ouest,* nos. 3–4 (1993): 183–97.

Niqueux, M., ed. *La Question russe: Essai sur le nationalisme russe.* Paris: Editions Universitaires, 1992.

Niqueux, M., and L. Heller. *Histoire de l'utopie en Russie.* Paris: PUF, 1995.

Nivat, G. *Russie-Europe, la fin du schisme.* Lausanne: L'Age d'Homme, 1993.

Parland, T. *The Extreme Nationalist Threat in Russia: The Growing Influence of Western Rightist Ideas.* New York: RoutledgeCurzon, 2004.

Pribylovskii, V., ed. *Russkie natsionalisticheskie i pravoradikal'nye organizatsii, 1989–1995: Dokumenty i teksty.* Moscow: Panorama, 1996.

Ramet, S., ed. *The Radical Right in Central and Eastern Europe since 1989.* University Park: Pennsylvania State University Press, 1999.

Rancour-Laferriere, D. *Russian Nationalism from an Interdisciplinary Perspective: Imagining Russia.* Lewiston, N.Y.: Edward Mellen Press, 2000.

Reddaway, P., and D. Glinski. *The Tragedy of Russia's Reforms: Market Bolshevism against Democracy.* Washington, D.C.: United States Institute of Peace Press, 2001.

Ree, E. van. "The Concept of National Bolshevism: An interpretative Essay." *Journal of Political Ideologies,* no. 3 (2001): 289–307.

Reznik, S. *The Nazification of Russia: Antisemitism in the Post-Soviet Era.* Washington, D.C.: Challenge Publications, 1996.

Rogachevski, A. *A Biographical and Critical Study of Russian Writer Eduard Limonov.* Studies in Slavic Language and Literature 20. Lewiston, Maine: Edwin Mellen Press, 2003.

Rosenthal, B. G. *The Occult in Russian and Soviet Culture.* Ithaca, N.Y.: Cornell University Press, 1997.

Rossman, V. *Russian Intellectual Antisemitism in the Post-Communist Era.* Lincoln: University of Nebraska Press for Vidal Sassoon International Center for the Study of Anti-Semitism, 2002.

Scherrer, J. *Kulturologie: Russland auf der Suche nach einer zivilisatorischen Identität.* Göttingen: Wallstein Verlag, 2003.

Shenfield, S. D. *Russian Fascism: Traditions, Tendencies, Movements.* Armonk, N.Y.: M. E. Sharpe, 2001.

Shlapentokh, D. "Bolshevism, Nationalism and Statism: Soviet Ideology in Formation." *Cahiers du monde russe,* no. 4 (1996): 429–66.

Shnirelman, V. *The Myth of the Khazars and Intellectual Antisemitism in Russia, 1970–1990s.* Jerusalem: Hebrew University of Jerusalem for Vidal Sassoon International Center for the Study of Anti-Semitism, 2002.

———. *Intellektual'nye labirinty: Ocherki ideologii v sovremennoi Rossii.* Moscow: Academia, 2004.

Simonsen, S. G. *Politics and Personalities: Key Actors in the Russian Opposition.* Oslo: PRIO, 1996.

Struve, G. *Russkaia literatura v izgnanii.* Paris: YMCA Press, 1984.

Struve, N. *Soixante-dix ans d'émigration russe, 1919–89.* Paris: Fayard, 1996.

Tolz, V. "The Radical Right in Post-Communist Russian Politics." In *The Revival of Right-Wing Extremism in the Nineties,* ed. P. H. Merkl and L. Weinberg. London: Frank Cass, 1997.

Tsygankov, A. *Whose World Order? Russia's Perception of American Ideas after the Cold War.* Notre Dame, Ind.: University of Notre Dame Press, 2004.

Umland, A. "The Post-Soviet Russian Extreme Right." *Problems of Post-Communism* 44, no. 4 (1997): 53–61.

———. *Toward an Uncivil Society? Contextualizing the Recent Decline of Extremely Right-Wing Parties in Russia.* Weatherhead Center for International Affairs Working Paper 02–03/2002. Cambridge, Mass.: Harvard University.

Urban, J. B., and V. Solovei. *Russia's Communists at the Crossroads.* Boulder, Colo.: Westview Press, 1997.

Urban, M. "Remythologising the Russian State." *Europe-Asia Studies,* no. 6 (1998): 969–92.

Verkhovskii, A., E. Mikhailovskaia, and V. Pribylovskii. *Politicheskaia ksenofobiia: Radikal'nye gruppy, predstavleniia liderov, rol' tserkvi.* Moscow: Panorama, 1999.

———. *Rossiia Putina: Pristrastnyi vzgliad.* Moscow: Panorama, 2003.

Verkhovskii, A., A. Papp, and V. Pribylovskii. *Politicheskii ekstremizm v Rossii.* Moscow: Panorama, 1996.

Verkhovskii, A., and V. Pribylovskii. *Natsional-patrioticheskie organizatsii v Rossii,* Moscow: Panorama, 1996.

Verkhovskii, A., V. Pribylovskii, and E. Mikhailovskaia. *Natsionalizm i ksenofobiia v rossiiskom obshchestve.* Moscow: Panorama, 1998.

Yanov, A. *The Russian Challenge and the Year 2000.* New York: Basil Blackwell, 1987.

———. *The Russian New Right: Right-Wing Ideologies in the Contemporary USSR.* Berkeley: University of California Press, 1978.

Zimmerman, W. *The Russian People and Foreign Policy: Russian Elite and Mass Perspectives, 1993–2000.* Princeton, N.J.: Princeton University Press, 2002.

General Theoretical Works on Nationalism

Anderson, B. *Imagined Communities: Reflections on the Origin and Spread of Nationalism.* New York: Verso, 1983.

Balibar, E., and E. Wallenstein. *Race, nation, classe: Les identités ambiguës.* Paris: La Découverte, 1988.

Birnbaum, P., ed. *Sociologie des nationalismes.* Paris: PUF, 1997.

Crapez, M. *La Gauche réactionnaire: Mythes de la plèbe et de la race.* Paris: Berg International, 1997.

Delannoi, G. *Sociologie de la nation: Fondements théoriques et expériences historiques.* Paris: Armand Colin, 1999.

Delannoi, G., and P.-A. Taguieff, eds. *Théories du nationalisme: Nation, nationalité, ethnicité.* Paris: Kimé, 1991.

Duranton-Crabol, A.-M. *L'Europe de l'extrême droite : De 1945 à nos jours.* Brussels: Complexe, 1991.

Gellner, E. *Nations and Nationalism.* Ithaca, N.Y.: Cornell University Press, 1983.

Girardet, R. *Mythes et mythologies politiques.* Paris: Seuil, 1990.

Godechot, J. *La Contre-révolution: Doctrine et action.* Paris: PUF, 1984; orig. pub. 1961.

Guillaumin, C. *L'Idéologie raciste, genèse et langage actuel.* Paris: Mouton, 1972.

Gusdorf, G. *Le Romantisme.* Paris: Payot, 1993.

Hobsbawn, E. *Nations and Nationalism since 1780: Programme, Myth, Reality.* Cambridge: Cambridge University Press, 1992.

Kohn, H. *Nationalism: Its Meaning and History.* Princeton, N.J.: Van Nostrand, 1955.

Milza, P. *L'Europe en chemise noire: Les extrêmes droites en Europe de 1945 à aujourd'hui.* Paris: Flammarion, 2002.

Milza, P. *Les Fascismes.* Paris: Seuil, 1985.

Olender, M., ed. *Pour Léon Poliakov: Le racisme, mythes et sciences.* Brussels: Complexe, 1981.

Perrineau, P. *Les Croisés de la société fermée: L'Europe des extrêmes droites.* Paris: Éditions de l'Aube, 2001.

Poliakov, L. *The Aryan Myth.* New York: Basic Books, 1974.

———. *A History of Antisemitism.* New York: Vanguard Press, 1975.

Remond, R. *Les Droites en France.* Paris: Aubier, 1982.

Rogger, H., and E. Weber, eds. *The European Right: A Historical Profile.* Berkeley: University of California Press, 1965.

Sternhell, Z. *The Birth of Fascist Ideology: From Cultural Rebellion to Political Revolution.* Princeton, N.J.: Princeton University Press, 1995.

———. *Neither Right nor Left: Fascist Ideology in France.* Princeton, N.J.: Princeton University Press, 1995.

Taguieff, P.-A. *La couleur et le sang: Doctrines racistes à la Française.* Paris: Mille et Une Nuits, 1998.

———. *La force du préjugé: Essai sur le racisme et ses doubles.* Paris: Gallimard, 1987.

———. *Sur la nouvelle droite: Jalons d'une analyse critique.* Paris: Descartes & Cie, 1994.

Taguieff, P.-A., and G. Delannoi, eds. *Les nationalismes en perspective.* Paris: Berg International, 2001.

Winock, M., ed. *Histoire de l'extrême droite en France.* Paris: Seuil, 1993.

———. *Nationalisme, antisémitisme et fascisme en France.* Paris: Seuil, 1990.

Other Works Cited

Balci, B. *Missionnaires de l'Islam en Asie centrale: Les écoles turques de Fethullah Gülen.* Paris: Maisonneuve & Larose, 2003.

Bazin, L., S. Kançal, R. Perez, and J. Thobie. *La Turquie entre trois mondes.* Istanbul: IFEA–L'Harmattan, 1998.

Bennigsen, A., and C. Lemercier-Quelquejay. *Sultan Galiev: Le père de la révolution tiers-mondiste.* Paris: Fayard, 1986.

Cahun, L. *Introduction à l'histoire de l'Asie: Turcs et Mongols des origines à 1405.* Paris: Armand Colin, 1896.

Copeaux, E. "Ahmed Arvasi, un idéologue de la synthèse turco-islamique." *Turcica,* no. 30 (1998): 211–33.

———. "De la mer Noire à la mer Baltique: La circulation des idées dans le triangle Istanbul-Crimée-Pologne." *Cahiers d'études sur la Méditerranée orientale et le monde turco-iranien,* no. 15 (1993): 107–20.

———. *Espace et temps de la nation turque: Analyse d'une historiographie nationale, 1931–1993.* Paris: CNRS Éditions, 1997.

———. "L'Invention de l'histoire." *Les Turcs, Orient et Occident, islam et laïcité* (Autrement Monde HS, Paris), no. 76 (1994): 160–76.

———. "Le Mouvement prométhéen." *Cahiers d'études sur la Méditerranée orientale et le monde turco-iranien,* no. 16 (1993): 9–46.

———. "Les 'Turcs de l'extérieur' dans Türkiye: Un aspect du discours nationaliste turc." *Cahiers d'études sur la Méditerranée orientale et le monde turco-iranien,* no. 14 (1992): 31–52.

———. *Une vision turque du monde à travers les cartes.* Paris: CNRS Éditions, 2000.

De Tapia, S. "Türksat et les républiques turcophones de l'ex-URSS." *Cahiers d'études sur la Méditerranée orientale et le monde turco-iranien,* no. 20 (1995): 399–413.

Dudoignon, S. A. "Le Réformisme musulman en Asie centrale: Du 'premier renouveau' à la soviétisation, 1788–1937." *Cahiers du monde russe* 37, nos. 1–2 (1996).

Dudoignon, S. A., D. Is'haqov, and R. Mohämmätshin, eds. *L'Islam de Russie: Conscience communautaire et autonomie politique chez les Tatars de la Volga et de l'Oural, depuis le XVIIIe siècle.* Paris: Maisonneuve & Larose, 1997.

Dumont, P. "La Fascination du bolchevisme: Enver Pacha et le parti des Soviets populaires, 1919–1922," *Cahiers du monde russe et soviétique,* no. 1 (1975): 141–66.

———. "La Revue *Türk Yurdu* et les musulmans de l'Empire russe, 1911–1914." *Cahiers du monde russe et soviétique,* nos. 3–4 (1974): 215–331.

Fuller, G. E., and I. O. Lesser. *Turkey's New Geopolitics: From the Balkans to Western China.* Boulder, Colo.: Westview Press, 1993.

Georgeon, F. *Aux origines du nationalisme turc: Yusuf Akçura (1876–1935).* Paris: Institut d'Etudes Anatoliennes, 1980.

———. *Des Ottomans aux Turcs: Naissance d'une nation.* Istanbul: Isis, 1995.

Gökalp, A., ed. *La Turquie en transition.* Paris: Maisonneuve & Larose, 1986.

Goodrick-Clarke, N. *The Occult Roots of Nazism: Secret Aryan Cults and Their Influence on Nazi Ideology.* New York: New York University Press, 1992.

Imart, G. *Islamic and Slavic Fundamentalism: Foes or Allies?* Bloomington, Ind.: Research Institute for Inner Asian Studies, 1987.

"Istanbul—Oulan Bator: Autonomisation, mouvements identitaires, construction du politique." *Cahiers d'études sur la Méditerranée orientale et le monde turco-iranien,* no. 16 (1993).

Khalid, A. *The Politics of Muslim Cultural Reform: Jadidism in Central Asia.* Berkeley: University of California Press, 1998.

Kushner, D. *The Rise of Turkish Nationalism, 1876–1908.* London: Frank Cass, 1977.

Landau, J. M. *Panturkism in Turkey: From Irrendentism to Cooperation.* London: Hurst & Co, 1981.

Laruelle, M., and S. Peyrouse, eds. *Islam et politique en ex-URSS (Russie d'Europe et Asie centrale).* Paris: L'Harmattan, 2005.

Laruelle, M., and S. Peyrouse. *Les Russes du Kazakhstan: Identités nationales et nouveaux États dans l'espace post-soviétique.* Paris: Maisonneuve & Larose, 2004.

Laut, J. P. *Das Türkische als Ursprache? Sprachwissenschaftliche Theorien in der Zeit des erwachenden türkischen Nationalismus.* Wiesbaden: Harrassowitz Verlag, 2000.

Malashenko, A. *Islamskoe vozrozhdenie v sovremennoi Rossii.* Moscow: Carnegie Endowment for International Peace, 1998.

Mastny, V., and R. Craig Nation, eds. *Turkey between East and West: New Challenges for a Rising Regional Power.* Boulder, Colo.: Westview Press, 1996.

Raviot, J.-R. "Identité régionale et identité nationale: L'émancipation politique du Tatarstan de juin 1988 au 21 mars 1992." *Revue d'études comparatives Est-Ouest,* no. 1 (1993) : 101–30.

Schlanger, J. *Les Métaphores de l'organisme.* Paris: L'Harmattan, 1995.

Sedgwick, M. *Against the Modern World: Traditionalism and the Secret Intellectual History of the Twentieth Century.* Oxford: Oxford University Press, 2004.

La Turquie en Asie centrale: La conversion au réalisme (1991–2000). Dossiers de l'IFEA 5. Istanbul: IFEA, 2001.

Üstel, F. "Les Foyers turcs et les Turcs de l'extérieur." *Cahiers d'études sur la Méditerranée orientale et le monde turco-iranien (CEMOTI),* no. 16 (1993): 47–62.

Winrow, G. *Turkey in Post-Soviet Central Asia.* London: Royal Institute of International Affairs, 1995.

Zenkovsky, S. A. *Pan-Turkism and Islam in Russia.* Cambridge, Mass.: Harvard University Press, 1960.

Index

Adzii, M.,186, 194
Ağaoğlu, A., 189
Aitmatov, T., 150, 178
Akaev, A., 10, 85
Akçura, Y., 189–90
Akhtaev, A., 146–47
Alekseev, N.: and the Clamart group,
     21–22, 24, 57, 225–26; and the
     classic Eurasianist movement, 19,
     57; and Dugin's rendition, 115
Almaty, 178
alter-globalization, 83, 114, 141, 235
anti-Semitism: in Dugin's works, 108,
     132, 250; in Gumilëv's works,
     74–76, 78, 234; the "Jewish
     question" in Duginian thought,
     135–38; and the Nazi past, 112,
     129, 142
Arctogaïa, 108–9, 115, 168
Artamonov, M., 52, 75
Aryanism: and Asia, 2–4; in Dugin's
     works, 108, 130, 137–38, 142–
     43; and Germany, 30; and Russia,
     40, 104, 240; and Tajikistan, 85;
     and the Turkic steppic past, 186,
     194
Ashirov, N., 156, 161
Assembly of Peoples, 181–82
Astana, 10, 178–79, 181, 183, 208
Atatürk, 190–91, 197. See also Kemal

Atlanticism, 118–19, 132, 154, 201
Auezov, Mukhtar, 176, 185, 249
Auezov, Murat, 176
Avrasya, 171, 195–98, 201, 207
Az i Ia, 173, 249

Baburin, S., 112, 127
Bagramov, E., 60, 84–86, 160, 179,
     206, 235
Balkans, 20, 26, 117, 192, 197, 220.
     See also Serbia
Barkashov, A., 112, 240
Bashkortostan, 12, 55, 118, 162, 168,
     247
Benoist, A. de, 94, 126–29, 142. See
     also New Right
Bernshtam, A., 57
Bibarsov, M., 146, 148, 156
biology, 64–66, 70, 139, 209
Blok, A., 4, 84, 148
Borisov, A., 168
Borodin, P., 150
Bromberg, Ia., 19, 136, 241
Bromlei, Iou., 53, 70, 80–81, 141
Buddhism: in Dugin's works, 123,
     149; in Gumilëv's works, 71; and
     Kazakhstan legacy, 176; in
     Panarin's works, 98, 102–3; as a
     religion in Russia, 6, 37, 118–19; in
     Russian thought, 4, 45, 220

Buriatia, 168
Byzantium: in Gumilëv's anti-Semitic conceptions, 75; and Orthodoxy, 43, 236; as a predecessor for Russia, 42, 44, 183, 229; as a super-*ethnos,* 71

Caspian Sea, 53, 66, 232
Central Asia: in Eurasianist thought, 205; as independent states, 162–63, 172, 187, 194–96; and Kazakh identity, 176, 186, 251; in the Mongol empire, 53, 102; as part of the post-Soviet space, 218–19, 250; during the Russian colonization, 43, 166; and Turkish identity, 190–92, 194, 197, 199–200
Chaadaev, P., 2–3, 223
Chechnya, 118, 148–49, 222
China: and contemporary Russia, 99, 104, 219; in Eurasianist thought, 45, 85, 117, 216; and Mongol and Turkic peoples, 52, 169, 194
Chivilikhin, V., 78
Chizhevskii, A., 67
Christianity: in Dugin's works, 116, 118, 123–24, 137–38; and Islam, 156; and Judaism, 76, 154; during the Khazar and Mongol empires, 43, 75, 176; and Oriental religions, 44–45, 227; in Panarin's works, 99–101, 104
Chubais, A., 9, 224
Communist Party of the Russian Federation. *See* Ziuganov
conflictology, 12, 216
conservative revolution: as a definition of Eurasianism, 26, 210; in Dugin's works, 115, 131, 134–35, 239; and Gumilëv and Panarin, 82, 99; as a Western tradition, 31, 58, 142
conspirology, 12, 120, 216
continentalism, 34, 132, 241
culturology, 10–12, 55, 91, 216, 224

Danilevski, N., 4, 88, 91, 93, 105, 233
Demirel, S., 195, 199

Den', 4–5, 109, 115, 127, 154–55
determinism: cultural, 203, 224; ethnic in Soviet tradition, 58, 206; geographic in Eurasianist thought, 31–32, 88, 205; in Gumilëv's works, 59, 65–66, 78, 81–82; in Panarin's works, 93, 96; racial, 129, 138
differentialism, 129, 138, 141, 201, 212, 214
Dostoyevsky, F., 3
Dugin, A. G.: biography of, 11, 108–11, 141–43; and the Eurasianist movement, 2, 5, 9, 13–15, 107, 170, 205–8; as a fascist thinker, 131–35, 210; geopolitical theories of, 115–20; and Gumilëv, 60, 82, 105; influence on Zhirinovsky and Ziuganov, 6; and Judaism, 135–38, 214; and Khakimov, 167; and Muslim Eurasianist parties, 146, 149, 151–55; and Panarin, 82, 86, 88–89, 95–96, 100, 102, 104; presence in Turkey, 194, 197–200; as a proponent of ethno-differentialism, 138–41, 211–12, 216; and Vladimir Putin, 7, 8, 114; and the Rodina party, 111–13, 240; as the Russian version of the New Right, 126–31; success in Yakutia-Sakha, 168–69; and Tadzhuddin, 160–61; traditionalism of, 120–26; as viewed in Kazakhstan, 179, 250
Dzhemal, G., 121, 146–48, 155

Erasov, B., 88, 91, 96
Ermolaev, V., 70, 78
esotericism: in Dugin's works, 109, 112, 132, 153, 179, 207; and Nordic theories, 129–30, 133, 137, 210; in Panarin's works, 98; and traditionalism, 121, 123–25, 131, 136–37, 142–43
ethno-differentialism. *See* New Right
ethnos: as an anti-Semitic argument,

75–76, 231–33; and culturalist theories, 220; in Dugin's works, 139–40; and Eurasian super-*ethnos,* 50, 59, 72, 78; and Eurasianist determinism, 206–7, 214, 216, 221; in Gumilëv's theories, 61, 65–72; in Kazakhstan, 185; in Khakimov's works, 167; in Russian publications, 10; in Soviet ethnology, 53, 80–82

Eurasianist Party of Russia (EPR), 146, 149–54, 161, 167, 245

Evola, J., 121–23, 129, 214

Evraziia (party): and the Eurasianist Party of Russia, 146, 153–54; founding of, 86, 110, 240; Jewish members of, 135–36; Muslim members of, 118–19, 160–61; Panarin's participation in, 89; place in the public scene, 179, 206; and the Rodina party, 111–12

Evraziia (weekly), 21–24, 26

Far East, 3, 8, 16, 43, 103–4, 168–69

fascism: and classic Eurasianism, 18, 24, 31, 205, 210; and Dugin, 2, 109, 128, 131–35, 142, 179; and Dzhemal, 155; as a Eurasianist vision of Italy, 25, 30; and Gumilëv, 58; and neo-Nazi groups, 152; and traditionalism, 121

Fedorov, N., 23, 67, 226

Fukuyama, F., 86, 92

Gainutdin, R., 153, 156–61

Galiev, S., 163

Gaspraly, I. (Gasprinsky), 165, 189, 199

genetics, 66, 209

Genghis Khan: in classic Eurasianist thought, 41–42; in Dugin's works, 129; in Gümilev's works, 53, 60, 72, 231; and Kazakhstan, 183; in Turkish historiography, 193–94; and Yakutia-Sakha, 168–69

geography: as a definition of Russia-

Eurasia, 31–35, 46–48; and Duginian sacred geography, 131, 168; as a Eurasianist science, 18, 47, 202, 228; in Gumilëv's works, 54, 64–67; and Leningrad University's Institute of Geography and Economics, 52

geopolitics: in Dugin's works, 2, 11, 108–11, 115–18, 125, 129; in Muslim Eurasianism, 147, 167, 198–99; as a nationalist science, 12, 34, 206, 216, 220; in Panarin's works, 88, 90, 92, 96, 105

Girenko, F., 84

Glaz'ev, S., 111, 132, 240

Gökalp, Z., 190

Golovin, E., 108, 121, 155

Gorbachev, M., 54, 87, 151, 218

GRECE (Groupe d'Études et de Recherche sur la Civilisation Européenne), 127, 129

Guénon, R.: and Dugin as a post-Guenonist, 123; in Dugin's works, 122, 124, 133, 142; as a founder of traditionalism, 15, 115; on the idea of sacred traditions, 120–21; on Judaism, 136; on race, 129–30, 133

Gumilëv, L. N.: the anti-Semitism of, 74–77; biography of, 50–55, 81–82; and classic Eurasianism, 55–60; in Dugin's works, 116, 141; ethnic conceptions of, 65–70, 206, 209, 212–14; and Eurasianist history of Russia, 70–73; and the Eurasianist movement, 2, 13, 170, 205–8, 216; in Kazakhstan, 178–81; and Muslim Eurasianism, 150, 163–64, 167; in Panarin's works, 88, 96, 104–5; the scientific assumptions of, 60–65; and Soviet ethnology, 77–81; the success in Russia of, 10–11, 14, 83–84; in Suleimenov's works, 173, 175, 249

Huns, 52, 57, 63, 185

Huntington, S., 93, 119, 219

Index

International Eurasianist Movement:
the foundation of, 113, 160; in
Kazakhstan, 179; political goal of,
143, 206; in Turkey, 199–200; in
Yakutia-Sakha, 168
Iran: in Aryanist theories, 130–31;
Dugin on Iranian Shiism, 117; in
Eurasianist theories, 85, 185–86; as
a partner of Russia, 6, 8, 200;
religious influence among Russian
Muslims, 147, 152, 155; and
Turkism, 192
Islam: and Dugin, 15, 117–18; in
Eurasianist thought, 37, 44–45,
174, 176, 205, 208, 218, 220; and
Evraziia party, 136; in Gumilëv's
works, 59, 72, 75; as an
international ally of Russia, 6–7; in
Kazakhstan, 183; Muslim parties in
Russia, 146–62, 207; and other
world religions, 4; in Panarin's
works, 85, 92, 98–100, 102–4;
place in Russia, 12, 14, 145; in
Tatarstan, 162–70; and
traditionalism, 122–23; in Turkey,
188–90, 192–93, 198–99, 201
Islamic Party of Rebirth, 146–47, 154
Islamism. *See* Islam
Israel, 135–37

Jadidism, 165–67, 189, 190. *See also*
Ottoman Empire; Tatarstan
Japan, 117, 142, 241
Judaism: and Iakov Bromberg, 19;
in Dugin's works, 120, 135–38,
142; in Eurasianist thought, 214,
233; Gumilëv's theories of, 71,
75–76; and Muslim Eurasianism,
154, 185; in Panarin's works,
100
Jungar, 180

Kafesoğlu, I., 192
Kaskabasov, S., 183–84, 251
Kazan: bust of Gumilëv in, 11, 164; as
a Eurasianist capital, 163, 177; in

the history of Russian expansion,
102, 166, 189; Islamic University
in, 159
Kemal, M., 190–91
Kemalism, 190–93, 195, 197
Khakimov, R., 164–67, 208
Khazaria, 75–77
Khomiakov, A., 4, 129, 242
Kievan Rus, 41, 71, 102, 157, 174
Koran, 45, 99, 164
Koreniako, V., 77
Kozhinov, V., 5, 53, 76, 109
Kozlov, V., 53–54, 70
Kozybaev, M., 184
Kozyrev, N., 61
Kuchum, 152, 181, 245
Kurginian, S., 5

Lamanskii, V., 3–4
Lavrov, S., 55
Lay of Igor's Host, 72, 78, 174, 234
Leont'ev, Konstantin, 3, 88, 91, 116,
236, 241
Leont'ev, Mikhail, 111
Liberal Democratic Party of Russia.
See Zhirinovsky
Likhachev, V., 163, 247
Limonov, E., 109, 127, 142

Mamleev, Iu., 108, 121
Manchuria, 117, 168, 189
Medzhlis, 148
Mialo, K., 78
Middle Ages, 101, 128, 159
Molodaia gvardiia, 5, 173
Mongolia: in Dugin's works, 115, 117;
in Eurasianist thought, 4, 40, 205,
223, 247; in Gumilëv's works,
53–54, 57, 59–60, 70–73, 81, 234;
in Jakobson's and Trubetzkoy's
theories, 36–37, 227–29, 231; and
Kazakh Eurasianism, 186; in
Khakimov's works, 165; and Evgen
Khara-Davan, 19; and Muslim
Eurasianism, 158; in Panarin's
works, 102; rehabilitation of the

Mongol Empire in classic
Eurasianism, 41–45; in Russian
history, 3; in Suleimenov's works,
174–75; and Turkism, 194, 229
Muscovy, 23, 41, 43–44, 71–72

Nash sovremennik, 53
Naturphilosophie: call for synthesis of,
47, 105, 125; and German
Romanticism, 31, 91, 188; and
harmony between humanity and
nature, 59, 69, 185
Nazarbaev, N.: and Dugin's presence
in Kazakhstan, 113, 179, 250; and
the Eurasianist University in
Astana, 177–78; as financier of
Eurasianist publications, 85–86; on
Gumilëv, 10; historical conceptions
of, 186; and Muslim Eurasianism,
150; place in Eurasianist thought,
206–8; as president of Kazakhstan,
172–73, 176, 187; proposal of
Union of Eurasian states, 152, 163,
177, 183; on the Slavic question
and Kazakhness, 180–82, 184
Nazism: as a Duginian reference, 117,
129, 133–34; in Dugin's racial
thought, 130–31; Eurasianist
condemning of, 23, 30; Russian
emigration facing, 18, 25; and
Turkish Nationalism, 189, 191
neo-Paganism, 121, 123–24, 130, 142,
154, 244
Nestorianism, 44, 53, 60, 75, 176, 185,
234
New Right: and Alain de Benoist, 126;
and Aryanism and neo-Paganism,
124, 130–31; in Dugin's works, 5,
15, 115, 142; ethno-differentialism
in, 138–39, 212–14; history of, 127;
influence in Russia of, 7; and
interchangeability of left and right,
126; Jewish question in, 136; in
Panarin's works, 94
Niiazov, A.-V., 146, 148–53, 156, 161
Nikolaev, M., 168

nomads: cult of (in classic
Eurasianism), 36–37, 94;
Eurasianist historiography on,
40–42, 229; in Gumilëv's works,
52–53, 57–59, 66, 73; "Jewish
nomadism," 100, 137; and Kazakh
Eurasianism, 176, 180, 183,
185–86; in Russian history, 3; and
Turkism, 189

Old Believers, 44, 124, 233, 242
Orthodoxy: in Bagramov's
publications, 85; in the Communist
Party of the Russian Federation, 6,
112; among converts to Islam,
154–55; as Duginian esotericism,
122–24, 130; in Dugin's
geopolitics, 117–118, 199; in
Eurasianist geopolitics, 207, 220;
in Eurasianist historiography on
Muscovy, 23–24, 43, 53; as a
foundation of the Panarinian "Great
Tradition," 98–103; in Gumilëv's
works, 71–73, 233–34; and Islam
and Judaism, 136–37; and Kazakh
Eurasianism, 176, 184; in Muslim
Eurasianism, 147, 149, 151, 156;
and the Muslim Spiritual Boards,
156–62; and Oriental religions,
41, 44–45, 60; in Panarin's works,
86, 88–89, 93–94; in the Rodina
party, 111; and Russian identity, 35,
209, 226–27, 233; and Spas
orthodox channel, 108; as a
"specific civilization," 8–9, 11, 46,
59, 105; in Tatarstan, 163, 248; and
the Union of Orthodox Citizens,
150
Ottoman Empire: as an Eurasianist
empire, 183; Jadid intellectual
circles in, 188–89; in Kazakh
historiography, 185; and
Ottomanism, 189–90; and the
Romanov empire, 199, 236; and
Turkic geopolitical thinking, 194,
220

Pamiat, 4, 78, 108, 155, 240
Panarin, A. S.: biography of, 86–89; on definition of civilizations, 89–95; and Dugin, 86, 115, 140; and the Eurasianist movement, 2, 13, 170, 205–9, 212, 214, 216; and Gumilëv, 60, 82; and the Orient, 101–5; and rehabilitation of empire, 95–101; success of, 11, 14, 83–84, 105–6
pan-Mongolism, 18. *See also* Mongolia
pan-Turkism: as an anti–Russian geopolitical axis, 118; in contemporary Turkey, 195–99, 201; and Kazakh Eurasianism, 185–87; in Kemalist Turkey, 171, 187–95; Panarin's fear of, 102–3; rejection by the Islamic Party of Rebirth, 147; and Tatar Eurasianism, 165–66
Pashchenko, V., 84
passionarity: in Dugin's works, 134; as an explanation of Russian history, 72–73, 233; Gumilevian theory of, 67–69; in Gumilëv's works, 58; and Judaism, 76; in Russian publications, 10
Perinçek, D., 199
Podberezkin, A., 11
Primakov, E., 7, 87–88, 110, 141, 162
Prokhanov, A., 109, 127
Pulatov, T., 84–85, 235
Putin, V.: Dugin's attitude toward, 111, 113–114, 143; and "Eurasianist" conceptions of Russia, 7–8, 10–11; and Muslim Eurasianism, 148, 151; Panarin's attitude toward, 88; as president of Russia, 110, 141, 218, 222; Shaimiev's attitude toward, 162, 164

race: and accusations of racism made by Dugin against Rodina, 112; in classic Eurasianist thought, 24, 30–31, 35, 38; and cultural racism or ethno-differentialism, 138–39, 142–43, 211–14; as a definition of

Europe by Panarin, 89; in Dugin's theories, 60, 129–132, 137, 206; and Kazakh Eurasianism, 184; and Nazism and Judaism, 134, 137; as a synonym for Gumilëv's *ethnos,* 10, 76; and Turkism, 191–92
Refakh, 148–49, 161
relativism: as a definition of Eurasianism, 212–13; and Europe, 37, 41, 233; in Panarin's works, 91, 105; philosophy of, 82
Rodina, 111–13, 132, 141, 240
Rogozin, D., 111
Romanov, 27, 72, 97, 102, 199
romanticism. See *Naturphilosophie*
Rome, 96, 117, 134, 172, 229
Rybakov, B., 77

Savel'ev, A., 112
Savitsky, P. N.: in Dugin's works, 105, 115, 120; and the Eurasianist movement, 19–22, 24–25, 205, 225; as founder of "topogenesis," 32–33, 36, 211; and Gumilëv, 56–60, 63, 230–31; and Muslim Eurasianim, 150, 225; on Orthodoxy, 43; in Panarin's works, 84, 90, 102; and the USSR, 26, 230
Scythia: and Eurasianism, 194; in Gumilëv's theories of the Khazar empire, 75; and Kazakh Eurasianism, 185–86; in Suleimenov's works, 174
Scythism, as a literary trend, 4, 18. *See also* Scythia
Seleznev, G., 11, 110
Serbia, 8, 85, 88, 100, 222. *See also* Balkans
Shafarevich, I., 76
Shaimiev, M., 158, 162–64, 167, 208
Shiism, 137
Shirokogorov, S., 80
Shnirelman, V., 77
Siberia: and Dugin's Aryanism, 129–31; in Dugin's geopolitics, 118; in Gumilëv's biography, 52; in

Gumilëv's works, 69, 72; and
Kazakh Eurasianism, 180–81; and
Muslim Eurasianism, 152, 161,
165–66; in Panarin's works, 102–3;
in Russian geopolitics, 8; in
Savitsky's geographical theories,
33; and Yakutian Eurasianism,
168–69

Slavophilism: as culturalism, 211–13;
in Dugin's works, 122, 129, 138,
143, 242; and Eurasianist thinkers
as futuristic Slavophiles, 47; as an
intellectual movement, 2–4, 226,
233; and Orthodoxy, 59; and
Panarin, 88, 104–5; as a
predecessor of Eurasianism, 16, 18,
27, 34, 202; in the Soviet Union,
77–79; and Turkism, 188–189

Suleimenov, O.: and the Eurasianist
movement, 2; Eurasianist writings
of, 172–75, 249; and Gumilëv, 72;
and Gumilëv's meeting with his
father, 84; and Kazakh Eurasianism,
185, 187; and Muslim Eurasianism,
150

Sumer, 174–75, 193, 194

Sunnism, 118, 126, 137

Tadzhuddin, T., 119, 156–61

Tamerlane, 43, 59, 194, 251

Tatarstan: in classic Eurasianist
thought, 34, 43–44; in
Dostoyevsky's formula, 3; in
Dugin's geopolitics, 118–19; as an
Eurasianist state, 12, 15, 55,
145–46, 158, 169, 208; and
Euro–Islam, 162–64; and Gumilëv,
11; in Gumilëv's works, 71–73, 81,
234; Jadid legacy in, 189–91; and
Kazakh Eurasianism, 171, 175, 178;
Muslim political parties in, 146–47,
149; Muslim Spiritual Boards in,
157, 159; and nationalism, 6; in
Panarin's works, 102; and Tatar
history in Khakimov's works,
165–68

tellurocracies, 89, 116

Tengrism, 157–58, 161, 178

thalassocracies, 89, 116–17, 137

theocracy, 29, 95, 98, 126, 211

Third Rome, 42, 95, 101, 134

Thiriart, J., 128

traditionalism: and Aryanism, 130–31;
in Alain de Benoist's works, 127,
129; Dugin's criticism of, 123; in
Dugin's works, 15, 108, 111, 115,
142–43, 189, 200; history of,
120–21; and Islam, 155, 207; and
Judaism, 135–37; at the New
University, 107, 114, 122; and
political ideologies, 125–26, 133;
reception in the Soviet Union,
121–22; the religious question in,
124

Trubetzkoy, N. S.: and the classic
Eurasianist movement, 19–26, 40,
226; in Dugin's works, 115, 120,
169; Eurasianist theories of, 33–38,
228; and Gumilëv's works, 57–59,
231; and Muslim Eurasianism, 150;
and Oriental religions, 45–46; in
Panarin's works, 105; place in the
Eurasianist movement, 205

Tsiolkovskii, K., 67

Turan: as a definition of Russianness
or Slavness, 3–4, 35, 236, 241;
Eurasianist theories on Turanian
languages, 36–37, 223, 228; as a
mythical space, 219; place in
Russian history, 39–41, 43–44; and
Turkism, 190, 194

Turkeş, A., 192, 195

Turkey: and Central Asia, 195–96; and
Eurasianism, 172, 188, 198–201,
205, 207–8; and Islamism, 147,
153; and Russia, 103; and Russian
alliance, 2, 200, 254. *See also*
Turkic peoples; Turks

Turkic peoples: in comparison to the
East and West, 40, 188, 195, 247;
and Dugin's Aryanism, 129; and
Dugin's geopolitics, 118; and

Turkic peoples (*continued*)
the Eurasianist movement, 206,
208; Eurasianist theory on the
languages and cultures of, 35–37,
39, 47, 223, 227; in Eurasianist
thought, 5, 79, 85–86, 241; in
Gumilëv's works, 52–53, 55, 75,
79, 233; inter-Turkic relations, 112,
196–97, 201; in Kazakh Eurasianist
historiography, 179, 183, 186; in
Muslim Spiritual Boards, 158, 161;
and Muslim Eurasianism, 146, 151,
155; in Panarin's works, 85, 102–3;
in Russian history, 2, 169–70, 203,
251; Russian perceptions of, 11,
145–46; in Suleimenov's works,
172–75, 249; in Tatar Eurasianism,
161, 163, 165–66; in Turkish
historiography, 189–195. *See also*
Turkey
Turkish International Cooperation
Agency, 196, 201
Turks: and Gumilëv, 73, 75; and
Islamism, 37; against Latins, 4,
233; and national identity, 15,
188–95; Old Turks, 52, 59; Young
Turks, 190. *See also* Turkey

universalism: ambiguity of
Eurasianism toward, 212–13; in
classic Eurasianist philosophy, 31,
41–42, 73; and Kazakh
Eurasianism, 176, 184; and Muslim
Eurasianism, 169; in Panarin's
works, 81–82, 93, 96, 104; the
Roman idea of, 90

Valikhanov, T., 145, 186, 251
Vernadsky, Georges: and the classic
Eurasianist movement, 19, 21, 25,
225; and Eurasianist theory of
space, 205, 228; and Gumilëv, 56,
60; in Panarin's works, 102
Vernadsky, Vladimir, 55, 59, 67
von Liebenfels, J. L., 130
von List, G., 130

Wirth, H., 130

Xinjiang, 117, 251

Yakutia-Sakha, 168–69
Yassavi, A., 186, 198, 251
Yeltsin, B.: and Chubais on empire,
224; and Eurasianists against
economic reforms, 87, 141, 208;
and federal questions, 139; on
foreign policy, 7–8; and Glaz'ev,
240; and Nazarbaev, 177; and
Shaimiev, 162
Yermak, 58, 181, 230
Yugoslavia. *See* Serbia

Zavtra, 107, 109, 127, 154
Zhirinovsky, V.: Dugin's criticism of,
127–28, 142, 211; Dugin's
influence on, 109, 118; and Duma's
Advisory Council on National
Security, 110; as a fictitious
opposition, 141; and Muslim
nationalists, 154; and nationalist
parties in Russia, 5–6
Ziuganov, G.: Dugin's criticism of,
127–28, 132, 142, 211; Dugin's
influence on, 11; Dugin's personal
relation to, 109; and nationalist
parties in Russia, 6; as a non-
efficient opposition, 141